The Working Class in American History
Editorial Advisors
David Brody
Alice Kessler-Harris
David Montgomery
Sean Wilentz

A list of books in the series appears at the end of this volume.

Upheaval in the Quiet Zone

Upheaval
in the Quiet Zone

A History of Hospital Workers' Union, Local 1199

Leon Fink
and Brian Greenberg

University of Illinois Press
Urbana and Chicago

This book is dedicated to the memory of Elliott Godoff, the example of Leon Davis, and the dreams of health care workers, past, present, and future.

All photographs provided courtesy of the *1199 News*.

© 1989 by the Board of Trustees of the University of Illinois
Manufactured in the United States of America
1   2   3   4   5   C   P   5   4   3   2   1

This book is printed on acid-free paper.

Library of Congress Cataloging-in-Publication Data

Fink, Leon, 1948–
    Upheaval in the quiet zone : a history of Hospital Workers' Union, Local
    1199 / Leon Fink and Brian Greenberg.
        p. cm. — (The Working class in American history)
    Includes index.
    ISBN 0-252-01545-2 (cloth). ISBN 0-252-06047-4 (paper)
    1. Trade-unions—Hospitals—United States—History. 2. Montefiore
Hospital and Medical Center—History. 3. Collective labor
agreements—Hospitals—United States—History. I. Greenberg,
Brian. II. Title. III. Series.
RA971.35.F56 1989
331.88'113621'10—dc19   88-20743
                                                              CIP

Contents

Introduction

During the past thirty years American intellectuals have become increasingly disillusioned with the labor union as an instrument of social change. Despite a renaissance in the study of working people and their communities, "scholarly and intellectual interest in American trade unions has been at a low ebb since the 1960s."[1] It is fair to say that even to sympathetic observers the daily work of unions appears at best routine, narrowly self-interested, and politically uninspiring. In part this perception reflects real changes in the behavior of unions and in the social status and interests of their members. It occurs against the backdrop of a sharp decline in the unionized sector of the labor force and, more recently, of mounting industrial defeats and political setbacks. Yet the current view of union irrelevance also carries with it the arrogance of middle-class political fashion as well as a general ignorance of the inner workings and varieties of action within the trade union movement. Despite their weaknesses, labor unions in the post–World War II period have continued to represent a major force for social reform. Most notably they have remained the key vehicle by which the working poor might pass from silence to an active voice in American public life. Whoever would seek to understand both the promise and disappointment of contemporary America can ill afford to ignore labor's influence on our history.

In this volume we tell the story of one of the liveliest, stormiest organizations on the recent American labor scene. For nearly three decades the local, then district, and finally national union bearing the numerical designation 1199 has played a role in American labor affairs out of all proportion to its size. Primarily this is because the history of the hospital workers' union continually has intersected with major social movements as well as structural transformations within postwar American life. An initial clue to the union's distinctiveness lies in the timing of its "takeoff." In 1958 a small union of New York pharmacists and drug clerks with a left-wing political past set out to organize the city's huge private, nonprofit (or "voluntary") hospital system. At the time, American hospitals were a virtual no-man's-land for trade unionism. An aura of philanthropic voluntarism still shrouded the hospital as employer, while the low-skilled service work force, increasingly black and Hispanic and overwhelmingly female, was commonly regarded as the province of the unmotivated, benighted poor.

In the space of one decade the unionization movement—sparked by 1199's New York example—became a powerful new factor in hospital industrial relations. By 1968 a once weak and divided labor force of unskilled service workers had emerged with collective bargaining rights, an enhanced economic status, and a determined public voice. With a secure foothold of organized strength in the New York metropolitan area, 1199 ventured out into a much more varied national terrain, even while it attempted to defend and extend its gains in the midst of shifting fiscal fortunes in its home city.

The achievements of this union were linked to at least three larger shifts in postwar urban labor relations. The first concerns the changing social content and consciousness of the labor force itself. For this portion of the "new working class," the organizing process increasingly involved not only economic and job-related issues but a larger civil rights identity, a sense of community empowerment, and moral-political appeals directed to a larger audience. Perhaps more directly than for any other group of urban workers— and in a way that connected their efforts to the struggles of California farm laborers in the same period—the developing tempo of the civil rights struggle would redound repeatedly upon hospital labor organization. By the late sixties the rank-and-file mobilization of hospital workers developed using what 1199 leaders dubbed a "union power, soul power" model.

A second vital feature of the breakthrough in hospital unionism was its connection to the larger dynamic of public-sector collective bargaining. Although 1199 members were employed by theoretically private, nonprofit institutions, the financial solutions both to rising worker demands and to generally expanding claims on the contemporary health care system derived from public—that is, governmental—sources. In hospital organizing and contract campaigns dating to the late 1950s, municipal and then state authorities emerged as a crucial third party to hospital labor relations. As an example of a new dynamism within the public sector, the unionization of New York City hospital workers in 1958–59 offered a prologue to what one observer has called "the decade of the public employee revolution." Alongside an otherwise stagnant, even shrinking command of the labor force, American labor unions from the early sixties through the mid-seventies substantially supplemented their organizational and political strength by the infusion of public-sector service and professional workers, ranging from municipal sanitation workers and teachers to federal employees.[2]

Third, like other public-sector disputes, hospital labor conflict quickly spilled out beyond the workplace into a communitywide *political* issue. Given the critical nature of the "industry" involved, together with the mobilization of a low-paid minority work force, big-city hospital strikes were particularly volatile events. Even the threat of a strike necessarily involved the contending parties in an intricate round of political maneuvering among the media, public officials, and other organized interest groups.

It was 1199's manner of handling the political question—both in mobilizing a previously unorganized labor force and in capturing public support for the hospital workers' cause—that singled out the union on the contemporary labor scene. Erupting between the abatement of McCarthyism in the late 1950s and the renewed urban fiscal crisis of the 1970s, the rise of hospital unionism can be viewed as a reassertion of a labor-based vision of social reform. Among the subthemes: 1199's hospital drive offered one of the first post-McCarthy initiatives to reknit ties between Old Left "progressives" and anti-Communist American liberals both within and outside the labor movements; a traditionally exclusionist labor movement adopted the hospital workers as a symbol of its larger commitment to a minority, low-skilled laboring poor; and, as an overwhelmingly black union led by secular-Jewish radicals, the union itself became an experiment in urban sociology and ethnic politics.

While we may locate the story of the hospital workers in relation to larger structures, outside forces, and even "the spirit of the times," we do not slight the significance of the specific actors themselves. On the contrary, it is our belief that historical change begins with the thoughts and acts of individuals, that national stories begin on a local level, and that it is the duty of historians to try to reconstruct big events with an eye to the contributing force of many smaller ones. That, at least, is what we have tried to do here. Aided by the tools of oral history, we have sought to chronicle the experiences of a specific group of working people (and others with whom they interacted) in a particular time and place. Indeed, precisely by allowing for the complexity of a specific industry, local circumstances, and individual capacity and motives, we hope realistically to have addressed the larger promise and perils facing modern-day labor movements.

The establishment and consolidation of Local 1199 is dealt with in the first six chapters of this book. Chapter 1 sets the stage for the study with a retrospective look at the nature of hospital work, personnel relations, and organizing attempts in the preunion era; it closes with the fortuitous entente between Leon Davis, head of the tiny drugstore union, and the exiled hospital organizer Elliott Godoff. Chapter 2 examines the first fruits of the

Davis-Godoff strategy through a close look at the organizing campaign at Montefiore Hospital in the Bronx. Although in many respects an atypical and extraordinary chapter in labor relations, the battle to unionize Montefiore defined a range of basic issues that would reappear in later years. Chapters 3 and 4 together explore the takeoff of the hospital union through the event of the 1959 hospital strike, an unprecedented disruption of the traditional "quiet zone" around hospital personnel relations. Through a twin focus on rank-and-file mobilization and the competing political strategies of union leaders, hospital officials, and government mediators, we seek to set political change in an appropriate interpretive context. Chapter 5, focusing on the battle for incorporation of hospital workers into state labor legislation and collective bargaining rights, takes up a crucial, if ordinarily invisible, transition in the unionization process. Chapter 6 pursues the union as a secure and aggressive political entity. Internal organizational consolidation, contract negotiating strategies, geographic and occupational expansionism, and union political initiatives are assessed against the backdrop of the social ferment and comparative economic affluence of the 1960s.

The latter half of this book is concerned with more recent developments as well as with the larger meaning of the 1199 union experience, essentially a story of new initiatives in a changing social, geographic, and political environment. By testing its strength outside the boundaries of metropolitan New York, and by reaching out from its service and blue-collar base to a pink-and-white-collar professional constituency, what had by 1969 become District 1199 attempted to combine movement building with the consolidation and institutionalization of past achievements. At the same time the union felt the world changing around it. During the 1970s the hospital expansion boom fizzled. Faced with growing financial constraints, hospital managements devised new, more sophisticated antiunion strategies. The same period witnessed the national exhaustion of the liberal agenda, with even the civil rights coalition's favored constituencies beginning to dance to new tunes. The spirit of interracial cooperation and a progressive-liberal political alliance again became more scarce public commodities. Ethnic factionalism, racial mistrust, and political self-promotion emerged as political staples in an era of welfare cutbacks and urban fiscal crisis. The mixed results of the union's efforts post-1968—a combination of brilliant success and most painful failure—point to critical problems in the path of contemporary health care workers and, more generally, of American trade unionism. At an abstract level, 1199's troubles speak to the dilemmas of any social movement seeking to sustain its spirit as well as its power over the long haul. At a more concrete level, the turmoil invading the union's highest councils points to the role of individuals of most human frailty in determining the course of big events.

Specific chapters explore diverse facets of the balancing act the union has sought to perform since 1968. The problem of "going national" with an organizing strategy bred within the circumstances of New York first confronted the union in its joint management of a labor and civil rights crusade in Charleston, South Carolina (chapter 7). Events during the decade of the 1970s, the subject of chapter 8 challenged 1199 to reassess its goals and its mode of operation on a number of fronts. Changing managerial tactics, a new legal framework for hospital industrial relations, an unfamiliar set of organizing targets, the impact of fiscal crisis and budgetary freezes, and, finally, belated grappling with the problem of union succession and bitter internal disagreements described a new uncertainty beneath the apparent material health of the organization. Chapter 9 locates the distinctiveness of 1199's first thirty years in the hospital field within a collective portrait of the Leon Davis administration. Emphasizing the adaptation of a prior political culture to new circumstances, this treatment pays particular attention to questions of union structure and decision making, bread-and-butter goals versus a larger political vision, and, more generally, the gap between the understanding of the union by its pioneers and the mass of its rank and file. Chapter 10 chronicles the descent of 1199 in the 1980s, a bitter period of internal division occasioned by a struggle for leadership in the post-Davis years. While the rise and fall of the Doris Turner regime and the equally troubled regency of Georgianna Johnson in New York City provide the narrative thread for this story, these recent events also serve to highlight earlier themes, connecting the questions of style and ideology of union leadership to matters of structure as well as the larger political context. We conclude on a cautious note, convinced of the significance of unionism as a force for both social welfare and democratic change in American life, yet troubled by the underbrush of personal, ethnic, and political conflict that hobble many an effort toward movement building.

Touching as it does a multitude of characters, scenes, and institutions affecting postwar American society, the history of the hospital workers' union not surprisingly strides into several arenas of contemporary historical inquiry. In recent years the history of American health care systems has received a delayed but rewarding examination by social historians, sociologists, and economists. So far, however, study has focused on the health professions and their relation to the rise of medical schools and hospitals. While telling us much about the culture of modern medicine, its relation to developments in technology and business enterprise, as well as the peculiarly retarded development of national health insurance and public medicine in the United States, the new scholarship rarely ventures beyond the physician and almost never beyond the registered nurse, ignoring developments in hospital boiler rooms, kitchens, parking lots, and laundries that sustained the advances of modern, "scientific" medicine. Where the rise of hospital unionism and collective bargaining has been taken into account, it is treated not as a historical subject but as an adjunct of hospital administration or as a new equation within labor economics. Moreover, even some of the most penetrating criticisms of the American health care sector have subordinated the lived experiences of health care workers and their unions to a more abstract critique of the logic, function, and ideology of the system. One might hope, therefore, that a closer look at "the labor problem" in hospitals would contribute to a more general institutional reemphasis in health care studies, one that would explore both present realities and tangible possibilities for reform.[3]

As a chapter in post–World War II labor history, the story of the hospital workers has until now been eclipsed by a general neglect of the contemporary era of labor relations. The "new labor history," which in the past twenty years has dramatically opened the doors between "union history" and larger social and cultural developments affecting American working people, has rarely stepped across the twentieth-century divide. The few scholarly treatments of postwar events focus on the traditional industrial sector, slighting the critical development of largely female white-collar and service industries as well as the expansion of public employment. As a case study of unionization within the "new working class," the 1199 story treats the altered physical and political terrain with which organized labor has had to contend.[4]

This study also adjoins an extensive literature on the black urban experience. While much attention, both historical and sociological, has focused on Afro-American (and, to a lesser extent, Hispanic) migration to northern cities, the areas of concentration have been community conditions, family life, culture, and politics. Few researchers have treated racial minorities as workers or have studied their workplaces.[5] Indeed, until most recently, the black women who comprise the single largest segment of hospital union membership formed part of a historically hidden citizenry and work force.[6] The intimate connection between the rise of 1199 and the civil rights movement itself redirects historical questions along new paths, offering a striking exception to the conventional wisdom that assumes a sharp break between the social movement of the 1930s and that of the 1960s. The leadership of the hospital workers' union personally experienced and continued to embrace the sustaining social idealism of the thirties; at the same time, their campaign for "union power" drew its moral fervor from the insistent trumpet of "soul power." That an element of Old Left ideology could still inspire the latter-day union builders — but could less effectively be translated to the mass of union members — highlights the peculiar position of the American radical as reformer.

An institutionally centered labor history, particularly one in which many of the participants are still active, public figures, runs some obvious risks. For one, as social historians have repeatedly emphasized, a focus on formal organization tends to exaggerate the role of union or political leadership at the expense of rank-and-file workers. An institutional study may generally overemphasize the minority of formally "organized" workers and ignore the experience of the vast majority of people employed outside the realm of unionism. There is, as well, in union histories, the tendency by sympathetic scholars or in-house chroniclers to accept at face value the union's own assumptions about its past. Union hagiography thus regularly exaggerates organizational and contract "victories" while it rarely penetrates the organization's inner tensions. Such intellectual provincialism derives in no small measure from the traditional neglect of labor unions by the larger academic community as well as the almost unbending hostility of the media. The result, in any case, is a general suspiciousness among most union staff toward outside, "independent" researchers. Still, in our opinion there are compelling reasons to undertake the historical investigation of labor unions. The emphasis in working-class social history on social structure, protest movements, and popular culture leaves a gulf between its subjects and the world of political events, institutions, and strategic decision making. It is, after all, around institutions and through individuals acting together that social conflicts are both fought and contained. And it is through unions that working-class Americans have most often exercised leverage over society.

A word is in order about the sources for this study, particularly the use of oral evidence. We have, of course, made use of the available written record, which includes secondary works, many newspaper and journal reports, and numerous documents, minutes, and publications drawn from the union's own files. But we have also undertaken extensive interviews with those who helped shape the events discussed in these pages. Indeed, precisely because we could locate quite specific events and questions, and then examine them through the lens of diverse, often opposing perspectives, oral interviews have proven an invaluable and indispensable aid in the writing of this book. A grant from the National Endowment for the Humanities allowed us to transcribe the bulk of the interviews and the tapes and transcriptions (or, in some cases, detailed summaries of the interviews) are available for scholarly use at the Labor-Management Documentation Center at Cornell University, in Ithaca, New York. In the interests of simplicity we have refrained from repetitive citation of the interviews in note references. Where a source is clearly cited or quoted in the text, the reader should consult the alphabetical list of interviews for the full reference. Where a source is not explicit in the text, or, as in the final chapters, where vital information was gathered via telephone interviews, full note citation is used.

Our experience with the fast-changing world of the hospital workers' union has led us to a sobering modesty about the capacity of "contemporary" history to get "on top of the present," let alone predict the future. Our oral history interviews, for example, framed by the insight of the current moment, in hindsight often appear confined by ignorance of events that lay just around the corner. In particular, the eruption within 1199's high command in 1979–80 sent us scurrying back to earlier notes and sources for an explanation. But pursuing the most recent events is like holding a tiger by the tail. As keen observers of the play, and occasionally even bit players themselves, contemporary historians must wait (impatiently) for the curtain to rise on the next act.

Finally, our stance as authors should be made clear. Ours is an independent and unofficial history of 1199, though it was carried out with full cooperation of the union in terms of access to sources and research materials. The project began in 1976 as a small-scale effort to compile an oral archive for the union, a move stimulated by the death of organizing director Elliott Godoff and the imminent retirement of many of the old guard.[7] Within the first year of work, however, we glimpsed the potential for a larger historical work and began to direct the project toward that end, entirely on the basis of outside financial assistance. Grants from the Ford Foundation, the Office of Research and Development of the U.S. Department of Labor, and the National Endowment for the Humanities allowed us to complete our research. While asserting our authorial autonomy, we nevertheless gratefully acknowledge the fact that without the help of union leaders, members, and their friends, this book could not have been written. It is to their credit that Leon Davis and Moe Foner (and whoever else may have passed judgment on the matter) decided that a serious, even critical, scholarly portrait would ultimately be for the union's good. Likewise, it is to the credit of a multitude of other willing informants, inside and outside the union, that we could tell this story.

Those who work in the hospital field and/or are already acquainted in some way with 1199 should find here a broader context in which to place their own experiences and observations. We also deem it important that the history of the hospital workers' union be brought to a larger audience, thus raising public understanding of the experience and needs of the millions of people who themselves sustain America's largest life-sustaining institutions. Finally, we hope to persuade readers that the state of the labor movement is one of the vital signs of a democratic society and, therefore, that the fate of unions like the hospital workers' has widespread implications. As such, we have tried not only to tell the story of how an organized group of people tried to change something about the world around them but to interpret it as well. If our understanding is imperfect, we trust that others will come along to set the record straight.

This co-authored project has necessarily involved a division of labor.

Original research and interviews in New York were conducted concurrently and with a rough equality of effort. Research outside New York City was divided on a practical basis, with Fink pursuing the Charleston events and Greenberg covering the national union elsewhere. When it came to organizing and writing, academic schedules and personal commitments dictated the following assignments: Greenberg wrote chapters 5, 6, and 8 (and co-authored an earlier version of chapter 2); Fink wrote the remainder of the chapters. Despite this specialization of task, we have asserted a common analytic perspective throughout the project and as such assume joint responsibility for the completed work.

We express our deep appreciation to all those individuals, within and outside 1199, who gave of their time and thoughts in the course of our research. In addition to the people cited in the text, we acknowledge the invaluable assistance and criticism of Karen Kearns, Pamela Brier, David Slavin, Barbara Melosh, David Rosner, Susan Reverby, Mark Naison, Fred Siegel, Jules Bernstein, Marshall Dubin, Louise Jonsson, Peter Agree, Walter Licht, Nelson Lichtenstein, Eric Schneider, Janet Golden, Lawrence Goodwyn, Susan Greenberg, Donald Reid, Carol Smith, and David Paskin. We are also indebted to Richard Strassberg of the Labor-Management Documentation Center for facilitating our work. Susan Levine contributed enormously to the book with a merciless editing of an earlier draft. We have also been aided by a critical reading from Alice Kessler-Harris and two anonymous readers. Theresa L. Sears, associate editor at the University of Illinois Press, substantially improved the final presentation of the manuscript; Mary Woodall and Ella Phillips helped prepare copy along the way. Finally, Moe Foner, executive secretary emeritus of the National Union of Hospital and Health Care Employees, deserves special mention as the patient godfather of this project.

CHAPTER 1

Before the Union:
The Hospital Worker as Involuntary
Philanthropist

When you inquire at the information desk of a hospital for the room number of your convalescent friend, you are probably conjuring up a picture of long halls and nurses in white on the floors above. Under your feet, in the bowels of the hospital, down to a depth of perhaps forty feet, men and women go about tending fires, mending uniforms, slicing loaves of bread, driving sheets through a mangle, roasting joints of lamb, feeling the pulses of dynamoes. There is a carpenter shop and sometimes a machine shop. Above, in a part of the hospital that many of the maintenance workers rarely see, men and women expire; babies are born, smart ladies sit up in bed, dressed in silk negligees, and write thank-you letters for the roses and tulips and gladioli that lend fragrance to their sunny rooms.[1]

In post–World War II America hospitals became big business, albeit a special kind of big business. The money and human resources invested in health care between 1945 and 1970 burgeoned along an arc that no other economic sector could match. While the absolute number of institutions rose only slightly in this period, hospital budgets increased more than tenfold. During the fifties and sixties more than 2.5 million employees were added to the nation's health care work force; of nearly 4 million people employed in the health care industry, as it came to be called, some 2.3 million worked in 7,100 hospitals, dwarfing employment in steel and railroads combined. The major surge in hospital growth occurred between 1960 and 1975. During a period when manufacturing employment rose by 17 percent and all services by 74 percent, hospital employment jumped 114 percent. The growing dominance of large institutions within the industry also signaled an important change: by 1969 the largest hospitals (those with over 400 beds) controlled nearly 60 percent of the industry's bed capacity, even as middle-sized institutions (with 200 beds) still employed 70 percent of all hospital personnel. In many communities the local hospital became the area's single largest employer, and by the 1970s hospitals in general had become the most dynamic sector of the nation's largest industry—health services.[2]

Amid what some have labeled a general "medicalization" of American life, the private nonprofit, or *voluntary* hospital experienced its golden age. Distinguished in governance from *proprietary* (for profit) and *public* (munici-pal, state, and federal) institutions, the voluntaries usually derived from religious, philanthropic roots. In the postwar period voluntaries continued to function as self-governed, semiautonomous institutions despite the fact that charitable endowments (except for long-term building funds) were replaced by third-party payments as the major operating resource. By 1980 voluntary hospitals employed 2.3 million people or approximately 60 percent of the nation's total hospital personnel.[3]

Superficially, hospital trends seem to follow the general tendencies of business and bureaucratic expansionism. However, gross figures of hospital growth and concentration hide the real peculiarity of the industry. As sociologist Paul Starr has noted, hospitals represent "blocked institutional development." Instead of following a clear line of consolidation in size and authority, hospitals—largely because of physicians' power to shape, or forestall, national health policy—only partially overcame their precapitalist legacy of divided power, institutional autonomy, and administrative back-wardness. Even the great leap forward in the postwar years occurred largely without systematic managerial reorganization of the industry. According to Starr, that period was characterized in the fifties and early sixties by "growth without [social] redistribution" of resources followed by a decade of social redistribution (e.g., Medicare, Medicaid) without "fundamental reorganiza-tion of the system." Only in the last decade have the pressures of a general fiscal crisis prompted moves—often more rhetorical than real—to reorga-nize the medical system from above in order to forestall growth and cut costs.[4]

Defined neither by market forces (as with business enterprises) nor by public control and planning (as with most social services), hospitals devel-oped along an anomalous institutional path. Decentralization was one key to hospital particularism. While large voluntary hospital complexes (called "medical empires" by critics) did eventually grow up in most cities—particularly through affiliation agreements with area medical schools—the terrain remained varied. The lack of a national health or insurance plan forced each hospital to become an entire business unit. Unlike other public services, individual hospitals had to raise funds, set fees, provide public relations, and recruit staff, often in the absence of clear-cut internal lines of authority and decision making. For historical reasons, policy-making responsibilities in the postwar period shifted uneasily between professional administrators, department heads, and trustees.[5]

Demands on an already ill structured hospital administration were stretched further by the growing problems of personnel management. Hospital expansionism in the postwar period was a labor-intensive process that led to the growth of a semiskilled service sector. More than 60 percent of hospital budgets, according to American Hospital Association figures for the early 1960s, were consumed by payroll costs; in addition, the ratio of hospital personnel to number of beds for all U.S. hospitals grew from .58 to 1 in 1946 to 1.57 to 1 in 1970, an increase of 171 percent. The hospital labor force was also becoming more complex, as the postwar period witnessed an extension of new technologies—with a consequent elaboration of "elite" practitioners. A distinct "hourglass" profile, with the labor force bulging simultaneously at the most- and least-skilled ends, thus marked personnel recruitment during the voluntary hospital's boom years.[6]

Hospital employment needs were influenced by many factors. On the whole, the years between 1940 and 1960 were characterized by a trend toward "substitution" of less-skilled for more-skilled positions, including the introduction of licensed practical nurses (LPNs) and the hiring of aides. However, the next ten years saw a reversal as changes in capital equipment, such as data processing, material handling systems, and disposable linen, led to the replacement of unskilled workers by a semiskilled labor force; simultaneously, highly trained technicians were required to assist in new therapies. Excluding interns, residents, and registered nurses (RNs), New York City's voluntary hospital work force in 1957 was 70 percent "unskilled." By 1970 the number of unskilled workers had dropped to 59 percent.[7]

The mass of nonprofessional, less-skilled employees provided vital support services to hospital patients and medical-administrative staff and generally were grouped by administrative departments: nursing (including aides, orderlies, and LPNs), dietary (cooks, aides), housekeeping (formerly maids and janitors, later aides), and building and maintenance (engineers, craftsmen, laborers). Traditionally, the separation of estates within the hospitals was reinforced by measures such as designated uniforms or patches and distinct dining and recreational facilities, while clerical workers as well as the growing phalanx of medical technicians formed an occupational buffer zone between professionals and service employees. Aside from the general layering of talents, however, each department had its own skill ladder. The dietary or nutrition department, for example, ranged from unskilled dishwashers and pantry workers to skilled meat-cutters, cooks, and professional dieticians.

A hospital's medical staff and its work force represented opposite poles of

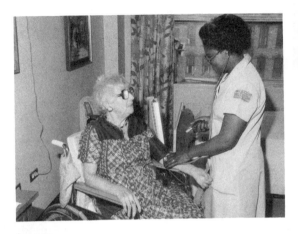

The variety of skills and assignments associated with hospital work is suggested here: a nurse's aide with an elderly patient; a dietary worker in a hospital kitchen; laundry workers ironing hospital gowns; an engineering or maintenance worker in the boiler room; and a laboratory technician.

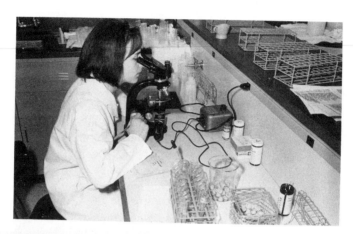

America's social structure. On one end were the twentieth century's most upwardly mobile, successful, and esteemed professionals; on the other were the unskilled, unrecognized ranks of the working poor. Before World War II, many hospital workers not only had been recruited from the lists of social agencies but performed their work under sheltered conditions, including living in hospital dormitories. In 1937 wages were reported to be as low as $25 a month with maintenance. Citing the lack of privacy, supervision away from work, and split shifts expected of live-in workers, one report noted the "paradox that a charitable institution should tend to treat its employees in such a manner as to make them potential objects of charity."

While extended paternal practices gradually died out in the postwar period, the basic, subsistence position of hospital workers continued. In 1959 untrained women started hospital work in New York City with an average wage of $0.90 per hour; unskilled men started at $1.03 per hour—both well below the national minimum wage of $1.30 per hour. Hospital representatives argued as late as 1962 that extension of national minimum wage legislation to the heretofore exempt nonprofit service sector would affect nearly half of all hospital nonprofessionals. Hospital authorities did not contest the fact that even with full-time jobs many service workers were forced to seek public relief. They simply pointed out that the hourly hospital wage in 1959 was two and a half times what it had been in 1947.[8]

Effectively if unintentionally an employer of last resort, big-city hospitals were a window on the changing demography of the working poor. A 1937 description of hospital nonprofessionals called them "very much like the cooks, laundresses, charwomen, and kitchen help that you will find wherever you go. They include Negroes, Irish, Italians, Poles." Hospitals of the postwar period, like the city's labor force more generally, reflected the massive influx of southern blacks and, by the early 1950s, Puerto Ricans into unskilled jobs. The immigrants' impact on the hospitals was, if anything, even more dramatic than on the city as a whole. For example, while blacks and Hispanics increased from one-quarter to one-third of New York City's population between 1960 and 1970, they made up 80 percent of the hospital service and maintenance work force. Often recruited through familial chain migration patterns, the newest employees were bunched in the least-desirable jobs.[9]

Labor relations was one of the last areas of hospital operation to be subjected to postwar administrative "modernization." Personnel management, which in private industry had emerged at the turn of the century as a key component of corporate efficiency, came both belatedly and fitfully to health care administration. With little to offer in the form of wage incentives and ever able to tap a reserve of female and minority labor, hospitals only slowly and unevenly altered traditional ways of treating workers. In 1959, for example, less than 10 percent of voluntary hospitals reported full-time personnel directors. Coordination of employment policies was often in the hands of an "efficient executive secretary with little professional education." When Dr. Martin R. Steinberg became director of Mt. Sinai Hospital in 1945, the personnel operation consisted of the personnel manager and a secretary: "There was a lady who had been there some fifteen years, clipped speech and very dictatorial and matronly." The personnel office did little more than try to coordinate the demands of departmental fiefdoms. Steinberg discovered that secretaries were getting "anywhere from 'A to triple-A' in salaries—it depended upon the forcefulness of her boss, you know, to get her a raise he'd go down and fight it out with Personnel." Initial moves away from the administrative chaos of departmental autonomy usually amounted only to centralized hiring and record-keeping with the tools of newspaper help-wanted ads, interviews, referrals to specific departments, and simple testing procedures, including a physical exam. As late as 1969 the incremental progress toward systematic hospital management was evident in the self-congratulation conferred in an industry publication on the meager basis of "the increasing numbers of pictures in local newspapers showing the hospital administrator placing a pin on the uniform of a smiling and proud aide, kitchen helper, maid or porter."[10]

Working within a tightly limited annual operating budget, and mindful of the need to attract skilled personnel, administrators paid relatively little attention to the conditions of nonprofessional workers. General wage increases, Steinberg remembered, depended on a trickle-down effect:

> The nurses would write a letter to the Greater New York Hospital Association to say "that we want more money." This would be discussed thoroughly and we would sort of make a decision. [The decision was practically dictated by six or seven large hospitals.] We would decide, "Alright, instead of what they'd ask for we'd give them X." And so that's the nurses. Now the other employees—porters, maids, the kitchen men, etc.—we would make up the budget and then we would include an increase for the unskilled help. But their priority was not high. We were paying their salaries twice a month, and the average [annual] raise through the fifties was about four dollars, maybe five, a month, so their weekly increase was less than a quarter of that and by the time you took off the deduction they had very little.

In addition, the quality of work life for the service worker was, in important respects, dependent on one's lower-level crew chief, head nurse, or supervisor, who handed out task and shift assignments, granted leaves, and exercised "spot firing" authority. Personal relationships with superiors might also affect one's pension. Steinberg recalled that during the preunion years "there was no pension fund, but when an employee retired because of illness or age, Social Service would come in and investigate the situation, his home situation and assets, his needs . . . then the Board would receive a recommendation for a small pension for him."

As a classic response by an underpaid, unorganized work force to a paternal and arbitrary employer, hospitals faced high, even astronomical, absence and turnover rates. In 1956 the annual general labor turnover in hospitals was 60 percent; two years later the Catholic Hospital Association reported 83 percent annual employee exodus.[11]

The experience of New York City hospital workers in the preunion years confirms the image of an institution awkwardly suspended between informal paternalism and bureaucratic routinization. At the same time, health care employees were encountering changes in their own lives—changes that uprooted them from the world in which they had been born and raised; changes that, in many cases, had already led them through other work environments. Their later collective union experience was conditioned in important ways by this "prehistory" of individual adjustment.

The post–World War II voluntary hospital might be regarded as a giant sponge soaking up surplus, unskilled labor. At the individual level, however, a combination of accident and conscious decision conditioned workers' entry into the hospital labor force. Economic need, family or friendship connections, and the search for personal fulfillment played important, if uneven, roles in the motivations of nonprofessional hospital job applicants. For many, especially black women, this expanding service sector offered an attractive alternative to domestic work. Edith Garcia, following her mother and sisters, came to New York City from St. Croix, Virgin Islands, in 1947. Initially on welfare, she quickly found domestic employment, then sought "steady work" in the housekeeping department of Bronx-Lebanon Hospital. Hilda Joquin, a native of Bermuda who was raising three children on her own, sought employment at Beth Israel Hospital in 1951 following jobs as a charwoman in the Empire State Building and a housekeeper in a sanatorium. Mae Harrison, widowed in her early twenties, left the farm country near Greenville, South Carolina, in 1952 to join her mother in New York and through a friend got a job as a nurse's aide at Beth Israel Hospital.

This pattern of chain migration also accounted for Cassie Cosby's entry into the Mt. Sinai dietary department as a "pantry maid" in 1947. Mrs. Cosby left mill-town life in High Point, North Carolina, and with her husband moved into his mother's apartment on 101st Street in Manhattan. "At first I didn't think I was going to stay," she remembers, "but somehow. . . ." For Cassie Cosby, a momentary decision to find a job established her occupation for the next thirty years. Eddie Sanchez also sought the promise of a regular pay envelope when in 1959, at the age of twenty-two, he left Salinas, Puerto Rico, for the greener pastures of New York City. Living with his brother, he at first found only odd jobs; then, a cousin who worked in the

Mt. Sinai laundry passed along word of an opening. By 1977, Eddie Sanchez had been a presser at Mt. Sinai for eighteen years.

There were, of course, exceptions to the pattern of unconscious career choices. Mildred Reeves, who grew up in Barbados under an aunt's tutelage, joined her parents in New York City to attend high school. One summer, while still in school, she took a job as a hospital clerical assistant and from that time on knew what she wanted to do. Upon graduation in 1954 she filled out an application, was hired the same day, and after a week's apprenticeship began her job as a ward clerk in the Mt. Sinai nursing department.

For others, including those workers cast out of the private marketplace, a job at a voluntary hospital represented an unanticipated "second career." Cornelius "Bill" Volk, a native of the Netherlands Antilles, promised his wife and young son that he would quit the U.S. merchant marines and seek a more stable outlet for his engineering skills. Unable to break into the union shop at the Brooklyn Schaeffer Brewery, Volk finally landed a job via an employment agency as fireman at Beth Israel Hospital. For Ramon Malave, what mattered most about Beth Israel in 1948 was that it had four walls and heat. One of twelve children born to a Puerto Rican plantation foreman, he had worked in the fields and also shined shoes. After moving in with his uncle in New York City, he tried unsuccessfully to complete high school at night while working days as a roofer and shingler. Suffering from cold and loneliness in a strange city, Malave finally accepted a job, arranged by his uncle, in the Beth Israel storeroom.

Hospital employment might also serve as a shelter from the crises of private life. In 1929, following her mother's death, Gloria Arana left her native Puerto Rico to join her sister in New York. She worked in a Brooklyn battery plant for $10 a week until she burned her hand; later, she got a job in a candy factory, then married a handyman and settled down to raise three daughters. When her marriage ended in 1942 she found full-time work in the Mt. Sinai laundry, straightening and pressing curtains for $60 a month. Elon Tompkins began at Mt. Sinai in 1957, at the age of fifty-eight. He had traveled from Philadelphia to Buffalo to New York City, working at a variety of jobs, including on the railroads, in the garment district, and as a superintendent for several Brooklyn private houses. When his wife died in 1956, he fell into a depression; a friendly Catholic priest in whom he confided then arranged employment at the hospital. Initially a bottle washer at $1 an hour, Tompkins quickly moved into an opening in the engineering department, advancing to $43 a week. "That was a great thing then, everybody congratulated me," he remembered.

If economic imperative most often accounted for a worker's entry into the hospital labor force, it did not necessarily explain why many workers chose to remain for years at their hospital posts. Pearl Cormack is probably typical of those recruits for whom hospital work quickly and in a positive sense became a way of life. One of eight children born to sharecropping parents in Ellery, South Carolina, in 1949 she joined the general postwar exodus of siblings and friends to the urban Northeast. Her early work experiences in New York mixed domestic service and child care, a stint as a hospital messenger, and a job in a brassiere factory. In 1954 she joined her husband, James, already employed as a surgical orderly, at Beth Israel Hospital. While economically only the latest in a string of low-paying, semiskilled jobs, being a nurse's aide offered her the satisfaction of "helping others." "It's not the easiest thing to face," she said, " . . . you face death, you face life . . . you face newborns, you face newborns dying . . . . there's just so many different things in life that you experience. It's not just another job, it's far more than that." Such commitment, typical of many hospital workers, may have contributed to the delay in collective efforts by the hospital labor force. According to Cormack, "This is why you're taken advantage of in the hospital. They realize that people going into this, if they don't like it, they're not going to stay very long, but if you really like the work you will endure a lot of hardships in order to continue doing it."

Compared to other workplaces, the voluntary hospital in the postwar period offered an uncharacteristically personalistic work regime. At its best this created a sense of belonging, of individuals pulling together, each held accountable for his or her own efforts on behalf of the hospital and patients. Indeed, some union stalwarts as well as hospital supervisors looked back with regret on the passing of the old regime. While proud of her role in building the union at Beth Israel, Mae Harrison fondly remembered that in the early fifties "it was like one big family . . . . People was much kinder then, you know, you all worked together." Mary Riley, a nurse's aide at Beth Israel, similarly referred to her first supervisor, Gustava Hills, as "not only a supervisor but a true friend. . . . And don't think she wouldn't blast you, oh yeah! But she knew, I knew, and they [other workers] knew she was our friend. If she blast you she meant you well. And from that I learned what I know today." Lucille Works, employed at Beth Israel in 1954 as a "kitchen maid," serving patients and washing dishes, before being elevated to a supervisory position, recalled a different atmosphere before additions to the physical plant, administrative layers, and unionism complicated the picture. "Everybody knew everybody," she said, "nurses, aides, everybody." A supervisor once took time to visit the sick, but "now we're so far apart because we've grown. Even people you know could come in and out and you'd never know it. We've lost that family touch." The older supervisors, she recalled, ran a tight ship. If too much food was mistakenly delivered to a floor, for example, the supervisor took immediate responsibility and would "holler like crazy." Today there is computerized accountability in the central kitchen.

Changes in the maintenance department reflect the larger pattern of hospital work reorganization. Here, the rise of professional subspecialties and multiple layers of licensing, apparent by the 1960s, transformed what had been the preserve of master mechanics and their helpers. Andrew Danielli came to the Mt. Sinai engineering department in 1949 as an unlicensed refrigeration mechanic, hired to help maintain the hospital's new air-conditioning system (which at first was limited to a few designated areas because of widespread public misgivings about its health effects). He emphasized that his fellow electricians, painters, plumbers, and carpenters were "tradesmen," not engineers, who brought "exceptional pride" to their work and ate lunch together every day in the basement "Mechanics Dining Room." Most were foreign-born, and before the private marketplace lured them away during the building boom of the late 1950s and 1960s, the hospitals reaped a windfall from these "grade-A men." In the power plant, Danielli recalled, one could find the "old spit-and-polish" stationary engineers overseeing the boilers. Frequently, a fellow would "go to sea" with the merchant marines in the spring, returning to the hospital in the winter. Unencumbered by formal job descriptions, the department chief and his foremen allocated the work to be done. "If a doctor wanted a lab renovated," Danielli remembered, "a gang of men would go up there with the foreman and work as a team." It was also not uncommon for maintenance personnel to service the homes of hospital administrators and trustees—"replace a fuse, put in an outlet, do some painting, things like that." By the mid-1970s, Danielli had advanced from mechanic to chief refrigeration engineer (foreman) to assistant director of the engineering department. Along the way he had adjusted, with seemingly serene detachment, to major changes in his corner of the hospital: a doubling, then tripling in size; master craftsmen replaced by graduate engineers; grades and licenses generally overtaking on-the-job training and promotions; and simultaneously replacement of rule by the supervisor with rule by "the union plus the foremen, it's more 50-50."

Hospital workers' dissatisfaction during the preunion era centered not only on an inadequate basic living standard but also on the underside of the hospital as "family." An employee's dependence on his or her immediate boss and the meager rewards that boss could dole out became sources of grievance. The "family" feeling easily took on an ambivalent meaning. While Pearl Cormack remembered that "everyone was very close," she also noted that many on the supervisory staff "did not see it that way . . . [and] this is where conflicts came in." "There are always some who feel themselves superior," she said, "who push people around or speak to them in any manner . . . who feel that because of their authority they should not just give [people] directions . . . but handle them." High turnover rates also worked against sustained feelings of "closeness." The problem of "command" was particularly exacerbated by the arrival of newer, younger supervisors who, Cormack recalled, would "feel they have to use an iron hand."

At best employees attained only roundabout or partial solutions to their problems. Ramon Malave initially checked food into the Beth Israel storeroom during twelve-hour days beginning at 4:00 A.M. "There was no way you would get something out of management," he recalls. To make ends meet most people took things home—"eggs, butter, they didn't have a choice." "The supervisors would say, 'My door is always open,' but you didn't know who was the [real] big boss." Malave once obtained support from his department supervisor for a raise of "a couple of dollars [a week]," which added a mere 30¢ to his paycheck. Still, the hospital parceled out pay raises to maximize individual loyalty to the employer. Mae Harrison recalled, "They'd take each one, like if I was gonna get a raise, they'd take me downstairs and say, 'Now, don't say anything to [your] co-workers.' "

For hospital workers to speak up as a group was most uncommon. "They would mumble and talk and complain among themselves or with themselves," remembered Pearl Cormack, "but when the time comes and you say, 'We all got to get together . . . and let them know what we expect,' they wouldn't do it. If you was strong enough then you would go by yourself." Edith Garcia recalled prevailing on her housekeeping work group at Beth Israel to go see Mrs. Kahn, the supervisor, after a lot of complaining in the washroom about a woman who didn't get paid for a sick day. But "when we got there they showed me up." She was left to do all the talking, and then "the lady [Kahn] asked what right I had as a new worker [to protest] and ran us all out of her office."

Occasionally a supervisor might show considerable flexibility. Bill Volk's first supervisor, a man named Smart, was ideal. "If anything happened we would all get together and then go see Mr. Smart about it." Whether it was allowing workers to leave as soon as their relief showed up or adding or subtracting a half hour to the (unpaid) lunch break, Smart seemed always willing to experiment, provided the work got done. "It makes you feel better to work for a man like that," said Volk. When Smart retired in the midsixties, Volk recalled that conditions deteriorated. "The place started expanding, . . . getting bigger and bigger [and there were] more bosses, more bosses, more bosses." Mr. Morris was the new supervisor, and talking to him was "like you talk to a piece of wood." Then came a series of edicts, tightening departmental rules: "You come in at eight, you work till four, regardless if your relief man is there. You don't punch your card without your uniform on. . . . it's a lot of rules and regulations now and I don't know, you go nuts!"

Above the immediate supervisors and even more remote from the ordinary hospital worker stood the hospital directors and upper-level staff, whom Ramon Malave called the "big bosses." Both their power and physical distance usually shielded these administrators from direct confrontation with employees and their problems. Indeed, in a manner not untypical of hierarchical organizations, workers often blamed middle management for unfairness or abuses in the chain of command. Cassie Cosby thus criticized the Mt. Sinai dietary department supervisors who would "always lie to the bosses about the workers." A friend of hers was once fired for talking back to the supervisor "with her eyes . . . she had big eyes" and the supervisor "got away with that." Against such arbitrariness, workers had few resources. Cosby did recall one occasion when complaints to management against a supervisor helped to get her removed, but ordinarily protest never went beyond "bathroom talk and locker-room talk." "To go directly to the [administrators], to sit down and go shake with them, like since the union's been here, no, that never happened."

Without formal rights or representation, workers nonetheless obtained a modicum of leverage by exposing institutional irregularities and sticking together. Doris Turner, a future union leader whose children were in school and whose husband was supporting the family on a policeman's salary, took a job in 1956 as a dietary clerk at Lenox Hill Hospital and soon became "involved with the people who worked there." The only black in her job classification, Turner formed a close friendship with the Italian woman who trained her. After several months the two discovered that Turner was earning $5 a week less than the white women working around her. Although the hospital quickly corrected the "mistake," the initial response of the supervisor was, "How did you find out?"

A second issue during the preunion period at Lenox Hill aroused the entire female kitchen staff. It seems that male dietary workers received free meals, while female workers did not. Turner recalled that the women's protest began with a lot of "bitching":

> You know how you commiserate . . . sometimes for long periods before you actually get up and do something about it. You talk about it a long time trying to get up your courage, really, like kids whistling in the dark. But you finally realize you gotta do something, so that's what happened. We had a meeting with Lewis Shenkweiler [administrator of Lenox Hill] in the auditorium. They said the meals were worth $10 and if they gave us meals, they'd have to take away some salary, so we said, since you're not giving us meals, [then] add to our salary. We can do crazy arithmetic too.

A spontaneous walkout followed. "It was just the women. We didn't ask anybody to support us. We said, foolishly it could have been, that if you won't give us any food we'll leave. Or if you won't give us any money we'll leave. And we left. And all the way home, all night we were all miserable because we felt we had lost our jobs. But we went back the next morning and, you know, they took us back." The women also began receiving free meals.[12]

The complexity of the female hospital worker's relationship to her employer in the preunion days is further revealed in the experience of a veteran Mt. Sinai laundry worker who took a hospital job in 1942 and emerged as "the floor lady of the laundry" by the early fifties. Born in San Juan, Puerto Rico, in 1913, the daughter of a carpenter and a woman who "sewed all the time," Gloria Arana was sixteen years old when her mother died and her older sister summoned her to New York. In 1942, the divorced mother of three girls under the age of ten, she found work in the Mt. Sinai laundry, first on the flat iron, and then as a linen press worker. For Arana, the hospital offered not just a wage but a world of new faces and a bittersweet experience into which she could pour herself. Among the hospital administrators she met over the years, she found a number of "good bosses." Early on, for example, she remembered crying in hospital director Joseph Turner's office until he granted her a $5-a-month raise. After that, "he was very friendly to me . . . [and] gave me an envelope with $3 at Christmas time." Dr. Turner also took a personal interest in Arana's family: "Everything I needed for my children [medicine, doctors, even once a summer camp program], honest to God, I got from the hospital." But there was also the time when she was sick for two months and was paid only for the first ten days. Or the time in 1949 when she fell in the snow in front of the hospital and couldn't walk for weeks, but "I didn't get a penny."

Unable to affect the "big picture" of their working lives in the hospital, Arana and her co-workers nevertheless sometimes drew clear limits as to how far they could be pushed. For example, one summer it became so hot in the second-floor pressing room, with "no air, no water, no fans," that one woman fainted. Arana "talked to the people [at the time she was pushing delivery carts around to the four floors of the laundry]. . . . Everybody stopped work. Mr. Markowitz [the assistant director] came, put in fans, water, frigidaire . . . also we have a big can of orange juice or pineapple juice." Tensions in the laundry department seemed to intensify in 1952 with the arrival of a new department head, Fritz Field, and his wife, who was also a supervisor. Mr. Field, who had considerable commercial laundry experience, oversaw the mechanization of the laundry as well as a transformation to an almost entirely black and Hispanic labor force. When the workers requested a cutback to a five-day, forty-hour week, Field finally accepted the idea but insisted that productivity improve to compensate for the loss of work time. Shortly before the New Year's holiday, "for three weekends straight [the workers] didn't work, then on New Year's weekend they were asked to work." Arana led a delegation into Field's office and declared, "You can fire me and everybody but we no work. . . ." She recalled that "he was mad. . . . he ran over to [the head of personnel] and said [pointed at her] 'And she's the leader.' " The justice of the workers' request was recognized, however, and the forty-hour week was instituted as the norm.

To many workers like Arana, labor unions, however desirable in the abstract, simply had no place in the world they inhabited. In the early 1940s a Spanish cook "who like too much the Russians" explained "many things about union" to Arana and even took her to a 1944 campaign meeting for the left-wing congressman Vito Marcantonio. When she asked Marcantonio, "Why you no try to help us over at Mt. Sinai 'cause we make so little money," she said he replied, " 'Why don't you try to get a union over there?' I said, 'But which union?' He said, 'Get a union.' " Some years later an Italian man in the laundry ran up to Arana and yelled, " 'Gloria go up to the fifth floor, there's a man trying to get the union inside.' . . I went upstairs but I never saw him 'cause the Irish woman supervisor of the floor summoned Dr. Turner who chased him away." Her next contact with unionism did not come until the late 1950s.

For decades the barriers to effective mobilization of hospital workers appeared insurmountable. On the whole, hospitals were much smaller than most industrial worksites, and were located in many small communities. Even in larger cities, hospital workers were isolated from other groups of industrial workers both economically and socially. Rapid employment turn-over, especially among poor women with no prior connection to the labor force, further complicated the agenda of prospective organizers. But it was the authority and work structure of the hospital itself that probably posed the biggest obstacle to unionism. A heterogeneity of skills and function created physical and mental "islands" with little sense of common identity; and a paternal-philanthropic condescension emanated from hospital trustees as well as much of the public. The antiunionism of conservative business people on hospital boards was matched by the professionally privileged self-identity of physicians and nurses. But the ultimate roadblock was the lack of enabling legislation for hospital worker unionization and collective bargaining rights.

To be sure, in exceptional periods of labor unrest, hospitals felt the pressure of new aspirations from a normally docile labor force. During the great strike wave of 1919, for example, unions won a temporary foothold in several San Francisco hospitals. In the 1930s and 1940s, unorganized hospital workers in major cities sometimes followed the lead of their industrial brothers and sisters—as when big union breakthroughs in San

Francisco and Hawaii included a few signed hospital contracts. The oldest continuing hospital local in the country, San Francisco Local 250 of the Building Service Employees International (now SEIU), dates from the late thirties. In Minnesota, enlightened labor laws contributed to an advance in hospital collective bargaining. However, a more common pattern of grievances and spontaneous protest appeared in New York City, where workers, stung by the death of a nurse in a dormitory fire, staged a sit-down strike at Brooklyn's Israel Zion (later Maimonides) Hospital in January 1937. Subsequent wage cuts triggered further sit-downs as well as picket lines at other New York City facilities, including Beth Israel Hospital, the Hospital for Joint Diseases, and Brooklyn Jewish Hospital. The city only barely averted a health service crisis the following year when the Funeral Casket and Ambulance Chauffeurs Unions called off their threatened walkout.[13]

Despite general advances for the labor movement during the turbulent 1930s, the hospital workers' protests ended with few tangible gains. Management resistance to workers' claims was undivided, encompassing even the most otherwise unconventional of hospital administrators. The reaction of E. M. Bluestone, director of Montefiore Hospital in the Bronx, himself an avid health care reformer, pioneer of "social medicine," and advocate of enlightened personnel policies, is representative. Bluestone was appalled by the strikers, who, he suggested, mistakenly assumed "that the philanthropist and [the workers'] traditional enemy, the capitalist, were one, and began to look upon the hospital as just one more sweatshop to be destroyed, if necessary, in the mad rush to revolutionize our national economy."[14]

If hospital employees stepped over an invisible barrier when they imported methods of protest from the private marketplace, health care employers, for their part, showed little hesitation in adopting an arsenal of classic antiunion measures for their own purposes. At Brooklyn Jewish Hospital, for example, the scene of the sharpest confrontation with unionizing employees, employer hostility was as bitter as at any private corporation. From early on a private detective agency maintained surveillance of all union organizing activity, and when the strike erupted the protesters were quickly arrested by police and summarily fired by the hospital. The courts, meanwhile, enjoined the union from further disruptions, including picketing, on the grounds that the employer was a charitable institution not subject to the nation's newly enacted labor laws. The hospital unions of the 1930s, which included a variety of independent, ad hoc groups, quickly withered.[15]

Effectively, New Deal labor reform excluded hospital workers, whose legal right to strike remained uncertain for ten years following passage of the Wagner Act (1935). When, in 1945, a federal appellate court upheld a local ruling from Washington, D.C., that a nonprofit hospital was indeed subject to the jurisdiction of the National Labor Relations Board, the decision was quickly nullified by the Tydings amendment to the Taft-Hartley Act (1947), which specifically denied collective bargaining rights to nonprofit hospital employees. In any case, hospital nonprofessionals had already been legally isolated from industrial workers and the legislation designed to meet their minimal social welfare needs. Along with restaurant workers, farm laborers, and domestics, hospital service workers were excluded from the Social Security Act of 1935 as well as the minimum wage provisions of the Fair Labor Standards Act of 1938 on the grounds that they did not engage in interstate commerce.[16]

The postwar period, generally a bleak one for left-wing unions kicked out of the labor movement during the Red Purge, did witness something of import for the future of hospital organizing. In New York City the United Public Workers of America (UPWA) established outposts in both voluntary and municipal hospitals (as well as other sectors of the municipal labor force) during the late forties before succumbing to anti-Communist prosecutions and the combined muscle of the city's Democratic administration and the rival unionism of District Council 37, American Federation of State, County, and Municipal Employees (AFSCME). One tangible product of the UPWA hospital drive was a collective bargaining contract at Brooklyn's Maimonides Hospital, primarily the achievement of Elliott Godoff, an exceptional labor organizer who might well be described as the "father" of present-day hospital unionism. In 1923 his paternal uncle, Harry Godoff, a wealthy dress manufacturer who lived in a twenty-four room house with servants in the Boro Park section of Brooklyn, secured passage from Russia for fourteen-year-old Elliott and his older brother. The boys were raised in Patchogue, on Long Island, by Harry and his sister. After two years at Cornell University, Elliott transferred to the Columbia School of Pharmacy, from which he graduated in 1934. The following year he married Lillian Ratick, who recalled that the decision to switch to pharmacy school had been made by Uncle Harry, because Elliott "had no idea what he wanted to do, really." Godoff was a trustee and important donor at Israel Zion Hospital, and he arranged a job for Elliott in the pharmacy. "It was a riot," remembered Lillian. "He made all kinds of ointments and everything else by hand. The pipes overhead, the hot water pipes, were dripping [while] he had things going. And boxes were coming down from the floors, and he had to fill the orders. And when he got through with the boxes, there was a line at the clinic. He had to dispense drugs too."

Elliott Godoff became director of the pharmacy in 1935 and began to step out from under the guiding hand of his conservative Republican uncle. In association with a Russian-born colleague named Rae Ginsburg, Godoff became actively involved in Communist party labor circles. Soon the pharmacy was dispensing not only drugs but the *Daily Worker* and other sheets from would-be hospital worker organizers, which helped lead to the abortive sit-down strike in 1937. Such behavior did not please Uncle Harry. "It's ok for you to help organize the people," he reportedly said, "but do you have to be the leader? Why does *my nephew* have to be the leader?" For a long period the two men did not speak to each other, and Elliott forfeited any inheritance that might have come his way.[17]

In 1945, following a brief fling with Local 218 of the State, County, and Municipal Workers Union (now AFSCME), Godoff became the full-time hospital organizer for Local 444 of the UPWA. By the late forties the Communist-led local had organized a few thousand hospital workers, mostly in city-run institutions. Morris Hodara, a Montefiore lab technician remembered about one hundred enthusiasts, including white-collar employees, RNs and even a few sympathetic physicians. The Montefiore chapter elected black janitor Ben Holland, a former coal miner who learned his union principles directly from the legendary Mother Jones, its local president.

Into the inhospitable climate of the early 1950s Godoff pursued his health sector organizing dreams. In point of fact, aside from the Maimonides contract—gained through a combination of his own persistence and the relative indifference of the hospital administration—he had little to show for years of effort. Elsewhere Local 444 secured at best an informal negotiating role over worker grievances. Meanwhile, public investigations hounded the union leadership, activists faced harassment at work, and even the local Jewish Community Center shut its doors to 444 meetings.[18] Still, Godoff and a few other activists continued their rounds of meetings with the city's hospital union loyalists. To observers, Godoff seemed to possess an unshakable air of confidence and unending resourcefulness. In the worst of times, he dreamed up new strategies, not all of them, according to Hodara, "exactly kosher." (Godoff reportedly told his friend that "even Stalin robbed banks to keep the Revolution going.") Local 444 officers regularly played the numbers game, and once, in the face of salary cutoffs due to lack of funds, Godoff hit on $500, which he then spread around. Speaking with a slight accent, he would entertain his comrades with Jewish humor, with stories and talk of music and theater as well as political dreams. He once joked that his wife almost didn't marry him because to mark a special personal occasion he invited her to a political meeting, thinking that would be the highest form of courtship.

In the mid-1950s Godoff and the Maimonides local, together with a few other remnants of the sinking UPWA, sought refuge within Teamsters Local 237, which was then competing with AFCSME for the allegiance of the city's municipal workers. Uneasy with the new union's style of operation, Godoff felt isolated and abandoned by the front office. In November 1954, for example, he was forced to call off a drive at Montefiore Hospital because, despite "reasonable prospects of success," the union, preoccupied by fights at other institutions, was "not ready to concentrate on the organization of voluntary Hospitals." The strained association did not last long, however. In 1957, with AFCSME District 37 leader Jerry Wurf continually sniping at "the Reds" hiding within the Teamster organization, Local 237 president Henry Feinstein dismissed Godoff but charitably left him the old Maimonides local as a calling card for future union employment, as well as $1,000 in severance pay "because we are a union with a heart." Out of work, Godoff wandered into the hiring hall of the small pharmacists' and drugstore workers' union, Local 1199, Retail Drug Employees. Whether he really had any intention of trading full-time union work for a pharmacy job is debated by those who tell the story. In any case, instead of being interviewed, Godoff ended up in conference with Leon Davis, president of 1199, who proposed that Godoff join the union's staff as an organizer and begin a new drive in the city's hospitals.[19]

A small but proud unit, Local 1199 already had a twenty-five year history of its own. The Retail Drug Employees Union was one of a cluster of Jewish- and Communist-led New York City unions that had carved out a sector of the retail trade during the 1930s. Facing isolation and potential extinction as the political winds shifted and "progressives" became personae non grata in the mainstream labor movement, Local 1199 struggled to survive as an autonomous union. By the mid-fifties its leadership, having weathered the worst of the storm, formed a tight-knit, battle-hardened crew, confident of their own abilities but instinctively mistrustful of others, both within and outside organized labor.

The individual most responsible for the union's endurance was Leon Julius Davis, its president since 1934, who was born on November 21, 1906, in Pinsk, a peasant village near Brest-Litovsk in White Russia. His parents were religious Jews and relatively well-off. He remembered his mother, who came from a family of rabbis, as "a very religious woman with a modern touch—she smoked cigarettes." His father had more entrepreneurial ambitions: he kept a store, held a contract to deliver mail, and rented land. During World War I when the Germans occupied Pinsk, Davis recalled that they "made farmers out of us." Amid the revolutionary ferment of the times, religious traditions lost their hold on the family's nine children. While his parents took no direct interest in the struggles between uniformed Polish troops and barefooted Bolsheviks, economic and political uncertainty led them to send Davis and his older brother to America, to live with an aunt in Hartford, Connecticut. Within months fifteen-year-old Leon was enrolled in high school while helping to support himself by selling newspapers. (He would later regret not learning to spell or write well.) Upon graduation he experimented with a variety of jobs, waiting tables and even working on a tobacco farm. Through a local debating society he began to immerse himself in politics, and a local strike of upholsterers became his baptism into the world of labor unionism.

In 1927, already professing radical political sympathies, Leon Davis moved to New York City to enter the Columbia School of Pharmacy. He worked as a porter and a stock clerk in Harlem drugstores and developed his first friendships with blacks. As a student he led a typically Bohemian life-style, moving frequently with his future wife, Julia, to avoid paying rent. Because his political commitment interfered with his studies, he never completed his pharmacy degree. Instead, Davis channeled his early political energies into the Trade Union Unity League (TUUL), the labor organizing arm of the Communist party.[20] Along with a few other TUUL activists and sympathizers drawn from *Daily Worker* support groups, he was part of a bold effort to organize "all workers in the pharmaceutical industry." On March 31, 1929, the first issue of *Voice of the Mortar and Pestle* proclaimed the goals of the New York Drug Clerks Association (NYDCA): to gain union recognition and better working conditions, and generally to "organize and develop a militant spirit of struggle against wage cutting, speed-ups, unsanitary conditions, etc." The NYDCA met twice a month at the Stuyvesant Casino, 142 Second Avenue, but, according to Davis, was "highly sectarian and had no substantial following"—though its publication carried an endorsement from the Scientific Vegetarian Restaurant on Madison Avenue, a place to "meet for a good meal after the dance." A like-minded organization, the Pharmacists' Union of Greater New York, complemented the NYDCA and shared some of the same organizers. The pharmacists' union established chapters at drugstores and local hospitals, including Maimonedes, where, according to one reminiscence of these years, Elliott Godoff was counted among the early activists. In 1932 the two left-wing groups merged with Local 1199, Retail Drug Employees Union.[21]

The flavor of the pioneering years of drugstore unionism is captured in the recollections of Phil Kamenkowitz, who would later serve as vice president of 1199's drug division. Kamenkowitz first received a circular from the Pharmacists' Union of Greater New York when he visited a city employment office, having lost his own drugstore early in the Depression. Although both his father and his uncle had been members of the Amalgamated Clothing Workers Union, the family was thoroughly Republican, and for several years Kamenkowitz served as Republican chairman of the county elections board. The pharmacists' union office (which Local 1199 later took over) on Forty-second Street and Third Avenue, was a "sloppy cubbyhole" with a desk, a wooden bench along the wall, and "four guys playing chess"—conceivably including Leo Barrish, union president until he left to open a candy store; Leon Davis, general organizer; and Eddie Ayash, treasurer, a position he would maintain for decades with 1199. Dues were posted at 10¢ per month for unemployed members, 25¢ for the employed.

On the surface, 1199's experience in New York's drugstore industry beginning in the 1930s was altogether different from its encounters a quarter-century later in metropolitan hospitals. Yet there were both social and political commonalities that spilled over from one experience to the other. An important early lesson of drugstore unionism—and an abiding theme of 1199 agitation—was the necessity of interracial and interethnic solidarity. Partially as a response to the anti-Semitic quota system affecting medical schools, Jews dominated the pharmacist trade in New York City. During the thirties, drug clerks were also overwhelmingly Jewish, though perhaps 20 percent were Italian or Irish. Drugstore porters and stockmen were predominantly black, almost invariably so in the larger chain stores. In 1937 the union launched a successful campaign in Harlem, beginning with open-air meetings of the unemployed and ending with strike threats, to secure jobs for black pharmacists and to promote the "invisible" porters to the position of "sodamen." This agitation, in line with the generally aggressive stance of the American Communist movement toward Jim Crow in northern cities, had its counterpart in the interior life of the union. Local 1199 was one of the earliest unions to annually celebrate Negro History Week, and as president, Leon Davis, from the first, assured members that "in 1199 we mix and live as one."[22]

Another important principle in the early development of 1199 was militant, industrial unionism. According to Kamenkowitz, the local remained overwhelmingly a "pharmacists' organization" until 1936, when it adopted the industrial unionist idealism of the Congress of Industrial Organizations (CIO) and resolved to add porters and stockmen to its ranks. Generally excluded from National Labor Relations Board (NLRB) jurisdiction—again, a useful preparation for latter-day hospital campaigns—because most drugstores employed fewer than four persons, 1199 developed a creative, participatory approach to organizing. Davis remembers that "to organize you had to convince each individual to join. There it was, store by store, worker by worker." With 4,500 stores to cover in Greater New York, the union devised a decentralized system of discrete "areas" to allow for flexibility in organizational method and to be able to adapt to the sentiments of affected neighborhoods. A Works Progress Administration (WPA) program for unemployed pharmacists proved to be one of the prime recruiting grounds for union members, emphasizing the value of appropriate political contacts and governmental legislation. Thus, early on, both the ideological vision of its leaders and the burdens of practical experience inclined 1199 toward an appreciation of diverse terrains of struggle: at the workplace, in the community and union hall, and among the broader counsels of formal political life.

Leon Davis leading a picket line during a 1941 strike by Local 1199 against the Whelan Stores Corporation.

A small but scrappy outfit, 1199 fought a variety of battles in its early years and proved its organizing mettle in repeated confrontations with the Whelan Stores Corporation, owner of the national drugstore chain. After a bitter, fourth strike against the firm in 1953, the workers finally won a banner forty-hour, five-day-a-week contract. The union also did battle within the trade union movement. In 1937 it joined the American Federation of Labor (AFL) as part of the Retail Clerks International, quickly linked up with John L. Lewis's New Era Committee, then participated in the formation of the Retail, Wholesale, Department Store Union (RWDSU), CIO, in 1938. An ill-fated merger in 1943 with another CIO retail union, Local 830, almost killed the drugstore union at a time when a thousand of its members were doing wartime service. Local 1199 "reorganized" as an independent in 1945, after membership reportedly had dropped from a peak of 4,000 to 1,400.[23]

Much of the postwar history of the drugstore union was shaped by the contemporary political assault directed from both within and without the labor movement on the left-wing remnant of the CIO. Politically, 1199's hopes, like those of other constituents of the Popular Front, depended on a continuing identity with Roosevelt's New Deal. "The forward march of our country," Leon Davis declared before drugstore delegates in 1947, "has been led not by the reactionaries and big business but by George Washington, by Lincoln and of late by our great President Roosevelt." "That day when Roosevelt died" retrospectively symbolized the end of a dream for the CIO radicals of the late 1940s. For 1199 and other Communist-led unions, the next several years witnessed a series of hostile governmental-sponsored investigations, withdrawal (in the face of expulsion) from the main body of organized labor, subsequent raiding by both the AFL and the CIO, and employer tests of the unions' will to survive. That 1199 emerged with nearly 4,000 members and over half the independent drugstores in New York City under contract was no small achievement.[24]

A key factor in 1199's survival may have been its compact size. Too small and insignificant to attract sustained public attention, it weathered the worst storm by relying on the trust the union leadership had built up with the members. Called before the Hartley Committee (Congressional Committee on Labor and Education), which was investigating communism in the distributive trades in August 1948, Leon Davis sparred with committee members while invoking constitutional privilege as to his political affiliations. He was grilled for one and a half hours by Congressmen Charles Kersten of Wisconsin and John F. Kennedy of Massachusetts (which did little to enamor the Kennedy name among 1199's high command) but stuck by his political guns. Claiming as a trade unionist to have read too little "economics or social philosophy" to determine "whether Lenin was right or somebody else was," Davis nevertheless asserted that the Communist party had done more good than harm in the American labor movement, that the capitalist system could be "improved a darn sight," and that the government should promptly cease its support of the "reactionary Fascist monarchy" in Greece. (While maintaining a permanent public silence about his own political ties, and allowing others to entirely disclaim such connections, in 1979 Davis acknowledged that for the good of the union he had officially—and permanently—resigned from the Communist party a few weeks prior to being called before the Hartley Committee.)[25]

Like Davis, the rank and file of 1199 seemed content to separate personal political beliefs from accountability of trade union officers. Although it did not ignore domestic and foreign policy issues, the union usually took care to relate political stands to the economic interests of its members. A rank-and-file committee accompanied Davis to the hearings and dismissed as irrelevant much of the questioning, countercharging that the investigators were "out to do a job on our union and other unions, something the employers have attempted to do for years." Several months earlier, on February 19, 1948, the union leader had been supported in a similar fashion when, in a moment of uncommon cooperation, 1199 and the Bronx County Pharmaceutical Association joined forces and closed down all 650 Bronx drugstores to celebrate the establishment of the state of Israel.[26]

Three legacies of the defensive, postwar period carried particular weight for the future of 1199. First, union ties to the Communist party grew increasingly irrelevant and largely disintegrated in the 1950s. As Davis's own actions suggested, union members were expected to give up political work before taking union staff positions; in any case, he insisted on independence from all outside political directives. As early as 1948, for example, he ignored a party-backed resolution that Theodore ("Teddy") Mitchell, a black porter, become union vice president, giving the position instead to former sodaman William J. Taylor, who would guide the union's benefit and pension programs for decades to come. Davis also refused to adopt a unilateral position on the Julius and Ethel Rosenberg case. Fearing union division, he characteristically deferred the matter to a stewards' assembly and only then joined the demonstrators. Throughout the 1950s a contingent of party loyalists continued to operate as a cell within the union, with at most forty members clustered in activist steward positions. By 1958, however, when organizer Jesse Olson himself quit, the party and its influence had measurably faded. Elliott Godoff's son recalled his father scoffing that the party people were "losers." Olson himself had come to believe that the party "was not an organization that would advance the cause," that "it was too alien, too undemocratic." What remained were habits of mind, a disciplined behavior, and a network of associations based on "the old days."[27]

While to some extent moving away from old moorings, the siege years bound the drugstore union more closely to its civil rights commitment and its black membership. In 1948 and 1949, when the union faced a fierce attack from the government and rival CIO locals, black Harlem pharmacists stepped in to protect 1199's jurisdiction. Leon Davis recalled that the North Harlem Pharmaceutical Association, led by 1199 member Howard Reckling, "closed up a hundred stores" rather than see them certified by a raiding union. Retired 1199 vice president Teddy Mitchell, the union's first black officer, remembers when the "Harlem pharmacists actually hid Davis and treasurer Eddie Ayash in the 135th Street YMCA" to delay the serving of a subpoena. Indeed, an almost ritualistic homage to "the time the Harlem membership saved this union" has become part of 1199's historical self-consciousness. When Davis was invited by black professionals to address the National Pharmaceutical Convention in 1951, he lashed out with characteristic verve at those who "advise caution and tact" in eliminating "discrimination, Jim Crow, segregation, and the whole vicious system of white supremacy." The 1199 leader claimed to speak for a "union of 5000 men and women who have learned through bitter experience that real progress cannot be achieved unless there is progress for all the people, Negro and white, Jew and gentile."[28]

Less dramatic than the civil rights theme but hardly less important for 1199's future was the connection the drugstore union made, beginning in 1949, with the New York City distributive trades, especially District 65, Wholesale and Warehouse Workers, under the leadership of Arthur Osman. A commanding presence, Osman sought to group and protect a number of left-wing CIO units cast adrift during the McCarthy era. In 1950 his Distributive, Processing, and Office Workers of America (DPOWA) united District 65, 1199, and other New York locals with the militant, southern-based Food, Tobacco, Agriculture, and Allied Workers (FTA), which had just been expelled from the CIO. Conforming to the general guidelines of the DPOWA, 1199 refashioned its constitution based on the 65 model, complete with a general council (executive), divisional administrative units, and election of shop stewards according to the principle of "approximately one steward for each fifteen members." It also decided to comply with the non-Communist affidavit required by the Taft-Hartley Act—"not because we approve of this vicious law, but because we recognize that we must protect ourselves against the raids of the AFL and CIO."[29]

Perhaps the most significant impact of the District 65 connection was personal. Determined to stimulate more rank-and-file participation in union affairs, the drugstore local worked to improve its social and cultural programming. A move into new headquarters in 1954 created space for such activities, while the impetus was provided by Moe Foner, recruited from 65 to serve as activities director and editor of the *1199 News*. Born to immigrant, Polish-Jewish parents (his father was a seltzer man in the Williamsburg area of Brooklyn), Foner and his three brothers gravitated from an early age toward an active, politically engaged life. A basketball player at Brooklyn College in the mid-thirties, he joined the young radicals of the American Student Union who were agitating over conditions in Spain and after graduation took a job in the registrar's office at City College. In 1941 the accusing finger of the state's Rapp-Coudert Committee began pointing out academics suspected of Communist associations. Two of Foner's brothers lost their instructorships in the history department at City College, and he himself was suspended and then dismissed. (With characteristic spunk the family regrouped as the Foner Brothers Band and, with Moe on sax, played dance music in a style they dubbed "suspended swing.") By the time he was hired at 1199, Foner had lost neither his sociable good humor nor his indefatigable sense of commitment. For the next three decades he would make full use of both as the union's de facto political strategist and director of public relations.

Local 1199's defensive alignment alongside District 65 lasted for five years. Legitimacy for labor's self-styled "progressives" did not come easily. After facing disabling legislation as well as grand jury harassment, in 1954 the DPOWA accepted a general statement of policy opposing "all forms of totalitarianisms" and managed to regain admittance to the CIO, with its various locals reintegrated into the RWDSU. Although 65 and 1199 continued to cooperate as a kind of left flank within the international, tensions occasionally surfaced between the two. For example, Osman and his successor, David Livingston, anticipated a merger with the smaller 1199, though Davis stubbornly stuck to his own, independent path. On the whole, however, both unions had reason to greet the mid-fifties with a sigh of relief. The end of McCarthyism meant that the worst years were over.[30]

In 1957, when Elliott Godoff met with Leon Davis, he found the union leader restless and hungry for new ideas. Peaking in the mid-fifties with nearly 6,000 members, the Retail Drug Employees Union had all but exhausted its organizational potential in New York City drugstores, while the jurisdictional claims of AFL-CIO affiliates prevented outreach to other metropolitan areas. Under the circumstances, 1199 pressed forward with a number of modest initiatives. The union entered Nassau and Suffolk counties, took on HIP (the city health insurance plan) drug dispensaries, and probed the variety chain stores carrying pharmaceutical products. It was within this framework of cautious experimentation that Davis welcomed Godoff into the organization.

Godoff's plans to organize hospital workers initially fell on receptive if only modestly enthusiastic ears. "We were looking for a challenge," Davis recalled many years later. "We had an industrial organization [but] were not going out of New York City. He had a contract at Maimonedes with 125-50 workers." With the help of a few volunteers, Godoff first investigated several small proprietary hospitals and nursing homes on the grounds that these profit-making institutions would be covered by the NLRB. That effort went nowhere. As Foner recollected, no one that first year had "a vision of the future"; there was as yet no real thought of the hospitals as "an industry" susceptible to mass organization. It was, he said, strictly small scale—"basically one guy [Godoff] creeping around."

Phil Kamenkowitz, at the time busy with his own organizational duties, remembered the early hospital effort as a kind of benevolent sideshow indulged in by the drugstore members. "We didn't know how low they [i.e., hospital workers' living and working conditions] were. . . . If we had known we probably never would have entered the hospitals." When Davis introduced Godoff to the union's general council in 1957, the veteran hospital organizer offered a brief rundown of the early history of hospital workers—"how the first workers were prisoners, prostitutes, the poorest people . . . like slavery. We looked at [Godoff] like he was crazy." Still, the delegates gave their quick approval to the Davis-Godoff initiative. Claude Ferrara, a pharmacist and drugstore steward at the time, recalled Godoff's appearance and endorsement before the larger assembly of New York union stewards: "Davis says, 'We've taken Godoff onto our staff.' It was put to a vote. No one spoke opposed." Kamenkowitz remembered that "the staff was always a very good staff . . . we went along with everything." While some pharmacists later expressed resentment that their interests had been slighted by a shift in union priorities away from the drugstores and toward the hospital field, no one at the time, according to Ferrara, "really dreamed it would come to where we're at now."

CHAPTER 2

Awakening at Montefiore: The Hospital That Refused to Fight

In December 1957 Elliott Godoff turned his hopes for a break-through in hospital unionism to Montefiore Hospital, a large voluntary institution located on Gun Hill Road in the north Bronx. The decision proved most auspicious, setting off a chain of events with broad repercussions for hospitals and hospital workers alike. Years later, Local 1199 members tended to recall the Montefiore events as the early swelling of one big wave of unionism, a wave that ultimately swept over the entire metropolitan New York area. Such a view has superficial validity. Union recognition by the Montefiore administration, sealed on December 6, 1958, resulted in the postwar era's first openly negotiated contract in the hospital industry and raised expectations for workers across the city. Six months after the Montefiore settlement, 3,500 workers from seven hospitals staged an unprecedented forty-six-day strike that ended without formal union recognition but nevertheless created an opening for union presence at the workplace. Continued workplace-centered agitation and an active political campaign culminated in 1963 in crucial changes in the New York State labor law permitting collective bargaining in the city's voluntary hospitals. By the end of the decade three-quarters of the metropolitan hospital labor force was unionized; 1199 had some 30,000 members at dozens of institutions.

Reviewed more closely, the breakthrough at Montefiore was marked at once by typical and exceptional circumstances. Compared to what followed, the Montefiore campaign proved to be a kind of dress rehearsal, with the basic themes of the 1199 story being played out before a relatively friendly audience. Those themes divide into three areas for analysis: the worker-union dynamic, the union-employer dynamic, and the union-politics dynamic. Each was present at Montefiore—hence, the circumstances were typical— but it was the distinctiveness of the situation that accounted for the historic opening.

It required no great genius to think that Montefiore might be more amenable to collective bargaining than many other hospitals. Founded as a chronic care home in 1884 by an ex-Confederate Jewish surgeon and Ku Klux Klan member, Montefiore had nevertheless gained a liberal and innovative reputation by the 1930s. In addition to placing many refugees from Nazi-occupied Europe into full-time salaried positions, the director, E. M. Bluestone, was the first to accept women on the house staff and blacks as resident physicians. Seeking to extend concern for health care "beyond the hospital, into the community," he assigned young Dr. Martin Cherkasky from Philadelphia to pioneer programs in home care and group practice and in 1949 named him head of the nation's first hospital-based division of social medicine. As successor to Bluestone in 1950, Cherkasky presided over the final transformation of the "custodial" Hospital for Chronic Diseases into the acute care–focused Montefiore Hospital and Medical Center.[1] Within the administrative fraternity of the hospitals of the 1950s, Cherkasky was undoubtedly as much a black sheep as Leon Davis was within the trade union movement. Influenced by the social-democratic currents of the 1930s, Cherkasky liked to think of himself as a "radical" and a political progressive as well as a general menace to the medical establishment. During the McCarthy era, in fact, Montefiore became a haven for left-wing physicians who could count on administrative protection.

No one knew better than Elliott Godoff that Montefiore's liberalism did not extend to the organization of its salaried or wage-earning work force. Indeed, prior to 1958 Godoff had made at least two attempts to organize Montefiore workers. After initial explorations the previous year, Local 444 of the United Public Workers of America (UPWA) attracted roughly one hundred inter- ested employees during a summer campaign in 1949. But when the hospital administration ignored the workers' demands the movement "simply col- lapsed." In 1953 a group operating under the Teamsters' jurisdiction forced an end to separate dining rooms for professional, clerical, and service workers but got not further.

These early drives centered on a politically conscious core of white-collar workers who looked at labor organizing as only one aspect of a larger political agenda. From the beginning, however, their efforts were hampered by the very real racial and occupational divisions within the hospital labor force. Grosvenor Cooper, a hospital mortician and one of the few black UPWA activists, recalled that union meetings were often held at the homes of sympathetic doctors and that discussion focused as much on issues like segregated housing in the surrounding neighborhood or the platform of the American Labor party as on the hospital itself. Clearly, the activist minority had trouble communicating their vision of change beyond a limited circle. A Montefiore service worker recalled the early union drives as "some lab workers who used to try to organize us," while a Puerto Rican cook made the point more graphically: "White-collar workers are OK. . . . if they lost their jobs they could work elsewhere; we belong to our stomachs." One latter-day union activist remembered the would-be organizers as "not quite strong enough to do anything about the hospitals, so we lost faith in them."

The political enlightenment lodged in the upper reaches of the Montefiore administrative structure generally meant little to the workers at the bottom. Indeed, personnel policies at Montefiore—as at most other hospitals—simply did not receive much administrative attention. Cherkasky recalled, "No one thought about the nonprofessional area then. My own program was to make this the best scientific institution for the care of the sick and, even more so, to make this the most uniquely responsive social institution . . . I didn't have much of a clue in the personnel area." Workers at Montefiore had few rights and were treated in certain respects as dependent members of an extended family. Their "free" meals were deducted in advance from their paychecks, and as late as 1958 some workers continued the old practice of "living in." While the administration claimed that job security compensated for the workers' inferior pay, departmental supervisors exercised nearly arbitrary authority. Al Kosloski, who worked in the engineering (mainte-nance) department since 1937, believed that "your job depended on being cooperative." He knew he was expected to be available on Saturdays and to help supervisors or administrators build driveways or make other home repairs. Because the supervisors did not hide their antiunion feelings, one hospital messenger who joined the Teamster effort in 1953 recalled "how hard [it was] for us to get going. . . . most of the workers were too scared, afraid to be fired."

There is no evidence to suggest that Montefiore was particularly "ripe" for organization in 1958. While Godoff was drawn to the hospital on the basis of his old contacts there, much of the earlier union base had in fact eroded. Only two people, Betty Rosoff—a lab technician with political experience dating back to the American Student Union—and a clerk showed up at a preliminary meeting. Many of the earlier activists, including UPWA chapter president Ben Holland, Morris Hodara, and Grosvenor Cooper (who started his own funeral home) had left the hospital. Together with a few of Godoff's friends at Maimonides Hospital, they offered at best peripheral support to the new campaign.

Of the earlier union leaders, only Marshall Dubin played a major role in the 1958 campaign. The son of Russian-Jewish immigrants from Chicago, he combined medical-technical skills with passionate political interests. Following World War II service in the Pacific engineer corps, Dubin wrote a master's thesis at Berkeley on the development of the labor movement in the South. The death of his mother and the need for a steady income called him back to New York, where he became chief technician of the bacteriology lab at Montefiore and made common cause with the active left-wing circle at the hospital. He met Godoff during a 1948 UPWA campaign and from that time on became a loyal friend and admirer of the man he later referred to as "the father of us all." Although Dubin left Montefiore in 1955 for jobs at Lenox Hill and then Jacobi hospitals, he returned to Godoff's side as an informal assistant for the Montefiore drive. A small, gentle man of literary bent whose poems regularly spiced organizing efforts, Dubin later joined 1199's staff and ultimately served as union education director.

What lay behind Godoff's success in 1958? In retrospect, three mutually reinforcing developments distinguished the campaign: changes in work relations within the hospital; a more concentrated organizing focus on hospital service workers; and the effective integration of union organizers with indigenous work-group leaders. Montefiore was undergoing a major transformation in the late 1950s from a chronic-care home to a general hospital with an acute-care focus. Symbolically, it closed its tuberculosis sanitarium in 1956, even as it was building new pediatric, psychiatric, and nursing centers. As an acute-care facility, the hospital experienced a much more rapid turnover of patients and required enhanced flexibility to serve multiple patient needs, in turn placing new emphasis on the service component of the institution. Cherkasky remembered the 1950s as a period of transition from a time when the hospital admitted some 200 patients a year to one in which it processed nearly the same number of new patients each day. "It was like going from slow down to speed up," he said. "The needs of the patients were more acute and the personnel, the facility, and the pace began to change."[2]

The hospital's business style quickly reflected its change in operations. "We recognized the new demands set by the new pace," Cherkasky recalled. "Costs per day had risen to $27 [per bed] in 1958 from $8 or $9 in 1950. We needed large infusions of money and I had to turn my attention there. . . . I was always prepared to accept new ideas." To promote greater efficiency in its operations, Montefiore, like other hospitals, hired people with outside business experience to direct the expansion and upgrading of support services. Unintentionally, the move to enhance productivity upended the stability of past employee relations. Worker dissatisfaction tended to center precisely on those departments engaged in efficiency reforms. Irving Stern, for example, arrived at Montefiore in the early 1950s and proudly introduced a profit-and-loss consciousness into the laundry operations, which included the installation of a 500-pound washer and a flatwork ironer that handled 1,900 sheets and towels per hour. Jacques Bloch joined the food service department in 1954 with a background in hotel and business administration and within three years had centralized the dishwashing and tray-assembly systems, opened a new cafeteria, and, with the attitude that "food is money," eliminated the paternalistic "free food" system—which increased the amount of take-home pay for workers but still triggered resentments. Stern was dubbed "the Bull" for his dictatorial manner, and employees complained that Bloch was personally "remote" and that his task supervision interfered with a pre-established, more casual "workers' way of life."

Judged by the administrators' yardsticks, the progressive refurbishing of Montefiore's personnel policies offered tangible gains to hospital workers, yet the same policies looked different to those who lived with them on a daily basis. Complaints of speedups, closer supervision, and both direct and indirect harassment on the job were common. Union appeals to workplace "dignity" and "respect" responded to the workers' grievances, and the kitchen and laundry staffs, which had felt most directly the change in work rhythms, became bulwarks of 1199's organizing drive in 1957–58. For the first time the union self-consciously decided to focus on the service workers, which ipso facto entailed an appeal to blacks and Hispanics. Betty Rosoff recalled, "The technical people made a conscious decision to move to the background of this campaign." Grosvenor Cooper similarly acknowledged that "the 1958 effort was left to the newcomers."

The first clear-cut sign of a new emphasis in the unionizing campaign was the assignment of drugstore union vice president Teddy Mitchell to full-time Montefiore duty. The son of a traveling railroad fireman, Mitchell was raised by his maternal grandparents in Ahoskie, North Carolina, where his grandmother, a freed slave, had acquired a dozen acres of land from a wealthy mulatto neighbor. Mitchell first traveled to New York as a child to visit his mother, who worked as a maid for an actress. Following high school in Portsmouth, Virginia, he moved to New York and eventually took a job as a stockman at a Whelan drugstore. He joined Local 1199 when it first began to organize porters in 1936 and soon after was elected shop steward for fifteen stores. While working in a battery plant during World War II, Mitchell contracted lead poisoning and subsequently returned to working in a drugstore. In 1949, after five years as a clerk, he joined the staff of 1199 and became the union's first black official. He recalled that the only objection to his appointment came from black pharmacists who resented the appointment of someone without adequate "professional" credentials. Mitchell brushed off such criticism: "The black middle class is a son of a bitch." Years later Leon Davis credited Mitchell not so much for strategic leadership in the Montefiore campaign but with strengthening the link between union "outsiders" and rank-and-file hospital workers. "The best organizer," offered Davis, "is one who has all the qualities and all the faults of a worker himself."

Mitchell's appointment signaled a new adaptation to the racial realities of the hospital's service work force. Instead of ignoring existing divisions and stratifications among hospital workers, the union turned an apparent obstacle to its advantage, seeking a kind of coalition of distinct social groupings. The strategy was to appeal to workers by specific department: "Special meeting of the Nutrition [dietary] Dept.," "Attention PNs and Nurse's Aides," read early leaflets. Only after the nonprofessional campaign was off the ground did lab worker Harold Garelick, for example, begin to build support in the white-collar sector. And Morris Hodara recalled that the appearance of twenty Puerto Rican workers at an early meeting first convinced Montefiore organizers that they stood a real chance.

The Montefiore organizing campaign worked because the union was able not only to inspire workers with a tangible sense of what they might win but to harness individual ambitions to a project for group advancement. The assignment of drugstore stewards to the picket lines, the opening of an office across from the hospital, and the scheduling of key meetings at the union's Manhattan headquarters were all calculated to transfer a sense of the union's collective strength to the workers. Perhaps the key accomplishment of the organizing staff lay in its ability to attract a core of exceptionally motivated individuals who actively carried the union message to all parts of the hospital. In fact, at least three of the 1958 rank-and-file organizers had taken peripheral roles in earlier Montefiore campaigns. Salvatore Cordero, a messenger in the nursing unit who had met Elliott Godoff during the Teamster effort, recalled how he was asked to rally a group of Spanish-speaking hospital workers. Emerito Cruz, an attendant at a Puerto Rican mental health clinic, came to New York in the early 1950s and joined Godoff's 1954 organizing drive. A "salad man" and then a special cook in the Montefiore dietary department, Cruz was uncommonly well acclimated to hospital unionism, having served as a union officer in Puerto Rico as early as 1944.

Harold Harris, the third of the unskilled recruits from earlier years, was the epitome of the early union pioneers: dedicated, ambitious, even entrepreneurial, yet frustrated by the system. Harris's Jamaican parents separated when he was an infant and his mother moved to Panama. His father, who owned a small grocery in Kingston, died when Harold was six years old, leaving him in the care of his teenage cousin, who raised him while his aunt and uncle worked all day on their farm outside Kingston. Harold joined them in the fields at age fourteen; before that he had helped with the housework, including cooking, cleaning, and sewing, the "ambitious" routine of his adopted family allowing little time for play. He read at night and looked forward to college, but he was forced to abandon that dream when his uncle died. His cousin married and moved to Kingston, leaving Harold to run the farm with his aunt, which he did, until he was eighteen. After a family quarrel and a generally "bitter time," he too left to seek a new life in Kingston, spending most of six years working for wealthy Americans—for example, as a valet, then waiter, then driver for a bank manager, all the while waiting tables at night in local clubs. Although directly dependent on the dispositions of his employers, Harris followed his own political and intellectual instincts. He joined a group of black nationalist followers of island hero Marcus Garvey ("The outside world didn't recognize the Garvey movement, but black people did") and participated in the nationalist insurrections that began to sweep the island in 1936 and that led to a general strike in Kingston. "I mean it was a strike," he recalled, "not a strike that you walk around with your hands in your pockets. This was a revolution." Years later he compared the spirit and community of the Garvey movement to "being in the union."

In 1944 Harris traveled to the United States to work on tobacco farms in Connecticut. Then, after nearly five years of work, agricultural "repatriation" to Jamaica, and an unhappy marriage, he returned to America and accepted a job as pantryman at Montefiore Hospital in 1950. Harris brought a rich background to this new and "more settled" life, taking his tasks seriously and priding himself on being a particularly conscientious worker. He considered his new job analogous to and just as important as that of the doctors, for "food is like medicine to the sick people." He lived in the hospital for two years, taking home $54 a month after meals and other deductions and getting only Thursdays off. By 1952 he was feeling "rebellious," committed to his job but desiring something better. He got his own apartment and, determined to set "things straight," took it upon himself to "get the boys together." Harris and his co-workers brought a series of grievances, including the six-day week and split shifts, to the head dietician and threatened "action" in two weeks if they received no response. Their efforts, he claimed, speeded the change to a five-day week, the most dramatic improvement the dietary workers remember having won in the preunion years. He also joined Godoff's band of Teamsters in 1954, though the movement never seemed to him to have the makings of "a fighting force."

Harold Harris's accumulated experiences and sensibilities collided with the managerial initiatives at Montefiore. Things had "tightened up," it seemed to him, ever since Jacques Bloch arrived to manage the food service. Harris admired the department director's attempt to replace the lax standards and poor morale that had previously dominated the section, but the new system seemed entirely designed for the benefit of management, not the workers—"it never fit in with us." Harris, whom Bloch remembered as one of his "brightest" and most responsible workers, began to regard his supervisor as both a model and an antagonist. "I decided to stay for improvement," he said. "Just the same as old Bloch came there for improvement on the part of management, I was there to improve the labor and working class, in my own funny way."

By 1958 Harris viewed the food service department in almost military terms, with Bloch directing the department "like an army" and Elliott Godoff and Leon Davis leading embattled union militants. With a real organization behind them the workers settled down to a permanent tug of war, with the union members trying always to keep "the rope tight." Both the administration and the workers had legitimate but differing purposes, in Harris's view. Local 1199 had become the equivalent of "General Motors or the Telephone Company," that is, a powerful, organized body that could get things done. The union gave him something to believe in, something that could provide leverage in the unpredictable world around him.

Like Harris, the rest of the inner core of rank-and-file activists in 1958 were workers who generally enjoyed their jobs, received good marks from their supervisors, and displayed a talent for advancement within their skill categories. Thelma Bowles decided to pursue a career in nursing despite her parents conflicting desires. She entered Montefiore's practical nursing program in 1951 and for five years was in charge of a floor during the night shift. Perhaps her working hours explain why she never encountered the union until early 1958, when she met Godoff and Mitchell outside the hospital, passing out leaflets. Bowles attributed her openness to the union message to her disgust at having to wear a special patch that distinguished the second-class "PN" from the all-white "RNs." For Al Kosloski, who came from a Polish family of hard-coal miners near Wilkes Barre, Pennsylvania, participation in unions was a natural part of working-class life. He exploited every opportunity, moving from pantryman to gardener to assistant head gardener, then parlayed World War II service into the training he needed to pursue an engineering license. (As late as 1976 his supervisor regarded him as "one of the best engineers in the plant.") "My dream," said Kosloski, "was to move up, keep movin' up."

Kenneth Downes, a native of Barbados with background as a fisherman, butler, carpenter, barman, painter, and merchant seaman, took a job as a dishwasher at Montefiore in 1950 and worked his way up by the rules. To earn extra money he ran the bar at the doctors' dances, and his West Indian cooking soon won him a raise and a new position—working the morning grill. He took pride in getting the staff off to a good day; indeed, with uncommon care he cleaned the grill with his "spade" after each egg, then applied fresh lard. Like Harold Harris, however, the self-motivated Downes ran afoul of the hospital's new efficiency programs. When a reduction in the operating hours of the grill nearly led to his dismissal, a friendly woman in personnel transferred Downes to the safety and traffic department. Circulating throughout the hospital on guard duty, he was able to sign up more workers for the union in 1958 than any other individual. After his retirement, he returned to Barbados but on a visit to New York recalled his instrumental role in the unionization campaign: "All I wanted is for my poor workers to get a proper salary . . . I fought, I walked all night with cards in my pocket getting them signed up and the bottom of my shoes burnin' like hot peppers."

Local 1199 organizers were, by August 1958, expressing enthusiasm and even amazement at the reception they were receiving among the Montefiore workers. Weak in the white-collar laboratory and pink-collar clerical divisions, the union drive had attracted overwhelming support in the largely nonwhite housekeeping, food service, and traffic and safety departments. With help from Kosloski and a core of activists who called themselves the "Four Horsemen," the engineering department was also solidly prounion. The large nursing division tended to split along racial and occupational lines, with the less-skilled aides and orderlies most effectively lined up in the union camp. Altogether, the organizers had collected over 500 signed cards from a work force of 900 employees. This paper majority meant nothing, however, because under the existing labor law hospital management could—and did—ignore the demands for formal union recognition and a contract.

Having reached the workers, the union was now compelled to devise a strategy for confronting the Montefiore administration. While it necessarily drew on the energies and talents of the hospital rank and file, the ensuing battle demanded a logic and a terrain distinct from the organizing drive. Workplace militancy, mobilization of public opinion, the hospital's liberal self-image, and political and financial intervention from the mayor's office all contributed to the victory claimed in December. Without the first two factors the Montefiore drive would have stalled like others in the past; but it was the last two that underscored the significance of the achievement and suggested the difficulty of reproducing the situation elsewhere.

By the end of the summer of 1958, the union strategists were ready, as Leon Davis put it, "to test the workers' discipline." Lab technician Betty Rosoff remembered, "The feeling was that this was our chance and we should make the most of it." Early, voluntary organizing committees became more formal, democratic structures, with union stewards elected in each department, and workers regularly marched with signs and passed out leaflets outside the hospital buildings. At one point Moe Foner decided to place a poster-sized petition in front of the hospital doors to give "people confidence once their names are down in public . . ." Meanwhile, the administration was "sitting tight"; it took "no action regarding the workers."

Local 1199 next appealed to the moral sympathies and sense of fair play of those who helped shape public opinion. Foner enlisted the support of columnist James Wechsler of the *New York Post* and editors of the *New York Times*, the *New York Amsterdam News*, and *El Diario* for a campaign that was conducted "like a crusade . . . good versus evil." Hospital administrators discovered the workers' depressing economic conditions laid out before them in regular installments in the daily press: service workers earned an average of $34–38 per week, less than half that earned by unskilled industrial workers and some $12 less than city hospital workers in the same grades. Accepting both the moral claims of the workers' protest and the hospital's claims of financial stringency, a *Times* editorial on November 21 appealed to administrative accountability and a larger public responsibility: "Isn't it unfair and inhuman to ask hospital workers to help meet hospital deficits by accepting substandard wages? Shouldn't voluntary hospital managements deal with unions that represent a majority of their employees — even though no state law compels them to? Shouldn't wages in them be raised at least to city hospital levels? Shouldn't the city increase its ward subsidies to meet city hospital standards? Shouldn't the state bring hospital employees under the provisions of the state labor laws?"[3]

Soon prominent public figures like Eleanor Roosevelt and Senator Herbert H. Lehman acknowledged the growing appeals "on behalf of 600 Negro and Puerto Rican workers . . . terribly exploited and . . . practically desperate unless something is done in their behalf." They were urged to use their "great influence to persuade Mr. Victor Riesenfeld, President of the Board of Directors of Montefiore Hospital, to sit down with a committee of the union and attempt to work out some of the problems." In her syndicated column "My Day," Mrs. Roosevelt commented on the severe hardship faced by hospital workers, and she and Lehman both wrote privately to Riesenfeld asking for some accommodation with the workers. While neither of these notables pushed openly for union recognition, Moe Foner has argued that the very fact that they said something "made what we were doing important."[4]

New York's organized labor movement also responded to 1199's call for help. In particular, Harry Van Arsdale, Jr., president of New York's Central Labor Council (CLC), offered a most welcome cloak of respectability for the hospital insurgents. Overriding the reluctance of some trade unionists to accept the legitimacy of unionism in the nonprofit health sector, and setting aside 1199's maverick past, Van Arsdale publicly placed the council's seal of approval on the Montefiore campaign. Faced with growing criticism by civil rights groups as to the exclusionary policies of many AFL-CIO affiliates, Van Arsdale seized on the hospital drive as a dramatic test of organized labor's good intentions with regard to the city's rapidly expanding nonwhite working population. Van Arsdale adopted the hospital workers' cause in press releases, personal appearances, and the activation of other locals to openly support the Montefiore picketers.

The most important contribution Van Arsdale made to the Montefiore campaign came by way of his influence with Mayor Robert F. Wagner, Jr. Wagner is identified with instituting a code for public employee bargaining as early as 1954, which was updated in March 1958 as the celebrated Executive Order 49 (or "Little Wagner Act") and formally recognized the rights of unions in dealing with the city. However, labor relations during his twelve-year administration generally danced to an older, personalistic, and very political tune. Acting through labor advisor Theodore Kheel, the mayor had, over the years, used connections to transit union leader Michael Quill, Teamster head Henry Feinstein, and Van Arsdale to set informal terms of labor peace. He regularly extended social invitations to trade unionists and attended countless bar mitzvahs and confirmation parties of labor leaders' offspring, establishing a personalistic style of conflict resolution. For those outside the inner circle, access to one of the power brokers—like Van Arsdale—was crucial. Although Local 1199 was not exactly a "public employees" union, in late November 1958 Mayor Wagner assigned labor commissioner Harold A. Felix to try to work out a strike-avoiding agreement. In and of itself, mediation from Gracie Mansion provided the hospital workers with a visibility and legitimacy they could achieve in few other ways.[5]

While continued worker militancy and the growing public campaign kept the union drive alive, there was no immediate resolution to the struggle. Administrative intransigency stemmed at least in part from an awareness that the confrontation with 1199 involved more than local issues: recognition of the union at Montefiore would be the first major breakthrough for hospital unionism citywide. Victor Weingarten, coordinator of Montefiore's public relations office, remembers being warned by other hospital directors of a continuous escalation of demands and the loss of administrative control should the union be recognized. The idea of unionization struck even the liberal Cherkasky as an imposition on legitimate managerial prerogatives. Antiunion letters from donors to the Federation of Jewish Philanthropies, with which Montefiore was vitally associated, convinced Weingarten that "it would be difficult to get philanthropic money if [we then appear to] give it all to unions."

The opposition of Montefiore's own board of trustees was a more critical obstacle to union recognition. Composed of bank directors, corporate attorneys, and industrial executives—men accustomed to dealing with unions as an inevitable but unenjoyable part of the private "business" world—the board found the special nonunion sanctum of the hospitals, to use

Cherkasky's word, "heavenly." However, these sentiments conflicted with Jewish notions of social justice and particularly with the hospital director's own well developed social idealism. For Cherkasky to deny the union was to deny his self-image as a sensitive and visionary administrator. Thus, as the impasse at the hospital dragged on, union leaders appealed to Cherkasky's conscience. On November 28, Leon Davis addressed him in writing as a man of "good will." Admitting that continuing recalcitrance on the administrator's part might well "destroy the union," Davis wondered whether the director could "rightly participate in this concerted effort to defeat these workers [and] destroy their hopes for better conditions now and in the future. . . . The question still remains whether [a union defeat] solves any problems for the management, for the workers, or for you who must assume a great share of the burden." Flattering the hospital director as "the most important factor in this whole situation," Davis implored him to take the steps necessary to avoid an ugly strike, to side with "reason against insanity."[6] Looking back, Davis's letter was, according to Cherkasky, the "final blow—there wasn't a chord in me that Leon didn't strike." In the director's opinion, the letter "turned the whole thing around." Cherkasky resolved to end the stalemate, and he soon persuaded Riesenfeld and other trustees that "if we win, we lose—we do not want to be a part of that."

Even before he decided to deal openly with 1199, Cherkasky had recognized limits beyond which he was unwilling to go in resisting the union. Local 1199 organizers, for example, were astounded at the ease with which they could penetrate the hospital, sometimes communicating with workers even when supervisors were in the same room. Sarah Goldstein, Montefiore's director of volunteer services, recalled the day when Pinkerton guards arrived to protect the hospital from the union picketers demonstrating at noontime. The employment (apparently by an administrative subordinate) of this notorious union-busting firm—one to which Jewish liberals of the thirties would have had an instinctual revulsion—"shocked" Goldstein. When she sought out the director, she found him so embarrassed by the episode that he ordered the guards removed, "and they were gone in twenty minutes." Weingarten also remembered interrupting a police captain about to arrest some unruly picketers with word that the hospital would not file charges. More significantly, the public relations coordinator was privately communicating with Moe Foner, who recalled: "After a while Weingarten was pulling for us, [he] would tell me that a meeting was called for the next day and that an editorial would be helpful. We assumed that he was speaking for Cherkasky."

The record indicates that financial calculations as well as private conscience figured in Montefiore's ultimate accommodation with 1199. From the moment of his original discussions with Riesenfeld concerning union recognition, Cherkasky linked a settlement with an increase in the reimbursement rate paid by the city to the voluntary hospitals for ward patients. In doing so the director displayed a long-range astuteness regarding the hospital's future development.

As in many industrial disputes, the final bargaining took place in an atmosphere of crisis. Even with the basic agreement already in place, Riesenfeld and the other trustees apparently required a dramatic moment to convince the hospital's financial patrons as well as other administrators that Montefiore had not simply "caved in" to union demands. The climax came once the union set Monday, December 8, at 6:00 A.M. as a strike deadline. Faced with the unwelcome prospect of disruptions and public protest, Mayor Wagner, urged on by Riesenfeld and Van Arsdale, called an emergency meeting to negotiate a settlement. With Van Arsdale representing 1199's interests, an agreement was reached a day and a half before the deadline. The hospital would recognize the union as "the sole collective bargaining agent pending a certification election and [would] negotiate an agreement dealing with all issues." Publicly the matter of reimbursement remained unsettled;

Montefiore workers celebrate winning union recognition, December 6, 1958. Union leaders standing in the foreground, from left to right, include Moe Foner, Teddy Mitchell, Leon Davis, and Elliott Godoff.

privately the city agreed to increase its support of ward patients in the voluntary hospitals from $16 per day to $20 per day, an implicit recognition of public responsibility for the welfare of the voluntary hospital system.

On December 30, 1958, a union election was held at Montefiore. Of 900 workers eligible to vote, 628 chose Local 1199 as their bargaining agent; only 31 opposed the union. Early in 1959 the union and the hospital entered negotiations, and by March they had initialed a contract. The terms represented modest gains — a $30-per-month increase in pay, time-and-a-half pay for work beyond a forty-hour week, establishment of grievance procedures, and the setting of minimum provisions for sick leave and vacation time. Most important, however, the contract offered visible proof of the power of organization — a union among hospital workers.

The events at Montefiore Hospital foreshadowed important themes for contemporary health institutions and their workers. A "new" working-class population, outside the traditional reach of trade unionism, had effectively mobilized in the face of nonunion managerial rationalization of the workplace. In particular, a growing sense of entitlement among racial minorities had emerged as a potentially powerful factor in urban industrial relations. The public nature of hospital organizing was also manifest in the union's dependence on a favorable outside political balance of power. Once isolated and little noticed, Local 1199 had suddenly entered a new realm of political alliances and public impact. Response of the local trade union movement, cultivation of the press and prominent public figures, and the pressuring of key political figures had marked the campaign. Finally, both managerial ideology and the financial restructuring of the hospital industry began to change with the Montefiore settlement. It became clear that unionization might itself play a role in the construction of a rationalized voluntary hospital complex — the kind of health care "empire" that, with the help of increasing tax dollars, came to dominate big American cities by the late 1960s. It was no coincidence that the hospital that could solve a labor dispute by effective appeal to municipal financial subsidy would also lead the way toward a more general expansion through public monies.

In 1958 Montefiore, like other voluntary hospitals, faced impending financial crisis. Martin Cherkasky and other administrators realized that neither private giving, like that from the Federation of Jewish Philanthropies, nor fee-for-service could provide the capital necessary for the extensive changes that the hospital was undergoing and had projected for the future. Indeed, rising costs and a shortage of paying patients had already forced some small institutions to close their doors. Some means had to be found to increase public funding to voluntary hospitals and generally make government a bigger participant in health care. In New York City, initial relief from the financial crisis was provided by the 1961 citywide affiliation system whereby voluntary hospitals and private medical colleges agreed to staff deteriorating municipal hospitals in exchange for substantial subsidies. Organized by the city hospital commissioner, Ray E. Trussell, and with key backing from progressive administrators like Cherkasky, the affiliation agreements significantly improved the planning capacity of the voluntary complexes. (Montefiore, for example, received $7 million per year from its connection to publicly owned Morrisania Hospital, since closed.) Together, these affiliations and a sharp increase in the number of payments by the city for inpatient services infused the voluntary hospitals with much-needed dollars.[7]

Throughout the 1960s the entire financial edifice of the hospital was shifted away from the austerity of fee-for-service and philanthropic contributions to other sources. Third-party insurance payments mushroomed with the expansion of health benefits in both private industry and public employment contracts. In the late 1960s Medicare and Medicaid, with their cost-plus reimbursement formulas, offered a golden opportunity for supplementing hospital budgets. No one took better advantage of these financial innovations in medical care than Martin Cherkasky. From the mid-1950s through the 1960s, Montefiore financed a fourfold increase in plant size while attracting an ambitious, research-oriented, salaried teaching staff. Dorothy Levenson reported that total costs at Montefiore were some $4 million in 1951, $10 million plus in 1961 and $75 million in 1971. By 1970 the complex now called the Montefiore Medical Center had also become the largest employer in the Bronx.[8]

In a 1959 *Modern Hospital* article, Cherkasky subtly alluded to the secret of the hospitals' future welfare when he noted that "hospitals will have to stop hiding their light under a bushel and find ways and means of bringing to the community an awareness of how hospital income is spent." By then the Montefiore director had, in fact, already discovered that a dissatisfied labor force could provide a useful wedge into the public coffers.[9] However, to suggest that he ingeniously transformed the "threat" of unionization into a sustaining vehicle of hospital expansionism imposes too grand a logic on the solution to Montefiore's labor problems in 1958. While the settlement there foreshadowed the transformation of voluntary hospital financing in New York, its full implications could not have been predicted at the time. It is more plausible to assume that once Cherkasky had privately made the "big" decision (i.e., to abide by a union election), he did his level best to sweeten the deal. The real sticking point in the conflict had been ideological and political: Was Montefiore prepared to become the first major hospital to share its managerial prerogatives with a union? Mayor Wagner, who appeared at the time to have miraculously resolved the conflict by coming up with the city subsidy, himself recalled that the money issue was not primary: "You can always find a little more here or there once you've got [the basic agreement] going." Local 1199 hoped to immediately spread the union message throughout the city, but beyond Gun Hill Road, "basic agreement" between hospital management and organized labor would not come so easily.

CHAPTER 3

The Brewing Storm:
Organizing from the Ground Up

The Montefiore settlement in December 1958 left union leaders exuberant. Leon Davis immediately announced "the beginning of a new day for all the workers in all the [city's] hospitals."[1] Within days, small groups of workers in at least three hospitals—Mt. Sinai, Lenox Hill, and Beth Israel in Manhattan—had taken the initiative to contact the union, and on New Year's Day, Local 1199 formally announced an organizing drive aimed at the 35,000 employees of New York City's voluntary hospitals. In March 1959 the union marked its annual black history celebration with a play entitled *The Montefiore Story*, written and produced by Ossie Davis and starring union supporters Ricardo Montalban, Ruby Dee, Lloyd Gough, and Robert De Cormier. The performance was capped by a rendition of the "Hospital Song of 1199," written by Moe Foner's brother and furworkers' leader Henry Foner, and an address by Congressman Adam Clayton Powell. In effect, the program served a dual purpose: to present the Montefiore agreement as a model for other hospital workers to follow; and to link the interests of the hospital workers with the general cause of freedom and progress for the black community.[2]

The dawn so keenly anticipated by Davis and others revealed only a brewing storm. Just as the union had hoped, the message of Montefiore spread throughout the city's hospital kitchens, laundry rooms, and nursing wards. This time, however, the union's efforts met determined resistance from management and ultimately resulted in the first major hospital strike in American history.

As in the early stages of most labor unions, the hospital workers' efforts in 1959 ultimately rested on the shoulders of rank-and-file leaders, workers whom historian David Montgomery has called the "Militant Minority."[3] In every social struggle, big or small, such workplace or community militants seem to emerge, as if from nowhere, as leaders. Precisely because they have no pre-established office or formal authority, and because they remain invisible to most outside observers, such people are usually lost to the historical record. In the case of the hospital workers, we focus here on several individuals who emerged in the early months of 1959 as union stalwarts. Their stories, in addition to shedding light on the organizing campaign, suggest the intricate connection between private lives and public actions.

With high hopes Local 1199 targeted forty of the city's eighty-odd hospitals and nursing homes, then handed over the task to a small but energetic staff. The drive began with only two full-time hospital organizers, Elliott Godoff and Teddy Mitchell. In mid-January they were joined by Godoff's old friend Marshall Dubin, drug (i.e., drugstore) organizer Jesse Olson, and licensed practical nurse and Montefiore steward Thelma Bowles. Olson's appointment was a typical Leon Davis move. Although the pragmatic Davis had tended to dismiss Olson's political preoccupations— "He [Davis] said my head was always in the clouds" — he knew a talented servant when he saw one. Going from a $175-a-week salary as a registered pharmacist to $110 as an organizer, Olson acquiesced because, he felt, it was "God's work." Bowles, the only woman on the team and one of the few female rank-and-file leaders to emerge from the Montefiore effort, expressed mixed feelings about her new job: "I didn't know whether I could cope with it or not. When you go among strangers, it's not like people that you've known for many years, working with them you know, but then. . . . I remember Elliott said to me, 'I'll be with you and you'll be alright, you'll do alright.' " Soon after the staff was in place, the "Crack of Dawn Brigade" was formed to help them. Drafted from the union's drug staff and steward system, these early-morning volunteers provided the first real muscle behind the union's extensive campaign.

Phil Kamenkowitz, then drug union director for the Bronx and Washington Heights (Manhattan), remembered that "we all had a good laugh" over the seemingly impossible task facing each organizer. Moe Foner handed him some cards that listed each institution for which he was in charge of leafleting, and Kamenkowitz recalled: "I took a look at my cards. I got [Columbia-] Presbyterian with 1,900 workers, Flower-Fifth [Avenue] with 800, and I got Joint Disease, and I got Women's Hospital, and I got Knickerbocker." With two stewards in tow, he started out at Knickerbocker Hospital in Harlem, arriving at 5:30 A.M. in order to catch the 6:00 A.M. shift change. At first the trio huddled in Kamenkowitz's old Buick, trying to keep warm and to figure out which entrance most workers would likely use. "We were starting from scratch, no contacts, no nothing inside. We were huddling there, it was freezing, man, freezing. . . . Then I see an old man walking down with a little bag toward the emergency room and I want to show my delegates what I can do. I run over to him, 'I'm from 1199 here to organize you.' He grabbed my hand, 'Thank God the Union's here.' Mr. Burns, I'll never forget him."

All over the city, drugstore employees used to working in small shops with a handful of people now converged on massive, alien hospital complexes, armed with leaflets and union membership applications. For many of the volunteers, the contact with poor, black, unskilled workers was eye-opening. Union steward Claude Ferrara, a pharmacist, normally worked an 8:00 A.M.–4:00 P.M. or 2:30–11:00 P.M. shift. During the hospital drive he set his alarm for 4:00 A.M., caught the subway to Manhattan by 4:30, then leafleted hospitals until it was time to go to work. Ferrara, the son of Italian immigrants, who had worked his way up through pharmacy school, explained, "These people had been pushed around all their life. . . . It was really amazing to me that they could have been excluded from the great social steps that this country [had taken] forward." The first month was exhilarating. "We were floating," remembered union vice president William Taylor. Membership applications were "coming in by the bushel basket." An early leaflet suggested the momentum on which the union was counting: "If Montefiore can do it, so can Beth Israel." Olson recalled, "It was as if people were just waiting for a 'moshiach' [messiah] to come."

A system emerged to the organizing effort: The union staff would gather a small group of sympathetic workers at each hospital and, to show its strength and seriousness of purpose, invite the group to a meeting at 1199 headquarters, where they would officially be designated as the "organizing committee." Then came the hard work. Olson recalled that at Beth Israel, "We met every week in the [nearby] apartment of an office worker to make our plans and give responsibilities for people to organize within their department. I set up a sub rosa organizing headquarters in the stockroom of a laboratory." Union membership grew, though signed declarations were little more than expressions of interest, since 1199 had stopped collecting the usual $3-per-month dues until workers could secure a "union contract." Active involvement of the members, not finances, thus became the chief mark of union commitment.

Local 1199 opened area headquarters near the larger institutions to coordinate strategy and as a symbol of the union's presence. As enrollment cards came tumbling in, general membership patterns began to emerge. While upholding in principle the "one big union" or industrial unionist vision of the CIO, the 1959 drive, to an even greater degree than the Montefiore campaign, focused on nonprofessionals. To be sure, even within the nonprofessional grades there existed differences among prounion enthusiasts. The dietary and housekeeping departments, for example, generally organized most quickly and developed solid, prounion sympathies. Hospital kitchens and laundries (in hospitals so equipped) offered work centers conducive to social ties as well as collective grievances, and, as at Montefiore, the centralization of services in these departments had had disruptive consequences. Most of these service departments were staffed by minority workers and were almost invariably controlled by white male department heads possessing broad authority over the workday lives of the individual employees.

Compared to the concentrated and relatively isolated service departments, the nonprofessional nursing division—numerically the largest section in each hospital—proved somewhat difficult to organize. More direct involvement in patient care placed aides, orderlies, and LPNs in closer contact with doctors and especially with the "professional" registered nurses. It was here that the doctrine "service before self" had the greatest impact. In addition, the administrative regime in nursing departments was heavily personalistic and quite arbitrary. Working conditions often depended upon which ward or floor one was working and to which nurse or supervisor one was assigned. The range in assignments naturally created considerable variations in attitudes toward work and loyalty to one's employer. Beyond the structural factors, unauthorized practices complicated work relations in nursing and did little to foster worker solidarity. One union organizer referred to the "private deals" that workers had negotiated for many years with certain nursing supervisors; another cited a common practice of "tips" from patients on certain wards. Yet the felt irrationality and petty injustices of nursing supervision also provoked grievances. Adding to the tension in nursing department relationships was the common racial division in most hospitals between the white supervisor and the black or Hispanic aide or orderly. Thus, if somewhat divided in their initial response to the organizing drive, nursing division workers invariably played a central role in the union campaign.

The maintenance (or engineering, as it was more often called) department also played a critical, if less predictable, role in the organizing drives. A sense of craft pride as well as functional independence from the rest of the hospital hierarchy characterized individuals in these all-male departments. Working in small, usually self-supervised crews throughout the physical expanse of the institution, the sympathetic maintenance man became a valuable resource in the organizing campaign and often took on a leadership role. Frequently, however, the potential importance of these individuals to the unionizing effort was offset by the impact of the special conditions of their work—their pride in skill and craft traditions creating a self-isolating snobbery. While the engineers in one sense assumed the role of "aristocrats of [manual] labor," the union stalwarts were almost invariably drawn from the nonlicensed "maintenance" side of the department. The line separating licensed and unlicensed workers also demarcated ethnic and racial differences, as it did everywhere else in the hospitals. Blacks and Hispanics took over the lowest-paying, least-specialized maintenance jobs, while eastern and southern European immigrants clung to the more skilled positions.

At root, the activation of departments depended on key individuals who seized the opportunity available at that moment. For the most part this early rank-and-file vanguard was predisposed by past experience and inherited values to a struggle for group advancement. Joseph Brown, for example, was ready-made for union activism. When he took a job as a handyman-mason at Bronx Hospital in 1954, his worldly attitudes were already well defined. Brown grew up with his mother's family during the Depression in a poor Philadelphia household. He knew of his father's "gift" as a self-taught automobile mechanic in Troy, New York, but early on he set his sights on a white-collar career. When he finished high school in Philadelphia, Brown headed to Baltimore's Morgan College (now Morgan State) on a football scholarship, with the ultimate intention of teaching physical education. In the midst of his college career, however, he became a husband and father and "had no other means but to move out and seek a job." Lacking the connections to secure one of Baltimore's higher-status black jobs in the steel industry, the shipyards, or the post office, Brown eventually found work as a general laborer in a white-run building union. He befriended a white compressor mechanic and learned to steer clear of racial confrontations without losing his self-respect: "Sometimes they'd get up and say, 'Hey boy, hey nigger,' you know, but they wasn't talking to me, 'cause that's not my name, and I wasn't going to say anything. Then when they see that I ignore what they say, then they call me by name, 'Joe,' or 'Brownie.' As long as you don't contest what they're saying, eventually they will get tired."

Joe Brown won the confidence of both laborers and mechanics, and soon became the acknowledged representative of blacks in the local union. Still, he wanted to be more than a laborer. In 1947, when his wife's family moved to New York, he took a job with a North Bergen, New Jersey, meat-packing firm, unloading hogs from freight cars. Quickly advancing to lard tender, he became a union shop steward. Then, in 1953, a skidding lard drum hit him in the back and ended his meat-packing career. After a frustrating year of inactivity, Brown filled out an application for what he thought would be a short stint in the slower-paced world of hospital maintenance work.

Joe Brown heard no more about unions until early 1959, when Dubin and Mitchell appeared at Bronx Hospital's back entrance passing out union cards. Brown agreed to take a handful of cards to "see what I can do."

I was well-known there, and by me bein' a mason and plasterer, I could go all over the building. And so I commenced spreading the news about how we need a union here and let's get together, you know. . . . I had a boss, the chief engineer, he was a union man himself, or had been, and he never hindered me from going around, but the others couldn't. So what I did, I would catch the nurse's aides and orderlies and dietary workers in the locker-rooms in the morning. That [first] day I signed up about thirty workers. The next morning Teddy was around and says, "Listen, Brown, . . . we could get a union in here."

The biggest obstacle Brown and other organizers confronted at Bronx Hospital was fear. The threat of retaliation centered on the hospital's assistant director, Abraham Friedman, who "could walk down the hall and see you doing something wrong and he would go to your department head. . . . or maybe even tell them to get rid of you." Fear among the workers spread when it was learned that the hospital's director, Dr. Arnold Karan, had already identified Brown as the chief union agitator. Thinking he could always go back to New Jersey, Brown resolved to confront the issue directly:

I told them, "You know, I'm going to sit down and talk to Dr. Karan." And so a couple of days later, I went upstairs to his office. . . . you go up on the elevator and before I left everybody was grouped around saying, "Watch, watch Joe Brown get thrown out of this hospital." . . . There's Dr. Karan, a little short man behind this long table. "Are you Mr. Brown?" he asks. "Yes, Dr. Karan, I'm Mr. Brown." He says, "Shut the door, have a seat." He had leather chairs and what not. . . . I had on my white overalls, you know, mostly caked with plaster. "No Dr. Karan, I don't want to sit down, I'm dirty." "Have a seat, Mr. Brown. What can I do for you?" "Dr. Karan," I said, "I'm here to tell you that I know you know what's happening. We, the workers here, want a union, and we have organized." Oh, my God, when I said that, I might as well have shot him. "Now what are you talking about? Don't bring no union in here. Young man, you have the audacity to come visit me and tell me that? Mr. Brown, as long as I am here, there never will be a union. You can go back and tell your people." I said, "No, they're not my people, they're yours. They work for you. Dr. Karan, remember this, I'll be back to see you again. Thank you for your time."

Brown went downstairs and told the others about his meeting with the director. There was no retaliation, and in early April 1959 Bronx Hospital service workers, led by chief steward Joe Brown, voted 337 to 34 to strike for union recognition.

As Brown's experience indicates, the very presence of unions within the larger political culture could make an impression, even among a totally unorganized labor force like the hospital workers. Mt. Sinai nurse's aide Mildred Reeves, for example, had never heard of Local 1199, but she was predisposed to believe that a union "brought good things" because, as she recalled, during the 1940s, her father and two of her brothers had fought to bring a union to their baking company. Soon after organizers appeared outside Mt. Sinai, she began to pass out leaflets and talk up the union during coffee breaks, lunch, and in the locker-room. Ironically, Mt. Sinai maintenance worker Elon Tompkins was familiar with unions as a result of his experience as a strikebreaker in the terminal commissary during the fierce 1922 Buffalo (N.Y.) railroad strike. By 1959, he had invested the local union with a faith adapted from his Baptist upbringing: "I believe in religion and I believe in myself. . . . If I trust in Him I can make it, if I get up and try, that's the reason I been here all these years and I'm still fighting. . . . The union is the next thing, my next religion. I trust in the union, to the extent that they help me along in my daily life. You can't just say and pray all the time, and not hustle. I pray and then try to hustle."

In many ways the hospital union drive spoke to personal struggles for survival. Julio Pagan, who grew up on a small farm near Ponce, Puerto Rico, where his family hired out as domestics, had no previous experience with unions. Following a half-dozen years of schooling in New York City, Pagan returned to the island to train as an orderly at San Juan City Hospital. Then, in 1958, at age nineteen, he moved to East Harlem and signed on at neighboring Mt. Sinai Hospital, where he spent six months in training— "how to make a bed, give enemas, that sort of thing." Just over a year after his arrival he became an active member of the Sinai Organizing Committee. Asked why he got involved, he responded: "Because of working conditions. . . . My boss, he treated me like an animal. I knew the way to bring something that you want, you have to fight for it. If you don't fight you get nothing. When I came to the meetings at the union headquarters . . . when I learned that other workers had unions, it just came to me that that was the only way." Like Pagan, Mt. Sinai operating room attendant Leonard Stovall also joined the union because he was tired of being "pushed around." He told a reporter in 1959 that he had been threatened with dismissal for speaking to a patient, telling her to "trust in God" as she was wheeled under the operating room lights.[4]

Lenox Hill Hospital diet clerk Doris Turner, who eventually moved from rank-and-file organizer to become the union's chief executive, shared a background of struggle with Pagan, Stovall, and Tompkins. Turner's motivation emerged from a willing identification with two important groups of people around her—her family and her fellow kitchen workers. Although her parents divorced when she was only a year old, Turner learned a sense of striving from both sides of her family. Her maternal grandmother, with whom she lived for several years in Pensacola, Florida, was an ardent Baptist who could not read or write and had been raised by her own grandmother, a slave-midwife who had seen all but one of her children sold. Turner remembered her grandmother as "one of these salt-of-the-earth women who believed in trying to be helpful to everybody. . . . ." Her father, with whom she lived during high school, was a skilled and literate shoemaker whose home was a busy social meeting place for card players as well as civic groups. "Whatever initiative I might have . . . has come from my father . . . and his ability to do things," Turner said. "He always seemed very sure of himself. Discriminated against as a black female employee, Doris Turner discovered the uses of solidarity well before 1959 (see chapter 1). Through an Italian friend whose husband was an officer in the International Union of Electrical Workers, she learned that "what we need is a union." Within hours after the appearance of an 1199 organizer at Lenox Hill, Turner and almost 200 co-workers had signed up: "You see, we'd had so many miseries and we'd talked about 'em for so long and we'd even mentioned having a union."

For the dietary workers at Mt. Sinai, like those at Lenox Hill, joining the union was a collective decision. Cassie Cosby, a twenty-year veteran of numerous skirmishes in the food service, recalled that by the time Local 1199 arrived, "Amongst ourselves, we was very much organized"; each floor "was like your own kitchen or apartment," with a "good community" growing up between aides and most nurses. The supervisors, in Cosby's opinion, spoiled things, especially Miss Hoffman, head dietician in Hausman Pavilion: "She had no feeling for the girls, nothing nice to say, no 'good mornings,' nothing. We wanted to work but we were really getting pretty peeled up. Of course, we didn't know nothing about no union, but we'd talk about it and talk about it." According to Cosby, the union appeared at Mt. Sinai "out of the blue sky." "We run into the pickets out there, and they give us cards and talked to us." She remembered "just being glad to see someone come along and recognize us as human beings. I guess that just pushed me right on." Later, she and her co-workers "ran all over the hospital with cards. At first we was kosher [i.e., secret] with it. The main thing was to get people to come to the meetings."[5]

Prior union and work experience, workplace grievances backed by group solidarity, personal strength derived from familial and religious influence, and individual pluck and ambition seem to define the prospective rank-and-file activist. These qualities neatly converged in Beth Israel nurse's aide Pearl Cormack. Attracted to the hospital in 1954 out of a positive sense of service and because her husband, James, already worked there as an orderly, she nevertheless chafed under petty supervisor tyranny and administrative high-handedness. Miss Blake, Cormack's first supervisor in the dietary department, had once admonished her, "People like you we can get a dime a dozen." That kind of talk and the arbitrary raises based on "good behavior" and "personality" led Cormack to request a transfer to the nursing department, but again she grew unhappy. She believed that she was once unfairly reprimanded for malingering, and on another occasion she almost lost her job when she refused to help a special-duty nurse with an assignment. Cormack said that she was busy with her own duties, helping six to eight patients in oxygen tents ("I had to turn them back and forth, bathe them, change their beds, all by myself"), while the nurse had only one patient to care for. The head nurse saved Cormack's job, even while her supervisor circulated a petition to get rid of her for "insubordination." "My patients liked me," she recalled. They "sometimes preferred me to going into a home, some wanted me to come home with them." Other patients sent letters of praise for her work, and a few even refused special duty nurses "just to get my care."

Pearl Cormack had previously depended on her own resources to cope with work-related problems. For example, shortly after arriving in New York City she had taken a job in a metal-plating factory, making lipstick cases and watchbands. One day one of the Puerto Rican workers got burned with acid and the company let him go without compensation. Cormack took it upon herself to organize a protest, charging the company with negligence for supplying short gloves. "After that everything I did was picked on. Then one day the super got on me for something, came after me cursing, calling me a son of a bitch. I grabbed two knives [used to cut boxes] and I jumped across the table at him and I ran for him but he closed the office door." She was fired the next day, and "as I was leaving I reached up and grabbed every cabinet and threw them down on the floor and slammed the door." The factory in question had a union, but to Cormack it seemed weak, even "silly."

In 1959, during the union organizing drive, David Livingston, president of the Wholesale and Warehouse Workers Union, District 65, was confined to Beth Israel with hepatitis. Cormack was working on his floor, and "while he was there I went into his room one day giving him fresh water. He said they were trying to organize these voluntary hospitals, and what did I think of it. I told him I thought it was a great idea. While he was there we did a little secret talking to different people and so from that I started talking to others. He told us to do it quietly so long as he was in the hospital, and then to go with it after he left."

Pearl Cormack, Cassie Cosby, and the others were part of a solid phalanx of supporters recruited by the union in a bare six weeks of effort. Claiming 6,000 adherents by early February 1959, Local 1199 pointed excitedly to "one of the fastest organizing drives in history." However, without exactly saying so, the union then began to modify its original wide-open attack in favor of a strategy of consolidation. In part the change was simply a recognition of the uneven pace of organizing in different hospital settings. Local 1199 abandoned its campaign at New York Eye and Ear Hospital, for example, when Olson reported "very little activity by late January." Similarly, continuous coverage at Women's Hospital was withdrawn after three leaflet distributions brought "no response." University Hospital organizers reported slow but steady progress, declaring a majority of employees signed up on March 2, yet two weeks later Olson found the workers "completely unprepared for a strike vote," and by April the drive there was declared "dormant." After high expectations Local 1199 also threw in the towel in mid-March at Knickerbocker Hospital because of "very weak leadership." The union revealed its real organizing strongholds on February 4 when it demanded recognition from the directors of Mt. Sinai and Beth David hospitals in Manhattan, Brooklyn Jewish Hospital, and Bronx Hospital. By early March, Manhattan's Lenox Hill, Beth Israel, Flower–Fifth Avenue and (briefly) Knickerbocker hospitals, as well as Beth El Hospital in Brooklyn, were added to the list.[6]

Local 1199's strategic targeting of a few institutions was both a pragmatic response to reports from the workplace and a reflection of a new urgency brought on by a competitive race with other unions in the field. The rival unions, drawn to the once-barren but now apparently fertile hospital environment, appeared on the scene by the beginning of February 1959. Teamsters Local 237, State, County and Municipal Workers Union (now AFSCME) Local 302, and Building Service Employees International Union (now SEIU) Local 144 all made ambitious noises in the direction of the voluntary hospitals. Local 1199 enjoyed good relations with none of them, but the competition was most bitter with the Teamsters. Local 237 was Elliott Godoff's old affiliation, and his cohorts, still distressed at 237 for giving up on the hospitals years before, considered Teamster local leaders Henry Feinstein and his son Barry "liars," "scoundrels," and "the scum of the earth" for jumping back into the hospital field. However, based on their early entrée among public-sector workers in the city, 237 claimed a charter in the voluntary hospital sector, and there were reports that the Teamsters had reached an accord with their old nemesis, AFSCME, in order to beat out 1199 at the giant Columbia-Presbyterian Hospital in Upper Manhattan. In a scarcely veiled denigration of 1199, AFSCME regional director Jerry Wurf asked for public support of "decent trade unions" for workers long "left out in the cold." In mid-April AFSCME claimed majorities at five hospitals, but the intransigence of the hospitals had been made clear by then, and AFSCME, whatever its real strength, did not push for a showdown.[7]

In the end, only the hotel workers' union, Local 144, proved an enduring competitor to 1199 in New York City. Late in February 1959 it began leafleting Beth Israel Hospital, where 1199 had already sunk rather firm roots; immediately the 1199 organizing committee moved "to discourage the return of these intruders." To head off open warfare, Leon Davis ultimately offered Peter Ottley, Local 144's new black president, the right-of-way in the smaller proprietary hospitals and many of the city's nursing homes. While not airtight, the agreement allowed each union to productively develop its own turf.

The hardening of 1199's strategy was also a response to a united show of resistance to the organizing drive by the hospitals. In trumpeting the Montefiore effort, union leaders initially had hoped to uncover other willing negotiating partners from among the diverse managements of the city's voluntary hospitals. The fact that the seventy-member Greater New York Hospital Association (GNYHA) had, since its establishment in 1904, never addressed personnel matters suggested the possibility of direct communication channels with individual employers, a situation the union might be expected to exploit to its advantage. Thus, when workers reported threats of dismissal for organizing activity, 1199 publicly blamed "eager-beaver supervisors," not top management, for the harassment.[8] The union dusted off and recirculated old statements by some hospital directors that they would never interfere with the rights of expression and association of their employees.

All hopes for employer moderation soon faded. The agreement with Montefiore had done little to incline the rest of the hospital community toward collective bargaining. Indeed, the attorney for several wealthy Jewish donors complained both to the Montefiore trustees and to the Federation of Jewish Philanthropies about the "weak and pusillanimous manner in which Montefiore capitulated to Local 1199." After a month of delay, postponement, and official silence before worker and union appeals, the besieged hospitals announced on March 3, 1959, a joint, hard-line decision: "We hereby state our unwillingness to recognize any union as the collective bargaining agent for our employees," read GNYHA acting director John V. Connorton. The next day Fred K. Fish, president of the association, elaborated that while unions might be appropriate instruments in profit-making institutions, totally different rules must necessarily be applied in the hospitals: "Voluntary hospitals have accepted responsibility of the sick and are committed to this obligation. They cannot delegate any part of this responsibility to a union or any other medically unrelated organization. . . . There should be no intervention when the issue may be life or death."[9]

The "special" nature of the hospital and its presumed immunity from collective bargaining and strikes on humanitarian grounds formed the basis of the employers' official antiunion policy. In April, Dr. Martin Steinberg, director of Mt. Sinai, publicly elaborated the employers' position to a city hall representative: "A hospital is not an economic, industrial unit. It is a social unit. . . . Human life should not be a pawn in jousting for economic gain or power."[10] Later he described a basic, ideological antiunionism that also affected hospital thinking: "I went to the [Mt. Sinai] Board [of Directors] and told the board, 'Look, our wages are low, much too low, I'm not proud of them, all they're asking for is recognition and that means that they will make demands, of course. But my own feeling is that I could be swayed either way and this is a problem I'm going to leave to you.' And the board [members] were all businessmen who were all tired and sick to death of the dealings and restrictions that the union had placed on their factories and businesses [and they] said, 'No, we will not have a union.' "

Even before announcing their official position on the union question, the hospitals had launched an internal campaign of resistance. Beginning in February 1959, field organizers for the union reported a variety of hostile incidents. In one extreme case, frightened administrators at Knickerbocker Hospital had ordered Puerto Rican workers who were suspected of organizing to speak English while on the job. As the organizing committee became more vocal and conspicuous, the danger to union militants intensified. Organizers told the union's executive council on March 23 that "management is holding firmly to its opposition . . . and is intimidating, threatening and firing Union members." Dietary workers at Mt. Sinai had no doubts about Steinberg's position: "He said he would eat shit before he'd see the Union in here," one recalled. At Knickerbocker Hospital, Congressman Adam Clayton Powell, offering unqualified support to the workers, lashed out at the "union-busting conspiracy" among the voluntary hospitals' boards of directors.[11]

As it had at Montefiore, the union moved swiftly to raise the stakes of confrontation elsewhere. Beginning on March 6, and for five days thereafter, union members demonstrated for recognition in front of the narrowed group of targeted hospitals. At Mt. Sinai, 800 workers boycotted the cafeteria in a lunch-hour demonstration, demanding that the hospital "stop stalling and recognize our union." Placards and leaflets denounced the $32/44-hour/ 6-day week, which represented a minimum wage of less than $1 per hour for nearly a thousand service workers, and split shifts that kept many employees at the hospital from 8:00 A.M. to 7:00 P.M. In an attempt to broaden the union's base, organizers also appealed to the wounded professional pride of senior lab technicians with doctorates who worked for a paltry $55.50 a week. Several days after these first demonstrations, hundreds of gelatin capsules containing prounion messages, printed fortune-cookie-style, turned up all over the affected hospitals.

Union rhetoric grew tougher and more pointed. Seeking to force some individual accountability out of the faceless antiunion hospital front—and reflecting as well the union's growing knowledge of local working conditions—union leaflets singled out specific administrators and supervisors for censure. A leaflet distributed at Lenox Hill Hospital on March 10, for example, expressed shock "that this enlightened management should turn out to be most vicious"; specifically, it charged pharmacy head Robert Bogash with threatening the revocation of licenses of union members and referred to a "take-it-or-lump-it edict" from hospital president Theodore Childs as "the kind of talk that no free American worker is going to take." Soon the union extended its taunts to Benjamin Buttonwieser, chairman of the board at Lenox Hill and chief officer of the New York Urban League, who, while "claiming to be a liberal" and even supporting arbitration of a recent citywide gravediggers' strike, "apparently does not believe that his employees are entitled to the same fair treatment."[12]

Ultimately, Local 1199, like other unions, resorted to the strike threat to try to force the issue of recognition. As early as March 9 Leon Davis informed the union's executive council that he would push negotiations with management only where "we have a strong group within the hospital that can be depended upon to put up a struggle if necessary." During the last week of March the union proceeded to call for a strike vote at each of its best-organized hospitals. Of the five institutions polled—Mt. Sinai, Beth Israel, Beth David, Bronx, and Brooklyn Jewish—the verdict was overwhelming: 2,258 to 95 in favor of walking out. The vote, monitored by an independent election management firm, testified to the effectiveness of the union's first phase of activity, particularly the strength of rank-and-file organizing committees. At Beth Israel, for example, the organizing committee sent union staffer Jesse Olson away while it deliberated the wisdom of the strike call. Then, with the committee's endorsement, Beth Israel workers proceeded to vote 349 to 8 to strike. Within days of the first vote Lenox Hill was also added to the list of prospective targets. The strike date was set for April 22 at 6:00 A.M.

Within the hospitals workers readied themselves for a show of force. After observing several general membership meetings in mid-March, journalist Dan Wakefield concluded that the problem for the union "was not so much to urge [the workers] on as to keep them in line." "Private" strikes reportedly broke out among workers in the oxygen room and animal labs at Mt. Sinai, and union organizers had to step in to enforce discipline.[13] Meanwhile, Local 1199 held out an olive branch: if management would sit down with the workers' designated representatives, effectively acknowledging the union, they would sign a no-strike pledge and submit all unresolved grievances to binding arbitration. In retrospect, Leon Davis asserted that the arbitration offer, anathema to most labor leaders, was "a policy, a tactic, not a principle." "As an organizing instrument the workers position was so low, you [know you will] make advances in arbitration. . . . to win a strike in a hospital you have to have a very positive public posture. You just can't win on the right to strike."

With the stakes rising, the union had to reckon with its dependence on outside opinion. City labor leader Harry Van Arsdale, for example, had lent crucial weight to the union's cause during the Montefiore campaign, but concern for the reputation of organized labor as well as the costs involved persuaded him to seek to avoid an ugly confrontation if at all possible. District 65 president David Livingston was also influential and was regularly consulted during this period by Leon Davis. The leader of 1199's "older-sister union" demonstrated his commitment to the hospital campaign with a $10,000 grant and the "loan" of ten organizers on the eve of the strike. The hospital union took account of other potential allies as well. Union correspondence confirms that a no-strike pledge upon union recognition was crucial to endorsements from such liberal public leaders as Eleanor Roosevelt, Senators Herbert H. Lehman and Jacob Javits, Thurgood Marshall, and Congressman Emanuel Celler.

Just as it had at Montefiore six months earlier, the threat of a strike resulted in immediate intervention from the mayor's office. At the prodding of both Van Arsdale and GNYHA director Connorton, each with close personal ties to city hall, the labor commissioner began sounding out the parties with an eye toward compromise. Felix quickly discovered, however, that the hospitals were in no mood for a Montefiore-style settlement. Indeed, Connorton remembers that hospital leaders bristled at the very idea of negotiations with the union, and "some didn't want to talk even to Wagner," given his prolabor reputation. When talks did begin, they went through Van Arsdale's Central Labor Council, not the hospital workers' own representatives. Mt. Sinai counsel Howard Lichtenstein recalled that "Charles Silver of Beth Israel and Joe Klingenstein of Mt. Sinai [took] us out to dinner one night and they agreed to raise about a half a million dollars to provide scholarships for children of the employees. Anything but actual recognition."

Caught in the middle, the mayor requested a delay in strike plans and mutual acceptance of an official city fact-finding mission. In the meantime, Felix met with hospital representatives then returned to sit with Van Arsdale, CLC Secretary Moe Iushewitz, District 65 vice president Bill Michelson, Leon Davis, and 1199 vice president William Taylor. The latter soon offered this grim review and recommendation to the union's executive council: "Hospital management does not want to budge an inch and will do everything they can to prevent organization of the hospital workers into the Union. They are obviously convinced that the workers will not go out on strike— certainly not in enough numbers to affect hospital operation. . . ." Officials at the target hospitals refused to endorse the fact-finding commission but did consent on April 21 to placing the proposal before their boards of trustees during the next two weeks. At 1:00 A.M. on April 22 the union agreed to postpone the strike pending the hospitals' decision. Davis made his displeasure with the mayor's passive approach clear to his own staff, but he argued that "our acceptance [of fact-finding] and its rejection by the hospitals puts us in a better [public] position."[14]

While the diplomatic exercises were played out, tensions continued to mount within the hospitals. Doris Turner recalled that in the Lenox Hill dietary department a white man on the night shift was interrogated by his white female boss, for whom he regularly fixed coffee. "You're not going out on strike with those blacks and Puerto Ricans, are you?" taunted the supervisor. When the man threatened the woman with his hot coffee, she broke out in tears. Some hospitals asked employees to fill out questionnaires as to their personal intentions regarding the strike. Mt. Sinai's director recalls, "About 95 percent of them said yes, they were coming in, but when the day came about 90 percent of them did not come in. They gave you the answer they thought you wanted." At Beth Israel the administration stepped up an established practice of meetings between departmental supervisors and individuals workers. Aimed at intimidating potential strikers, such meetings were sometimes equally uncomfortable for the supervisors. According to Pearl Cormack, one administrative nurse who had expressed sympathy with the workers and who had only recently recuperated from an operation was nevertheless required to take part in the discussion sessions with the employees. At the end of a pressure-filled week she was found dead in her kitchen chair. By contrast Beth Israel supervisor Gustava Hills "didn't say, 'You shouldn't be going' or 'I think it's disgraceful,' she said, 'You all have your minds . . . ,' " remembered Mary Riley. Engineering assistant director Andrew Danielli and Mt. Sinai union activist Elon Tompkins likewise pointedly avoided antagonizing each other over the strike issue: "He had a dog, I had a dog," was how Danielli put it.

As the hospital dispute neared open confrontation, another, largely unspoken source of tension contributed to the climate of mutual hostility. Five of the six hospitals slated to be struck were Jewish-endowed—Mt. Sinai, Beth Israel, Brooklyn Jewish, and Bronx were linked to the Federation of Jewish Philanthropies, while Beth David operated independently—which raised the issue of whether they had been "singled out" as strike targets. In addition, the board president of the sixth hospital, Lenox Hill, was the socially prominent Jewish financier Benjamin Buttonwieser. Instead of provoking a "crisis of conscience," as it had with Cherkasky at Montefiore, union pressure on the Jewish hospitals seemed instead to have struck a nerve of insecurity among hospital directors and trustees. Philanthropic leaders of the Jewish community appeared determined to show their mettle to gentile colleagues in the GNYHA.

The six targeted hospitals, through their boards of directors, did in fact represent a cross-section of upper-class New York Jewry at a period of generally rising Jewish economic and social respectability. Mt. Sinai, by far the largest of the strike-threatened institutions, represented the pride and joy of the city's older German-Jewish elite. Begun as the Jews Hospital in 1852,

Mt. Sinai moved to its present uptown site in 1901. The reputation of the hospital was vouchsafed in 1953 when it officially became the major teaching affiliate of Columbia University's College of Physicians and Surgeons. For research, technological sophistication, and quality of care, Mt. Sinai boasted with some justification that it had no superior in the country. The hospital board, headed by investment firm and department store owner Joseph Klingenstein, included blue-chip financiers as well as partners in some of the city's most distinguished law firms.[15]

Beth Israel Hospital, by contrast, reflected the hard-won achievements of its eastern European founders whose original tenement dwellings still lay sprawling just to the south of the medical center. Forty Orthodox Jewish tailors and other workingmen chartered the institution in 1889 on 25¢-a-month contributions to relieve the "horrible conditions existing in the downtown area for those who wait indefinitely for medical attention."[16] Although Beth Israel's directors liked to think that their institution was oriented toward "community service," they were dramatic evidence of the upward social mobility of the original Beth Israel community. Seymour Phillips, a third-generation owner of Phillips–Van Heusen Shirts, noted defense attorney Louis Nizer, and Mrs. David Podell, widow of the New Deal brain truster, at one time or another all served on the hospital board. The most powerful presence, however, was seventy-year-old Charles H. Silver, who in 1959 was in his thirteenth year as board president. Born in Romania, the youngest of six children, he had worked his way up from office boy to chief executive in the American Woolen company. He possessed an "extraordinary vitality and enthusiasm for work" and in 1959 was also serving his sixth term as president of the New York City Board of Education as well as remaining active on the governing board of Yeshiva University and within his orthodox synagogue. Silver enjoyed extensive political contacts (he was mentioned only a few years earlier as a potential mayoral aspirant) and served as the key Jewish liaison to the Catholic hierarchy in New York City.[17]

Whether or not a "Jewish strategy" was operating in the hospital campaign remained a hotly contested issue for years after the fact. To many, the strike decisions seemed cruel and unfair; there were even charges of anti-Semitism. Said one letter-writing remonstrant, "You strike only against Jewish hospitals. You wouldn't dare touch a Roman Catholic one."[18] Mt. Sinai attorney Howard Lichtenstein recalled: "We resented bitterly the fact that [Leon Davis] chose primarily the Jewish hospitals to organize first. I suppose he did it because, on his own feeling, well, Jews had more responsibilities to their fellow men and so forth, employees and what not; whether it's true I don't know but that was his reason." Connorton, Wagner, and *New York Times* labor editor A. H. Raskin all more or less shared Lichtenstein's perception of the decision-making process.

Unions officials dismissed such imputations. The ecumenical scope of their original canvas, together with the uneven workers' response from the city's institutions, does seem to belie the notion of a preexisting religious strategy. Retired union vice president William Taylor insisted simply, "We struck where we had the strength to strike." Moe Foner elaborated: "What was at the time stumbling through appears later as evil genius. . . . We expected the response, other than from the Catholic hospitals, to be uniform and it stands to reason that we should go after the biggest places. In the end the choices were made by looking at the scorecard, at where we had a majority. . . . the hospitals didn't seem any different in the way they were run. In the Catholic hospitals there was greater fear among the workers. In major hospitals like New York and Presbyterian they paid better."

There is no doubt that, once in gear, the leaders of the hospital drive searched for any chink they could find in the armor of their adversaries. Clearly, they hoped to derive some advantage from the liberal Jewish leanings of some of the hospital directors. On the model of his intercession to Martin Cherkasky, Leon Davis sent letters to the trustees of Beth Israel Hospital pleading for "an amicable settlement," and for a time he tried to sort things out by telephone with Charles Silver. However, any expected special understanding ultimately proved misplaced. As the strike deadline approached in late April, Silver conveniently extended a Florida vacation; meanwhile, Beth Israel workers were informed that in the event of a walkout, nuns from St. Vincent's Hospital would be available to replace them. The union, for its part, proved equally deaf to special pleading. Active in the Congress of Racial Equality (CORE) and other liberal causes (his wife, Helen, had been a defender of Alger Hiss), Lenox Hill's Benjamin Buttonwieser made a direct appeal to Davis. "He came down one day [to my office] without an overcoat on," Davis recalled; "he looked like a guy who had come off the Bowery. He came down with his building plans . . . [and] told me 'I have priorities' and that 'As soon as I get through building I'll sit down with you and see about a union.' I looked at him and I said, 'Do you think this [building] is a priority over the workers?' That ended the conversation. He became very bitter and violent."

By whatever combination of reason and circumstance, a union largely led by Jews had squared off against hospitals directed by the scions of the city's Jewish community. In the middle lay the people of New York City, themselves of many different national and ethnic backgrounds but all to some extent influenced by the Jewish metropolitan presence. To the degree that it was a "family affair", the 1959 hospital fight thus took on the bitterness of a civil war.

On May 5 representatives of the six targeted hospitals returned to the mayor with a unanimous verdict: the proposal that wages, working conditions, and union recognition be submitted to third-party fact-finding was "neither wise nor necessary." The principles of collective bargaining, in the hospital trustees' view, simply had "no place in the administration of the affairs of voluntary non-profit hospitals." They offered no "technical theory . . . that hospital employees may not be organized" but insisted that experience proved that such "should not" be the case. Discrediting the union's no-strike pledge, the hospitals claimed that "organization without the right to strike is a contradiction in terms. . . . The strike weapon exists wherever unions represent employees no matter what the protestations of the union." Finally, the voluntary hospitals' spokesmen pointed to the "problem of underfinancing" as one more reason why they had to oppose a union among the workers. "Perpetual deficits and. . . tormenting dependence for survival on charitable contributions have always distinguished [the voluntaries] from tax-supported governmental hospitals and from profit-making proprietary hospitals." Under these circumstances, it would be folly for the hospitals to abandon their long-standing policy and submit to a review by outsiders.[19]

While unbending on the key issue of union recognition, the hospitals counteroffered a positive program of improved wage and working conditions. As of July 1, 1959, they announced, there would be a $1-an-hour minimum wage, overtime pay after forty hours, and seniority privileges. In addition, the hospitals promised to establish, by October 1, 1959, equitable job grades and wage schedules, improvements in fringe benefits, and formal grievance and appeal procedures regarding "individual wage adjustments." Finally, the new program would create a "permanent administrative committee" of seven hospital trustees to supervise and review the total package. With these changes, the hospitals argued, they had moved substantially to enhance the workers' welfare; further agitation, they charged, would serve only "the naked purpose" of unionization.

Space for negotiation had been squeezed out. After a final, mostly rhetorical offer to throw all outstanding issues to arbitration or fact-finding, Leon Davis castigated the "callous and stubborn men whose opposition to unions leads them to endanger the entire community." The union set a new strike deadline 6:00 A.M., Friday, May 8. The hospitals immediately sought and obtained a temporary restraining order through the municipal courts on the grounds that a hospital strike was unsupported by law and likely to damage life and property. To avoid subpoenas, Davis and union secretary-treasurer Edward Ayash went into hiding. At city hall there was one last attempt to avoid a strike. Bill Michelson of District 65 remembers that the night before the strike two hospital attorneys (Howard Lichtenstein and Len Roven) invited him to address an assembly of hospital trustees in a final appeal for union recognition: It was "like speaking to a graveyard . . . the most unsuccessful speech I ever made in my life." With apparent remorse the two experienced labor-management attorneys told Michelson that they had sought the injunction against Davis only in the hope that it might "serve as a rationale and excuse for Leon not to proceed with the strike."

On the other side of the city the union's entire staff received news of the break-off of negotiations in a solemn but determined mood. All knew that the union was laying its future on the line. Davis asked for comments from anyone who had doubts about the propriety of a strike. No one spoke. Most of the staff sat up together through the night. At 5:00 A.M., remembered Marshall Dubin, "Davis looks around, says, 'Get going, that's it, get going, the strike is on.' " Dubin later captured the tension of these last prestrike moments in verse:

> Let there be no doubt among us now
>   and no illusion
> The struggle that we face is grave
>   the end uncertain
> The prison doors are open for us all
> If this you fear
>   then speak and beg off now
>   but recognize among us gathered here
>   that flight betrays the faith of working men
> For myself the line of march is clear
> Fight, fight again Whatever the cost,
> We'll go, we'll beg or borrow
> I swear you'll have your picket signs tomorrow.

And so the real battle began.

CHAPTER 4

The Battle of '59:
Anatomy of a Hospital
Strike

At 4:00 A.M. on May 8, 1959, twenty-one-year-old Julio Pagan, an orderly at Mt. Sinai Hospital, stopped work in the middle of his shift and with the help of a nurse's aide began to dismantle and "hide" the trays and place settings he had just laid out for the patients' breakfasts. Then, without informing his supervisor or most of his co-workers, he walked out of the hospital to Local 1199's basement headquarters two blocks away. Two hours later Pagan and three other Spanish-speaking employees from the housekeeping unit reemerged, outfitted with picket signs. "At first, I was a little afraid, because, you know, I didn't know exactly what would happen to me," Pagan recalled. "But then I told myself, 'I'm going to take a chance.'" Most of the other workers on his shift joined him, and by 8:00 A.M. they had effectively blocked the hospital's three main entrances. By then "things were getting pretty rough."

Summoned to maintain order around the hospitals, the police seemed to share management's view that a hospital strike was illegal. They established outposts on hospital property and, until the union protested, accepted coffee and donuts from the hospital administration. They also tried to impose severe restrictions on picketing. For example, ten Beth Israel strikers were arrested the first day for breaking a police limit of five pickets per entrance, while at Lenox Hill, Willa Mae Buckum was picked up for shouting on the picket line after a rule of silence was imposed. At Mt. Sinai, Pagan was shoved by New York City police commissioner Michael Kennedy and was grabbed by another policeman. His friend from the housekeeping department, Lorenzo

Santiago, was arrested amid much scuffling and hustled off in a paddy wagon. Workers quickly dubbed the police sentry box at Mt. Sinai "the toilet."

Gloria Arana and her daughter left their Bronx home early that first morning to prepare for the strike at Mt. Sinai. By 8:00 A.M. Madison Avenue, near the emergency entrance, was full of people, traffic was stopped, pickets were yelling, and incoming office workers hesitated, "afraid to go inside." In the middle of the commotion stood Elliott Godoff, shouting encouragement and directions to the picket captains. "I was so emotioned," remembered Arana, "I run over and said, 'Elliott, look at this!' " It was the first strike she had ever seen, "a beautiful day."

It was not on emotional grounds, however, that Elliott Godoff directed the first day's events. In contrast to the workers' sense of power and elation at Mt. Sinai, for example, the same hours were fraught with confusion for the union militants only blocks away at Lenox Hill. Just before the strike deadline, Godoff declared that the Lenox Hill workers "were not ready to go"; the union staff, concentrating on Mt. Sinai, needed more time to plan and prepare the troops at Lenox Hill. "That broke my heart," remembered Lenox Hill organizing committee leader Doris Turner. "It seemed to me that unless we participated in that strike, we'd never get out from under." Angrily, she called Godoff a "traitor" and accused the union of selling out the Lenox Hill workers. To Turner's relief the delay at Lenox Hill did not last long; by afternoon Lenox Hill workers had joined those at Mt. Sinai, Beth Israel, Bronx, Beth David, and Brooklyn Jewish in the thick of the action.

The 1959 hospital strike can be divided into three parts: the initial confrontation between the union and the hospitals; an extended siege combined with rising outside pressures; and the political events that ultimately produced a negotiated settlement seven weeks after it began. Throughout the conflict the workers, Local 1199, and the hospital administrators were preoccupied not only with the problems of conducting (or resisting) the strike but with the search for public legitimation of their actions.

Confrontation

The 1959 strike involved an immense human as well as financial investment by Local 1199. Maintenance of around-the-clock picket lines, relief to the strikers, internal morale building, and external publicity stretched the resources of the union to their limits. In and out of hiding from process servers through much of the conflict, Leon Davis shared decisions affecting overall strategy, negotiations, political contacts, and support services with a small circle of trusted advisors. Despite the unprecedented circumstances confronting union leaders, they assembled a well-disciplined strike operation after little more than a week of frenzied activity.

While 1199 could offer no strike benefits, with financial help from other unions it quickly assembled food kitchens near each hospital and provided food packages, carfare, and free medical service to strikers and their families. In addition, Julia Davis, wife of the union president and a former city welfare worker, took charge of a welfare committee to deal with individual cases involving rent, evictions, food, or family problems. During the strike the committee helped some 600 workers apply for emergency public assistance.

Direct control of field operations fell to Elliott Godoff. An "organizer's organizer," he inspired less with fiery oratory than with quiet strength and total personal trust. He was also a nuts-and-bolts man who approached organizing much like a military commander, surveying the field on the eve of battle with a sure eye for the physical strength or weakness of a particular position or maneuver. During the strike Godoff made the union's uptown headquarters near Mt. Sinai his base camp, but he continually visited each embattled hospital. One striker from Beth Israel in Lower Manhattan incorrectly but tellingly remembered Godoff's "daily" appearances there on the picket lines. Thelma Bowles recalled, "We would call him in and discuss how we're going to do this. But he had it all in the back of his mind just how it should be. . . . nobody went ahead of Elliott."

For the strike operations at each hospital, Godoff relied on a staff consisting of reassigned drug union officers (the "Crack of Dawn Brigade"), organizers on loan from District 65, and elected hospital stewards. Despite strains and minor conflicts, this makeshift chain of command held remarkably steady throughout the strike. There is no evidence, for example, of a single major figure from the strike committees quitting in pique or being ousted for incompetence or insubordination—a fact that can only be explained by the pervasive spirit of sacrifice and the overwhelming sense of adversity. Phil Kamenkowitz, the drug area director assigned to Bronx Hospital, generally left strike conduct in the hands of the Bronx rank-and-file committee headed by electrician Joseph Brown. But Kamenkowitz acknowledged, "I had to straighten him out a couple times. It was [a matter of] discipline, he was an easy-going guy, and I said either you do it [i.e., tighten up the picket lines] or else." Brown, who would later become an organizer, respected the authority vested in the union command.

In the first few days of the walkout, hospital union leaders went to dramatic lengths to reassure the untested ranks of their right to strike and also to fend off fear of employer recrimination. At Bronx Hospital, for example, on the first evening of the strike, picket captain Brown was arrested and charged with the assault of a scab worker. "I told the pickets not to worry, they wouldn't do nothing to me. I was back on the line by 10:00 P.M." In another incident two young women ran into strike headquarters claiming that the hospital personnel director had pushed them into the street while a police officer had looked the other way. Kamenkowitz ran back to the lines, the women in tow, and approached the policeman, calling him "Mr.," a form of address to which the law enforcement officer immediately objected. "I'll call you 'officer' when you do your duty as an officer," the strike captain responded. Kamenkowitz and the personnel director then squared off in front of the strikers, and while no blows were exchanged, the former proceeded to swear out an arrest warrant on behalf of the picketers. Soon the hospital responded by having papers alleging disorderly conduct served on the women who had returned to union headquarters upset and frightened. Kamenkowitz grabbed the papers, tore them up, and sent the women back to the picket line. He was eventually fined $300 for his part in the incident, but his bravado raised the morale of his troops.

For Karl Rath, like other drugstore veterans assigned hospital duty, the 1959 strike quickly became a full-time job. Born into a German iron-working family in Mansfield, Ohio, Rath had quit school at age sixteen to haul scrap iron and by 1959 had already seen plenty of excitement in his life. A paratrooper for the 507th Airborne, he had jumped on D-Day and was wounded during the Battle of the Bulge. After securing work in the Whelan drugstore chain during the mid-1950s, Rath had played an active role in several strikes. In 1959 the union's storefront office near Manhattan's Beth David Hospital became his home for forty-six days, twenty-four hours a day; he slept on an air mattress for only three to four hours a night and lost thirty-five pounds. Rath's wife visited him daily, bringing him a change of clothes and clean sheets smuggled out of the hospital.

Leaving administration of the daily strike routine to the Beth David workers, Rath concentrated on bolstering the morale of 200 strikers, about equally split between blacks and Hispanics. "The first week is a lark, let's not kid ourselves, but it's after that first week goes by and you go into the second week and nothing happens and then you go into the third week, you start getting friction from people who had never had to get along before, people who are now living together." Once, for example, Rath intervened when a domino game degenerated into a knife fight. For the most part, however, he left long-time Beth David employee Maria Munoz in charge of discipline. Like other female strike activists, Munoz played both a supporting role, as cook, and a more subtle, directing role. According to Rath, "She had a hell of a lot of pull with the Spanish people. . . . she would give the Spanish men the business and get them to pull in their horns a little bit." Over the long weeks it was, in Rath's view, people like Munoz who saved the strike:

You always find a number who are aggressive, believe in what they're doing, are always talking to keep spirits up, that's the big thing. Especially when a strike hits a lull you got to start talking, "You're in this thing now, you're gonna have to fight it off to the finish." Constantly you hammer this, you get the newspaper clippings, bring editorials to peoples' attention . . . to show that these sons of bitches, you know, this is the way you talk even to the women, you have to be honest and they know it, that these wealthy trustees are grinding you down and they don't give a shit about you and they're trying to starve you out. . . . More and more as the strike went on, these people started to get the feeling that we're out, goddamit, you're not gonna drag me down anymore.

Walking the picket lines was the principal work assignment for those on strike. Besides keeping out scabs, the lines bound strikers together and gave them a sense of common identity and purpose. Workers registered at each hospital's strike headquarters for daily picket duty during their normal work shift. "Walk two hours, rest two hours," was how one striker remembered the routine. While a few close friends might march together, picket duty necessarily threw together workers from different departments. It was often at their strike station that workers who had toiled for years in the same building met for the first time. Even so, there was some bunching at picket locations by race and sex. Stewards, for example, made sure to have a cordon of burly men working the truck entrances, and black and Hispanic picket captains reportedly sometimes brought "their people" together at distinct locations.

While sustaining the spirits of those out on strike, picket duty, of course was meant to dissuade others from going back to work. In addition to supervisory personnel, a combination of "loyal" employees, volunteers, and, eventually, groups of new hirees ignored the walkout. Stopping the leakage from their own ranks became particularly important to the striking workers, who, despite tight security around the hospitals, quickly learned a range of persuasive tactics in dealing with strikebreakers. The strike committees kept systematic tabs on who was working or not picketing, and the picket sign-up sheets helped to identify scab workers; those who did not sign up were soon contacted by postcard. For example:

Dear _____:
We did not see you on the picket line today. Please report for duty tomorrow.
Fraternally yours,
Mt. Sinai Strike Committee

One response, by a young woman named Bertha Moore, read as follows: "I regret to say that, before the strike begun, I had resign from Mt. Sinai and have another job. I been receiving letter from the union quite often, but never-the-less, I still with you 100%. And I do hope in the near future we will win."

The union had surreptitious sources of information as well. While visiting a hospitalized relative, for example, a worker might secretly survey a given department. It seemed to Marshall Dubin that Godoff "knew more what was going on in the hospitals than the bosses did." From sympathetic secretaries and other undisclosed sources the union sometimes gained access to lists of strikebreakers. Strikers also reached out beyond the hospital doors. Mt. Sinai's education committee, for example, tried to pick out strikebreakers near the subway turnstiles. Groups of four or five male workers, as Julio Pagan remembered, also used the time-honored union tactic of home visits to convince reluctant employees "to stay out there like everybody else."

"Scab patrol," as Godoff called it, could be a source of great excitement. Although the basic routine was simple, specific situations called for some ingenuity. Cassie Cosby remembered that she always got herself assigned to the emergency entrance, "'cause I knew that that was the way the Hausman [Pavilion] people used to come to work. . . . I used to stay there and watch [and when] some workers tried to get in, I [ran up] and just pulled 'em on down." Pagan recalled the arrival of strikebreakers in trucks escorted by police. It was almost impossible to stop them from entering the hospital, although a melee erupted one day when an elderly striker from the laundry lay down in the entrance. Godoff, who regularly coached the stewards on picket tactics, once sent a group of pickets into Central Park, near Mt. Sinai. Suddenly, shrieking and screaming was heard from the park, the police ran over, and that "gave us a chance at the entrances to do our business."

At Beth David Hospital, Karl Rath described picket duty as a game of hide-and-seek with policemen who were perched every fifty to one hundred feet around the building. Once the workers identified strikebreakers, they kept track of them. Rath estimates that "90 percent of the time we would catch 'em the next day and they wouldn't come back. A good part of [dealing with] scabs is if you give 'em the business enough, and show 'em that you're mad, show 'em that they can possibly get hurt, a good part of the scabs don't come back." The Beth David strikers especially liked scab patrol on rainy days—"then you could carry umbrellas." According to Rath, "a little Spanish fellow named Garcia" became something of a legend. With one blow of his fist he felled a scab who then required sixteen stitches. On another occasion a scab known for rough play approached the hospital with a rolled-up newspaper in hand. In clear view of the police, Garcia walked up to the scab and began to reach inside his shirt. Certain that Garcia was pulling a knife, the man pounced on him and began beating him with the newspaper. When the police intervened, Garcia demonstrated that it was only his hearing aid he had been reaching for. That was good enough to get the scab carted off.

Among the hospital labor force the strike's impact varied with one's commitment and personality. For Mt. Sinai orderly Henry Nicholas, the 1959 events became not only a personal testing ground but ultimately the beginning of a new career. Throughout the spring organizing drive, Nicholas had shied away from all talk of a strike. Having left the navy in 1957 and not wishing to return to his native Mississippi, he dreaded the thought of losing his first foothold in the city. His friend Julio Pagan practically had to drag him out to the picket lines when the strike started, and Nicholas remembered his initial embarrassment when he was first spotted by his supervisor. Yet from the time he visited Marshall Dubin on the second day of the strike to sign up as a picket captain, he was with the strike twenty-four hours a day. His sharecropper father had counseled him to be prepared to survive on his own, "without depending on anyone." Now Nicholas and the white superiors he had come to resent were on "separate sides of the street." "I knew my only salvation in terms of a job was to win and that I had to do what was necessary to make sure a win came about." The struggle at Mt. Sinai, he believed, was part of the same fight for survival faced by black farmers in Mississippi or black GIs—the threat of being run off the land, blacklisted by a dishonorable discharge, or fired by the hospital reflected the same "administration of things."

The union's collective social discipline weighed heavily on those who did not or could not identify fully with the movement. Arthur Landsberg, for example, had worked as a supplyman in the Beth Israel chemistry lab since 1943 while he looked after his aging Jewish mother: "It was very nice. Everybody knew each other by their first name—it was just like a family." But the hospital grew, the workers changed, and then "the strike broke." Landsberg was caught in the middle. His bosses told him not to go out: "They said to tell the union you're with them but you can't go on strike." At the same time he thought, "How can you not go out when the rest of the workers went?" So Landsberg, one of the few whites in his department, reluctantly walked out with the others. Pearl Cormack remembered pressuring him: "I threatened him so bad. . . . he was more afraid to go back in than to stay out."

For Lucille Works, a pantry supervisor in Beth Israel's dietary department, the strike also proved trying. Hired as a kitchen maid in 1954, she had been promoted to supervisor only months before the strike occurred. Not only did she have friends among the strikers, but her husband, a cook in the same department, was dutifully walking the picket line. Works approached the strike philosophically. Like other supervisors she did double duty during the strike and even took pride that "not once were meals to patients jeopardized." She insisted that she was treated with understanding by the strikers: "Really, I wasn't that fearful of something happening to me with [my husband] being out." Works added, "They knew supervisors had to go to work." Although some workers called her "scab," both during and after the strike, a barely concealed humor softened such insults. Not so for Anna Mateo. She and her husband, Sixto, both employees of the Mt. Sinai laundry and natives of Puerto Rico, walked out with everyone else on May 8. After two weeks they could not make ends meet, however, and Anna went back in, braving insults and invective from the picketers.

Amid the initial period of confrontation the union and the hospital management both dispensed wildly varying estimates of the walkout's effectiveness. On the second day of the strike, for example, a Greater New York Hospital Association (GNYHA) spokesman claimed that less than a third of the nonprofessional employees had stayed out, while the union counted only a dozen or so at each institution who had gone in.[1] Although both sides were doubtlessly exaggerating, Mt. Sinai director Dr. Martin Steinberg's retrospective declaration that "90 percent of nonprofessionals" walked out is probably accurate, at least during the strike's first month.

As during the Montefiore campaign, the strike message was clearly aimed at nonprofessional employees (notwithstanding a few appeals to physicians to "talk to management" and the taunting of nurses—"Proud professionals . . . how does it feel to wash the dishes?"). Early invitations to hospital technicians to "take an active part . . . otherwise [you] will not share in the gains received" were ignored. Although a majority of Mt. Sinai lab workers, for example, had signed union cards and even voted "yes" in the strike balloting, the hospital administration convinced them to stay on the job. (According to one observer, only two Mt. Sinai lab workers actually walked out on May 8.) The solidarity of twenty Mt. Sinai social workers who joined the strike (and later faced hospital reprisals) proved a rare exception among white-collar employees.[2]

Among service workers, commitments varied by department. Dietary, laundry, and housekeeping employees were solidly behind the strike. Eddie Kay, a veteran 1199 organizer, found such worker responses consistent with subsequent behavior patterns: "The kitchen is a very hard place to work in. Now the laundry is even more hard but they half kill them in the laundry and they beat them down. You see, when a laundry worker fights back, he's gonna kill you. That's because he works in 120° in the summer." The nursing auxiliary staff, despite some racial division, was also generally strong, while engineering workers were less predictable. At Mt. Sinai, unlicensed black engineers gave strong support to the strike, but at Beth Israel the department was ambivalent about allying with service workers and ultimately negotiated a separate contract with the building service union.

The Mt. Sinai laundry was representative of the strike's impact on a well-organized department. The overwhelmingly Hispanic work group there quickly followed Gloria Arana out on May 8. Supervisor Fritz Field remembered that two workers came in that first morning but were so hazed by the strikers that they quit by the end of the day. Such unity went beyond racial and family ties; indeed, perhaps the bravest displays of solidarity came from a few older European women who had not only made the laundry their daily place of work but the hospital dormitory their nightly home. For them the institution was a holdover from an earlier era of hospital philanthropy. To a remarkable degree, however, the live-in employees were union loyalists and their identity lay with their fellow workers, not their employing "benefactors." Arana remembered only one live-in worker who did not strike, "she was a scab." Another, Jenny Sternberg, "made a strike in her room" because she was afflicted with ailing feet and could not walk the picket lines. She rebuffed personal entreaties of hospital assistant director Andrew Mazei: "Gloria told me I don't work, I do the strike here." After two weeks, however, the hospital toughened its position and issued ultimatums to the live-in workers to report to work or lose their "homes." Reluctantly, Sternberg abandoned the strike, while her friend Ida Ullman, who also worked in the laundry and had walked out with the others, refused to return and found her possessions deposited on the street.

Despite overwhelming numerical support, the union suffered a strategic weakness in its limited ability to "halt production." Local 1199 walked a fine political line on this issue, insisting that the strike made quality patient care intolerable while at the same time taking pains not to hurt anyone. Beth Israel elevator operators, for example, chained open their doors before they walked out, while other strikers set up a telephone hotline to render assistance in case of emergency. Realistically, however, the strikers could not have shut down the hospitals even if they had wanted to. Each institution was able to count on the overtime effort of nursing and administrative staff as well as a unique "reserve army of labor" in the form of spouses of the house staff, relatives of patients, and wealthy society matrons. Letters to hospital contributors, appeals to the Girl Scouts, and, in the case of Beth Israel's Charles Silver, contacts with the public schools were all used to recruit volunteers, and through newspaper ads and employment agencies management sought to attract potential new employees.

At Lenox Hill Hospital Mrs. John S. Willim, wife of a public relations executive, and her two postdebutante twin daughters worked twelve hours a day, seven days a week, for one month (until the family moved to its summer home in Connecticut). Mrs. Richard Gardner left her five-year-old son with his nurse and gave up her Monday afternoon shopping trip to help out as a receptionist at Mt. Sinai. Sherry Hackett, wife of comedian Buddy Hackett, worked as a nurse's aide. Mrs. Henry J. Mali, a Bryn Mawr graduate living on the Upper East Side, responded to a Lenox Hill appeal and became a dishwasher. She readily admitted that the position held no long-term attraction: "While I enjoy very much doing exactly what I'm told and not, for the moment, having to use my head, I think that would pall." It should be noted, however, that the volunteers were not necessarily unsympathetic to the union presence. "I'm strong for the union," commented Mrs. Gardner, "but why should the sick be neglected?"[3]

Such sympathy was hardly reciprocated by the strikers. Some spoke scornfully, even twenty years later, of "dames riding in on taxi floors" to avoid the taunts of picketers and of "a lady daily accompanied by her butler arriving at Sinai." The union's *Strike Bulletin* was vitriolic on the subject of "volunteers": "It will be a pleasure to see some of these 'ladies' in the hospital with hernias they got from scabbing."[4] Gradually the number of volunteers diminished, a function both of the difficulty of the work and the hiring of new full-time help.

On the whole, the hospitals were able to make good their claim that the strike had caused "no interruption of services." Although the union demanded that the hospitals be closed down and patients transferred, state welfare department inspections confirmed (despite union charges of political bias) a basically "normal" level of operation. The ultimate antagonists—hospital trustees and boards of directors—suffered no tangible losses from the work stoppage. The union, which maintained spirited, sometimes militant picket lines around each of the struck hospitals, was forced to turn its attention to other sources of pressure.[5]

The Siege

The first major test of the union's claim on worker loyalties came eleven days into the strike. Mayor Robert Wagner, prompted by both John Connorton of the GNYHA and city labor leader Harry Van Arsdale, enlisted veteran municipal labor relations troubleshooter and transit arbitrator Theodore Kheel to arrange a compromise settlement. To the package of improvements for nonprofessional workers offered by the hospitals on May 5, the Kheel plan added two new twists: an expanded review body selected by the mayor, the governor, the hospitals, and the city's Central Labor Council (CLC); and a grievance procedure with some allowance for third-party representation. Adamantly rejecting any dealings with the union inside their institutions, a hospital negotiating team of Connorton, Benjamin Buttonwieser (of Lenox Hill), Jesse Frieden (of Beth Israel), and Msgr. Patrick J. Frawley (representing nineteen Catholic Charity hospitals) reportedly accepted a version of this plan that allowed for union representation—by the CLC, not Local 1199—only in the final arbitration phase of grievance appeals. Essentially, this was a substitute for unionism, a kind of public protectorate for the hospital workers and a way around what negotiators called "irresponsible, emotional, and radical groups."[6] By avoiding full union recognition, the hospital directors clearly expected that they could at least dispose of the immediate threat from Local 1199.

The mayor had placed the drug union in a difficult position. To reject the plan summarily cast the union as the public troublemaker, the main obstacle to stability in the health care field. Yet to accept it was to give up the commitment to fight to win. In the end 1199 agreed to submit the plan to a referendum of its members. On May 18, before the balloting, Leon Davis emerged from hiding and predicted rejection of the compromise. Likewise, shop stewards interviewed at the struck hospitals argued forcibly for a "no" vote, citing union recognition as the key issue in the strike. The vote of the membership was overwhelming: 1,784 to 14 to reject the plan. As if to prove that union members had only begun to fight, Davis coupled his report on the referendum with a declaration that the strike might spread momentarily and unannounced to any of several other hospitals. Within a week 1199 members at nine new institutions approved strike votes.

Officials at the struck hospitals were furious and somewhat taken aback by the union's intransigence. After all, hadn't they proven they could withstand a strike? Weren't the strikers clearly hurting? Even the mayor, a Democrat and nominally prolabor, had essentially sided with the hospitals, while the hospitals saw themselves as having taken concrete steps toward improving conditions by upgrading personnel relations and by laying the groundwork for modest wage increases for nonprofessional employees. Administrators, in their own minds, had been patient with the strikers, using volunteers, nurses, and supervisory staff to hold things together while the workers let off steam. Now it was time for the workers to do their part. However, the hospitals' most loyal employees, pressed and unhappy as they must have been out on the picket lines, had seemingly turned sullen and hostile. "This is not a strike," proclaimed the GNYHA after the vote, "but a revolution against law and order." By the end of the week the hospitals announced plans for the permanent replacement of the recalcitrant employees, offering $1-per-hour wages for general hospital service work. The employers also stepped up their legal offensive. On May 21, Leon Davis was served with an injunction for the Brooklyn Jewish Hospital shutdown; two days later, Judge Charles Beckinella ruled him in contempt of court and sentenced him and business agent George Goodman to fifteen days in jail and a $250 fine. While the union moved to appeal the verdict, Manhattan Justice George Tilzer granted temporary injunctive relief to five borough hospitals, and hospital attorneys immediately sought further contempt citations.[7]

The siege had begun. By refusing a diplomatic surrender the union had opted for a war of attrition, one that the hospitals might still win but that the union could not afford to lose. The strikers plodded on, sacrificing what little they had on an uncertain and increasingly pessimistic future. Their means were limited, their reserves low. Nearly 3,000 families who normally lived on the margins of subsistence had gone without paychecks for four weeks. The *New York Times* captured the trials of one striking Beth Israel porter:

> Benito Nieves is a slender volatile man in his thirties. He lives with his wife and seven children in a three-room basement apartment on East Sixth Street. The tidy, barren living room has a lumpy couch and two dumpy upholstered chairs. These are covered with clean, threadbare slipcovers. Besides a few religious pictures, the only other furnishing is a table on which there is a television set, draped with a cretonne curtain. The floors are unpainted cement. The walls are gaily painted. . . .
>
> In good times, which are bad enough, Mr. Nieves . . . takes home a salary of $72.64 every two weeks. But his need is so great that the Department of Welfare pays him $134.43 every two weeks in supplemental relief—nearly twice his salary.
>
> The relief includes payment for his daughter who needed a special diet at Bellevue Hospital, where she underwent surgery and had one of her father's ribs grafted on for a back injury. She is now home and still requires extra attention. She looks healthier than her brother and sisters.
>
> Mr. Nieves says the family "ate pretty good" before, but now it's not so good. The kids run through their shoes with regularity and a grocery bill of nearly $200 has been run up in the last month.
>
> The Nieves' credit at the store has now been cut off. Luis Martinez, owner of the Spanish-American grocery near the Nieves' apartment on Avenue B, said he had done it reluctantly. "My shelves are getting empty," Mr. Martinez said, waving at the gaps on the shelves in the tiny store. "They are my people, I give them as long as I can," he said. "But everything goes up. There are too many in the family. They have always paid before but now they wait for checks from the Welfare. I don't know."[8]

The lengthening stalemate, Mt. Sinai aide Mildred Reeves remembered, elicited many different reactions among the workers: "Some was getting tired. Some felt they had a job to do and let's get it over. A lot of them thought it was fun to be out there, want to show their supervisors they would stick it out. Some got other jobs or got welfare. Some went back in; [others] just stopped picketing."

Gritty resolve was no formula for success or even survival. What saved the union and the strike was a massive infusion of outside support—both material and political. The sources of salvation, in evidence since the Montefiore campaign, were the city's labor movement, a liberal civil rights network, and the political power of the big-city press. The conflict had, in fact, gradually changed character. As *New York Times* labor editor A. H. Raskin wrote on May 24, the strike had originated in a series of moves and

(top) Maria Cruz and her children march outside Mt. Sinai Hospital. (bottom) Beth Israel rank-and-file strike leader Hilda Jocquin (in apron) and Joseph Brown (with sign) from Bronx Hospital join balladeer Joe Glazer in song. AFL-CIO Labor Council president Harry Van Arsdale, in the rear, offers his support, as does 1199 organizer Jesse Olson, on the right.

countermoves that no one involved apparently expected to last more than a week. Now it had been transformed into a "sociological struggle" involving some of the most powerful forces in the city.

The most tangible and important source of intervention was the active support of the city's AFL-CIO Central Labor Council. For the leaders of the municipal labor federation, the hospital conflict struck an emotional chord reminiscent of the 1930s and their voices took on an uncommonly charged tone. Only a few years before, Charles Silver might have counted on substantial labor support had he chosen to run for mayor; but at a labor march and rally at Beth Israel, he was attacked as a "union-buster" and a "reactionary," and some union leaders even suggested that he be dumped from the New York City Board of Education. Only months before, Benjamin Buttonwieser had settled a citywide gravediggers' dispute by getting both parties to enter binding arbitration. Now he and other hospital officials were assailed by David Dubinsky, International Ladies' Garment Workers' Union (ILGWU) president, as "phony liberals." Both the ILGWU and the Jewelry Workers Union even threatened to withhold their substantial annual contributions to the Federation of Jewish Philanthropies because of its rigidity toward the strikers.[9]

Aside from the special organizing help from District 65's David Livingston, labor support for 1199 was almost entirely orchestrated by Harry Van Arsdale. From the beginning the venerable city labor chieftain had adopted the 1199 fight as "our strike" and eventually turned his own bailiwick, Local 3 of the International Brotherhood of Electrical Workers (IBEW), into a major benefactor of the hospital workers, first with a $28,000 cash contribution and then with a $50,000 loan to Local 1199. In an equally significant move Van Arsdale convinced traditionally conservative construction unions to walk off digging sites at three of the affected hospitals, and by the beginning of June, IBEW members were assessing themselves $1 a week for the hospital strikers. Beyond monetary assistance Van Arsdale lent physical support, twice leading marches of his union to hospital picket lines; he also paid early-morning calls to the strikers, riding aboard union secretary Arnold Beichman's motor scooter. Those close to the gruff Irish-American union leader from Manhattan's Hell's Kitchen found him unusually affected by a tenacity and discipline he had never before seen in the labor movement.

While no one admitted it publicly, the past political radicalism of Local 1199 clearly upset trade union leaders. This is hardly surprising, given the bitterness of political infighting during the CIO Communist purges of the late forties. As Beichman, himself an ardent anti-Communist with alleged ties to the C.I.A., later put it: "Davis' problem was his ex-Party record and he knew it."[10] The hospitals themselves never openly "red-baited" Local 1199, although talk of an "irresponsible," "militant," or "radical" union appealed to anti-Communist fears. As the strike approached, the conservative city press—especially the *World-Telegram* and the *Journal-American*'s Westbrook Pegler—played up the Red Scare aspect, resurrecting Davis's testimony before the Hartley Committee and the similarity of the union's past political stance to Communist party policy.

Early in the strike Van Arsdale tangibly lifted the political burden of the past from 1199's shoulders when, at a hastily assembled emergency meeting of CLC representatives on the steps of city hall, he told his associates that he had received a private disavowal of Communist ties by Leon Davis and announced that "the issue is now closed." Davis found it necessary to reiterate to a May 21 meeting of 300 CLC delegates, "The union is not Communist-controlled, and I, personally, am not an issue in this strike."[11] Davis was still far from being "one of the boys," but the statement was sufficient for Van Arsdale's purposes and he made it suffice for everyone else, effectively wrapping his own public respectability around the hospital workers' cause. In a dramatic demonstration of ultimate acceptance, Beichman reached George Meany, AFL-CIO president, for a national endorsement of the hospital strike.

The results of labor approval were dramatic. Shortly after Meany's statement was issued, Moe Foner nervously answered a telephone call from Victor Riesel, the staunchly anti-Communist labor columnist with whom Foner had disagreed since their undergraduate days. "What have you got against me?" asked Riesel. "How come you give everybody material but me? I'd like to help." It seems that a renewal of positive liberal-labor idealism had begun to thaw the antagonists from labor's cold war.

The hospital workers received endorsements and contributions from trade unionists across the city. Aging firebrand Michael Quill, leader of the Transport Workers Union (TWU), declared that the fortunes of the entire city labor movement rested with the strikers, and at a May 17 rally he attacked the hospital trustees as "worse than Gov. Faubus" in their treatment of blacks. The TWU followed Quill's words with thousands of cans of donated food, $2,600, and a sympathetic picket line at Lenox Hill Hospital; by the third week of the strike there were biweekly grocery packages. The International Union of Electrical Workers delivered 4,000 dozen eggs and 4,000 chickens to Local 1199 storefronts, while the Amalgamated Meatcutters and Butcher Workmen of America, Local 400, provided two weeks' worth of meat to every striker as well as "thousands" of pounds of cold cuts to be divided among strike headquarters. Local 32B of the Building Service Employees Union (SEIU), which included many black building superintendents, also showed strong rank-and-file support. At Bronx Hospital, for example, 1,500

32B members arrived one day, each loaded with a bag of groceries, which they placed in one great pyramid on the hospital steps. Local 1199 required two storefronts and a church basement to store the food.[12]

The hospital strike prompted what AFL-CIO regional director Michael Mann called "the finest display of labor unity in the City's history." A total of 175 union locals officially voted aid to the hospital workers, the largest gifts coming from the IBEW ($28,115), the RWDSU, Local 1199's international ($17,000, including $10,000 from District 65), ILGWU ($15,000), and the Amalgamated Clothing Workers Union ($11,000). In addition, $9,000 was sent to 1199 headquarters from individual trade union members, such as S. Grupski ($5), Giovanni Restaurant ($9.50), Lobster Box ($12), and Paddy's Clam House ($12.50), all part of Dining Room Employees Local 1 of the Hotel, Restaurant, and Bartenders International. Approximately $110,000 of the $123,000 received by Local 1199 came from unions and union members, a significant figure in view of the cost of the strike: nearly $195,000, 80 percent which went for food and medical and financial aid for the strikers and their families. With these contributions, two weeks into the strike 1199 was able to begin paying benefits of $10 per week. More than one observer reported workers who counted themselves better off materially during the strike than before or after it. The strike headquarters often functioned as community centers, attending to the workers' all-around needs, and organizer Thelma Bowles even remembered ordering a high school graduation outfit for the daughter of a proud but indigent striker. Joe Brown reported "four or five fellas with large families" who were actually sorry to return to work at the end of the strike.[13]

Alongside labor solidarity, civil rights emerged as a public rallying cry for the strikers. Outside sympathizers, in particular, expressed a special concern for the hospital workers as both an economically and racially oppressed group. Indeed, as the strike lengthened and became increasingly a public issue, the racial overtones of the conflict became more prominent. To be sure, the hospital strike did not exactly match the gathering storm in places like Selma or Montgomery, Alabama; and neither the situation nor the behavior of the participants made for a direct translation of southern organizing strategies to northern soil. In 1959 public opinion in cities like New York held that racial inequality was essentially a southern problem. Yet there were some cries for nationwide social reform as well as the exposure of instances of outright discrimination at home. In Harlem, for example, charges of police overreaction pointed to simmering areas of discontent, and a public flap ensued when U.S. Under Secretary of State Ralph Bunche was denied membership in Forest Hills's West Side Tennis Club. But no New York City black feared conviction for swearing in front of a white woman, as was the case in Fayette, Georgia, and even the Reverend Martin Luther King, Jr., appealed to New York City blacks only to support the southern campaign of passive resistance to segregation.[14]

The hospital strike was nevertheless one of the first northern struggles to directly tap a growing civil rights constituency comprised of leading members of the minority community as well as white liberal and labor allies. Local 1199, a union with an extensive history of struggle against race discrimination, deftly appropriated in 1959 the moral tones of a "fight for emancipation." The *New York Amsterdam News* and *El Diario,* for example, opened their pages to prounion reports and editorials, often reproducing verbatim the press releases of 1199 public relations director Moe Foner. Early on the powerful black congressman Adam Clayton Powell personally adopted the strike and on May 24, as part of Operation Humanity, led 200 Abyssinian Baptist Church parishioners to the picket line at Mt. Sinai. That same day delegations from the National Association for the Advancement of Colored People (NAACP), the Federation of Hispanic-American Societies, and the Urban League marched together at Bronx and Brooklyn Jewish hospitals to demonstrate their outrage at racial exploitation in the hospitals. Behind the scenes Local 1199 gained an invaluable long-time ally in Bayard Rustin. The black socialist and civil rights activist, a key lieutenant to both A. Philip Randolph and Martin Luther King, Jr., worked tirelessly to coordinate community support for the strikers.[15]

Liberal establishment leaders also picked up on the civil rights theme. Public supporters of hospital union rights included the Association of Reform Rabbis, the American Civil Liberties Union, the executive committee of the Protestant Council of New York City, Eleanor Roosevelt, Mrs. Albert D. Lasker (widow of the famous scientist), former senator Herbert H. Lehman, Congressman Emanual Celler, and City Councilman Stanley Isaacs. In early June individual liberals joined forces in the Citizens Committee for a Just Settlement of the Hospital Strike, cochaired by A. Philip Randolph, president of the Brotherhood of Sleeping Car Porters, and theologian Reinhold Neibuhr. The committee's sixty signators, including Kenneth Clark (author of *Dark Ghetto,* an influential report on the social effects of racial discrimination), Gen. Telford Taylor (presiding American judge in the Nuremberg war crimes trial), and A. J. Muste (long-time peace and labor activist), supported 1199's claim to union recognition combined with arbitration machinery and a no-strike pledge. The low wages and "shameful working conditions" endured by hospital workers, warned the committee, "threaten the health of the infants and children of these workers" and indirectly "breed juvenile delinquency, crime and violence."[16]

The strikers enjoyed spontaneous, grassroots aid as well, especially in the immediate vicinities of hospitals situated in minority neighborhoods. Gloria Arana remembered picking up food packages at the East-Side Democratic

Club, where she had met Vito Marcantonio years before. Similarly, the Bronx Democratic Club on Boston Road offered money and other support to Bronx Hospital strikers, while school teachers from nearby P.S. 2 joined the picket line. Joe Brown gratefully recalled contributions made by Bronx neighbors, who brought food and other articles to strike headquarters, and one of Brown's picketers even convinced the minister at the Morissania Baptist Church to enlist the whole congregation. A most extraordinary demonstration of support came from critically ill Lilly Popper at Lenox Hill Hospital. When a friend called on the sixty-seven-year-old pianist and music teacher (who in the thirties had helped to found a music school for workers), Popper "gave to understand that she expected all her visitors to support the strikers. When I left her ward, I did indeed march with pickets, and I followed up by picketing with them several more times afterward."[17]

Despite widespread public support for the strike, the city's mainline press remained skeptical. The task of conciliating the media fell to Moe Foner, who, by the time of the strike approached public relations as a political struggle that depended on who knew whom and who could talk to whom with what information and when. The 1959 strike revealed Foner to be a master of the politics of the press. Condemned by all but one of the major metropolitan dailies when it began, the unprecedented hospital strike eventually received almost as much positive as negative publicity and editorial judgment.

Of the major papers, the *New York Post* was most supportive. While voicing a general abhorrence of the hospital strike, it tended to place a larger burden of responsibility on hospital management. James Wechsler, who had backed the union in the Montefiore dispute, was again unstinting in his support, and there was also pressure on the hospitals from *Post* owner Dorothy Schiff, a member of New York's German-Jewish elite and a close personal friend of Benjamin Buttonwieser. Before the paper's editorial staff was allowed to write favorable reports on the strike, Schiff insisted on a face-to-face interview with Leon Davis. Davis remembered being anxiously escorted up to the newspaper heiress's penthouse office by Wechsler: "I don't know what the hell she wanted to see. . . . I am not a well-spoken guy, but evidently I passed muster." As the strike progressed, the *Post* became a sharp critic of the hospital trustees: "Rarely have we seen a union more reluctant to pull its members off their jobs than Local 1199. Rarely have we seen citizens of high repute and progressivism . . . so incapable of responding to the influence of reason and good sense in a situation where a minimum of rationality could avert disaster. The strike is a municipal calamity. Yet it was made inevitable by the incredible intransigence of the hospital directors."[18]

More than any other single institution, the *New York Times* both framed and reflected the moral and political perspectives of the city's policy-making elite. Given that Jewish institutions were the main targets of the strike, 1199 privately feared rough treatment from the *Times,* which was the organ of the Sulzbergers, one of the city's most respectable German-Jewish families. According to Foner, Alfred Rose of the Mt. Sinai Hospital board regularly walked to work in the morning with Arthur Sulzberger and "was always bending his ear about how the *Times* [was] being unfair to [the hospitals]." In addition, the union had reason to believe that the hospital association was pushing the paper to oppose the strike. True to its best traditions, however, the *Times* editorial board stayed remarkably independent. While initially condemning the strike as immoral, it contradicted the hospitals' main claims and, in contrast to the *Daily News, Mirror, Herald-Tribune,* and *Telegram,* tentatively endorsed the rights of worker representation and union recognition in hospitals. Demanding an immediate end to the walkout, the *Times* suggested revision of state labor law that would incorporate voluntary hospitals within the normal machinery of collective bargaining. Foner privately communicated throughout the strike with an influential and sympathetic editorial board member, Evans Clark, operating on the maxim, "If you can get the *Times,* however reluctantly, to print something that the *Post* would gladly take no questions asked, give it to the *Times.*"

As the hospital strike entered its second month, Local 1199 appeared as determined and confident as ever in its struggle for full recognition. On June 5, Leon Davis called Flower–Fifth Avenue Hospital workers off their jobs; simultaneously, the union began picketing private business establishments owned by prominent hospital trustees, including Macy's (Roosevelt Hospital board chairman Jack Straus) and Blumstein's Department Store (Bronx Hospital trustee J. Blumstein). In another important development, contempt citations against the union's chief officers (which had, in any case, been ignored) were overturned. On June 12 State Supreme Court Justice Henry Epstein declared the strike a bonafide labor dispute, subject to the rights of hospital workers to organize, engage in collective bargaining, and strike. The hospitals' position, in Epstein's words, was "more an echo of the late 19th century than the last half of the 20th century." Local 1199 hailed the decision as "historic" and "victorious." [19]

The hospitals nevertheless maintained their hard-line stance. In one of a conflicting set of retrospective analyses, Mt. Sinai counsel Howard Lichtenstein recalled the situation as one of basically conciliatory attorneys like himself and Beth Israel's Jesse Frieden rather uncomfortably serving "hardnosed" antiunion hospital boards of directors. By contrast, District 65 president David Livingston remembered Lichtenstein as a thoroughly, albeit surprisingly, unbending negotiator: "He should have been a positive force, because he represented Bloomingdales, with whom '65' had a contract, but he wasn't a positive force at all." Frieden also confounded union expectations of moderation. "Once," said Leon Davis, "he pointed to me and said 'I'm going to nail you to the cross.' "

Aside from competing decision-making centers within each major hospital, there were diverse hospital factions to contend with. One theory held that the Jewish hospital directors came under heavy pressure from antiunionists in the non-Jewish hospitals. In the midst of the strike Harry Van Arsdale thus decried what he understood as "Catholic pressure" on the affected hospitals to hold out against the union. Msgr. James Fitzpatrick, chief executive in 1959 of the four Brooklyn diocesan hospitals, likewise referred in retrospect to a "paranoid" antiunion hostility within the New York and Brooklyn archdioceses. Despite papal encyclicals on behalf of collective bargaining, he noted, financial and managerial considerations took precedence at the time. The monsignor also believed that both the Jewish and Protestant-funded hospitals "were in a better position to take a financial kick than we were." He claimed that St. Luke's (Episcopal) Hospital had an endowment of $7 million, while the total endowment for fourteen Catholic institutions was only $600,000.

By no means were the Catholic hospitals isolated in their single-minded resistance to hospital unionism. David Livingston, for one, blamed the allegedly noncombatant Protestant institutions like Columbia-Presbyterian and St. Luke's for stiffening the backbone of GNYHA president John Connorton. In constant attendance at the city hall talks, Local 1199 vice president William Taylor also saw these unstruck, prestigious (and largely Protestant philanthropic) institutions as holding an effective suasion over the beleaguered Jewish hospitals. Mayor Wagner himself underscored the influence of wealthy spectators to the strike: "All through the negotiations there were observers from the other voluntary hospitals—New York Hospital, Columbia-Presbyterian, Roosevelt—boy, these fellows were really conservative! The struck hospitals were not acting on their own. . . ." Mt. Sinai's Martin Steinberg recalled the vehemence with which Sammy Schwarz (of toy empire F.A.O. Schwarz) declared he "would take apart 'Presbyterian' brick by brick" if the union ever got in there. Bill Michelson, the negotiator from District 65, nevertheless believed that the ideologues met little resistance from the Jewish hospital directors themselves: "The three most vicious [when they spoke at city hall] were Jack Straus, [Benjamin] Buttonwieser, and [Charles] Silver." Clearly, whatever their private qualms and their differences in emphasis, the New York City hospital hierarchy effectively acted as one unyielding body throughout the strike.

By early June, despite growing outside criticism of the hospitals, the strike was visibly weakening from within. The affected institutions had begun to replace the strikers, thereby relieving pressure on an overextended staff and tired volunteers. Mt. Sinai, for instance, reportedly hired over 200 new workers, while Beth David retrained an entire kitchen staff. Meanwhile, the unexpected length of the strike was producing increasing discomfort and uncertainty among a significant portion of strikers. Twenty-two Mt. Sinai strikers announced to the leadership in late May that they were returning to work and that the strike had failed. Union stewards subsequently confirmed serious morale problems during the strike's final weeks. Even the union's high command showed the strain, despite contrary outward appearances. A continuing strike threatened not only the financial solvency of the union but the loyalty of 1199's drugstore rank and file. The cost of the strike by June 1 had reached $20,000 per week, and despite the infusion of outside funds the union could not make ends meet. In late May 1199's executive council asked drugstore members to vote to double their dues with drug division president George Glotzer chastising the membership for not doing "anywhere near as much as other unions are doing . . ." and declaring that "it would be criminal to permit such a state of affairs to continue." While the motion sailed through, grumbling continued among drug delegates that their organization had been consigned to endless sacrifice; that in a year of citywide drugstore negotiations, all of the union's energies had focused on the hospitals. Worried about communication problems between the overwhelmingly white drugstore membership and the predominantly black and Hispanic hospital workers, vice president William Taylor counseled drugstore stewards on June 3 that "it is not sufficient to just go out and picket. . . . make them feel you consider them fellow Union members."[20]

The dramatic escalation of the strike proved costly. Pressed as it was to maintain the existing campaign, an overworked union staff had not been able to adequately prepare the Flower–Fifth Avenue workers who were ordered out in early June. Tensions on those picket lines were especially high. On June 9, for example, one hundred strikers interrupted the academic procession during graduation ceremonies of the New York Medical College. During the ensuing melee they were beaten with nightsticks and seven strikers were arrested in what the police department labeled "the worst picket line violence in ten years." There were also intimations that Van Arsdale, pushing for mayoral intervention in the dispute, opposed any tactical escalation that would make reconciliation that much more difficult.[21] And, to make matters worse, Local 1199 faced renewed territorial threats from other unions, especially SEIU Local 144 and AFSCME Local 302. Six proprietary hospitals agreed on June 5 to recognize Local 144 and begin contract talks, and on June 8 Local 302 threatened to strike nonprofit Brooklyn Hospital. The militancy of Local 1199 had generally cast it as the last choice of any hospital administration forced to deal with a union. Thus, the possibility existed that the drug union would become the martyr in the hospital campaign, effectively clearing the way for other unions to reap the harvest.

While holding publicly to the demand for full union recognition, 1199 and its CLC allies began privately looking for some face-saving compromise with the hospital representatives. Leon Davis later recalled the painful realization that "you couldn't break the back of these guys. . . . you just couldn't do it."

Toward Settlement

At the urging of Harry Van Arsdale, Mayor Wagner launched a new initiative in early June aimed at terminating the hospital conflict. From every point of view it appeared the optimal moment for compromise. The union faced exhaustion of its financial resources, erosion of worker enthusiasm, court prosecutions, and pressure to settle from its chief labor allies. The hospitals faced staff morale problems, daily loss of revenues, and unwanted public notoriety. The mayor himself had for weeks been criticized by all parties for not doing enough to end the strike. Still, there was no easy way to wind down the confrontation. While both sides were anxious to end the walkout, neither could politically afford to surrender.

Beginning on May 25 Wagner entrusted the city government's leverage in the dispute to a new fact-finding panel headed by seventy-nine-year-old William H. Davis, a "soft-spoken deliberate Yankee" and one of the nation's most prominent mediators and arbitrators since his direction during the forties of the War Labor Board.[22] Constrained only by two considerations—that hospital workers should not strike but that they should be entitled to some collective grievance and bargaining procedure—the panel, which also included mediators Aaron Horvitz and Joseph McMurray, took separate testimony from both sides over a two-week period, then submitted its recommendations on June 8.[23]

Initially, the proposals of the panel suggested a victory in principle for the union. As befitted their experience in union-management relations, as well as their general commitment to collective bargaining, the city mediators challenged several assumptions underlying the hospitals' position. It was a "natural and inalienable right," argued the panel, for employees "to unite for their mutual aid and protection and to address their employers through representatives of their choice." In William Davis's view, the right to representation, protected by the First and Fourteenth Amendments as well as by the Wagner Act, was the most basic of political freedoms: "Short of enforced slavery there is no way to prevent employees from exercising their right to unite and to choose representatives to petition their employer for redress of grievances and for consideration of their proposals as to conditions of employment. Employers may, of course, refuse to listen."[24]

The "representation system" spelled out by the panel stopped just short of union recognition and collective bargaining. It called for the introduction of a third phase of the existing hospital grievance procedure — after presentation of individual grievances to the immediate supervisor and the personnel manager — in which a worker-selected "adjuster" (a euphemism for the shop steward) and one other adjuster selected by the hospitals would meet to settle the grievance. If the impasse was not resolved, a third adjuster, selected from an outside panel, would attempt to mediate, with ultimate recourse to professional arbitration. William Davis argued that the presence of an employee representative (or adjuster) would allow for "a good chance for give-and-take negotiations with full mutual opportunity for responsible freedom of choice between available alternatives" — an opportunity he realized was lacking in dealings between a lone worker and his or her supervisor or in a remote and costly arbitration procedure.

In other respects the Davis proposals closely resembled the hospitals' own "program for improvement" announced prior to the strike. To supervise employee relations, for example, they recommended, with minor revisions, the "permanent administrative committee" proposed by the hospitals, building into it an annual presentation of wage demands and grievances by worker representatives but leaving disposal of these issues in the hands of management. The hospitals, in turn, would be rewarded with a two-year no-strike, no-slowdown guarantee from Local 1199 and the Central Labor Council.

Eight days after submission of these proposals, hospital and labor representatives sat down and agreed to make the report a "basis for negotiations." At 3:30 A.M. on June 19 the ensuing joint talks yielded a "Memorandum of Understanding" to end the strike, subject to union membership approval. The memorandum bore little resemblance to the original Davis proposals, however, the most significant difference being the absence of the adjuster plan, the one guaranteed locus of union activity within the hospitals: the right to third-party representation was acknowledged only in the final arbitration phase, that is, outside the hospital workplace, of the grievance procedure.[25] The hospitals would contractually commit themselves to rehire all strike employees "unless guilty of violence" (a judgment itself open to arbitration) and to drop all litigation except for its appeal of Justice Epstein's decision (which was soon overruled). In addition, the hospitals' proposed Permanent Administrative Committee (PAC) was expanded into a twelve-member body to include six hospital trustees from the GNYHA and six "representatives of the public not associated with the Hospitals or Labor to be designated by the Chief Judge of the New York Court of Appeals." As in the original offer, the PAC would supervise a citywide upgrading in the treatment of nonprofessional employees and engage in annual reviews at which "any interested person, including representatives of any union," might appear. Any recommendation of the PAC would require the concurrence of at least three of the six "public" representatives.[26]

What had happened between the Davis panel's proposals and the final agreement? The evidence suggests that the hospitals effectively stonewalled the panel and forced both city and union negotiators to agree to quite different terms. Initially, Local 1199 insisted that the annual wage and job-grading reviews of the PAC be subject to arbitration in the event they did not win concurrence from employee representatives, thereby forcing the PAC to engage in de facto collective bargaining. The union also insisted on the democratic election of employees' adjusters who would act as the designated employee representative in all grievances. In this first, tough negotiating stance 1199 accepted the proposed no-strike clause but only on condition of being recognized as "full collective bargaining agent of the employees." The union's anticipated fall-back position dropped all talk of "unions" in the hospitals and substituted nonbinding fact-finding missions for arbitration in the event of appeals of PAC decisions.[27]

That the final settlement reproduced neither the Davis proposals nor the union's amendments to those proposals was testament to the upper hand held by management. Throughout the strike the hospitals had consistently vetoed any suggestions of worker-based grievance machinery, including the "adjuster" concept, fearing that such grassroots democracy would provide a ready-made haven for union organizers. Indeed, hospital negotiators counter-offered an "outside" route of arbitration following exhaustion of all internal management-based grievance procedures, no doubt figuring that the union could be kept at a distance, irrelevant to the day-to-day operations of the hospitals.

On first inspection the PAC was a well-conceived, employer-based compromise that signaled no major shake-up within the hospitals. It received strong philosophical endorsement from Monsignor Fitzpatrick and the Catholic Archdiocese, among other supporters. Harry Van Arsdale remembered the rising pressure in the final days of negotiations as the mediators themselves tilted more and more toward the hospitals' position. At one point he openly confronted Aaron Horvitz: "I expressed myself quite plainly, and he thought I was casting aspersions on his great record and got himself all excited. In my opinion he didn't seem to realize hospital workers were entitled to the same consideration as any other worker. [He took the attitude,] 'These people, if we give them a crumb they ought to be happy with it.' " Leon Davis said simply, "The hospitals wrote the PAC."

The settlement also bore the mark of Mayor Wagner, who took an expedient but ultimately rather passive approach to labor deadlocks. District 65 president David Livingston observed: "You have to know Wagner. He ran the city by never seeming to come in conflict with anybody. The strike settlement was typical. He didn't care if it was good, bad, or indifferent. If it was a way out of the crisis and it could be settled that way, great." The mayor himself looked back on the settlement in not dissimilar terms: "What you're always trying to do when a labor situation is tense. . . . you're seeking something and maybe you're not saying if it's going to be good for five or ten years—you're trying to find out if it's going to be good next week. The point is to get the people back to work."

While no one said so publicly, the hospital union leaders privately acknowledged that the 1959 settlement terms contained little to celebrate. The first imperative was to get out from under the crushing burden of the strike. They accepted a face-saving package that included the speedy return of strikers to their jobs, minimal material improvements (announced by the hospitals prior to the strike), a formal grievance mechanism, and the possibility of the union appearing at a public forum once a year—effectively no more than the Kheel plan that the union had rejected ten days into the strike. Leon Davis recalled, "Nobody was happy with it. The strike was defeated. I think you have to understand the PAC was a result of whatever could be resurrected from the strike. . . . I thought initially we were through." Bill Taylor, who had sat up night after night with the CLC negotiating team, knew that a similar plan in Toledo, Ohio,[28] "wasn't working"; that no union grievances had been processed through the PAC-like public body there. But "after forty-six days there was no place to go," he explained. "The realities of life dictated settlement."

The final push for acceptance had come from Van Arsdale, who made clear to the hospital union leaders that labor had played its last card. Hospital attorney Lichtenstein asserted that "Davis needed Van Arsdale desperately and I think he was shoved into the settlement. . . . by political considerations." Moe Foner remembered: "Elliott [Godoff], Davis, and I sat in a hotel room [discussing the settlement] in terms of whether we could put our imprimatur on it, 'cause it was Van Arsdale [who] had been involved in the discussions on it originally. . . . We agreed that we pretty much had gone as far as we could go with it, and the question that was raised in the hotel room was 'Can we survive with this settlement?' The estimate was, 'Yes, we can survive.' "

Despite their apparent triumph, hospital representatives accepted the 1959 agreement with mixed feelings. Publicly, John Connorton was all smiles, insisting that the settlement not only stopped short of union recognition but created a durable alternative to any kind of "union structure" within the hospitals. Management, he emphasized, had not signed a collective bargaining agreement at city hall, only a statement of policy.[29] Privately, however, the hospitals were less than certain about the settlement. From Lichtenstein's perspective the creative impetus had derived from directors Charles Silver of Beth Israel and Joe Klingenstein of Mt. Sinai, who "had the willingness to work out some accommodation to give the employees something. . . .

[They] realized in 1959 that you couldn't go on paying employees 35¢ an hour expecting them to live on it and be happy." As far as the lawyers were concerned, the PAC "was a stopgap—that was all."

For some of the hard-liners on the hospital boards, however, the PAC was not good enough. Simply put, they wanted no outside interference. Powerful voices at Roosevelt, Columbia-Presbyterian, Manhattan Eye and Ear, and New York hospitals ultimately convinced those institutions not to sign the "Statement of Policy" binding them to the PAC and the 1959 strike settlement. Thus began a serious policy split within the GNYHA, which would be exacerbated a few years later when a core of the PAC signators became the first hospitals to sign recognition agreements with Local 1199.

By most standards the strike of 1959 was a failure. The hospital workers returned to their jobs without the crucial ingredient that had triggered the strike and sustained it for seven weeks: there would be no union recognition and no collective bargaining in any real sense. If the PAC worked as planned—as a *permanent* administrative committee—the strike, at best, would have been responsible for the improvement of hospital workers' lives through a substitute for unionism. Yet we know that the events of 1959 did not signal the end of hospital unionism but rather its beginnings. How could this defeat launch a union?

The hospitals workers' strike did not, in fact, end in the conference room but on hundreds of hospital floors, just as the fate of the union hung less on written intentions than on the subsequent desire and activity of the mass of workers. Having held the whole city at bay for two months, the strikers themselves did not *feel* defeated. Those used to taking orders had defied their bosses with impunity and, by their own initiative, had improved their working conditions. Together they had created a hospital union and, recognized or not, no one could take that away from them. If the 3,000 employees going back to work and the rest of the New York City hospital workforce made these the lessons of the strike, then the union might well survive to fight again. "You see," Moe Foner recalled, "we'd been through forty-six days with these people, and we knew that they wanted our union, they were prepared to go to hell and back for this union."

In the few days between the initial private agreement and its formal ratification by both sides, Local 1199 took every opportunity, and occasionally bent the facts, to put the settlement in the best possible light. Foner played a key role in this process, having already developed close relationships with media representatives throughout the city. Now he played his trump card:

> Even though Van Arsdale said that he wanted nobody in the press to know what was in there . . . I was concerned that the press might hurt us by the way they would evaluate [the agreement]. . . . since they didn't know the terms, I

decided, without leaking the terms to begin to evaluate it for different people. I would call Jack Turcott of the *News* . . . and Stanley Levey at the *Times,* and the *Post,* well, with Wechsler, he would help us, you know, trying to build what we wanted. They would say, "Hey, what's in it?" "Well, you'd better read that plan [from the Davis panel] very carefully, and you won't be far wrong if you stay with what's in there." And they began to describe the settlement in terms of the Davis plan. . . . And when the *Times* says something, and they say it twice, it's the gospel. Even the *Times* believes it. You can't back off it. Everybody else is saying it, then you go on the radio and say the same thing, and you have a way of reaching your members and creating what you want to create on it.

The evidence bears out Foner's story. On June 22 the *Times,* with the terms still secret, erroneously claimed that (as in the Davis plan) workers would "elect" a representative to sit with management to mediate grievances, "thus paving the way for de facto union recognition." The *Herald Tribune* followed the same path the next day, referring to "a masterpiece of compromise." In general, the press repeated Leon Davis's public characterization of the settlement to a remarkable degree—an analysis that looks more accurate in retrospect than it had a right to be at the time. "Backdoor recognition" Davis called it, and he promised, "We'll be in the front door before long."

The major sales job was conducted inside the union itself, aimed at convincing staff, drugstore members, and hospital workers that the fight had been both heroic and crowned with tangible triumph. Contradicting his private thoughts, Leon Davis acted confident and upbeat before the 1,000 workers assembled on June 22 at the Hotel Diplomat to vote on the settlement. Following the singing of the National Anthem, he pledged that after a "slight pause" Local 1199 would tackle all eighty-one voluntary hospitals in New York City. Presenting the proposed settlement to the strikers, the exact terms of which had still not been made public, he announced that "the hospitals have agreed to recognize representatives of the workers to handle grievances in behalf of the workers; any grievances which cannot be settled will be submitted to an impartial arbitrator for decision." But for one loud "no," the strikers jubilantly ratified the agreement and, amid general pandemonium, hoisted Leon Davis and Harry Van Arsdale onto their shoulders and marched them around the room. Moe Foner's brother Henry, a leader of the furworkers, led the meeting in a rendition of "We're Just Wild about Harry." Bill Michelson of District 65 proclaimed, "You have learned what labor leaders all know—that many Negroes and Puerto Ricans never had an opportunity to look upon whites as their fellow-people; on the picket line you found you were friends for the first time. Until this brotherhood and unity was established, you had no chance for victory. Only this gives you the opportunity to see a better day."[30]

Following ratification, and even after the settlement documents were made public, Local 1199 continued to trumpet the agreement. Union members were assured that the hospitals were "not happy" with the terms of the settlement and that "time and time again" they had to "eat their words."[31] As when John L. Lewis stretched President Roosevelt's paper commitment to the right of worker representation (Section 7[a] of the National Industrial Recovery Act of 1933) into an endorsement of mass union organizing, 1199 sought to expand the meaning of the 1959 accords. On July 9 the union's newspaper claimed with some exaggeration that the settlement gave workers "the right to take up grievances through their own elected representatives of Local 1199" (the settlement in fact said nothing about worker or union participation in the hospitals' grievance procedures). "We looked at it," Foner explained, referring to the settlement, "and said, 'We're gonna do it this way no matter what the fine print says.' In a lot of labor-management battles things are very often not what they seem." Perhaps unwittingly, the American Public Relations Association confirmed Foner's point when it presented him with its annual award for exemplary service during the strike. Leon Davis also recognized the importance of the outside contacts cultivated by his public relations chief: "Moe knows three-fourths of New York personally, he knows who sleeps with whom and why, and if he doesn't know his brothers know 'cause everybody went to City College."

In one sense the union leaders were not straying far from the truth in their heady, somewhat calculated declarations, for in publicly acknowledging the right of individuals to join a union (even without agreeing to deal with that union), the hospitals in effect admitted that they could not stop workers, on their own, from electing representatives who might indeed press their interests within the workplace as well as before the PAC. The response to such activity, the 1199 leaders knew, did not depend on an official document that ignored the de facto organization of the workers. The future of hospital industrial relations would instead rest on a combination of disciplined activity by the workers and the hospitals' ultimate preference for eventual *real* compromise over continuing industrial strife.

In his first poststrike newspaper column, Leon Davis offered a candid commentary on the significance of the 1959 strike: "When the smoke of battle clears there come the usual questions: Have we won or have we lost? Was this fight worthwhile? The proper answer to these questions will be given by the hospital workers themselves: Will they build a great union, or will they slide back to where they were before?"[32] No one, in the strike's immediate aftermath, could be certain of the answers, though Henry Nicholas later captured the paradox of the 1959 events: ". . . it was a defeat, but the greatest defeat the union ever encountered." The struggle, he reasoned, had convinced the hospital workers that they "were part of a movement," and in the end that was the most important result of the "Battle of '59."

CHAPTER 5

Staying Alive:
The Search for Legal
Recognition

Even as they tried to make the 1959 strike settlement look like a victory, Local 1199's leaders understood that the union had failed to achieve its basic objective—recognition of hospital workers' collective bargaining rights. While they accepted the Permanent Administrative Committee (PAC) as a temporary, if unavoidable, compromise, 1199 worked hard to establish a tangible presence in New York City's voluntary hospitals and to fashion the political forces needed to change the state's labor law and gain formal union recognition. Ultimately this strategy would pay off.

Avoiding the Trap

Publicly confident, hospital management realized, as did the union, that the struggle for the hearts and minds of hospital workers had not ended with the strike settlement. To win the "cold war" that followed, union leaders and hospital administrators both devised tactics aimed at securing the workers' loyalty. The first priority for the hospitals was to convince returning workers that nothing had changed. Hospital officials advised all employees that the settlement was not a contract but a statement of policy; that the plan did not "provide either for union recognition or for a union structure within our hospitals."[1] During the strike Mt. Sinai's director, Martin Steinberg, had told supervisors at the hospital that the workers must be made to understand that in the future "positive acts of loyal and good performance are the best ways to restore our faith in them. Inadequate performance or disloyalty cannot be tolerated." The hospital director especially cautioned supervisors that "no one is to be recognized as agent for anyone else. The employee himself is to be encouraged to air his problem in order that justice will out."[2] For Steinberg and his fellow administrators, loyalty was defined as fealty to the "hospital family."

To demonstrate to their employees that the union was powerless and that management remained in firm control, hospital officials refused to simply recall the workers, as had been stipulated in the settlement. Instead, they subjected workers to physical examinations, fingerprinting, and screening by the personnel department before allowing "eligible returnees" back to work.[3] Each returning worker also was given a list of rules that specified disciplinary action for such infractions as "unauthorized solicitation or distribution of literature on Hospital property at anytime"; "unauthorized possession, use, copying or reading of Hospital records or disclosure of information contained in such records to unauthorized persons"; "acting in a disrespectful manner toward any supervisor anytime whether on or off Hospital premises"; and "threatening, intimidating or coercing another employee by word or deed or both."[4] Although some of these rules involved conduct improper by any standard, clearly a particular objective was to suppress potential union-related activities.

To forestall unionization, hospital management extended to workers a carrot as well as a stick. The citywide forty-six-day strike and unwelcome publicity given to the service workers' low wages and poor working conditions convinced the hospitals that they had to pay greater attention to the needs of their employees. Nevertheless, management continued to maintain that any improvements were matters of hospital personnel policy and not labor relations.

Before 1959 few voluntary hospitals in New York City, or elsewhere, had a personnel department let alone a coherent, institutionwide personnel policy. Norman Metzger, who became Mt. Sinai's director of personnel in January 1960, credited the threat of unionization for prompting the hospital to hire him and give him virtual carte blanche in setting personnel policy. He readily admitted that "the reason I was able to do what I was—what I did in the first years—was because the institution really felt that maybe they would keep the union out." In the absence of a union contract, personnel managers like Metzger had a free hand in establishing new procedures.

Metzger recalls that Mt. Sinai wanted him "to do certain things such as a wage and salary program, personnel records program, personnel policy," and so on. He adapted the system used by the National Electrical Manufacturers Association and the National Metal Trades Association and developed standard job descriptions, assigning points to each task. Personnel evaluations rated such factors as a job's required level of education and experience; its physical, mental, or visual demands; working conditions; and the employee's initiative and ingenuity. Metzger also prepared a policy manual that codified employment procedures for the entire hospital.[5]

Before he could institute common personnel practices at Mt. Sinai, Metzger understood that he had to restructure the hospital's administrative hierarchy. Mt. Sinai, like many other hospitals, contained a number of departments run with impunity as little "fiefdoms." He recalled one pavilion (or building) head, a nurse, who had tremendous power ("She even had her own benefit structure"). To replace such areas of autonomy with a clearly delineated authority structure, Metzger centralized top-level policy decisions under the hospital's director. He also assigned to assistant directors responsibility for the pavilions and made all matters relating to personnel the sole responsibility of his office. By upgrading personnel management, Mt. Sinai expected to forestall employee grievances and ensure "a stable personnel force of maximum efficiency."

Tighter management control in the hospitals was, however, more than a matter of introducing some personnel practices borrowed from private industry. Hospital administrators, like corporate leaders in the early twentieth century, used "welfare work," or nonwage incentives, to promote active employee identification with the institution. A loyal work force, management presumed, would also be a hardworking one. Thus, in poststrike issues of *Mt. Sinai News* (itself an example of a house organ intended to enhance employee identification with the employer) there are reports of an overhaul of the hospital cafeteria. Improvements initiated by the hospital administration included a new menu, better service (a fourth cashier was hired), and piped-in music. *Mt. Sinai News* also reminded workers that for them the hospital's gift shop operated like an army PX and they would not be charged sales tax. In addition, the hospital introduced new employee nameplates, designed, according to management, to promote courtesy and visible on-the-job identification as well as to add "dignity to every staff member and employee."[6]

Beyond the new personnel policies and benefits introduced at individual institutions after the strike, hospitals citywide turned to the PAC to coordinate their antiunion efforts. Participating hospital officials regarded the committee as a perfectly acceptable substitute for unions and collective bargaining. Msgr. James H. Fitzpatrick, director of Brooklyn Catholic Charities, recalled that he was "gung-ho" for the PAC: "I thought if we had this ongoing arbitration, mediation mechanism that you would be able to prevent [third-party intervention and strikes] from happening." Along with management at the seven hospitals struck in 1959, New York City's Catholic hierarchy was the PAC's biggest booster.[7]

As originally constituted, the PAC had twelve members—six hospital representatives appointed by the Greater New York Hospital Association

(GNYHA) and six "public" members not associated with the hospitals or with labor unions, appointed by the chief justice of the New York State Court of Appeals. The committee's mandate was to supervise the policies adopted under the "Statement of Policy" and provide an annual review of wages, rates and ranges, job grades, fringe benefits, seniority rules, and personnel policies. By July 1 each year the PAC, after collecting data and hearing testimony from any concerned person or the representative of any interested group, was to make public its (nonbinding) recommendations to the voluntary hospitals.

In October 1959 the GNYHA announced nine appointees, of whom six would serve as members, to the PAC, including Jack Straus of Roosevelt Hospital, Benjamin Buttonwieser of Lenox Hill Hospital, Monsignor Fitzpatrick, Msgr. Patrick Frawley of Catholic Charities, and Charles Silver of Beth Israel Hospital. Chief Justice Albert Conway named only attorneys to the committee, including the former presidents of the American Bar Association and the New York State Bar Association. The PAC members chose John Connorton, executive secretary of the GNYHA, to be secretary to the committee.[8]

Public hearings began on May 31, 1960, with Local 1199 representatives in attendance to express the union's hope that the committee would address hospital workers' immediate problems. Specifically, the union submitted wage proposals calling for "the same pay rates, pay ranges and fringe benefits in voluntary hospitals as those received by workers performing identical jobs in city hospitals."[9] Spokespersons for the hospitals testified to their institutions' good faith in carrying out the "Statement of Policy" guidelines as well as their willingness to implement PAC recommendations regarding future improvements in wages and working conditions.[10]

The PAC report in 1960 echoed hospital management's position on unions: patient care depended on "close and effective teamwork," which precluded third-party (i.e., union) intervention. The committee noted that hospitals could encourage good teamwork only by empathizing with their employees' problems and viewpoints and by being responsive and "scrupulously fair and honest" in their dealings with workers. Among its specific recommendations, the PAC outlined a "model" grievance procedure and suggested a minimum wage of $1.23 per hour (the same base rate paid workers in supposedly comparable jobs in the motel, restaurant, and laundry industries).[11]

In 1960 participating hospitals confidently anticipated that with a functioning PAC and their own upgraded personnel activities they held the best cards and only had to stand pat—to wait until 1199 faced the inevitable and folded. Metzger aptly characterized the union's dilemma: "They knew that if [the PAC] continued to work as it did in its first recommendations . . .

[workers] would start to say, 'Well, what do we need the union for? If we're going to have our wages raised each year, [if] we're going to get a new benefit each year' — [which was] what the PAC did, slowly, temperately — 'then what did the union do?' " In fact, if anything worried hospital management it was that they might prove to be their own worst enemy, inadvertently provoking the workers into joining the union. Thus, Martin Steinberg had warned Mt. Sinai's department heads "to beware of being tricked into precipitous unwise acts which disregard established employee relations policies." [12] The road to success for the PAC hospitals required that they be both tough (i.e., show workers that management was in control in the hospitals and that the union had no legitimate function) and accommodating (i.e., respond to workers' legitimate, according to management, grievances and slowly increase wages and benefits).

Before the end of 1962, however, the PAC hospitals were forced to recognize the union they thought they had defeated. What went "wrong"? In the first place, management failed to comprehend workers' feelings about what they had accomplished by striking. Ernestine Bowens, a dietary worker at Mt. Sinai, pointed out that although both hospital and union officials might have known how bad the settlement was for 1199, the workers themselves had little or no experience with such matters. As they saw it, not only had they managed to stay out on strike for forty-six days, but they had been able to return to work afterward. Bowens recalled that when the strike began supervisors at Mt. Sinai told workers "to take our things out of our lockers. We didn't. I have the same locker I had when I came here right now." Mary Riley, a nurse's aide at Beth Israel Hospital, expressed similar sentiments about returning to work. She found that even the supervisors were pleased to have the workers back: "Everybody wanted you to come back. But to come back, you found, you know, that in this place — the way it was — we were needed."

For workers who had experienced little power or status in the hospitals, just to be able to return to work after the strike represented great progress. In retrospect, Bowens recognized that the settlement was no more than "crawling . . . in the back door." But at the time, she insisted, "it was enough" to have had management "pay attention" at all. The workers felt that 1199 had enabled them to break the hospitals' "monopoly" control over them.

In the second place, beneath the surface calm following the 1959 strike, Local 1199 had been busy building a union in the hospitals. As Metzger pointed out for Mt. Sinai, "The Union did not give up the plant. [They] continued their meetings, continued their organization." Even before the strike had ended, Leon Davis was telling the union's staff that their ultimate success would depend on maintaining the substantial organization they had developed in the seven struck hospitals — this was to be 1199's "primary objective." Officially without legal standing, the union was determined nonetheless to make the best of the circumstances and forge a de facto organization within the hospitals. Before that could happen, however, 1199's leaders knew that they had to put their own house in order. In September 1960 the union set up separate drug and hospital divisions, the latter comprising four distinct geographical areas—the Bronx, Upper Manhattan, Lower Manhattan, and Brooklyn—as well as the professional, technical, and office workers' unit that had been started seven months earlier. Each area had its own director and assistant director. The drug division, which had a similar structure, would continue to service the existing membership as well as cooperate in the effort to build the new hospital division. The hospital campaign's overall leadership was provided by an executive council comprised of 1199's president, vice president, and secretary-treasurer; the director of the hospital division; and the director of each hospital division area.[13]

Initially, much of the hospital division's staff was drawn from 1199 organizers who had been active in the 1959 campaign. In addition, over the next few years ten experienced organizers from District 65 of the Retail, Wholesale and Department Store Union (RWDSU) joined the hospital division staff. The unions agreed to participate "on an equal, cooperative basis" in the organizing drive; however, David Livingston, president of District 65, insisted that long-time 65 organizer Bob Burke be made the head of 1199's hospital division, rather than Elliott Godoff who became the assistant director. Burke's appointment, generally unpopular among the hospital workers and 1199 staff, reflected Livingston's hope that his union would eventually lead a merged 65/1199 organizing drive in the hospitals.[14]

The staff of 1199's hospital division placed a high priority on giving workers a concrete sense of the union. As former guild director Jesse Olson observed, "it was a question of being seen." This meant bringing the union as close to the workers as possible—maintaining local offices opened during the strike and setting up new branch headquarters throughout the city, staffed by union-appointed organizers. Among their many duties union organizers assumed primary responsibility for collecting dues and handling grievances (both formally and informally). As a way of "maintaining contact," Moe Foner noted, organizers also called frequent meetings, scheduled at local headquarters as often as six times a day to correspond to workers' shift changes. Ramon Malave, a strike leader at Beth Israel who subsequently joined the union's staff, stated that after the strike "we kept talking union and we kept building. . . . And that's the only way to convince them. A leaflet never convince[d] anybody. You have to talk to them."

Local 1199 had a long-standing, deep commitment to rank-and-file leadership and, as a matter of course, relied on its battle-scarred veterans to keep the union campaign alive in the hospitals. Leon Davis believed that hospital workers would have a union only "when they develop[ed] their own leadership, coming from the ranks."[15] Rather than have the organizers appoint stewards, he insisted that the workers elect them, one for every fifteen to twenty-five workers in a department.[16] Just as most early 1199 organizers had at one time worked in a drugstore, hospital worker-stewards now formed "the guts of the union." According to Foner, "the staff can't reach the members; you need internal leaders."

Those workers elected stewards were likely to be individuals who had earned "a lot of prestige during the strike. . . . There were certain natural leaders that emerged," observed Marshall Dubin, who in 1959 was an organizer at Mt. Sinai. Elected a union steward at Beth Israel in the early years, Mary Riley stated that when her co-workers have a problem, they "come to me because they know that I [am] going to go all the way with them. . . . To get this kind of respect—every person look[s] to you as a leader—you have to do this." Stewards received no pay from the union for the added responsibility and work they took on, but, as Riley noted of these pioneers, "Somebody [had] to keep pushing . . . talking to them, . . . and if we would get one member a day. . . . You've got to feel for other people

Mt. Sinai laundry workers' leader Gloria Arana points proudly to her union button and delegate's badge.

otherwise you couldn't do it." For such individuals building a union in the hospitals became their mission.

At the base of the new hospital union were the rank-and-file leaders. Jim Bryant, a steward at Mt. Sinai, remembered going around on his break or during lunch, "catching a worker" to remind him or her to pay dues. When the worker stopped by later to pay up, Bryant would ask the individual to attend a union meeting after work at the local headquarters across the street from the hospital. Another Mt. Sinai worker, Gloria Arana, showed us her dues book, in which she had carefully noted each payment from her co-workers in the hospital's laundry. "The union wasn't here," she said, "but we want[ed] the union, so we paid . . . everybody in the laundry paid."[17] Rank-and-file leaders like Arana, Bryant, and others gave 1199 the day-to-day presence in the hospital that the union needed to survive.

Each month the stewards would meet to discuss reports from the union staff and carry that information back to the workers. They also attended classes, conducted by the union in both Spanish and English, to learn how to succeed as organizers. Local 1199 realized that while obviously dedicated, most newly elected stewards had little actual union experience. As Davis told the executive council in April 1960: "Stewards must be taught to participate in all activities and share the leadership."[18]

To ascertain the union's real strength in the hospitals, new stewards were held accountable for meeting specific goals. For example, late in 1959 the union initiated a petition drive aimed at revising state labor law to include workers in the voluntary hospitals. Each steward had to collect at least 200 signatures and involve five to ten workers in the project. When the campaign fell far short of its intended goal, Godoff told the stewards that they had only themselves to blame. "We have many tasks ahead of us," he said, and the failed petition drive was no way to win the struggle for a union.[19]

Because it lacked sufficient staff, 1199's commitment to actual member participation was a practical necessity. Any campaign to sign up new members had to rely on volunteer as well as staff organizers. In 1960, 1199 launched a "union builders" campaign that awarded prizes at a banquet to those worker-volunteers who signed up the most new members. Still, in all such drives success depended on leadership, on the ability to rally the troops. As the director of 1199's hospital division told the stewards' council: "It is a fact that a union like ours cannot function unless hundreds of rank-and-file members assume leadership as stewards and rally the membership to build the Union."[20]

As a supplement to staff and volunteer efforts, a continuous flow of union newspapers and leaflets dramatized worker grievances.[21] Frequently playing off themes related to slavery, the union linked everyday workplace issues to larger themes of civil rights and human dignity. For example, an 1199 flier of the period highlights charges by Mt. Sinai workers against Charles Valas-quez, the straw boss of the hospital's elevator operators, and refers to problems with "Mr. Charlie's Orders."[22] When another straw-boss super-visor was let go at Beth Israel in February 1960, the union let the workers know that the hospital had been "forced by the pressure of exposure and the indignation of workers" to act.[23] In one leaflet, 1199 greeted Mt. Sinai's poststrike rules, which provided that a worker showing disrespect toward a supervisor either on or off hospital premises be punished, by asking, "How far off hospital premises should the worker take his hat off to management? Does the rule apply to the sea and air as well as the yard?"[24] In another leaflet responding to the hospital's new rule book, the union was even blunter: "Heil! Mt. Sinai."[25]

Still, Local 1199 needed to do more than just exhort workers; it had to have real victories with which to encourage the membership. Union leaders understood that the workers had to see "the union in action, [even] without a contract," otherwise the organizer became "just another bill collector" going around collecting dues. To bolster the workers' sense of collective security as well as to demonstrate 1199's effectiveness, the union dramatized to the hilt any concession it gained from management. A favorable award in an arbitration would be quickly trumpeted in *1199 News*—for example, "Mary Jones, Dietary: Is back to work and has been told her vacation next year will be based on ten months' work."[26]

Not surprisingly, getting union activists back to work was a post-strike priority. At Bronx Hospital, Joe Brown, who had been arrested for allegedly beating a scab, was told not to return to his job in the engineering depart-ment. Local 1199 arbitrated his case and Brown was reinstated, but only after the courts had found him not guilty on the assault charge. In addition, he was awarded $2,500 in lost pay, something the union played up. Brown recalled, "They want[ed] to use that to organize other things."

In fact, *1199 News* kept a running score: "Our Own World Series—Arbitration Results To-Date 1199—10, Management—1."[27] Yet, for the union, it was nearly as much of an achievement for a grievance to reach arbitration as it was to obtain a satisfactory decision. Union leaders regularly accused the hospitals of having devised an "obstacle course" through which grievances had to be run in order to discourage workers from even initiating the process. Although frozen out of the grievance process until the arbitra-tion phase, 1199 organizers were able to teach the workers how to file grievances and have them heard. By the end of 1959, hospital workers had already filed over one hundred grievances.

Although a grievance might arise from many causes, 1199 responded most vigorously whenever a worker was fired for engaging in a union-related activity. When most hospitals failed to set standard wage rates and ranks for workers in different job classifications, as had been recommended by the PAC, the union designated certain activists to ask management "embarrassing questions" about when the standards would be put in place. In February 1960 Doris Turner, then a dietary worker at Lenox Hill Hospital, confronted her supervisor on this issue and was fired for insubordination.[28] The union responded quickly, vowing to do everything in its power "to see that justice is done." Turner's case was eventually arbitrated in her favor, and when she returned to work her co-workers spread their aprons down for a "red-carpet" entrance. "I was queen for a minute," she remembered. The lesson was clear for Turner, as it had been for Brown: the union could get results; "it could do things."

One of 1199's most spectacular early victories involved Hilda Joquin, a dietary worker at Beth Israel. Joquin was one of those outspoken activists— union lightning rods—who openly challenged management and rallied other workers to support the union. Her dismissal in May 1962 for collecting union dues while on the job instantly became a "test case."[29] She believed that she was reinstated because the hospital found that, rather than undercutting workers militancy, her firing "made it worse. So, therefore, I was reinstated . . . brought back." As it did after every victory, the union quickly moved to capitalize on its success. Along with stewards at Beth Israel, Jesse Olson met Joquin outside the hospital on the day she returned to work. "We had a big to-do," he stated. "It was always by dramatizing these things that the workers were encouraged to stick by it." Soon after her reinstatement, Joquin addressed a meeting of 1199's hospital division stewards' council, proclaiming: "United we stand; divided we fall, and we will back Mr. Davis, who God chose to make sacrifices for us and to lead us."[30] Joquin willingly made herself not only a symbol for "sticking by it" but for sticking by 1199 and the union's leadership.

A sense of theater pervaded many 1199 activities. In 1961, for example, Brooklyn Jewish Hospital gave workers what amounted to a 2¢-per-hour raise. Elliott Godoff seized on the paltry sum as an issue around which to rally workers, orchestrating an elaborate "burial" of the raise. Workers at Brooklyn Jewish formed a funeral procession, complete with a coffin covered with wax flowers and carried by pallbearers, and marched up the hospital's front steps. Management, obviously lacking Godoff's sense of humor, prevented the cortege from entering the building. The *1199 News* reported on the demonstration and insisted that management take its pennies back: "We Demand a Living Wage!" When the hospital subsequently accepted the PAC guidelines calling for an increase of $2.50 per week, the union could legitimately claim a big victory. And just so that the point of this "union victory" would not be lost, *1199 News* quoted a steward at Brooklyn Jewish who reminded his co-workers that the most important thing about the

In a mock funeral, Brooklyn Jewish Hospital workers "bury" a two-cents-an-hour raise. Union organizer and poet Marshall Dubin is on the left. Such theatrics helped keep the union presence alive even without formal hospital recognition.

raise was not the money but that the situation "proved once again that we need Local 1199 at this hospital and every hospital. Without the union, we are nothing; with it, we are strong."[31]

The elaborate ceremony to bury the two-cent raise was vintage Godoff. His many frustrating years trying to build a union in the hospitals had prepared him well for the difficult circumstances Local 1199 faced after the 1959 settlement. Building on the experience of a lifetime, Godoff devised the day-to-day strategy that 1199 hoped would generate more and more victories and make the union a reality for hospital workers and, ultimately, for hospital management as well.

There is much evidence that 1199's poststrike strategy paid off. While senior hospital administrators refused to legitimate union activity in their institutions, frontline supervisors, who were responsible for the day's work getting done, had to be more flexible. For many hospital supervisors self-interest meant establishing a good relationship with union rank-and-file leaders in their departments. "Certain supervisors," Marshall Dubin recalled, "found it expedient—in an unofficial way— . . . to give us de facto recognition." He cited in particular the Mt. Sinai laundry, where "anyone with half a brain" would know that to run the laundry meant dealing with Gloria Arana, an active union supporter. To ignore her might mean that "there just wouldn't be the right kind of washing that day . . . [laundry]

might get stuck in the mangle." Mary Riley remembered being able to sit down with supervisors at Beth Israel and discuss worker grievances: "I've never been rejected in no way by no one." Unlike remote hospital administrators, supervisors could ill afford, even before 1199 became "official," to ignore the very real authority union stewards exercised in the workplace.

For all of the union's "symbolic" victories in the PAC period, negotiated contracts to raise wages and guarantee basic benefits remained in the future. Thus, to counteract the hospitals' push for employee loyalty and to give members a sense of identification with the union, 1199 extended its usual service activities. Hospital workers' housing, credit, legal, and welfare problems had to be handled "within the framework of the union," 1199 vice president Bill Taylor told the stewards' council in January 1960. Under Taylor a social services department, staffed with qualified volunteers, met one night a week at local headquarters throughout the city.[32]

A commitment to social justice also pervaded the union's recreational and leisure programs. It sponsored dances, lectures, and theatrical performances all designed, as articulated in a 1961 statement of union goals, to heighten members' "sense of belonging to and participating in our social environment so necessary for creating a fuller and happier life."[33] Secretary-treasurer Eddie Ayash captured 1199's perception of the significance of off-hours activities in his report to stewards on a successful boat ride: "Just think back for a minute: Only two years before these hundreds of people, Negro, white, and Puerto Rican, were strangers to each other. They worked together day in and day out, but were disunited and never mingled together socially and now all these people were brought together in a spirit of friendship. This is 1199."[34]

Ever conscious of the racial makeup of New York's hospital work force, 1199 shaped social functions into an organizing tool. For example, on its annual boat ride the union had both Latin and black bands perform. Of course, the union's support for minority civil rights had been vital to its success in the hospitals from the first. During the early 1960s individual staff members belonged as a matter of course to the NAACP, the Urban League, and the like. The union regularly sponsored programs, such as its own "Negro History Week," at which Ossie Davis, Ruby Dee, or Pete Seeger might perform. Proceeds from these events went to support Martin Luther King, Jr.'s, Southern Christian Leadership Conference (SCLC) and other civil rights groups.[35] In 1960, in sympathy with the sit-in movement in the South, union staff and membership participated in the picketing of Woolworth's in New York City to protest lunch-counter segregation at the chain's southern stores. Individuals in the union also joined or contributed money to the Freedom Ride campaigns throughout the South.[36]

More than any other national civil rights figure, King publicly identified himself with the unionization efforts of New York City's hospital workers. During the 1959 strike he stated that their struggle "is more than a fight for union rights. . . . It is a fight for human rights and human dignity." In the 1960s he was a frequent visitor to 1199's New York City headquarters and each year spoke before or sent recorded messages to union rallies. Having long referred to 1199 as "my favorite union," King would, three weeks before his death in 1968, tell participants at the union-sponsored "Salute to Freedom," "I don't consider myself a stranger here, I consider myself a fellow 1199er." [37]

Even with the constraints imposed by the PAC, 1199, by involving the rank-and-file, holding meetings, issuing leaflets, and running dances, and by pursuing and occasionally winning redress of some grievances, made the union a material part of hospital workers' lives. By 1960, 1199 not only managed to fulfill Davis's "primary objective' of consolidating the union's substantial organization in the seven struck hospitals but also had launched chapters at fifteen other institutions in New York City. [38] Having established itself as a viable de facto organization, the union was poised to fight for full recognition. [39]

The Campaign Heats Up

Between 1959 and 1963, Local 1199 seized every opportunity to win union representation in New York City's voluntary hospitals. Particularly at the smaller institutions, the union, once it signed up a majority of workers, would threaten a strike and thereby "encourage" collective bargaining. In March 1960, Local 1199 announced a breakthrough in the heretofore solid antiunion front—the Home and Hospital of the Daughters of Jacob had signed a union shop agreement.

By taking advantage of every possible opening, 1199, less than a year after the 1959 strike ended, represented some 3,000 workers at a total of seven institutions in New York. One agreement, at Trafalgar Hospital in Manhattan, was offered publicly by Leon Davis as a "model for future hospital-union relations." In return for recognition and a contract, 1199 had given the management of Trafalgar Hospital a no-strike pledge and guaranteed five years of labor peace. [40]

Davis alternated between saber rattling—threatening to strike over the fact that fewer than half of the city's voluntary hospitals had joined the PAC—and peaceful coexistence under the "truce" created by the "Statement of Policy." [41] In early May 1960 he wrote to the trustees of the hospitals in which the union claimed a majority, offering them the same "perpetual never-strike commitment" given to Trafalgar. [42] Thus began what 1199's hospital division director referred to as the "Spring Offensive," under which the union eventually threatened to strike at ten hospitals. On May 23 the executive council requested from District 65 a $50,000 interest-free loan to meet the expenses of the projected strike.[43]

Despite their preparations for war, union leaders had good reason to prefer peace. Davis knew that if 1199 again went out on strike it would do so without the extraordinary help of the trade union movement "which we got last year."[44] The union was hardly in a good position to go it alone, nor is it likely that Davis wanted to do so. In fact, through the spring he kept Harry Van Arsdale, president of the city's Central Labor Council (CLC), and District 65 president David Livingston apprised of Local 1199's activities.[45] Moreover, in early June, even as the strike vote proceeded, Davis wrote to New York governor Nelson Rockefeller outlining hospital management's refusal to discuss with 1199 any proposals that included union elections and affirming the union's willingness to respond to any effort by a city or state agency to find a peaceful solution.[46]

Behind the scenes both Van Arsdale and Livingston worked to avoid a strike. In June, Mayor Wagner initiated discussions with Van Arsdale, Livingston, and representatives of hospital management, including Charles Silver of Beth Israel, who already had been approached by Livingston to see if an acceptable compromise could be reached. On June 30, 1960, the mayor announced revision of the 1959 "Statement of Policy," the most important change being the restructuring of the PAC to exclude the six hospital trustees, leaving the six public members, and adding three representatives from labor and three from the hospitals to act as advisors. Other changes involved streamlining grievance procedures and permitting mediation as well as arbitration as a means of resolving disputes. Having forced hospital management to make some concessions, Local 1199 agreed not to strike for five years.[47]

The union praised Silver and Livingston, as well as the mayor and Van Arsdale, for their roles in arranging the compromise. Silver had apparently convinced the Catholic hospitals—the most ardent supporters of the PAC— to accede to the changes. In fact, a *New York Post* profile claimed that without Silver's direct intercession the Catholic church would have vetoed the new PAC setup.[48]

Livingston's role in the negotiations was more complicated. Local 1199 and District 65 had referred to the organizing effort both in public and to their members as a "joint campaign" of the two unions, but beneath the apparent comradeship lay strong personal differences and conflicting organizational ambitions. Livingston's goal, which he has acknowledged, was to use the hospital drive as a springboard to a consolidation with 1199 either through absorption or formal merger. He later conceded that he was "naive" and realized that Davis was not "about to enter into a partnership with anybody." Knowing what Livingston wanted, Davis nevertheless accepted him as a labor advisor to the PAC (along with Van Arsdale and William Bowe, treasurer of the CLC). When full collective bargaining rights were finally won, Davis expected that Local 1199 alone would lead New York City's voluntary hospital workers.

Looking beyond New York City, union leaders focused their attention on the state legislature. According to Livingston, Davis realized all along that union recognition could never be won simply by manipulating the balance of political forces in the city. Victory for 1199 ultimately depended on finding "a path from Van Arsdale to Rockefeller," and Davis's letter to Rockefeller was, in fact, part of the union's long-term strategy. Mayor Wagner repeatedly revealed himself to be unwilling to pressure hospital management into accepting 1199. Therefore, even as the union campaigned to modify the PAC, it continued to press for revision of state labor law to include hospital workers. The slogan for the legislative campaign, Davis told union staff, was, "We, the hospital workers, want the same legislation other workers benefit from."[49]

Under Moe Foner's direction, each chapter and area of 1199 formed a legislative committee to meet with state senators and other representatives, organize petition drives, and otherwise lobby for a change in state law. The union designated February 13, 1960, as "Hospital Workers' Day" and urged members to go to every large shopping area in New York City and ask people to sign the union's petitions. By March some 18,000 signatures had been collected. The union also sent worker delegations to Albany to testify at legislative hearings and to personally lobby for the program.[50]

Foner once again formed a broad-based labor and civil rights coalition to demonstrate the union's community support. Over 200 prominent New Yorkers, most of whom had been members of the citizens' support committee during the 1959 strike, issued a public statement in January 1960 addressed to the governor in which they endorsed 1199's legislative program.[51] In 1962 Foner, along with key ally A. Philip Randolph, organized the Citizens Committee for Equal Rights for Voluntary Hospital Employees.[52] Like Van Arsdale, Randolph was close to Rockefeller and, according to aide Bayard Rustin, met informally four or five times with the governor on 1199's behalf.

Despite Foner's success in organizing public support for the union's legislative program—support that included the editorial endorsement of the *New York Times* and other city newspapers—the union failed to get the law changed. In 1962 a variety of bills with 1199's backing were introduced into the legislature. One of them, introduced by Senator Daniel G. Albert and Assemblyman Francis P. McCloskey, both Nassau County Republicans, lifted the exclusion of employees of nonprofit, charitable, religious, or educational organizations from the state labor relations law and, as the final step in any union-hospital dispute, provided for binding arbitration.[53] Opposition to these bills came from the expected quarters: hospital associations throughout the state argued that unionization diverted "employee interest from patient care" and led inevitably to "insubordination [and] infringement of management prerogatives."[54] The board of governors of the GNYHA called such legislation "a step backward" that would "create labor disturbances which do not now exist."[55]

The Catholic church remained adamantly opposed to any attempt to undermine or replace the PAC, which it saw as an alternative to hospital unions. Monsignor Fitzpatrick attributed Catholic opposition to collective bargaining by hospital workers to two sources: the church's concern over the financial viability of its own hospitals and its objections to injecting a third party into the hospital's chain of command. Reporting on the demise of the Albert-McCloskey bill, Murray Kempton of the *New York Post* cited Cardinal Spellman as a major source of the pressure against changing the law. Every legislator, but particularly Catholic legislators, according to one observer, felt "a lot of heat" from the Catholic church on the issue.[56]

Opposition at a critical juncture in 1962 also came from an unexpected source: Raymond Corbett, chief lobbyist for the New York State AFL-CIO. Corbett lobbied against the Albert-McCloskey bill ostensibly because of its provision for compulsory arbitration. Kempton—and 1199 officials—derisively dismissed Corbett's invoking such a "principle," concluding that Corbett was "a man who would violate every relevant one of the Ten Commandments to serve the aspirations of 20 plumbers."[57] Whatever Corbett's sincerity, by undermining labor unity he gave those legislators looking for a good excuse to vote against the bill an easy out.

Although unsuccessful in revising state labor law, Local 1199 had made progress. In particular, by 1962 Joseph Carlino, the Republican Speaker of the House, had thrown his considerable political clout behind the proposed legislation. During the debate over the Albert-McCloskey bill, Carlino, echoing 1199's "involuntary philanthropists" slogan, observed that hospital workers "subsidiz[ed] the operations of hospitals and nonprofit institutions. I can't see why the poorest people have to pay this subsidy."[58] Carlino appeared to be an unlikely ally for 1199, not having shown himself to be an advocate of either labor or civil rights legislation prior to 1962. How Carlino came to take up the gauntlet is illustrative of, among other things, Moe Foner's success at building public coalitions to support 1199's campaigns.

In feeling out union friends and enemies in Albany, Foner heard about Henry D. Paley, Carlino's legislative aide. Foner was only marginally aware of Paley's background, but "someone told me that Hank Paley was . . . a decent guy who came out of the labor movement [paper workers' union]. And I got to know Hank Paley, and I would go to his home in Albany and would sleep there . . . and we became very close friends." Through Paley, Foner gained access to Carlino.

With the defeat of the Albert-McCloskey bill, 1199's leaders felt that the union had reached a "dead end." The key had been "to get legislation" and that, Foner states, "was the crucial thing to us. Without legislation we would still be knocking our heads against the wall." Foner and Paley both understood that only through the governor's direct intervention could the legislative logjam be broken. The problem was how to get Rockefeller involved. Local 1199 found that the solution lay in its ongoing campaign to force management at Beth El Hospital to negotiate.

Davis had written to the mayor and to the leading participants in the PAC in August 1961, stating that the union was withdrawing its no-strike pledge from "nonsigners," that is, from the thirty-nine voluntary hospitals in New York that had not yet signed the amended "Statement of Policy."[59] A pattern had developed in which hospitals in the city that were confronted by a majority of their employees supporting the union would simply retreat under the PAC "umbrella" rather than face an election. Not surprisingly, the union found this pattern unacceptable. Davis did not threaten any specific action against these hospitals in his letter, but he told the *New York Times* that, if necessary, 1199 would not "hesitate to call a strike."[60]

Among the "nonsigners" was Beth El (now Brookdale Medical Center), long a target of the union's organizing efforts. Elliott Godoff took personal command of the Beth El campaign and in July 1961 began employing his usual tactics. Each day he visited the hospital in a vehicle that he advertised as the "1199 Union HQ on Wheels." After management responded to 1199's organizing activities by giving workers a small raise, Godoff designed leaflets that advised "Don't Work for Peanuts," to which he attached real peanuts. In December 1961, in an attempt to increase the pressure on Beth El's board, about forty workers picketed a hospital fund-raising dinner at the Waldorf-Astoria.[61] When hospital officials failed to respond, the union set February 12, Lincoln's birthday, for a strike vote. Benne Katz, president of Beth El Hospital, then promised to urge the hospital's trustees to recognize the workers' collective bargaining rights, at which point union leaders agreed to postpone the strike vote. Yet the only action Beth El trustees appear to have taken was to obtain a restraining order against a strike. After waiting over three months, Beth El workers walked out on May 23. Leon Davis was immediately arrested.[62]

The Beth El strike, which later spread to Manhattan Eye and Ear Hospital, was ostensibly waged against a leading nonsigner; however, the union's real objective remained to rid itself permanently of the PAC. The two strikes quickly became the requisite "dramatic struggle" that 1199 needed for Governor Rockefeller to come in as peacemaker. In contrast to events two years earlier, 1199 was now unwilling to accept a Livingston–Van Arsdale-negotiated compromise. The only acceptable ending was intervention by the governor and his support for revision of the state labor law to extend collective bargaining rights to hospital workers.[63]

Severely hamstrung by competing personal and political commitments, Mayor Wagner was unable to play a mediating role in 1962. He owed a large political debt to Van Arsdale, who in 1961 had launched the Brotherhood party in a successful effort to aid Wagner's re-election. Nevertheless, factors such as the presence of Abe Stark, Brooklyn's borough president and an important figure in the Brooklyn Democratic organization, on Beth El's board of trustees, as well as Wagner's strong ties to the Catholic church, constrained the mayor. Thus, when James Wechsler, editorial columnist for the *New York Post,* asked during the strike, "And where, by the way, is the mayor?" the answer was, "Out of the country."[64] In the middle of a sensitive strike Wagner had gone to Germany to visit his relatives and the sites of family graves. However surprising the timing of his trip, the mayor's departure helped clear the path for the governor to intervene. City officials asked that Rockefeller call a special session of the state legislature to enact a collective bargaining law and thus end the strike.[65]

As in 1959, Harry Van Arsdale's support was essential to Local 1199's success. He endorsed the union's decision to dump the PAC and, with the other labor members, formally withdrew from the committee's labor advisory board on June 21. Immediately thereafter the CLC publicly announced support, "with all the resources at its command," of the Beth El strike.[66] According to Davis, Van Arsdale's primary task remained to help enlist Rockefeller's intercession: "He had a very close personal and political relationship with Rockefeller. . . . Those guys deal with Van Arsdale." Local 1199 also maintained its alliance with important New York liberal and civil rights activists, especially A. Philip Randolph, who once again headed a support group, called the Committee for Justice to Hospital Workers. Randolph wrote to the governor on June 20, declaring that the hospital strikes had "again focused public attention on the urgent need for state legislation." In view of the city administration's failure to settle the strikes, "the committee call[ed] on Rockefeller's active intervention."[67]

Appeals to the governor were made on two levels: as the state's highest elected official and as a politician. Randolph emphasized that the repeated denial of rights to hospital workers, many of them from minority communities, had convinced the workers that they were special targets of discrimination, thus creating a potentially explosive situation.[68] The implicit promise of support from labor and civil rights groups during his re-election campaign was no doubt an added incentive to Rockefeller to step in and settle the strike. In a memo to Carlino, Paley noted the political rewards Republicans could expect from settling the hospital issue. In particular, he emphasized that it was an excellent opportunity "to crack off a substantial chunk of labor sentiment for the GOP."[69]

Paley became an important intermediary in the final negotiations, arranging a meeting during the Fourth of July weekend between himself, Davis, Foner, and Sol Corbin, the governor's attorney, at which the four men worked out the scenario for Rockefeller's intercession. Local 1199, as Foner recalls, had "to create an atmosphere for the governor to step in. . . . So we got every newspaper in New York to editorially urge the governor to step in on the grounds that this was a tragedy, a crisis, and this is out of hand, and it is necessary for Governor Rockefeller to step into the strike and settle it." After two weeks of mounting public "pressure," Rockefeller stated on July 17 that he had called a meeting of the representatives of all concerned parties, including Van Arsdale, Corbett, and the hospital trustees. As one indication that the union's careful strategy had worked, the governor cited the explosive racial situation in the city as the reason for his intervention.[70] While union leaders were not present at the negotiating session, they endorsed the outcome.[71] Local 1199 agreed to end the strike in return for Rockefeller's pledge to introduce and push for legislation granting hospital workers collective bargaining rights. Both sides also agreed that strikes would be barred in favor of binding arbitration as the means by which to settle union-hospital disputes.

By 1962 many leading civil rights figures besides Randolph had adopted the New York hospital workers' cause as their own. Speaking at a victory rally a few days after the settlement, Roy Wilkins, executive secretary of the NAACP, invoked the symbolic importance of the union's breakthrough for the civil rights movement: "Nobody gives you anything. You have to agitate, educate and sometimes you have to bludgeon people into giving you what is rightfully yours. The hospital workers have given New York an inspiration." Black activist Malcolm X celebrated Leon Davis's willingness to fight on even when facing jail: "If you aren't willing to pay the price, then you don't need the rewards or benefits that go along with it."[72] That two leaders in the black community who were usually thought of as adversaries could both celebrate the victory at Beth El and Manhattan Eye and Ear is a valid measure of 1199's ability to transform the campaign for hospital workers' rights into a moral crusade.

Governor Rockefeller abided by the strike settlement and on February 18, 1963, introduced a collective bargaining rights bill that became the basis of the legislation eventually adopted. Still, 1199 had to settle for half a loaf. Corbett, who had appeared to accept the Beth El settlement, did an about-face and announced that the state AFL-CIO would again oppose any legislation that included binding arbitration. The Catholic church's aversion

Malcolm X addresses a victory celebration by strikers at Beth El and Manhattan Eye and Ear hospitals in 1962. A. Philip Randolph, head of the Committee for Justice to Hospital Workers, is seated to the right.

Governor Nelson Rockefeller signs legislation on April 24, 1963, extending collective bargaining rights to New York City hospital workers. With him, left to right, are Leon Davis, Moe Foner, Elliott Godoff, and Doris Turner.

to hospital unions continued unabated, effectively coordinated by the New York State Catholic Conference. Finally, hospitals outside New York City, led by the Hospital Association of New York State, lobbied successfully to be excluded from the proposed legislation. Thus, the law that the governor signed on April 24, 1963, extended collective bargaining rights under the state labor relations act only to workers in nonprofit hospitals within New York City.[73]

Local 1199 had, by effectively organizing the workplace and molding broad-based support, freed itself from the PAC, but its victory was far from complete. Collective bargaining rights still waited to be extended to hospital workers throughout the state and union organization secured among their technical, clerical, and professional brothers and sisters.[74] Moreover, the union had yet to achieve a real breakthrough in wages, fringe benefits, or working conditions for its membership. Still, in having forced hospital management to acknowledge workers' right to a union, 1199 had taken an important first step.

CHAPTER 6

Coming of Age:
Building an Effective Union
in the 1960s

In Albany, on Capitol Hill,
The legislature passed a bill,
And that is why you'll hear us sing—
We won collective bargaining.

Chorus:

The Union has come, we're on our way,
We're building a new and better day,
The Union has come, it's here to stay:
Eleven ninety-nine.

"Eleven Ninety-Nine: Song of the Hospital Workers"

In May 1963 Leon Davis, recuperating at home from a heart attack suffered in February, met with a reporter from the *New York Herald Tribune* to discuss the future of Local 1199. Despite his physical infirmities, Davis was in a positive mood. At least in New York City, collective bargaining in voluntary hospitals was now the law, and workers at Mt. Sinai Hospital had recently voted, by a 20-to-1 margin, for representation by 1199. Surveying the New York hospital field, he expressed his belief that the Mt. Sinai vote would be the first of many union victories in the next several years. Yet for Davis and the rest of the union's leadership continued growth was linked to the struggle for broader social change in America. "This is the first big union to be built since the 1930s," he asserted, "but even more important than that

---

"Eleven Ninety-Nine: Song of the Hospital Workers," © 1963 by Henry Foner, sung to the tune of "The Blue-Tail Fly." Used by permission.

is the fact that it involves so many Negro and Puerto Rican low-wage workers. This is more than just another union, this is part of the freedom struggle."[1]

By the end of the sixties, much as Davis had predicted, 1199 had quadrupled its membership. Equally important, a significant number of its new members were professional and technical workers—laboratory technicians, social workers, therapists, and clerical workers—whom 1199 had organized into a separate guild. The union had won (in 1965) the right to represent hospital workers throughout New York State and in its collective bargaining agreements, first in 1966 and then two years later, had managed to nearly double hospital workers' minimum weekly salary.[2] Its progress on two fronts—extending union organization to professional and technical workers and raising the standard of living of hospital employees—truly represented the union's "coming of age."

"Bronxville, Mississippi"

Ever since its 1936 strike in Harlem drugstores, Local 1199 had allied itself with the struggle to fulfill the social and economic aspirations of black workers. In 1949 the union created a fair employment committee to combat discrimination in the drug field; the following year, it staged its first annual "Negro History Week" celebration."[3] In 1956 the union solicited funds from its membership in support of the Montgomery, Alabama, bus boycott, thereby fusing a friendship with the boycott's leader, Martin Luther King, Jr., that continued until his assassination twelve years later.[4]

Many national and local civil rights leaders had, over the years, been active in 1199's efforts to organize New York City's hospitals. Yet the strikes at Beth El and Manhattan Eye and Ear hospitals in 1962 marked a turning point in the union's relations with the civil rights community. As Davis told the executive committee, the union now had the advantage of "a strong community movement among the Negro and Puerto Rican leaders. This is the first time they have worked as closely together. . . . The fight of the hospital workers is symbolic of all the problems of the minority groups in the city and has become the focal point around which they are rallying."[5] Looking back, Doris Turner dated the full flowering of the alliance between 1199 and the civil rights movement to the 1962–63 period. Black hospital workers, she stated, saw an "amenity" between the struggles in the South and their own: "really and truthfully they were one [struggle], just being waged on different fronts, different places."

Throughout the 1960s the union continued to draw parallels between its organizing campaigns and the "freedom struggle." The civil rights anthem of "Freedom Now!" became 1199's rallying cry as well. For example, in 1963 the union called its lobbying campaign on behalf of collective bargaining legislation "Operation First-Class Citizenship," and after the law passed it set aside October 2 and 3 as "Freedom Days" to dramatize an organizing effort whose slogan was "Freedom and Decent Jobs."[6] More than 1,000 members of 1199 participated in the August 1963 "March on Washington," arriving on a special train chartered by the union.[7]

On March 10, 1964, more than 3,000 demonstrators, including many members of Local 1199, converged on the capitol in Albany to demand a $1.50-per-hour state minimum wage, legalization of rent strikes, substantial financial aid for quality, integrated education, and a law securing collective bargaining rights for workers in voluntary hospitals outside the New York metropolitan area. The rally was led by a cross-section of the state's civil rights and labor leaders, including A. Philip Randolph; Eugene T. Reed, president of the NAACP New York City conference; District 65 president David Livingston; and Leon Davis. Among other things it was the opening salvo in 1199's battle to extend the provisions of the 1963 collective bargaining law.[8] As in 1962, however, it would take more than peaceful lobbying to convince the state's political and legislative leaders to address the workers' demands. As a test case, the union chose Lawrence Hospital in the Westchester County community of Bronxville.

Suburban Bronxville was a wealthy, "lily white" community outside New York City that, according to 1199, only permitted blacks to come there to work "at the more menial jobs."[9] On January 16, 1965, after the hospital refused to accede to a demand by service and maintenance employees for union recognition, the workers went out on strike. Management said it saw no place for union involvement in the "hospital's responsibility [to deal] with life and death."[10] Echoing the position of the New York State Hospital Association, the president of Lawrence's board of governors, William A. Ritchie, opposed any revision of the state's 1963 collective bargaining law to make it more inclusive. He found it hard to accept that 1199 would allow itself to be bound by arbitration, as the law mandated, especially since the union had ignored a court injunction against the current walkout.[11]

All of 1199's actions during the Lawrence strike played up Bronxville as, in Moe Foner's words, "an enclave of the Deep South that happens to be in the North."[12] Through January and February, each Saturday the union transported busloads of its members to Bronxville for demonstrations. Picketers chanted "Freedom Now!" and "Jim Crow Must Go"; they also carried signs that read "Bronxville, Mississippi" and "Lincoln Freed the Slaves but Bronxville Hasn't."[13] Leaders of a local support group, the Concerned Citizens' Committee, told the *New York Times* that the strike made Bronxville "a symbol of outdated racial attitudes."[14]

Major civil rights groups, including the NAACP, the Urban League, and

CORE, took up the cause of the Lawrence Hospital strikers. Six civil rights leaders sent a telegram to Governor Rockefeller stating that "the strike of low-paid Negro workers at Lawrence Hospital, Bronxville, symbolizes the second-class citizenship status of thousands of Negro and Puerto Rican employees in voluntary hospitals throughout the state."[15] Ossie Davis, a longtime 1199 supporter, and Wyatt T. Walker, a former assistant to Martin Luther King, Jr. co-chaired the Citizens Committee to Aid the Lawrence Hospital Strikers. More surprising, among its few local supporters was John Richardson, Jr., an outspoken anticommunist and past president of Radio Free Europe, who championed the strike as a civil rights cause.[16]

Most New York newspapers also endorsed the workers' demand for union recognition and called on the legislature to extend collective bargaining to hospital employees throughout the state.[17] Finally, under mounting pressure to act, the Democratic legislative leadership as well as the Republican governor endorsed a revision of the 1963 law. After a fifty-five-day strike and on the eve of a planned civil rights march in Bronxville, hospital and union officials reached an agreement, with the union again having gained only the assurance that it would receive legislative redress.[18] Less than a month later, a bill was passed that extended the provisions of the 1963 collective bargaining law to hospital workers statewide, and Rockefeller promptly signed it.[19]

As a consequence of the strike in Lawrence, workers in voluntary hospitals throughout New York now had the rights to organize and to bargain collectively under the state's labor relations law — which did not mean that those rights would be granted in the workplace without a struggle. Through the sixties, Local 1199 made few inroads among hospitals in New York State, and even in New York City many battles had to be fought before the union represented a majority of the hospital workers. In the end, despite its apparent win at Bronxville, the union would not count the Lawrence strike among its victories. On January 21, 1966, blaming high worker turnover among service and maintenance personnel, Local 1199 withdrew its petition to hold an election at Lawrence.[20]

Peaceable Kingdom?

As a child of the militant trade unionism of the thirties, Local 1199 had a deep commitment to organize all workers in the health care industry, regardless of their skill or individual differences, into one union. But the early years of the hospital campaign convinced the union's leaders that they had no choice but to adopt separate divisions. According to Leon Davis, 1199 had tried "to accomplish the same thing" in the hospitals that it had in the drugstores, that is, industrial organization, "but we recognized that you can't . . . that we can't just put workers together regardless of their background and station in life, in their job and how they make a living." Union vice president Jesse Olson, looking back on the experience a dozen or so years after formation of the guild in 1964, insisted that "we would never have been able to organize 21,000 white-collar workers" if 1199 had not established a separate division.

Even though Davis was certain that the union's failure to engage professional hospital workers had been one of its "biggest weaknesses" in the 1959 strike, little was done to bring these workers into the union prior to 1963.[21] Elliott Godoff explained to the general council of the drug division in April 1963 that 1199 was slow in organizing professionals, "not because we didn't want to, but because they feared the militant struggles we were conducting and were not prepared to enter into them."[22] With good cause union leaders assumed that white-collar hospital employees would have serious reservations about mixing "professionalism" and "unionism."

Passage of the revised labor law created "new opportunities," however, and 1199 began anew its drive to organize professional and technical workers.[23] In leaflets and fliers the union hammered at the theme that the new law gave "all hospital employees the right to organize and bargain collectively through representatives of their own choice."[24] Local 1199 also focused on the potential for peaceful resolution of disputes. As Davis reminded professional workers, if "hospital management says no, no, no, and refuses to grant . . . decent improvements," the issue could be submitted to an impartial arbitrator whose recommendations both sides were legally bound to accept.[25]

The reluctance of professionals to strike does not, however, fully explain their resistance to joining a union. In the *1199 News* of August 1962, Harold Garelick, a research technician at Montefiore Hospital who had been a union steward since 1958, wrote that his co-workers wanted "an organization *of professional employees and for professional employees.*"[26] In response, the union announced in the same issue that it was forming a "separate group to deal exclusively with the needs of professional and technical workers."[27] Union leaders had become increasingly aware that the phenomenal growth of the hospital division was creating tension within 1199. "Young pharmacists," Davis told the executive council, could not "understand why they should be in the same union with other [hospital] workers." Although drug division members had "acted in a most commendable manner" in support of the hospital campaign, Davis felt that "there isn't and probably can never be a complete identity of interests between drug and hospital workers."[28]

Ratified by the membership in January 1964 as part of a new union constitution, the Guild of Professional, Technical, Office, and Clerical Hospital Employees would, like the drug and hospital divisions, keep its own records, collect its own dues, and create its own delegate assembly.[29] At the time it was officially launched the guild already had some 500 members, mainly technical and professional workers at Montefiore and Maimonides hospitals, as well as some at Mt. Sinai and Beth Israel.[30] The membership elected Jesse Olson, a former registered pharmacist and an 1199 organizer since 1959, as its first division director. Filling out the early guild staff was Fred J. Trippe, a technician since 1943 at Peninsula General Hospital on Long Island, who became a full-time organizer.[31]

Special literature was produced for guild organizing campaigns. In "a message to technicians and professionals in the voluntary hospital," the union outlined what the "GUILD CAN ACCOMPLISH." While acknowledging that "economic issues are uppermost in everyone's minds," the leaflet pointed out that the guild would work also "to give organizational expression on all professional issues." These issues included a fair job classification system based upon educational experience, salaries in line with responsibilities, educational opportunities for advancement made available through tuition-aid programs financed by the hospitals, and licensing legislation.[32] Guild publications tried to convince skilled workers that professionalism and unionism were fully compatible. Most of the literature included a picture of Albert Einstein along with his statement, "I consider it important, indeed urgently necessary, for intellectual workers to build an organization to protect their own interests." A leaflet entitled "Professionals and Economic Security" carried a typical endorsement: "As a pharmacist I know that 1199 has established standards for retail store Rx men which are 25 to 50% higher than what we receive in the voluntary hospitals." In addition to citing other benefits, the leaflet made special reference to union-sponsored social and cultural events under the heading "1199: A Swinging Union."[33]

Guild organizing proceeded slowly and mostly at institutions where 1199 already represented the service and maintenance workers. Olson recalled that the task was always somewhat easier when the organizer could point out to the professional staff how much more porters working in the same hospital were making since they had become members of the union. Nevertheless, fewer than 20 percent of the 5,000 hospital employees who joined 1199 in 1965 were guild members.[34] Unlike the hospital division, in which all of an institution's service and maintenance employees voted as a single unit, professional and technical workers in the guild usually voted by department—with one significant exception.[35]

A major advance for the guild occurred in the union's first entry into a medical school. In late 1966 workers at the Albert Einstein College of Medicine, led by Bernie Minter, an electrical technician, and Manya Shaffron, a research assistant in pediatrics, launched the Albert Einstein Employees Organization (AEEO).[36] An elected representative council met with college administrators to present the workers' modest demands: a 10-percent across-the-board wage increase, health coverage, and access to the institution's swimming pool. (The college had just closed the employees' health service facility at Jacobi Hospital, and, as one member of the representative council recalls, AEEO members found the denial of health coverage while working at a medical school to be particularly galling.[37]) Not surprisingly, the AEEO ran into a stone wall. By chance Minter met Leon Davis, an old friend, at a peace rally during the spring of 1967 and asked him if 1199 would help the AEEO. Minter found that convincing Davis was easier than convincing AEEO members to affiliate with 1199. As a research facility, Albert Einstein had a "flexible kind of atmosphere," and many workers expressed fears that "the union would come in and take over." They also were reluctant, as professionals, to join a union whose members were predominantly service and maintenance workers.

Minter used the college administration's hard-line stand as an argument for affiliation with the union. Diane Bianculli, then a recent high school graduate working as a trainee technician in the histology lab and known among AEEO members as "the Kid," recalled Minter ridiculing the college's claim that a 10-percent wage increase would lead to bankruptcy. All the employees really wanted was to be regarded "on the same level as [the] toilet paper," Minter argued, pointing out that even as the price went up Albert Einstein did not hesitate to pay for what it considered necessary. How could workers hide behind their "professionalism" and refuse to affiliate with 1199 when the college's administrators made it clear that the employees were not "as important to the functioning of the college as are supplies, furniture, etc."[38] Such arguments finally led to an overwhelming 5-to-1 vote in May 1967 to join the union, but because many of the workers still identified with their professional association, the new organization was called "AEEO/1199."[39]

Once the workers had affiliated with 1199, events at Albert Einstein followed a fairly predictable course. AEEO/1199 sent a mass delegation to meet with the college's administration while outside the medical school some 1,000 employees marched to demand recognition for the union. Yeshiva University, which governed the college, insisted that its status as a private, nonprofit, educational institution exempted it from "the obligations" of the New York State Labor Relations Act. While willing to abide by union elections at its affiliated institutions (the city-operated Jacobi, Van Etten, and Lincoln hospitals), university officials sought to exclude most of the workers—the medical researchers and higher-grade technical and clerical employees—at Albert Einstein from the union.[40]

Local 1199 rejected Yeshiva's claims.[41] On July 17, 1967, workers at the medical college and its affiliates voted to strike one week later for union recognition. As the deadline approached, both District Council 37, which represented other municipal hospital workers, and the college's doctors' association announced that they would honor an 1199 picket line. That prompted Deputy Mayor Timothy Costello to step in and help to arrange a last-minute settlement. The breakthrough apparently came after Charles C. Bassine, chairman of the college's board of overseers, intervened and agreed to a union election for all employees except supervisors and confidential secretaries.[42]

In preparation for what would later prove to be a successful union certification election, the executive committee of the AEEO/1199 issued "Sense and Commonsense." In this leaflet the executive committee stated that "it may be wise to pause at this junction, to sit and discuss some of the issues raised by some of our fellow employees" at Albert Einstein, particularly "Professionalism and Union Membership" and "Unions and Medical Schools." Workers who thought that they could "do all right" for themselves "by wheeling and dealing" were exhorted to "think about it the next time you pay for an X-ray or to be examined by a staff physician." The original leadership of the AEEO had recognized that forming "some kind of technical guild" would not work: "As long as any one group in this College remains alone and tries to better conditions for itself only, that effort is doomed to failure." Working conditions "affected everyone in the institution, from glasswasher to research assistant and from porters to senior secretaries. Our problems are common to everyone—the solutions are also."[43] Consequently, AEEO/1199 became the only chapter without a separate guild and hospital division membership, something Bianculli was proud of. She pointed out that all the workers at the AECOM meet to discuss the "particular demands" of any one group and asserted that because of this the union chapter has been a "training area," a model of "how to organize a democratic chapter."[44]

Despite the success of the AEEO/1199 affiliation, union leaders continued to argue for separate divisions. Differences in skill, race, gender, and ethnic background have historically fragmented American workers and the trade union movement. Yet Leon Davis insisted that by creating two divisions, 1199 avoided the conditions that prevail in, for example, the hotel or construction industries, where ten or twenty distinct unions are the rule. He wrote in 1963 that workers should vote for the union because "1199 has divisions for all hospital workers—the skilled, the unskilled, the professional, technical and office personnel."[45] For Davis, separate divisions were better than separate unions; or, as Olson observed, separate divisions represented not a failure "but a success" of industrial unionism.

Even as the guild was being established, 1199 was adopting other structural changes aimed at unifying the leadership. It was up to the union, Davis told the executive council, to build "a leadership of all three divisions, not just of any one division." Each division would be given a large measure of autonomy, but the union must be integrated "from the top. We want the top leadership to be '1199'—not drug, or hospital or Guild. As one union we must meet together, act together, have one point of interest, the union." Unity was the key, "If we succeed in this," Davis predicted, "we will have achieved the millennium. We will have proved that the lion and the lamb can live together."[46]

Despite the vigor with which 1199's leaders championed the divisional structure, there is evidence that they were also made uncomfortable by it. In 1967 the union engaged in another internal evaluation of its operations. At a meeting to review the administration of the guild, the staff discussed the current status of organizing among LPNs. Just two years earlier, Local 1199 had founded the Guild League for Licensed Practical Nurses, which by June 1967 had 1,500 members and two LPNs on the guild staff.[47] During the discussion Davis asked, "Should the LPN League be a separate entity?" Jesse Olson replied that there was no need for that: "As a matter of fact they enjoy mixing with other delegates at the [guild] assembly." The consensus of the staff was unequivocal: "DROP THE LEAGUE. Encourage the LPN's to mix with others."[48] Union organizing literature later referred to an LPN league but made it clear that the league was an integral part of the guild.[49]

Whatever misgivings they may have had over the LPN league, 1199's leaders obviously accepted the premise that the only way hospital workers would be organized in one union was through separate divisions. When Davis made this point in 1963 in reference to the need to revise the union's constitution, he stated that "the best we can work toward is mutual respect, interest and moral responsibility for each other."[50] If not quite the millennium, Davis still set a high standard of cooperation for the union to attain.

The Church and the State of the Union

The organizing of professional and technical workers was but one part of 1199's ongoing campaign to build up its presence in New York City hospitals. At the start of 1963 there were 6,000 union members at twelve PAC hospitals and twenty-three institutions that recognized 1199; by the end of the year the union had doubled its hospital division membership.[51] Many hospitals did not bother to go through the formalities of a state labor relations board election. In fact, during a four-year period, from July 1, 1963, through June 30, 1967, certification elections added only 3,000 hospital workers to 1199's membership rolls. Yet by January 1968 the union was able to report a paid-up membership of over 23,000 employees working in hospitals and nursing homes in the metropolitan area.[52]

Despite impressive advances, by July 1967 Local 1199 still represented only about one-third its potential membership in New York City hospitals.[53] The larger institutions, including New York University and Columbia-Presbyterian as well as the Catholic hospitals, continued to resist unionization. However, none was more resistant than Roosevelt Hospital in Manhattan. Even though 1199 waited until it could claim a majority at Roosevelt (the state labor relations law permitted a union to file for an election after 30 percent of the workers had signed membership cards), the union was defeated by a vote of 298 to 156 in June 1964. The outcome was the result of an "intensive brainwashing campaign, intimidation and vicious lies peddled by the [hospital's] management," union leaders charged.[54] When a campaign two years later also ended in defeat, 1199 filed charges of unfair labor practices with the state labor relations board. The union cited Roosevelt Hospital administrators for, among other things, trying to bribe workers by raising their wages three times during the organizing drive; by holding compulsory meetings at which the chief officer expounded on "how evil" the union was; by organizing an "I Am a Loyal American" committee, which portrayed 1199's leaders as Communists and criminals; and by using guards and supervisors to march workers to the polls on election day.[55] As far as the union was concerned, such practices made Jack Straus, Roosevelt's chairman of the board, "1199's no. 1 enemy."[56]

Between October 1967 and June 1968 the state labor relations board conducted forty-eight days of hearings on the union's charges against Roosevelt Hospital. In February 1969 the trial examiner, although rejecting some of 1199's accusations, agreed that a 10-percent across-the-board wage increase, coming one day after the union had filed for an election and on the heels of a 4-percent boost four months earlier, was meant "to seduce" workers. He found 1199's case so compelling, in fact, that he recommended union certification at Roosevelt without another election. But the full board failed to sustain the examiner's findings, and it was not until 1973 that 1199 would represent workers at Roosevelt Hospital.[57]

As a group, Catholic hospitals proved the most resistant to unionism. Teddy Mitchell, former vice president of 1199 and a union organizer in the 1960s, conceded that "the Catholic hospitals are tough. . . . The sisters run those hospitals and get to the workers." Julio Pagan, an 1199 organizer, indicted the Catholic hospitals for taking advantage of the workers' faith. He recalled that the sister-administrator of St. John's Hospital in Queens gave workers, most of whom were Catholic, little medals to wear, which they were told "descended from the Pope." Catholic workers, especially "the Spanish, . . . when they see a nun, think it's something high" and so "they went for that."

Much the same point was made by Monsignor Fitzpatrick, associate director of the Division of Health and Hospitals of the Catholic Charities of

Brooklyn during the 1960s. He ascribed the difficult time unions had organizing in Catholic hospitals not to anything "we did to oppose them" but to the "familial relationship of the religious there." As part of their vocation, Catholic nuns took a personal interest in the lives of the workers; they "would make soup for the sick wife. Sister would call the school if the kids were having trouble." By hiding their antiunion practices behind the veil, Catholic hospitals kept 1199 at bay during the organizing campaigns of the 1960s.[58]

Local 1199 suffered many defeats before achieving a breakthrough in New York City's Catholic hospitals. Mitchell recalled two election defeats at St. Vincent's Hospital and three at St. Clare's. In 1963, the union filed for an election at St. John's, only to have a majority of the workers vote "no union."[59] Finally, in 1968, after an intense year-and-a-half-long campaign by 1199, the administrators at St. John's agreed to recognize the union. However, it took a sit-in and a week-long strike at the hospital the following year before terms of a contract could be agreed upon.[60]

A Living Wage

Two complementary objectives dominated Local 1199's first decade of union building in the hospitals: expanding its organizational base and establishing its legitimacy as the collective bargaining agent for hospital workers. Inevitably, in its early years, the union had subordinated the winning of wage and other demands to the task of increasing its membership. But by 1966, having achieved a secure position in the New York City voluntary hospitals, union leaders decided that it was time to abandon their cautious approach to collective bargaining.

While the PAC operated, 1199 had only a modest impact on wages. Yet even at hospitals that recognized the union, like Montefiore, the minimum weekly wage for workers had, between 1963 and 1966, only risen from $40 to $63.[61] Norman Metzger, personnel director at Mt. Sinai Hospital, characterized labor-management relations during that time as "a piece of cake." In retrospect, he contended, 1199 was merely trying "to lull us into a sense of security that the union was not really a problem." For the hospitals, this modern-day "era of good feelings" proved short-lived: "1966," Metzger declared, "was the moment of truth."

With a special "Let's Fight Poverty" issue of *1199 News* in February 1966, the union launched its campaign to gain significant wage increases at nineteen of the city's voluntary hospitals.[62] As they did throughout the sixties, union leaders drew explicit parallels between wage demands and "the overall struggle of American Negro workers . . . to fight their way out of poverty and into first-class citizenship."[63] Seeking wage parity for its members with workers in the city's municipal hospitals, 1199 tried to arrange joint talks with the voluntary hospitals under contract. In June, workers at almost every institution gathered in front of the director's office each day for about two weeks to demand negotiations. Finally, on July 7, following a noontime walkout, officials at Maimonides Hospital agreed to bargain. An agreement was reached under which the workers gained a 24-percent wage increase: an immediate 10-percent raise, a 7½-percent increase the next year, an additional 2½ percent increase in June 1968, and a 4-percent payroll contribution for family health benefits.[64]

Local 1199 quickly announced that it would settle for no less than the "Maimonides formula" at the other hospitals. Employees at several institutions, particularly Montefiore and Mt. Sinai, began a series of on-again/off-again work stoppages. At Montefiore, workers on the morning shift reported four hours late on July 12; the following day they did not come in until noon; and two days later they stayed out for twenty-four hours. Mt. Sinai workers demonstrated on the morning of July 14 at the hospital's entrances and then rallied across the street in Central Park at noon. The next day, after a second noontime rally, the workers did not return to the hospital.[65] Union leaders obviously hoped that such actions would force a settlement, that they could stop short of a full-blown strike. State law as well as the reopener clause in the existing agreements required that the wage disputes be submitted to arbitration. Confronted by management with charges of flaunting the law, 1199 claimed that the work stoppages were the unauthorized, "spontaneous outbursts" of a dissatisfied work force.[66]

The hospitals never made a serious effort to force arbitration, and both sides hoped that continued unrest would ensure government intervention. On July 12, Mt. Sinai officials wired Governor Rockefeller, Lt. Governor Malcolm Wilson, and New York City's mayor John V. Lindsay, asking them to intervene in order to avoid a "catastrophe."[67] Lindsay as the first to act, assigning Deputy Mayor Costello to conduct secret negotiations with both sides. Lindsay was keenly aware that the civil rights movement once dominated by Martin Luther King, Jr.'s, philosophy of nonviolence had given way to cries of "Black Power" and "Burn, Baby, Burn," and the possibility of the wage campaign touching off a race riot had to be considered. The *New York Times* reported that during negotiations Leon Davis told Costello that the growing discontent of the black and Hispanic communities in New York could lead to "a blood bath that would make Watts look like a playground."[68] Whether or not Davis actually made this statement, it is unlikely that city officials needed to be reminded of the "long hot summers" then convulsing the nation.[69]

The possibility of violence lent a sense of urgency to the negotiations between the union and the hospitals. After a weekend of marathon bargaining, Mt. Sinai agreed to the "Maimonides formula," and the other hospitals quickly followed suit. Only Montefiore expressed open dissatisfaction, calling the agreement by Mt. Sinai's administrators a "disastrous surrender of principle." Martin Cherkasky, the director at Montefiore, publicly lamented "capitulating to Local 1199."[70] The *Times* agreed that the hospitals were bowing "to harassment by strike, exercised in defiance of both law and contract, [which] sets a precedent of great danger to the community." But what really raised the editors' ire was the inevitability that the hospitals would "pass their higher outlays on to patients and the community in the form of higher fees for all hospital services. All levels of government will feel the impact in inflation of the charges they must meet under the new Medicare and Medicaid program. Blue Cross rates will also feel the upward pull."[71] Under federal and state guidelines, increases in hospital wage rates and fringe benefits, as well as in expenses for personnel administration, were considered part of the legitimate cost of providing patient services and could be passed along to a third-party payer. In fact, within a year third-party payments covered more than half the nation's medical bills.[72]

Concern over the potential for racial violence as well as the vast expansion in health services contributed in 1966 to a greater receptivity among public officials to 1199's more ambitious collective bargaining demands. Also working in the union's favor was the rise in militancy among the city's municipal labor unions. During Mayor Wagner's long term in office (1954–65), municipal labor relations had generally been peaceful, albeit not very fruitful for the city's workers. But John Lindsay's mayoralty, beginning with a transit strike on January 1, 1966, the day he took office, was often disrupted by serious strikes, or threats of strikes, on behalf of greater economic gains for city workers. District Council 37 of AFSCME, which had just won a bitterly contested election with the Teamsters Union to represent most of the workers in the city's municipal hospitals, became increasingly tough in negotiations with the city. Under Lillian Roberts, whom Victor Gotbaum, then a District Council 37 field staff coordinator, had recruited from Chicago to provide aggressive leadership in New York, hospital workers would become in the 1970s the largest unit within AFSCME.[73]

After 1966, according to Norman Metzger, bargaining between hospital management and labor became something of a game, and both sides learned "that reimbursement was the name of the game and that negotiations had to take a certain form." From the hospitals' perspective, not only would the union not seriously negotiate, but once the talks reached a crisis, "ipso facto somebody would come in with a pile of money." As far as the hospitals were concerned, they were "a conduit" for the "public money" that paid the bills. In this regard the Metzger thesis might more accurately describe hospital-labor negotiations after 1968. Clearly, the response of Montefiore's director to the 1966 settlement is evidence that the participants had not fully learned the rules of the game. Moreover, the 1966 talks had at first involved bargaining only between hospital management and the union; it was not until 1968 that the hospitals began to press heavily for direct government and Blue Cross involvement in the bargaining process. Metzger may have been closer to the mark when he concluded that 1966 was a "sign of the future," whereas 1968, when a new agreement was negotiated, "was the future."

On March 7, 1968, in order to conduct joint bargaining with the union, fifteen local hospitals had formed the League of Voluntary Hospitals and Homes of New York. William Abelow, an attorney, was named executive director and acted as the league's sole public spokesperson throughout the negotiations with 1199. League hospitals employed a majority of 1199's membership, and both the league and the union expected that the terms they settled on would set the standard for the entire industry in New York.[74]

The league's position, articulated in a series of newspaper advertisements, was based on three premises: (1) Any work stoppage or strike was illegal; the main issue was "respect for the law." (2) Union wage and benefit demands would exact a tremendous price, pushing up the cost of hospital care by $25 per day. (3) The hospitals and patients both were innocent victims in that government and medical plan funds already had to provide a major share of the hospital costs. "It is not our money. . . . It is yours," league statements continually emphasized. Because the hospitals were only "custodians of public funds," the league called for direct participation by the mayor, the governor, and Blue Cross in the negotiations.[75]

For its part, 1199 was equally unyielding, announcing that its major demand, a $100-per-week minimum salary, was "not arbitrable, not negotiable, it's irreducible."[76] Once again the union linked its wage demands to the moral and social imperatives of the civil rights movement: as Leon Davis wrote in *1199 News,* "What sense, logic, reason or justice is there in talking about the abolition of poverty and making contributions to the Poor People's Campaign (as some of the hospital trustees have done) while opposing a minimum wage that would be a long step towards that objective?"[77] Union leaders, aware that in the hospital league they faced a tougher opponent than in 1966, appropriated $20,000 to cover the costs of a media campaign to explain why the workers "feel they must strike."[78] Headlined "Hospital Crisis," a June 24 union advertisement stated simply that hospital workers would no longer accept "poverty wages. . . . We want all the opportunities for advancement and education available to other Americans." Although recognizing that the demanded minimum wage would add to the hospitals' financial difficulties, the union insisted that the workers could no longer "act as involuntary philanthropists for the voluntary hospitals. . . . The hospitals cannot continue to balance their books on the shoulders of poor people any longer."[79]

At a strike rally on June 27, some 7,000 workers voted to stage work stoppages at any or all of the forty contract hospitals starting at midnight on July 1. Even more threatening was the union's announcement that the stoppages might take the form of worker sit-ins at duty stations, which raised the very real specter of violent confrontations between a largely minority work force and a mostly white police force.[80] The league responded by appealing to the governor and the mayor, announcing that "unless they act, we must capitulate to any demands the union will make and set no limit on the cost the public must bear, but insofar as our patients are concerned, we face disaster."[81] Speaking for 1199, Moe Foner stated that to avoid a labor conflict that "might stir up racial troubles," the union was prepared "to negotiate around the clock."[82] During the final weekend before the July 1 deadline, city and state officials intervened and all-night negotiations produced a settlement just one hour after the strike had begun. The league agreed to a two-year contract that established a $100-a-week minimum wage, gave those workers who already earned the minimum a 25-percent across-the-board

Demonstrators cheer the $100-a-week contract, thereby avoiding a strike in the summer of 1968.

increase, and funded a benefit plan for employees based upon 6 percent of the gross payroll, creating for the first time a pension plan and a training and upgrading program. The union made some concessions on fringe benefits and agreed to arbitrate three unresolved issues.[83]

Despite the dramatic conclusion, according to Metzger the 1968 negotiations showed, as did those in 1966, that the hospitals and the union were not engaging in adversary bargaining. In fact, he claimed, "the only thing different in 1970, '72, '74 was the hotel. . . . We both discovered what it was all about, and you just had to play it out." The brinksmanship of hospital and union, in Metzger's view, was more for effect; it was a means of applying pressure on government officials to step in and provide the financial wherewithal for a settlement, rather than a way to force the other side to compromise. The *Times* agreed. Its editors took note of the reluctance of the governor, the mayor, and Blue Cross to get involved in the talks and observed that "government officials have always been wary of entering private labor disputes, especially when they are asked, in effect, to bring the money."[84] Although concerned that rising hospital costs would cause an upward "inflationary spiral," after the settlement was reached the paper warmly praised Lindsay and other public officials for helping to "avoid a disaster."[85]

Metzger seems justified, then, in concluding that by 1968 collective bargaining between the union and the hospitals amounted to finding out how much the government was willing to pay. Yet it would be a mistake to view the 1968 settlement as no more than a cynical deal or an elaborate charade; to do so confuses means with ends. Both the union and the hospital league approached the negotiations knowing that nonparticipants held the keys to a settlement. From the league's perspective, the form of the negotiations was necessary to convince government and health insurance officials that the hospitals had no choice but to raise per diem rates. And if such tactics were required for the league to meet union demands, the leaders of 1199 were willing to play along.

For the union and its members the goal of collective bargaining was a better life, which was possible only through a substantial boost in wages. During the negotiations, 1199 advertisements had quoted Martin Luther King, Jr.: "Many of the poor people work in our hospitals. They work fulltime jobs at parttime wages. People are always talking about menial labor. But no labor is menial unless you're not getting adequate wages."[86] Ten years earlier, low wages had forced many hospital workers to supplement their salaries with public assistance. With the "breakthrough" in 1968, however, they finally earned a weekly salary that was more than the minimum established for a family of four on welfare in New York City.[87] One Mt. Sinai worker quoted in *1199 News* after the 1966 settlement observed,

"We had a time getting this pact but we can enjoy it with dignity. And after the next contract we'll hold our heads higher still."[88] As a result of the 1968 contract, hospital workers were, for the first time, earning a living wage.

Even before the ink dried on the 1968 contract, union leaders announced that they expected to use the settlement as a "springboard" from which to organize hospital workers in other major eastern cities.[89] Although worried about the resources needed to undertake a national campaign, no one on 1199's executive committee questioned that the union had the "moral right to organize hospital workers." Theirs was the only union that understood that organizing was not simply a trade union task but involved "human rights, civil rights." Local 1199, committing itself to a campaign with a "union power, soul power" theme, formed a national organizing committee and asked Coretta Scott King to be its honorary chair.[90] While 1199's leaders may have been overconfident in 1968, their self-assurance is understandable in light of the rapid and extensive growth of the union throughout the mid-sixties.

CHAPTER 7

Stayed on Freedom: A Labor Crusade behind the Magnolia Curtain

By the late sixties, enthusiasts within Local 1199 believed that the effective joining of "union power" and "soul power" would generate a new wave of labor organizing among the nation's poor and unskilled inner-city population. But there was cause for skepticism. In several respects New York City was particularly well suited to the union's style of crusadelike organizing. Historically, public officials there had been more liberal, the black community better organized, and the state more willing to subsidize social services than elsewhere in the country. Hospital managements, while not receptive to trade unionism, had at least moderated their antagonism in the face of a political culture long accustomed to collective bargaining. But could lessons learned in New York be applied elsewhere? The first national test of the "union power, soul power" strategy came in 1969 when a group of hospital workers in Charleston, South Carolina, sought 1199's protection. The formula that had begun to pay handsome rewards in the cosmopolitan North suddenly came up against a new antagonist, one equipped with a time-tested record of resistance to social change, and the ensuing confrontation left an ambivalent legacy for all concerned.

Accentuating the general pattern of the twentieth-century South, union organization in South Carolina not only failed to establish a mass base in the 1930s but experienced a precipitous decline following the ill-fated postwar Operation Dixie (1946–53). While the state's urban centers contained a relatively high percentage of manufacturing workers for the region, this did not redound to the benefit of labor organization. Indeed, during the 1960s South Carolina vied with North Carolina for the lowest rate of unionization in the nation. Aside from sizeable concentrations of communications workers, the metal trades council of the navy yard, and papermakers (all overwhelmingly white), the state's 50,000 union members were scattered among black longshoremen, white building trades workers, and small pockets of machinists and clothing, textile, and furniture workers. Antiunionism was one issue that united up-country industrialists, like the J. P. Stevens Company of the Greenville-Spartanburg area, with their traditional low-country political competitors. A statewide business and political consensus reinforced a state right-to-work statute and an official ban on public employee strikes with an extra, unofficial antiunion vigilance.[1]

Viewed against this background, the strike by Charleston hospital workers from March 20 to June 27, 1969, was one of the South's most disruptive and bitter labor confrontations since the 1930s. Less than forty-eight hours after the dismissal of twelve black union activists, 450 workers at the Medical College Hospital (MCH) of the University of South Carolina heeded a strike call by the newly formed Local 1199B. Eight days later, 60 workers walked out at the smaller Charleston County Hospital. All of the strikers were black; and all but twelve of them were women.

While already an important element of the union's message, the civil rights theme assumed an unprecedented centrality in the Charleston strike. Led by Ralph Abernathy, the Southern Christian Leadership Conference (SCLC), joined with 1199 in the fight for hospital workers' rights. As a result, a city that had generally escaped the heat of the civil rights movement belatedly experienced a kind of municipal civil war. After four months, nearly 1,000 arrests, and millions of dollars in lost property and boycotted sales, the strikers returned to work with some material gains but without official union recognition. Each side claimed victory, but the fact is that within a year of the strike the union movement among Charleston hospital workers had withered. "Charleston" proved to be more a codeword for what 1199 had become and where it planned to go than for what it had actually accomplished for hospital workers in the southern city.

The labor troubles in Charleston were tied to postwar economic and social changes in the area. Defense spending, commercial trade, and tourist dollars showed signs of awakening Greater Charleston from a long history of economic stagnation. But the fruits of recovery trickled down unevenly to the city's residents. Black citizens who made up nearly half the city's population and a third of the larger metropolitan area experienced little of the "revival of Charleston" after 1950. In 1970, 40 percent of black families lived below the poverty level and another 10 percent subsisted just above it.[2] Black women hospital workers formed the core of a new, low-wage service sector in the Charleston area, drawn from the expanding reserves of domestic and farm-related labor markets. These nonprofessionals worked for a sub-minimum wage of $1.30 an hour.

For many young women who had grown up on the truck farms of all-black island communities, hospital employment meant a stark encounter with the residual effects of a racial caste system. In 1968–69, the MCH had no black physicians on its staff and no black students in its School of Nursing, yet all low-paid nurse's aides and service workers were black. The same separation sharply distinguished the care offered to private (mainly white) versus public, nonpaying (overwhelmingly black) patients. Bed and waiting room assignments, as well as restroom use, were divided along racial lines, and certain practices seemed openly to reflect assumptions of black racial inferiority—for example, black husbands were not allowed in delivery rooms, yet whites were.[3]

If tradition still weighed heavily in some matters during the 1960s, the MCH was in other respects undergoing changes common to hospitals nationwide. Local modernization efforts took place under the watchful eye of college president and hospital director Dr. William McCord. The son of American missionaries in South Africa, he had served for twenty years as professor and chairman of the department of chemistry before being chosen in 1964 to lead the college through a period of ambitious expansion and upgrading. McCord embarked on a $15 million building plan, securing a $12 million grant in 1969 from the Department of Health, Education, and Welfare ($8 million for physical expansion and $4 millon for research). Among other administrative changes, he recruited John E. Wise, a business graduate from the University of Kentucky, as vice president for administration and finance. Wise found the tall, broad-chested, cigar-smoking director "authoritarian" in style but "responsive to new and modern ideas." Wise quickly developed a centralized personnel policy to uproot old departmental fiefdoms and moved to replace the subsidized employee cafeteria with higher take-home pay.[4]

Racial subordination in the Charleston hospitals reflected the area's long-standing social and political patterns. Although 32 percent of South Carolina was black, not one black state legislator had been elected since Reconstruction; indeed, it was one of only two states in which fewer than six of ten eligible blacks were registered to vote. Charleston, where older black males still doffed their caps to white passersby, seemed to fall well within Robert Coles's characterization of the entire state in 1968: "No southern state can match South Carolina's ability to resist the claims of Black people without becoming the object of national scorn." Not until 1967, for example, did the city have its first black council member, Saint Julian Devine.[5]

Committing few of the rhetorical or physical excesses of a Bull Connor in dealing with rising black expectations, the city's modern-day patriarchs had managed to preserve a relative social calm during the civil rights era. White political leaders (coordinated via the so-called "Broad Street Gang" of bankers and lawyers) tended to smother dissent with conciliatory gestures and an appeal for civic unity to a black elite of ministers, contractor-realtors, and funeral home directors. Reminiscing in 1985, one local black leader recalled earlier race relations as lacking overt hostility so long as blacks acquiesced in limiting themselves to "a certain place."[6]

During the 1950s the city had largely been spared social unrest as civil rights activists like Esau Jenkins and Septima Clark concentrated on education and voting rights in outlying island communities. Agitation within the city following the Supreme Court's 1954 *Brown* v. *Board of Education* decision was dampened by publication of the names of all integration petitioners in the *News and Courier*, a conservative daily. Charleston's only real trouble came during a 1963 summer desegregation campaign aimed at local merchants. The Charleston Movement led lunch-counter sit-ins, mass demonstrations, and night marches, including one major confrontation with police, and finally achieved a nondiscriminatory agreement with the city's major stores. Tensions had evidently eased in the city the next fall when, without major incident, a successful NAACP suit and court order enabled eleven black children to attend previously all-white public and parochial schools. Peaceful, if still largely symbolic, integration came to the entire city school system the next year.[7]

Advances in Charleston race relations were typically the result of slow but persistent efforts by middle-class white liberals working with a few black activists. Alice Cabaniss, who ran a small bookstore in the parish hall of the Episcopal Cathedral, helped to integrate South Carolina's League of Women Voters and also worked for racial progress through the United Church Women. "It all began," she recalled, "when I discovered, to my chagrin, at the age of fifteen, that my uncle by marriage was the Grand Dragon of the S.C. Ku Klux Klan." Her husband, Joseph, chaired the Charleston Council on Human Relations, "for which we had endured some social ostracism but not too much because both of us were guaranteed Southerners." In addition, he had been instrumental in recruiting the racial moderate John Conroy for Charleston police chief in 1964. Conroy and Cabaniss were old Marine buddies, and Conroy had married one of Mrs. Cabaniss's good friends from high school in North Charleston.[8]

The local style of handling racial tensions led to formation of a community relations committee to deal with the "long hot summers" of 1967 and 1968. The thirty-member committee, comprised of an equal number of blacks and whites, included banker Hugh Lane, liberal attorney Gedney Howe, a navy admiral, an air force general, and several older black businessmen as well as a representative of the younger militants in the person of William Saunders.

In committee sessions and before groups like the all-white Rotary Club and the Red Carpet Club—the "inner sanctum" of the Charleston Chamber of Commerce—black Episcopal minister Henry Grant tried to "interpret the community one to another." Yet in the end such efforts could not contain the frustrations welling up among younger working-class blacks. The years of talk and symbolic legal and legislative victories only underscored the substantive lack of change in the lives of poorer blacks and their daily domination by a variety of white authorities, as typified by conditions at MCH. In Charleston, "black power" ultimately combined with the long-standing grievances of black workers to break through a decade of containment of social unrest.

Charleston's first hospital organizers reflected the combined impact of the new "black power" impulse and an earlier political education garnered during the Korean War. A small circle of young racial militants formed around their elder statesman, thirty-seven-year-old William Saunders, who in 1968 was working as a foreman in a local mattress factory. Saunders had come out of the army in 1954 determined to change things for his people. His involvement in the Johns Island voter registration and integration fights convinced him that the nonviolent philosophy of the civil rights movement was a "sham," and he openly quarreled with older leaders. The situation became so tense, according to Saunders, that by 1966 the local black leaders interceded to have the governor nullify his election to the Office of Economic Opportunity's War on Poverty commission. Speaking through the *Low Country Newsletter,* Saunders soon voiced the rising anger within the black community. Malcolm X and the Student Non-Violent Coordinating Committee (SNCC) both influenced his sense of political urgency and prompted his hosting a 1967 Christmas visit to the Charleston area by SNCC leader Stokely Carmichael. In Saunders's view, SNCC was "the total black organization." He claimed, "every time that the power-that-be got rid of the person that they thought was bad, the next one was worse. They were structured in a way to dissolve, and that's the way we did the organization that we had." Together with Black Muslim Otis Robinson, Saunders fashioned a tight-knit, semisecret, self-defense group complete with code names and weapons. To avoid detection, he and his friends held meetings next to a loud jukebox. The level of daily fear reached its height in 1968 after the killings of three students at South Carolina State College in Orangeburg and the assassination of Martin Luther King, Jr. Saunders recalled, "We all planned to die."

Community organizing on Johns Island had put Saunders in touch with several hospital workers at the MCH, including twenty-six-year-old Mary Moultrie, the daughter of a Charleston navy yard worker. Moultrie had recently returned from working in a New York City municipal hospital as a licensed practical nurse, but the MCH would not recognize her New York credentials and slotted her at the less-responsible and lower-paid position of nurse's aide. While she had already done some work with civil rights crusader Guy Carawan of Tennessee's Highlander Center and with Charleston activist Esau Jenkins, Saunders was waiting for Moultrie and others at the hospital to recognize that "they had a problem" at their own workplace. It did not take long.[9] In February 1968 a white nursing supervisor gave orders to a group of five black nursing assistants without first sharing with them the contents of patient charts. Incensed at this violation of customary respect, the women walked off the job and were summarily fired. Moultrie and her co-workers alerted Saunders. Thanks in part to the intervention of black community leaders, who monitored compliance with Title VII (the employment provision of the 1964 Civil Rights Act), the workers won reinstatement.

This episode triggered a continuous, although still informal, organizing network among Charleston's hospital workers. Saunders, for one, initially "saw very little difference between George Meany and Richard Nixon. . . . I felt labor management was ripping off the workers." Instead, he and his friends at first envisioned a kind of broad-based association of community-owned businesses aimed at getting blacks into the "economic mainstream." Moultrie, who had only distant contact with a New York City Teamsters Union local at Goldwater Memorial, agreed: "At that time we didn't have a union in mind to affiliate with or anything like that. We just knew we had to do something to protect our jobs. We didn't want to be picked off one by one. So we sorta kept it a secret. We'd go around and whisper to people and we'd catch people during break time and on lunch hour. We kept it out of the ears of the whites. After we started having the weekly meetings we used to get community people to come in and meet with us."

Isaiah Bennett, president of Local 15A, RWDSU, became a key community contact on the way to formal organization. With roots in the militant 1945–46 strike of the Food, Tobacco, Agriculture, and Allied Workers—in which an old spiritual became the movement song, "We Shall Overcome"—the local still (in 1968) represented a few hundred workers at the American Tobacco Company in Charleston. Bennett provided the hospital workers a meeting hall and lobbied community leaders to establish a representation and grievance system for the MCH employees. As a black trade unionist, he occupied a precarious position within Charleston society: he could talk easily to local officials, yet he exercised little real influence. (So powerless were the black trade unionists, in fact, that the tobacco workers had never made a municipal political endorsement. "Hell," explained Bennett, "we always saw we got a fox and wolf running and both of them, they just alike.") Bennett initially recruited attorney Gedney Howe to represent the hospital workers; he also began meeting with Mayor J. Palmer Gaillard, Jr., and recalled, "I know that many times I go to him . . . you know, he's always sympathetic. But then when the pressure's really got down on him, he turns just like anybody else. He never would make a statement on our behalf on radio or TV or anything."

Bennett and others seeking a compromise settlement got nowhere. From the beginning the hospital turned a deaf ear to all talk of negotiation, referring interested parties to the interpretation of state statutes by Attorney General Daniel MacLeod, who said that without specific enabling legislation public employees had no right to collective bargaining and, further, that no state agency could authorize such discussions. Meanwhile, hospital administrators took countermeasures, hiring Greenville textile counsel and anti-union specialist Knox Haynesworth on an expensive consultancy basis. The MCH offered to discuss work-related problems only with small groups of workers selected at random; administrators promised to use "every legal means at our disposal — make no mistake about that," to resist the union. An early response to the organizing effort came in the form of a crude cartoon picturing a fat white union boss enjoying wine, cigars, and shapely female company at the workers' expense. With nearly 300 workers taking part in organizational meetings and community groups requesting mediation, the one, obviously insulting concession offered by the hospital to the black workers was an extra holiday on Robert E. Lee's birthday.[10]

Informal conciliation efforts were stymied, and union representation beckoned as the only alternative for the aggrieved workers. New York City's Local 1199 received an appeal from Charleston. The workers' organizing leaders had first asked Bennett to enroll them in his tobacco workers' union, but Arthur Osman, international vice president of the RWDSU, suggested instead that they contact the international's appropriate hospital affiliate. In late September or early October 1968, FTA member Lillie Mae Doster helped Moultrie draft a letter to Local 1199, which only months before had established a national organizing committee headed by Elliott Godoff, with Henry Nicholas as his top assistant. Staff members had been dispatched to Detroit, Philadelphia, Baltimore, and the New Jersey and Connecticut areas; now, the call from Charleston served to put the union's principles, as well as its national aspirations, to a sudden test.[11]

David White, Brooklyn area director of the hospital union, was sent to scout out the situation in Charleston. He had lived in the New Jersey–New York area since he was nine years old and was particularly uncomfortable about his mission to Charleston:

I'd heard all these war stories about the South and how it was and I had to take a plane into Columbia, South Carolina, and then had to get a connecting flight to Charleston. When I got there [Columbia] I found that that so-called connecting flight had been canceled a month before. So I said, oh my God, now I got to talk to some of these crackers. There was a Hertz desk in the airport and I told the guy I wanted a car to go to Charleston and I was shocked. He was as courteous to me as he could possibly be and then after we signed the papers for the car, he said to take Route 26 to Charleston. And I said, where do I find 26? So the guy got in the car and drove all the way out of the airport and showed me where Route 26 was and the way to Charleston. I expected to see like in the movies the southern roads with the trees and the vines hanging from the trees [but] then I came to this big modern six- to eight-lane highway and within an hour or so I was in Charleston. . . . what impressed me was the tremendous spirit of the people there—the determination, you know, to do something to improve themselves; so that I had to come back and report that I thought there was a possibility of organizing the people and I had to give a favorable report.

After other New York leaders confirmed White's impressions, Henry Nicholas was dispatched to Charleston in October 1968 to officially charter Local 1199B, the hospital union's first out-of-state local.[12] Over 400 MCH workers elected Mary Moultrie president; Isaiah Bennett stepped into a senior advisory position and William Saunders remained an important, unofficial presence among the workers. From New York, union officials offered advice to the Charleston workers but left early direction of the campaign in local hands.

Formal union backing quickly raised the stakes of the workers' demands for recognition, and "high noon" rallies demonstrated the solidity of support for 1199B among the black service staff. Delegations besieged local and state lawmakers, vehemently protesting the refusal of McCord to meet with the employees. Gov. Robert McNair and key legislators were courteous, but no progress was made. In response to what Moultrie characterized to Columbia legislators in February 1969 as an "explosive" situation, state officials could only point to plans for a long-term reclassification of all state jobs that might be completed within a year. "We're tired of asking and begging," Moultrie told the legislators. "Now we are demanding. We want union recognition." "We warn you, time is running out," added Bennett.[13]

South Carolina leaders did little to conciliate the hospital workers, despite a self-proclaimed "progressive" attitude. While the legislature had the power, in principle, to envelop the hospitals within the state labor law (as had happened in New York and a few other states), no public representative emerged to champion such an option. Without yielding substantive ground, the state tried to resolve the matter by fostering better communication between workers and administrators. On March 4 McCord unveiled a plan of monthly grievance meetings: one person, selected at random, from each department would represent fellow worker at the meetings. The situation was far beyond such cosmetics.

The rising demand for dignity and respect, which had first set off the worker protests at MCH, led directly to the strike on March 20. Two days earlier, at the urging of Mayor Gaillard, McCord agreed to meet with a workers' delegation that included union members. However, when Moultrie and six other workers arrived for the scheduled morning conference, they found that the director had invited eight "loyalists" to balance out the meeting. Within minutes nearly a hundred protesting prounion workers were packed into the hospital auditorium. An administrative assistant canceled the session and ordered the workers to return to their jobs. They did so, but only after huddling outside the hospital with Bennett. The next day twelve union activists, including Moultrie, were formally dismissed for dereliction of duty. One day later, March 20, after consultations between 1199B leaders and Nicholas, who had flown in from Detroit, the strike began. While the strikers made only two demands—union recognition and the rehiring of the twelve fired workers—McCord was economical in his reply: he was "not about to turn a 25 million dollar complex over to a bunch of people who don't have a grammar school education."[14]

The picketers who gathered in front of the MCH entrance faced the reality that, unlike any other strike in which the union had so far been engaged, they were taking on not only a rigid hospital administration but a city and state power structure that was overtly hostile to the union effort. A temporary state injunction banning all picketing was immediately issued, though on the advice of State Circuit Court Judge Clarence Singletary the order was amended to limit the number of picketers to ten, spaced 20 yards apart over a distance of 200 yards. "According to the injunction," scoffed Moultrie at a football stadium rally, "we could put only five people on this field from goal post to goal post. I think even the governor, as slow as he is, could get through a picket line like that." When union attorneys appealed Singletary's ruling to the federal courts, Judge Charles E. Simons, former law partner of Senator Strom Thurmond, declined jurisdiction in the matter.[15]

Throughout the strike the union was unable to play off competing power centers among state and local political authorities as it had in New York. Governor McNair was shielded from direct contact with the Charleston strike and set the state's overall pattern of response: "No agency of the state can be involved with a union." Perceived from the beginning as a provocation and threat to law and order, the strike led to the deployment of city police, then agents from the State Law Enforcement Division, and finally National Guard troops in full riot gear. Street demonstrations produced hundreds of arrests. The Dunkirk-like stand of state authority before the protesting workers was reflected in the governor's statement before the South Carolina Bar Association on May 10: "In a sense this is not a simple test of will or a test of strength. This is a test of our whole governmental system as we have known it in South Carolina."

Years later Judge Singletary reflected on the larger context of official reactions to the hospital dispute:

In the 1960s South Carolina was among the leaders in the South in attracting industry and our technical education program . . . and our development board had become a model for other southern states. Our governor and officials were going all over the world seeking industries and one of the inducements, obviously, was productive labor without the labor union problems that other areas of the country were experiencing. So I think that that was one of the reasons that we didn't want to give up. When I say "we," I think of the political leadership.

Unintentionally, Singletary's "we" probably also included whomever was involved in the attempted fire bombing of Henry Nicholas's motel room on March 27, an incident that forced the union to scatter its representatives in unannounced lodgings under armed guard for the strike's duration.[16]

In retrospect, one might well wonder why a small outside organization like 1199 would throw itself into the situation in Charleston. "I really don't think they knew what they were getting into," Isaiah Bennett would later suggest. Moe Foner indirectly confirmed that initial support for the Charleston strike was less a careful calculation than a moral and political imperative: "What do you do? You could either walk away from it, in which case you lose, or else you could scruff along. We couldn't walk away." However, the union's Charleston strategy was less naive than it appeared. While responding spontaneously to local developments and without a specific, prior battle plan, 1199 had nevertheless been preparing itself for some time for an escalating civil rights-based struggle. Its ties to the campaigns of Martin Luther King, Jr., and the SCLC, formalized symbolically in Coretta Scott King's honorary chairmanship in 1968 of the union's national organizing committee, now took on critical significance.[17]

The decision to support a strike in Charleston depended directly on the union's confidence in its working relationship with the civil rights organization whose roots lay in the Deep South. As Foner himself allowed, the union faced two decisions in Charleston: "The first key decision is to have a strike; the second decision is that this strike cannot be won in the strike alone, that this has to become a national issue. But before you make it a national issue, the other thing is that this strike can only be won if it's made a labor-civil rights issue. . . . The only way to do that is to convince SCLC to come in." On a personal level the bonds of trust between the civil rights group and the labor organization were secured by attorney and long-time activist Stanley Levison, a close friend of Foner and a former Communist still shadowed by the FBI who had served for years as a trusted adviser to King and to SCLC lieutenant Andrew Young. With Levison as go-between, the two organizations developed a coordinated strategy for the Charleston strike: the union would remain in charge of the workers' own activities and coordinate national support for the strikers, while the SCLC would direct a community-based campaign of civil disruption.

The Charleston strike, coming a year after King's assassination during the Memphis sanitation workers' strike, offered the SCLC the chance to renew its purpose and strength. Ralph Abernathy's efforts in 1968 to pick up the mantle of King's Poor People's Campaign were seriously hampered by the mud, indiscipline, and generally unfocused strategy of the Resurrection City encampment in Washington, D.C. Organizationally, the SCLC was in disrepair, internally feuding over Abernathy's leadership. Through Levison's mediation, however, the SCLC decided to make Charleston its priority battleground.[18] Andrew Young remembered:

> We began to see that having made significant social and political progress we'd have to take on the economic question of full employment, of the right to organize, of increasing the minimum wage, of guaranteed annual income. . . . Hospital workers came into the category of the working poor. . . . And so the Poor People's Campaign was also the first opportunity we had in a national way to try to reach out, to form a coalition between blacks, Hispanics, native Americans, and American Indians, the trade union movement, and, say, white workers in Appalachia and in the inner cities. It was really an attempt to overcome racial and cultural differences and move into a common economic effort to get our nation to eradicate poverty.

In certain key respects the SCLC approached Charleston as it had Montgomery, Selma, and other towns where it had faced a closed fist of opposition. "When you could not get the government to negotiate, either the state government or the local government," Young recalled, "you had to mobilize the entire community, the churches and the high school students in a total program of noncooperation or economic withdrawal."

According to the organization's own pragmatic ground rules, the SCLC's entry into the strike had to be ratified by the local black community, and such assent was by no means assured. Although people like Esau Jenkins and Septima Clark had ties through Highlander to the national civil rights movement, the SCLC had never developed a base in Charleston. The older black community leadership was, in fact, reluctant to involve itself in confrontation tactics, while younger Charleston militants also looked suspiciously at outsiders, particularly those still philosophically wedded to nonviolence.

David White, sent from Brooklyn to serve as community relations liaison, remembered a tense meeting of the citizens' support group sometime during the first two weeks of the strike. Carl Farris was at the meeting representing the SCLC, as were ministers, businessmen, and other black leaders who were trying desperately to negotiate a peaceful resolution to the dispute, several "expressing a very strong feeling against bringing [the SCLC] in" on the grounds that "wherever they go, they cause turmoil." White recalled: "SCLC did not want to come in unless invited by the local citizens . . . after all, they needed their cooperation. The meeting went on and on and quite a few people went home and then we—Farris and me—we were really working to delay . . . until we could get a yes vote. I didn't even know the guy but I realized immediately what he was doing and he realized what I was doing and together we got an invitation to ask the SCLC to come in and aid the strikers."

The 1199/SCLC collaboration came at a certain cost. More moderate local figures, shy of the projected strategy, separated themselves or were shoved aside from the ensuing events. The white-dominated South Carolina AFL-CIO, for example, effectively turned its back on a struggle waged on civil rights grounds, and even the mostly black Charleston branch of the National Maritime Union distanced itself from the strikers because of "racial overtones which we cannot accept." The escalation of social stakes also alienated early striker organizer Isaiah Bennett, who openly opposed the strategic arrangement with the SCLC. Bennett's continuing search for compromise through contacts with local authorities was monitored suspiciously by 1199 officials.[19]

The SCLC more than made up for local defections by its full-blown commitment to the Charleston campaign. Abernathy visited the strike-torn city for the first time on March 31 and committed the civil rights organization to an energetic display of "people's power" in the streets of Charleston. Thereafter, Andrew Young and staff members Farris, James Orange, and Hosea Williams made Charleston their second home, while Abernathy spent considerable time there as a lightning rod for mass mobilization, and Coretta Scott King arrived at carefully selected moments for greatest impact. Once involved, the SCLC drew on a network of several hundred contacts gained through what Young called the "underground work" of the state's citizenship or voter education schools.[20] Numerous signs of the spirit of community self-help engendered in other civil rights battles were evident. Surrounding black communities on James, Johns, and Edisto islands—indeed, all the way up to Columbia—expressed support through church donations. Within the city itself strikers received free haircuts, free meals at restaurants, and in some cases even had home and car payments made for them.

Under the SCLC's direction the campaign's physical focus immediately shifted from the union hall to black churches. White recalled:

> When they came in the first thing they did was to contact all the ministers in the city and start lining up churches so we could have mass meetings in the evening. They also contacted ministers where they would loan us their churches during

the day to organize the young people, kids all the way down to around eight and ten years . . . and they organized activities for these kids, classes where we had lectures on black history. I found out in Charleston, without the church you can't do a fucking thing. And everything we did was through the church, whether you believed in religion or not.

The truth is that the black religious community in Charleston was initially divided on the strike. But when the Interdenominational Ministerial Alliance, a citywide association for the enhancement of black welfare, refused to commit itself, younger black clergy like Z. L. Grady of the Morris Brown AME Church, J. T. Enright of the Plymouth Congregational Church, and Mack Sharpe of the Fourth Baptist Church formed the Committee of Concerned Clergy which openly sided with the strikers.[21]

The SCLC's strike strategy was ambitious. "It is only when you create the same kind of crisis in the life of the community as you have in the lives of workers," explained Young, "that the community will give in." By activating the local black community and simultaneously evoking the sympathies of an outside, liberal white audience, the SCLC hoped to force through shame, fear, or property loss a retraction of the official line of intransigence toward the strikers. As at Birmingham in 1963, the SCLC expected that disruptive but determinedly nonviolent crowd actions would provoke authorities into a massive counterresponse that would end up paralyzing normal operation of the city. In the end, the "economic power structure" (or self-interested business leaders) would bring the "political power structure" (state and local officials) "in line" (toward a compromise settlement).[22]

The civil rights aspect of the Charleston campaign was evident on April 21 when Abernathy promised to "sock it to Charleston." Demonstrators staged frequent mass marches through the city's central business corridors, past National Guard troops outfitted with rifles, bayonets, and riot visors. Invading the historic Battery district, strike supporters paused symbolically at the Old Slave Mart Museum. Learning from the bitter disarray that had marked the Memphis SCLC campaign, Charleston organizers effectively incorporated black youths into the official protests, even outfitting a young Ranger brigade in colorful costume. One Saturday morning demonstration featured scores of teenagers dribbling basketballs down King Street, the city's main commercial thoroughfare. An affluent local matron recalled the unpleasant disruptions: "It was horrible, absolutely horrible. . . . Why even today when I go downtown I can still see all those colored people marching around and singing and praying and everything." By the end of April the situation had grown tense: ten marches in six days, repeated confrontations with the police, and nearly 500 arrests, including Abernathy and visiting 1199 president Leon Davis. Abernathy called for a boycott of classes by schoolchildren, declaring; "Jesus said that a little child shall lead them [and] you are a traitor if you go to school." School officials said that attendance immediately dropped by a third.[23]

The nonviolent confrontations engineered by the SCLC required great self-control by both leaders and followers. As happened in other civil rights struggles of the late sixties, tensions developed between movement organizers and a fringe of supporters who wanted to increase the stakes of the conflict. William Saunders's "black power" group, for example, maintained an uneasy but close connection to the official union campaign. As an informal confidant of Moultrie, Saunders dispatched an armed "community militia" to strike meetings and demonstrations; he also functioned as both an ally and a critical observer of the national strike leadership. By his own account he sought to push beyond "the respected black leaders" in this citywide test of wills: "I wanted [to involve] everybody in the community that had been in jail before, that had a record, . . . the people that lived on the street." In Saunders's view the uncontrollable, unpredictable nature of individual acts — no matter how reckless — served as a powerful lever against white authority. "If you feel you have a contribution to offer," he said, "go ahead and offer your contribution [and] the less people that knows about what you're doing, the safer everythings are." Directly or indirectly, such thinking seemed to sanction the firebombings, gunshots, and breaking of windows that occasionally punctuated the Charleston events. Strike organizers took a dim view of these "spontaneous" measures, condemning such acts as the work of "thugs," "hoodlums," and even "agents provocateurs." In fact, at one point they reportedly paid Saunders and his group in an effort to maintain basic compliance with strike discipline.

On May 1, amid both planned confrontation and random violence, Governor McNair imposed martial law and a dusk-to-dawn curfew in Charleston. Alice Cabaniss later captured the feel of the disturbed city in a poem called "Strike and Curfew":

> Through the narrow, empty streets,
> trees and bees and birdcall line
> the concrete unexpectedly
> since fear in black sat down
> along the curb to mutter insurrection.
>
> Bivouacked in the suburbs,
> mothers mend what they might
> yesterday have thrown away,
> await the lifting of the curfew,
> to replenish larders, resume laughter.
>
> Merchants lounge in doorways
> cursing ease, grouping angrily,

> hawk-like where their mice have fled
> to cooler caves, patrolling windows,
> counting guardsmen going by.
>
> That friendly seethe, familiar faces,
> melts to vacuum. Denmark Vesey smiles
> with pleasure from another century;
> black shadows on the empty streets
> undo the handshakes of my friends.[24]

Martial law temporarily halted daily demonstrations, but it also attracted nationwide publicity to the strikers' cause. Reproducing in macrocosm the local alliance in Charleston, national civil rights and labor organizations rushed encouragement and tangible expressions of support to the strikers. Led by Abernathy, Davis, Coretta Scott King, and Walter Reuther, president of the United Auto Workers, a Mother's Day march and rally drew 10,000 participants. "You thought we'd just die out after a day or two of marching," Mary Moultrie taunted the governor. "You thought we'd say 'Sorry boss' and put those handkerchiefs back on our heads. Sorry about that governor, but we just had to disappoint you." On May 24 the SCLC called for an economic boycott of King Street businesses and for "shop-ins," whereby

Charleston strike leader Mary Moultrie walks arm-in-arm with United Auto Workers president Walter Reuther and Ralph Abernathy, president of the Southern Christian Leadership Conference, during the May 11, 1969, Mother's Day March.

demonstrators clogged grocery aisles and cash register lanes, blocking all transactions.[25]

While Moultrie and Abernathy talked of confrontation, Mrs. King underscored the moral claim of the unionizing effort. On April 29 she blessed the women leaders among the Charleston strikers, comparing them to Harriet Tubman, Sojourner Truth, Rosa Parks, and Fannie Lou Hamer. She assured them that "if my husband were alive today he would be right here with you tonight." A week later before a labor banquet honoring A. Philip Randolph, Mrs. King told of being greeted at the Charleston airport by a reporter just back from covering the war in Southeast Asia.

> He came up to me and said, "Mrs. King, welcome to Charleston, South Vietnam." The plain truth is that the city of Charleston is an armed camp. More than 1,000 national guardsmen wearing gas masks and flashing bayonets encircle the black community. Armored tanks rumble through the streets. Helmeted state troopers surround Charleston's churches and hospitals. And hundreds of decent men and women, young and old, black and white, have suffered jailings and mass arrests. Why? Simply because a courageous group of terribly exploited hospital workers have dared to stand up and say to the people who run the city of Charleston and the state of South Carolina that they are sick and tired of being sick and tired.[26]

Risking arrest and family hardship day after day, the Charleston hospital workers proved themselves one of the most dedicated groups of union men and women ever encountered in an American labor dispute. Their letters, many written from jail cells during the waning days of the strike, attest to the personal meanings of the struggle. The union was "like an oak tree in a petrified forest," wrote Mrs. D. P. Heyward, "standing with you through trials and tribulations and surrounding you with strength and love." She saw the strike as a matter of getting "all the little people together [to] decide now or forget forever the hope of becoming a real American citizen." Lattie Mae Glover, an aide at the MCH, wrote from jail, "I've seen sometimes in 1199B meetings and on the picket-line Satan comes our way. But it appear to me that whenever Satan comes 1199B has a prepared way to deal with him."[27]

Claire G. Brown, an obstetrics technician at MCH, had five children, some of whom accompanied her to jail. "It was one of the most exciting, hardest, and important periods of my life," she reflected.

> The walking, walking, and more walking. The hours and efforts spent trying to get programs together for mass meetings. The sacrifice to my husband and children. Many times my husband performed many of the duties that were mine as a wife and mother, and at times became quite upset, but beared with me. . . . There were days I wanted to cry, I was so depressed, because it seemed that in spite of all the hard work and sweat, we weren't accomplishing

anything, . . . but 1199 didn't lie to us, they laid it on the line and let us know just how hard it was going to be. . . ." [28]

Vera Smalls, a fourth-generation Charlestonian and the twenty-two-year-old mother of two young daughters, was one of the twelve nurse's aides whose discharge precipitated the strike. Her husband, a Lockheed assembly-line worker, had just returned to work after a layoff of several weeks. Three months into the strike she told a *New York Post* reporter, "I hear from my parents about times being hard, but I never experienced it before." Her living room furnishings (except for a picture of Martin Luther King, Jr., and a Lockheed calendar) were in danger of being repossessed, she had fallen behind on her rent, and she was only barely able to buy milk for her children. The SCLC had given her "the courage to go on," she said. "I need my job so we can live decently. But I won't go back until they realize black people are entitled to have a union too." [29]

The search for public dignity through the union campaign also drew on a private, religiously sanctioned identity. Donna and Virgie Lee Whack, County Hospital ward clerks, and a younger sister still in school together accumulated nearly two months of jail time during the strike. Virgie Lee Whack believed that "South Carolina is a sick society and maybe a strike like ours was God's way of making his people realize that. . . . In Church, the one thing I did learn was that salvation didn't come on a silver platter. There would be suffering and sacrifice like what Jesus spoke of and if [you] wanted victory you had to work for it and hold out to the perfect end." [30]

Many of the strikers sensed a dramatic role reversal as a result of their actions: with outside help the long-suffering acted-upon had become the actors. Donna Whack recalled that "a hidden slogan in my mind" was "if Mr. Charlie can have union representation, Annie Lou can have hers too." "I really enjoyed the hit and run demonstration," wrote Alma Harden, 1199B cochairperson at County Hospital, "especially blocking traffic on the historic Cooper River Bridge [and] finding out where the Governor was having luncheon, which I think was very funny. Charleston S.C. will never be the same. The historic sights will not be historic any more. The sacrificing Black people in Charleston has been historic." For Rosabelle Deas the strike "let the White men know that slavery is gone forever." Practical nurse Annie G. Fobbs penned this prayer: "O Lord God to whom vengeance belongeth, show thyself, Lift up thyself, Thou Judge of the earth, how long shall the wicked triumph?" [31]

In the 1199/SCLC way of thinking, however, it was the wrath of public opinion that might finally deliver the Charleston strikers from their sufferings, and to that end union leaders sought to combine press coverage, financial support, and political intervention at the national level, as it had in New York. If the city and state reactions looked bad to a national audience, the argument ran, then aid to the strikers would pour in from the outside until local authorities were forced into a settlement.

On the surface this strategy spelled success and signaled a new spirit in the American labor movement. Running for weeks as national news, the Charleston strikers drew support both from expected and unexpected sources. New York's 1199 members were the first to help, contributing some $52,000 in emergency funds. Brooklyn nurse's aide Annie Scott, for example, sent $50 to the Charleston struggle "because I remember ours." The national AFL-CIO and the fledgling UAW-Teamsters Alliance for Labor Action (ALA) competed as benefactors. Walter Reuther came forward with a $10,000 contribution to 1199 (along with $500 per week to the SCLC), prompting William Kirchner, the personal representative of George Meany, to show up in Charleston with a check for $25,000 — which the ALA ultimately matched.[32] Moe Foner observed to Andrew Young, "If the labor movement would only split two more ways, we'll make a profit here." A wide variety of groups and individuals responded to full-page newspaper appeals by contributing $13,000, which included the proceeds from a carnival at the New York City Brearly School for Girls, a cake sale from the eighth-grade honors English class at I.S. 70, and a declaration of support from the Psi Upsilon fraternity at the University of Rochester. In all some $185,000 was raised.[33]

Politically, the strike became a liberal cause célèbre. Twenty-five congressmen, led by New York's Edward Koch, urged President Richard Nixon in late April 1969 to appoint a special representative to mediate the Charleston dispute. The congressional initiative, politely rebuffed by the White House, likened the actions of the "power structure" in Charleston to "the kind of treatment that those who make up the great unions of the country were faced with in 1935." Two weeks later seventeen senators, led by Jacob Javits of New York and Walter F. Mondale of Minnesota, appealed for federal mediation in a situation that had become "a test of the principle of non-violence at a time when many in America are losing faith in that principle as a strategy for social change."[34] On May 11, in a show of northern liberal support, Koch attended the Mother's Day demonstration in Charleston, along with John Conyers and Charles Diggs of Michigan and William F. Ryan and Allard K. Lowenstein of New York. To a remarkable degree the hospital workers' campaign had revived a spirit of interracial cooperation at a time of otherwise intense polarization and breakdown of the traditional liberal (and especially Jewish liberal)-black coalition.

Among other impressions of the march, Koch seized on the young Rangers security guards, outfitted in red Stetsons, white bush boots, and red and black kerchiefs: "How different they seemed from the Black Panthers, who, had they been present, would have worn their black berets, leather jackets and dark glasses. My hostility toward the inflammatory Panthers made me feel an empathy, a rapport with these Rangers who clearly were capable of defending the march without scaring the marchers." As he listened to the speeches and the special presentation to civil rights heroine Rosa Parks, Koch wondered, "What has happened since the March on Washington? Why is there warmth and brotherhood here in Charleston and coldness and apartheid in New York City?" Earlier in the day he had been touched by a lunch with Reverend Abernathy and his ten-year-old son, Ralph Abernathy III. Responding to a question about what he wanted to be when he grew up, the youngster answered, "either a minister, an attorney or a freedom fighter." Koch wrote on his return to New York that he hoped the boy would not have to choose between his life goals and that, "sophomoric as it may [sound,] I intend to be a Congressman and a freedom fighter."[35]

Unfortunately, neither the endurance of the strikers nor the array of outsiders who came to their support swayed the Charleston hospital administrators or the state's political officials. Six weeks into the conflict the two sides seemed utterly deadlocked. The union's time-tested formula of confrontation followed by settlement had, in fact, hit some serious strategic snags, the most important being the ineffectiveness of the work stoppage itself. From the beginning, the Charleston strike probably created more trauma for the city than actual dislocation for the hospitals. Service at both the medical college and county hospitals was never severely curtailed because the MCH reportedly reduced its patient load from 450 to 300 beds, while County Hospital cut back by half. Also, 54 new workers had been hired at County Hospital by the end of the first month of the strike, and the medical college made do with 250 new employees and a volunteer labor force. Strikers Naomi White and Gloria Frazier remembered with bitterness the black men who drove their wives to work, right through the picket lines, some of them visibly armed. While the union forces were surely correct in claiming some disruption of normal services, the fact is that when Abernathy was treated in late May for an ulcer reactivated by a hunger strike, he went to County Hospital.[36]

Politically, the strike organizers discovered just how far removed they were from their traditional friends. Governor McNair, originally presumed to be open to compromise, simply would not budge on the issue of union recognition. Instead, he tried to avoid it by offering new material benefits to hospital workers. An early June news leak hinted that an ongoing review of all state employee relations would recommend that the state minimum wage for public workers be raised from $1.30 per hour to the federal minimum of $1.60. In addition the review panel promised to take a serious look at job classifications, holding out the hope of rational salary readjustment and work descriptions. State legislators registered their opinion of the strike in no uncertain terms, responding to the SCLC-organized school boycott with a bill that made it unlawful "to encourage or entice a child to stay out of school." First offenders could be fined up to $1,000 and given a prison term of up to two years.[37]

Resistance to union demands at the state level had a counterpart in the corporate consensus among Charleston community leaders. Early in the conflict Judge Singletary had set the mark for successful containment of the civil disturbance by restraining overzealous prosecution of the strikers. A graduate of the College of Charleston, the judge had taken his law degree at the University of Michigan and saw himself as an enlightened moderate on race and labor matters. To his dismay, however, hospital officials (who wanted a total ban on picketing) initially seemed to have "no idea" of the possible violent repercussions of the strike. Singletary had them meet with the mayor's legal counsel, Morris Rosen, Chief of Police John F. Conroy, and State Law Enforcement Division (SLED, a state investigative unit established in 1947) representative Leon Gasque "to make certain that the community understood the potential."

Relying on the city's experience with the 1963 sit-ins, Singletary and law enforcement officials coupled firmness with discretion in limiting violence and property damage. Several times, for example, the judge overlooked or delayed contempt citations; on principle he kept his rulings to a bare minimum. Chief Conroy, an articulate ex-marine from Niagara Falls, New York, complemented the judicial rulings with a cool, patient approach to the demonstrators. He refused to arrest picketers violating an injunction during Coretta Scott King's Mother's Day visit, explaining simply, "We don't want a holocaust." On other occasions SCLC veterans like Abernathy, expectantly equipped with Bible, toothbrush, tube of Crest, and ready-for-jail denims, and James Orange, with fifty-three arrests and ten jail sentences to his credit, were confounded by Conroy's exceptional patience.[38] In fact, white officials of the city and state were so temperate and civilized in their response that the expected crisis atmosphere in the local community was slow to materialize. Charleston's black citizenry, in particular, never fully rallied to the strikers' cause. Moultrie's castigation of the local black elite as "Dr. Thomases and Miss and Mrs. Ann" or Young's characterization of them as people with "black skins and white minds" reflected the strike leaders' own frustrations.[39]

One other aspect of police response to the strike—this one more ambivalent and inconspicuous than the public law enforcement of Chief Conroy—deserves mention: SLED director J. P. "Pete" Strom's subtle help in defusing the union coalition by undermining the mutual trust among its constituent parts. For example, Strom fortified community relations leader Rev. Henry

Grant's mistrust of the union and SCLC "outsiders" and encouraged him to play an independent role in settling the strike. Grant recalled Strom telling him, "You know, you don't have to be with [the union]. They don't have the troops. We have the troops."

Even a militant like William Saunders might have been swayed by SLED diplomacy. Saunders remembered times when he expressly resisted entreaties from the governor's office and SLED agents to announce the imminent resolution of strike issues, "when in fact it wasn't going to happen." But he also remembered a meeting with Strom at Dorchester Motor Lodge during a period of tense negotiation and increased street activity:

> When I got to the parking lot where I was supposed to meet him, I went to the trunk of my car. All the SLED agents got out of their cars, and I just stayed in the trunk and messed around for about five minutes and I just knew they didn't know what to do and I finally took my bag out and went over to the chief's car. They didn't know whether to shoot me or what to do then. And then, the chief told me, "You know, Bill, one of the reasons that I'm here is that I feel . . . we got proof that there's a group of people here in Charleston [who want to kill] you, and we want to protect you.

According to Saunders, the group reportedly out to get him were "white [craft] union people, who were anti some of the stuff that I was doing here." He believed that Strom was sincere in wanting to protect him but was surprised when, after complaining about petty police harassment—being stopped constantly and ticketed for "bad tires, . . . for lights," and so on—Strom said, "Here, I got a number I'll give you that anytime that you're having problems, the cops stop you, you call this number and then we'll handle it." In the end, said Saunders, "we got to be pretty good friends."[40]

As the forces of resistance gathered against the strike, the union was effectively painted by white Charlestonians as an unwanted intrusion. The county council (which oversaw County Hospital) officially protested "the unwarranted strike and unrest foisted on its citizens by a small group of individuals, many of whom are unrelated to this area, interested only in their own self-seeking ends." Some conservative Charlestonians went further: a paid public announcement signed by prominent businessmen and five clergymen linked the union to a campaign of worldwide Communist insurgency, which "in places like Algeria, China, and Cuba" has sought to divide the people "along racial lines, religious differences, or employer-employee relationships, as in the Medical College case."[41]

For many Charlestonians the assault on their city cut deeper than issues of trade unionism or civil rights. The message of deliverance and freedom carried by the SCLC in its oft-repeated refrain of "We Are Somebody" implicitly castigated the old ways of a city whose very historic-mindedness was both its pride and its chief economic selling point. In a paid "Letter to

Ralph Abernathy," Rev. Leon J. Hubalz, pastor of Blessed Sacrament Church, told readers of the May 7 issue of the *Charleston News and Courier:*

> Remember what you said when you came to Charleston?—about not wanting to see any more historic sites? When you said that I do not think you knew what it could mean to some of our Negro friends. . . . You have heard of the famous Gardens. Do you think any real connoisseur can walk through one of these gardens without appreciating the know-how and tender care of the Black man that makes it all possible? Have you ever seen the look of pride on the Black man's face as he watches these tourists admire these gardens? . . . What of the colored Mammy? Could all your speeches and marches ever replace the glow of pride on her face as she watches, day after day, as her little charge grows into a man of importance in the world?

The hospital workers' struggle was thus projected over a wide set of issues and symbols. It stood on one side for a rebellion against years of white domination and black subservience; on the other side it summoned up an almost chauvinistic civic loyalty, an instinctual defense of a way of life. In such a polarized setting, few white-dominated institutions dared break ranks with the antistrike forces. Indeed, those who called for conciliation risked real recrimination. White Methodist bishop Paul Hardin, Jr., for instance, forbade support by Methodist ministers for the strike; when three black ministers broke ranks, they were quickly transferred to lesser positions.

The Roman Catholic church was an exception. Since the church hierarchy's opposition to the New York hospital campaign in 1959, both the spirit of Pope John XXIII and a developing engagement with the civil rights movement had affected church responses in important ways. Ernest Unterkoefler, bishop of the Charleston archdiocese, continued the quiet but firm support he had lent to civil rights issues since his arrival in the city in 1965 (including marching at the head of the Poor People's Campaign caravan as it entered Charleston in 1968). He publicly blamed the strike on "constant refusals [of hospital officers] to communicate with the representatives of the non-professional workers in their organizational choice." The Charleston pastorate took an even more active role than the bishop. Rev. William Joyce of the all-black St. Patrick's parish was elected secretary of the prostrike Concerned Clergy Committee, which comprised approximately 30 of 265 ministers in Charleston who supported the workers' right to collective bargaining and union recognition. St. Zavier's, a small Catholic hospital, joined the black-owned McLennan-Banks proprietary hospital as the only institutions in the city prepared, if requested, to negotiate with the union. Joyce, Rev. Leo Croghan, a diocesan priest, and Rev. Thomas Duffy, director of Catholic Charities and a prison chaplain, were all arrested during nonviolent demonstrations on behalf of the strikers.[42] On May 15, in a critical commentary rarely heard in Charleston, the weekly *Catholic Banner* castigated city officials and the news media for "pulling a Magnolia Curtain down over their head and eyes," seeing only "what serves their emotional needs." "We have a curfew, militia and policemen making a great show of force, and all kinds of balderdash, to protect us from a few strikers, most of them very mild women indeed. One sometimes wonders whether South Carolina thinks it is a State of the Union or a banana republic."

Catholic support for the strike hardly went unnoticed by white Charlestonians. Popular local columnist F. B. Gilbreth, Jr., using his regular pen name Ashley Cooper, called the church's effective encouragement of illegal demonstrations "absolutely intolerable, unless anarchy is to be adopted as a way of life." Duffy found out that strike support meant a fall from public respectability, as invitations to the local Kiwanis Club and myriad other social organizations and functions were withheld. Moreover, the strike produced severe friction between the church and its wealthier white patrons, benefactors like real estate developer and Port Authority chairman Joseph Riley, who, according to Duffy, "washed their hands" of the church hierarchy. As a result, in 1969 — for the first time — the local United Fund deleted Catholic Charities from its list of community service grant recipients.[43]

During the first two weeks of May, 1199 leaders reluctantly (and privately) reached the conclusion that, as Moe Foner puts it, "we just did not have the cards." Relying as they were on daily transfusions of outside aid to maintain their operation, the union forces faced not only the depletion of their resources in Charleston but growing strains on their services to 1199 members in New York. A grim reassessment of the situation brought up the difficult question of how, after focusing so much energy and attention on Charleston, could the union disentangle itself without suffering a humiliating national defeat. Publicly, the first hint of a change in the union's position came on May 15 when Elliott Godoff said that 1199 might compromise its demand for direct recognition in favor of some independent intermediary voice for the hospital workers — a tactical move that directly evoked the union's acquiescence in the face-saving 1959 PAC agreement. While this initiative, in and of itself, produced no sudden shift in the state's hardline position, 1199's flexibility soon combined with the appearance of an unexpected outside force to raise the odds for a compromise solution.[44]

Escalating intervention by the federal government, first evident in a report from the civil rights division of the Department of Health, Education, and Welfare, Atlanta Field Office, transformed the situation in Charleston. Sometime during the latter half of May, through contacts with HEW under secretary (and former CORE leader) James Farmer and former under secretary Ruby Martin, union leaders learned that the Medical College Hospital was being audited under the terms of federal regulations governing millions of dollars in grants going to the medical complex. After informal contacts between 1199 officials and Atlanta Field Office director Hugh S. Brimm, the HEW noncompliance report of June 4, in addition to citing thirty-seven civil rights violations by the MCH administration, formally recommended the rehiring of the twelve union workers whose dismissal had touched off the strike.[45] As might be expected, the financial pressure implied by the HEW findings immediately triggered new moves toward a settlement.

Although the word "negotiation" was not publicly used, Andrew Young decided to make a direct effort to reach the MCH's William McCord. To everyone's surprise McCord took the phone call himself and quickly arranged a meeting. Young recalled: "Frankly we just listened to [McCord] for about two hours, telling us all that he tried to do for these workers and . . . how we were wrecking his hospital and so on. I didn't try to answer him or argue with him. I said, 'But Dr. McCord, what we're interested in is finding a way to go on from here, together.'" Unofficially, McCord agreed to dispatch the hospital's vice president for development, William Huff, for further exploratory talks with Young. (Huff had come to Charleston from New York, where he had worked in an 1199-organized hospital.) What ensued, Young remembered, was a kind of triangulated set of exchanges between the parties: "We began to just explore a kind of agreement. In the meantime we were calling this information to New York and they were calling this back down to the governor's office. And the governor then was calling McCord and the officials in Charleston. So we never really sat down in the same room with the governor or his people."

While the private contacts between Young and hospital administrators produced the outlines of a substantive compromise, another set of meetings took place, the goal being to hammer out an official public agreement. Preferring not to meet publicly with union or SCLC officials, hospital board members (acting for the governor's office) scheduled sessions with strike leaders and designated community representatives, including Reverend Grant and William Saunders. A June 5 meeting at the Santee-Cooper hydroelectric plant in Monck's Corner, some thirty-five miles north of Charleston, witnessed a significant softening in the board's position.[46] As Saunders remembered, the initial physical encounter of the women strikers with the hospital directors was tense and awkward, but "then the trustee board went and got chairs for the ladies to sit down . . . and the attitude began to change." Within days the basic pieces appeared in place to end the Charleston strike. On June 9, 1969, after cutting the city's curfew hours in half, the governor publicly accepted the state's responsibility to comply with federal guidelines. McCord then announced the hospitals' willingness to take back the strikers and to rehire the twelve fired workers. State and hospital officials, anxious to end the unrest in Charleston but politically constrained from appearing to appease the strikers, could now blame Washington for forcing concessions.

As in New York City ten years before, the longer-term issue of union recognition was purposefully left unresolved by the negotiators. However, without any formal reference to recognition or collective bargaining, the hospitals did agree to a new grievance procedure allowing workers to bring one representative to grievance sessions. Hopes were high in the union camp as the informal signing date of June 12 neared for a real agreement.

Then, only hours before the planned meetings, McCord reneged on his promise to rehire the twelve workers, claiming hospital staff opposition to the move. McCord's action, in fact, reflected a shifting of larger political forces. On the morning of the projected settlement-signing date, Congressman L. Mendel Rivers and Senator Strom Thurmond reportedly prevailed upon HEW secretary Robert Finch to postpone his threatened fund cutoff to MCH "pending a personal investigation" after he returned from a planned vacation in the Bahamas. This federal about-face was evidence of a larger conflict within the Nixon administration over civil rights enforcement. Liberal pressure for compromise and settlement of the dispute arose from a committed group of second-level administrative staff in HEW. Politically, however, Nixon's 1968 "southern strategy" had looked to a different constituency and was susceptible to different pressures. In this case the demands of state party leaders and political advisors crucial to Nixon's narrow national electoral victory could not be ignored. State Republican chairman Ray Harris had already placed Governor McNair and his fellow Democrats on notice for any waffling on the hospital issue. Now national Republicans were told to toe the line.[47]

Collapse of the projected settlement set off two more weeks of rising tension, including night marches, fire-bombings, and threats to tie up area telephones lines as well as transportation and major business arteries. Leaders of the International Longshoremen Association dropped hints that their union might close the port of Charleston, while 1199 sympathizers talked of union agitation spreading to the South Carolina textile industry. Pickets appeared overnight at the New York City headquarters of the J. P. Stevens, Deering-Milliken, and Manhattan Shirt companies, and Ralph Abernathy even raised the spectre of a national boycott of specified South Carolina manufactured goods.[48] For their part, strike leaders genuinely feared a breakdown of their whole operation in Charleston. Uncharacteristically, SCLC aide Hosea Williams gave vent to uncontrolled emotions at a June 20 rally at Memorial Baptist Church: "White folks are crazy. White America is insane. We have played around with Charleston long enough. We're going to march in Charleston tonight or we're going to die." Clashes with police and hundreds of arrests over the next few days were reported,

On June 21, 1969, a night march organized by the SCLC on behalf of the Charleston strikers brought a confrontation with the National Guard. Hosea Williams of the SCLC was among those arrested.

along with sporadic gunfire and dozens of suspicious fires. Andrew Young warned of a "violent fringe" within the movement: "They are short of money, it is hot, most have family responsibilities, and they see no relief in sight."[49]

Union leaders had all but exhausted their tactical supplies. Among his calculated leaks to the press and government officials, Moe Foner remembered the ultimate threat to bring Coretta Scott King and her family to Charleston to be arrested; rumor even had it that Joan Kennedy might accompany her. Playing out a final lead on a tip from *New York Post* writer James Wechsler, Foner called presidential counselor Daniel Patrick Moynihan and said, "Look, I'm not going to be responsible, but I think you have to know, the night marches are going to continue, and this town is going to burn." Moynihan promised to see what he could do.

For a second time the strike's deliverance issued from Washington. This time the White House transferred authority over the Charleston crisis from the vacationing Finch to labor secretary George Shultz. Armed with the renewed threat of a fund cutoff, and with Mayor Gaillard's acquiescence, Shultz sent federal mediator William Pierce to Charleston on June 24. On Friday, June 27, after a call to William McCord from White house aide and former state Republican chairman Harry Dent, invoking the national interest, the hospital director agreed to rehire the twelve fired workers along with strikers. At the same time Young paid a surprise visit to white nurses at the MCH and convinced them to drop their opposition to the return of the strikers. McCord initialed an agreement late that afternoon, then both sides proceeded to the Frances Marion Motel to announce the settlement. McCord's official statement was terse: "The strike is settled."[50]

Union officials knew that the strike drama was not over yet. As in 1959, they sought to extract a victory or at least a vital "foot in the door" from the strike's apparently stalemated ending. By selectively leaking details of the settlement and putting the best possible interpretation on the official language, 1199 once again finessed a public relations coup. The *New York Times*, for example, noted on June 28 that the settlement, which included wage increases, "appeared to meet the major demands of the hospital workers." Although no mention was made of union recognition or collective bargaining, the union pointed to the grievance procedure and the possibility of a voluntary dues checkoff via the employee credit union (a device that had been used to settle the Memphis sanitation workers' strike in 1968) as indirect evidence of union influence. The strike-ending terms prompted jubilant community celebration at the Zion-Olivet United Presbyterian Church, and to many observers Local 1199B appeared to have broken through the "Magnolia Curtain." Reverend Grant, for one, proclaimed the Charleston settlement "more than a compromise" — "It was a victory."[51]

Years later, black Charlestonians looked back on the tangible, positive changes achieved for the community through the hospital workers' strike. "It was like a revolution," remembered Grant. Black voter registration "shot up like mad," neighborhoods in Charleston County were substantially integrated, and in general "people were forced to take notice of the entire black community." In 1970 Herbert U. Fielding, a Charleston funeral home director, joined the first black delegation to the state legislature since Reconstruction; vocal strike supporter Rev. Robert Woods followed a few years later. Black representation on the city council went from one to six delegates in the ten years following the strike. William Saunders, who chartered a community service and organizing program called COBRA and later ran unsucessfully for political office, asserted in 1979 that the strike had made whites "respect blacks for having organized. They're a little scared now and will negotiate before they reach that same level of polarization."

Whatever its indirect "community" benefits, talk of "victory" proved premature for hospital workers' Local 1199B. At the time of settlement, many of the second-level 1199 and SCLC staff left the city still convinced that the foundation for a successful union local had indeed been laid. But during the months following the strike the MCH administration not only refused to authorize checkoff through the credit union but undermined the union's authority in the grievance system by limiting the number of times that the same person could serve as a grievant's representative. In addition, local union leaders faced an erosion of both outside support and internal goodwill. When County Hospital followed the MCH settlement with nearly identical strike-ending terms on July 19, outside aid to Charleston workers all but dried up. The money was gone, the issue had lost its national dramatic appeal, and, perhaps most important, the New York union and the SCLC had other priorities. The Charleston hospital workers had no office of their own, and organizers from New York visited only intermittently. Lone SCLC staffer James Orange was soon involved in new community campaigns, including a citywide organizing drive by black sanitation workers.

Under these circumstances the local leadership around Mary Moultrie proved unable to sustain difficult grassroots organizing. A national symbol of the Charleston cause who had addressed an AFL-CIO convention and even posed with Hubert Humphrey and Golda Meir during the strike, Moultrie was unprepared for the tasks that greeted her. When the real terms of day-to-day life in the hospitals reasserted themselves, long-simmering mistrust and jealousies among the Charleston activists burst forth in a destructive fury. Jubilation quickly turned to bitter recrimination and accusation against Moultrie, against Saunders, and against the union itself. Henry Nicholas echoed a common view among national union leaders in his assessment that Moultrie's problems revealed a basic tension between the union's metropolitan base and its provincial outpost. "Like the U.S. in foreign countries, we tried to prop up a leader," he explained. "But when you move the prop, the leader falls [and it's] dangerous." Acknowledging that Moultrie was a magnetic "Barbara Jordan type of speaker," Nicholas believed that the union may have pushed her beyond her limits: "She could do all things that had to be done at the moment, but the understanding of what she was really doing was missing."[52]

The poststrike disillusionment among the hospital workers took a heavy personal toll on Mary Moultrie. Her effectiveness as a strike leader had proved personally disorienting, and when she was voted out as chapter president not long after the strike's end, she withdrew from hospital organizing in discouraged confusion. The gap between Moultrie and national union leaders was highlighted in a family trip she took to New York City in 1973. With one of her cousins, an 1199 member in New York, Moultrie paid a visit to the attractive new headquarters of the national hospital workers' union, the Martin Luther King Labor Center. Her cousin led her down one hallway at the end of which she encountered a giant, blown-up photograph of herself marching arm in arm with Walter Reuther. Moultrie left the building without even making her presence known to officials upstairs. In the end she felt "hurt and disappointed with a lot of people" she had been involved with. "If I had it to do again I would. But then I'd be careful," she said.

The strike's failure to produce a solid victory also complicated the future of the southern-based civil rights movement. Tragedy in Memphis, ineptitude in Washington, D.C., chronic financial problems, and divisive internal wrangling raised the stakes for the SCLC's labor- and class-oriented strategy as applied to Charleston. Except for a few headlines, the SCLC could hardly draw strength, let alone a model for further actions, from the Charleston stalemate. In the world of what-might-have-been, Charleston might have served as an effective regenerator of the Poor People's Campaign, an inspiration for the broad labor and civil rights alliance that SCLC founders like Bayard Rustin, Ella Baker, and Stanley Levison had sought for years. Indeed, the possibilities were evident in August 1970 when an interracial group of steelworkers in Georgetown, South Carolina, sixty miles north of Charleston, walked off their jobs after demanding a union contract. Faced with a protracted strike and menacing state police, the strikers called on the SCLC for help. Aided by the showing of the 1199-produced film, *I Am Somebody* (drawn from footage of the Charleston events), visits by Mary Moultrie and other hospital workers, and a series of SCLC street demonstrations, the United Steelworkers' local emerged with a solid four-year contract. The experience convinced attending SCLC organizer Carl Farris that "black and white workers across the nation are ready to move together as brothers and sisters in the struggle."[53]

In the end, however, such dreams were not to be. Friction within the organization and failure to score truly dramatic victories with its economic organizing strategy left the SCLC increasingly demoralized. Charleston itself proved to be one more drain on the sinking civil rights organization's resources. By the end of 1969, Andrew Young was already expressing doubts about the viability of an "exhausted organization" and shortly afterward resigned to pursue a political career. Other resignations followed until in 1973 a once robust staff of 125 had been depleted to 17. The SCLC continued to involve itself in community efforts throughout the South, but its nonviolent and largely defensive campaigns failed to attract national attention and support. Surveying the overall civil rights scene in 1970, the *New York Times* reported "very little direct action . . . anywhere in the South today."[54]

Beyond the bittersweet local and regional effects of the Charleston struggle lay its impact on 1199 nationally. Here the returns for the union proved much more tangible. In the course of the Charleston campaign the hospital union, before a nationwide audience, had proved itself willing and able to take on any foe. Particularly for black urban workers the "union power, soul power" crusade broke down barriers separating labor organizing from the community-based black militancy of the era. If such tactics could exact concessions in the heart of the antiunion South, might they not utterly triumph in the urban-industrial North? In the weeks following the Charleston settlement, 1199 organizers confidently set up shop in a half-dozen cities. *I Am Somebody* became a staple in introducing the organized hospital workers to labor and community groups across the country. The mere threat of "pulling another Charleston" even extracted a union recognition agreement from the prestigious Johns Hopkins Hospital (see chapter 8).

With the Charleston campaign 1199 had strengthened its image as a "civil rights union." To be sure, the principles of interracial solidarity were evident during the early years of the old drugstore local, and they had been basic to the very creation of an organization among hospital service workers. Now, however, the connection between workers' rights and racial progress had reached a new stage and in the following years would prove both an asset and a liability as the hospital workers reached out across the country. At the end of *I Am Somebody,* strike steward Claire Brown declares: "If I didn't learn but one thing it was that if you are ready and willing to fight for yourself, other folks will be ready and willing to fight for you." She was right, of course. But, too often, the outcome of a political fight just as surely depends upon timing and location.[55]

High Expectations and Harsh Realities: Confronting a Changing Health Care System in the 1970s

The *Baltimore Sun*, which followed the drama unfolding in Charleston through the spring of 1969, predicted that the strike would send out "shock waves that would go far beyond South Carolina."[1] What the prognosticators did not realize was that the tremors had already reached Baltimore. Even before the strike in Charleston had ended, Elliott Godoff was contacted by James Griffin, president of the Baltimore chapter of the Congress of Racial Equality (CORE), who had been unsuccessful in his attempt to enroll black workers in that city's small retail shops in the Maryland Freedom Union. By 1969 the MFU was largely understaffed and underfunded, and Griffin turned to 1199 in order to build a more "self-sustaining" union movement.[2] Godoff assigned Bobby Nelson, a former field director for the Southern Christian Leadership Conference (SCLC) in Atlanta, to establish a "beachhead" in Baltimore. In March, dissatisfied with the lack of progress and believing Baltimore to be susceptible to its "union power, soul power" campaign, 1199 replaced Nelson with Fred Punch, who had recently led a successful organizing effort at St. Barnabus Hospital in the Bronx.

Most hospital service workers in Baltimore were black, and Punch, according to one union leader, "brilliantly orchestrated" the campaign so as to take full advantage of the local "black power spirit." Bob Muehlenkamp, the current national organizing director who began his career with 1199 in Baltimore, recalled that the union "never had an organizing committee" there because "things moved so fast." The city had experienced black power riots in the 1960s, and "Fred scared them" into dealing with the union.

The union concentrated its efforts on Johns Hopkins Hospital, which it felt stood as a symbol of Baltimore's elite white power structure. Located in a largely poor, largely black area, Johns Hopkins was the object of neighborhood residents' scorn because, they claimed, it neglected their health care needs. Punch continually hammered at Johns Hopkins, to the point where Dr. Russel A. Nelson, president of the hospital's board of trustees, publicly criticized 1199 for raising the "extraneous, emotional" issue of race.[3] When Nelson insisted that a union victory would push patient costs up by $20 a day, Punch branded the statement "typical of any other profiteer," adding that it "doesn't really weigh the true issues—poverty, dignity and respect."[4] In July 1969 the *Sun* reported that "with the grim reminder of recent events in Charleston, S.C., in the background," administrators at Johns Hopkins and at Lutheran and North Charles General hospitals had agreed to permit state labor board–supervised union certification elections for service and maintenance workers at their institutions.[5]

To underscore the "union power, soul power" theme, organizers sponsored a rally on the eve of the late-August elections at which Coretta Scott King told Baltimore hospital workers that she considered herself to be "a Sister 1199er." On August 31, Johns Hopkins's service and maintenance workers voted overwhelmingly in favor of the union, as exultant 1199 officials declared the victory a "major breakthrough in our organizing crusade to win union and human rights for hospital workers throughout the nation."[6] In less than a year, despite a setback at North Charles General, 1199E represented nearly 6,000 workers and had collective bargaining agreements with six hospitals in Baltimore.[7]

A decade after its Johns Hopkins victory, however, the union had not, according to Muehlenkamp, moved on "to other workers, white and black, beyond the initial movement core." Indeed, the local had "very little internal organization" and had failed to organize "a single guild or professional unit." Punch, while personally charismatic (much like Mary Moultrie in Charleston), had, as union leaders acknowledged, "zero trade union experience." Among the other 1199 organizers in Baltimore, one had come out of the civil rights movement in the South and another had worked in a luggage plant. Committed to expanding its national organizing drive, 1199 had had to "make the most of scarce resources," especially the few trained organizers willing to work outside New York City.[8]

The "union power, soul power" theme had been right for Baltimore, but it proved to be inappropriate for the situation in Pittsburgh. Beginning with its organizing drive in that city, 1199 would learn that to wave the "bloody shirt" of Charleston was not always enough to overcome the long-standing resistance of hospitals to unions. Before Pittsburgh took center stage, however, national organizers focused their attention on the other side of the state, in Philadelphia. John Black, an area director who had just concluded contract negotiations at a hospital in Trenton, New Jersey, was told by a former supervisor at Metropolitan Hospital in Philadelphia that conditions were ripe for an organizing effort. Friends of the supervisor even gave Black a complete list of employees' names. Thinking that Philadelphia was "a liberal town" very much like New York, Black ignored a warning from Leon Davis not to take the national campaign "across state lines" and decided to see if he could get something started there.

Inglis House, a large nursing home, was the site of the union's first victory in Philadelphia, in August 1969. Management there consented to an election because "as in Baltimore . . . it feared a repeat of the bitter, four-month Charleston strike if it resisted."[9] Having broken the ice in Philadelphia, Black targeted eight other hospitals in the city for organizing by Local 1199C. Before that campaign got underway, he received a call from a hospital worker in Pittsburgh, "a communist youth organizer," who claimed to have signed up twenty-six potential union members at St. Margaret's Hospital. Black overcame his initial skepticism and agreed to meet with interested workers. He first encountered Kay and Walter Tillow, both of whom had been active in civil rights and labor causes. Learning that Kay Tillow, whose communist politics he had "spotted right away," was unemployed, Black asked her "to help out this guy at St. Margaret's." Thus, by a curious—but not atypical—blend of chance and political connections an 1199 organizing drive was born. Unfortunately for the union, it would mark a major defeat in the national campaign.

Following the current 1199 strategy, Black told Tillow to concentrate on the city's most prestigious institution, Presbyterian-University Hospital. After things started moving in Pittsburgh, Black asked Elliott Godoff to assign Henry Nicholas to that city while he returned to Philadelphia. Encouraged by the "excitement" among the workers, Nicholas decided to expand the organizing campaign to all of the city's hospitals.

Local 1199 conducted a drive in Pittsburgh that one local hospital official depicted as "a bewildering blend of old-style union organizing and 'the tactics of the SDS and black militants.' "[10] As it had done so often before, the union characterized the struggle in Pittsburgh as a confrontation in which workers who earned "poverty wages" were arrayed against the "captains of industry," a wealthy elite who administered hospitals that, like Presbyterian-University, stood as symbols of the city's "big-money establishment." Denied their "basic human right" (i.e., a union representation election), Nicholas insisted that the hospital workers would strike "to prove that slavery will not be tolerated in Pittsburgh, to prove that workers cannot be sold to the lowest bidder. . . . "[11] Obviously, 1199 expected "union power, soul power" to be a winner in Pittsburgh.

Exhorting the faithful in Pittsburgh to ever-greater sacrifice for the cause,

Nicholas conducted union meetings much like down-home revivals. On a bitterly cold January night he told 250 assembled Presbyterian-University workers, "I am not a preacher, but I've got to give you the message." The union, he intoned, "is a very serous thing, and you've got to be serious about the union. . . . You must be ready to go to jail for the union. . . . For the union is a very serious thing. You've got to be ready to die for the union." To make certain that the workers got the message he added, "If you don't go out and win this fight, then Martin Luther King lies in his grave tonight in vain." "Fiery enthusiasm" notwithstanding, only half the audience reportedly was willing to follow Nicholas on a march after the meeting to Presbyterian-University Hospital, and the next day a prounion demonstration in front of the hospital attracted few workers.[12]

Local organizers continued to sense a "genuine" response from hospital workers in Pittsburgh when there was, in fact, "nothing there." According to Black, Pittsburgh was "never a viable campaign." Late in February 1970, feeling that they had "done it all," union leaders conducted a poll outside three of the targeted hospitals and claimed overwhelming support for a strike. A March 20 deadline was set, but at a rally on the evening before the threatened walkout, Nicholas announced that only workers at Presbyterian-University would strike. Kay Tillow recalls that fewer than one hundred workers responded to Nicholas's call for Presbyterian-University workers to get up and march around the hall in a show of strength. The following day confirmed the union leaders' worst fears: local newspapers reported only about seventy-five to one hundred picketers outside Presbyterian-University, many of whom did not appear to be hospital workers.[13]

Two days into the strike Godoff and Nicholas realized that the union's sole option was "to determine how . . . to get out of it." They agreed that only "by filling up the jails" could they get the third-party involvement they hoped would force a settlement. When 1199 defied a court order limiting the number of picketers, ninety-one persons were arrested; on the same day Kay Tillow led a sit-in at the corporate offices of Pittsburgh Plate Glass, whose director, David Hill, was a trustee of Presbyterian-University Hospital. These confrontations brought the strike before Judge Loran L. Lewis of the Common Pleas Court of Allegheny County. Lewis offered to mediate and both the union and hospital management accepted a truce. In a settlement similar to the one that ended the 1962 strikes in New York City, 1199P called off the strike at Presbyterian-University in exchange for a pledge from hospital officials that they would not oppose passage of a state labor bill guaranteeing hospital employees the right to a representative union election and, further, that they would allow strikers to return to work without reprisals.[14]

On October 21, 1970, Public Employees Law 195, which revised Pennsylvania's labor law to include nonprofit hospitals, went into effect.[15] But the new law had little impact in Pittsburgh. Tillow recalls that she and Nicholas met with workers after the strike and found "tremendous demoralization. . . . there wasn't the feel of victory." For reasons Tillow cannot explain, the union's organizing effort was successful only at the Jewish Home and Hospital, where workers voted 157 to 40 to be represented by 1199P.[16] In contrast to its previous campaigns, however, 1199 was unable to turn the Pittsburgh defeat into a victory.

Why did 1199P fail to gain mass support among Pittsburgh's hospital workers? Simply put, union leaders had misjudged the organizing environment there. According to Black, "Henry and Moe fooled each other. They believed what they wanted to—each escalated the other."[17] Looking back, Tillow observed that the union's experience in New York City had convinced its leaders that first "you unite the black workers" and then you might draw in a few of the white workers." These "central tactics," Moe Foner told the *Wall Street Journal* during the Pittsburgh campaign, logically followed from "the fact" that "hospital workers are predominantly black and poor."[18] In this instance he was only half right: hospital workers in Pittsburgh were indeed poorly paid, but they were not mostly black.

Some instructive comparisons between the racial makeup of each city and its hospital work force can be made for New York, where 1199 began; Pittsburgh, where it failed; and Philadelphia, where the national campaign best approximated the union's earlier success. In 1970 blacks comprised about 20 percent of Pittsburgh's population but accounted for less than 6 percent of the city's work force. In New York, 14.6 percent of the city's working people were black; in Philadelphia, 15.8 percent. Looking specifically at health care service workers (including practical nurses, nurse's aides, orderlies, and attendants), 44 percent of these workers in New York were black; in Philadelphia, 40 percent; and in Pittsburgh, less than 25 percent.[19] Whereas individual hospitals in Pittsburgh may have had a greater proportion of black workers, an organizing strategy directed solely at black service workers was bound to fail.

Following current national strategy, 1199 conducted a civil rights campaign in Pittsburgh that concentrated on public relations—on engaging the local black community—at the expense of organizing workers. The union's tactics, as Foner elaborated them, involved "enlisting the aid of local black leaders, civil rights groups and students, plus a big community relations push and dramatic demonstrations that generate publicity."[20] But once the union failed to rally the hospital workers, management was left free to ignore union demands, which is what happened. The unsuccessful campaign forced union leaders to reconsider their organizing strategy, to realize that, according to Bob Muehlenkamp, "you're not gonna get the public to win it for you, and you're not gonna get the bosses to run scared on that stuff."

The abortive drive in Pittsburgh was not the only setback 1199's national organizing campaign suffered in 1970. Union-backed efforts in Durham, North Carolina (1199D), and Dayton, Ohio (1199H), also proved futile.[21] As in Pittsburgh, the organizing situation in each city was more complex than the 1199 model allowed.[22] Realizing that it could not bully hospital management into holding elections, 1199 thus began to retrench and plan for the long haul. According to Nicholas, its first priority became "building membership." He and Godoff agreed that the union should remain in Pennsylvania "for the purpose of organizing," which meant Nicholas moving on to Philadelphia, where an organizing effort that became a testing ground for 1199's new strategy was already underway. John Black agreed to organize hospitals in the rest of the state.

Nicholas arrived in Philadelphia having calculated that "we had four years to survive, four years before the employers would become sophisticated enough to effectively combat the union." In October 1970, on the heels of passage of Public Employees Law 195, 1199C filed petitions calling for union elections at five of Philadelphia's largest voluntary hospitals—Children's Hospital of Pennsylvania, Episcopal Hospital, Hahnemann Medical College and Hospital, Metropolitan Hospital, and Wills Eye Hospital.[23] Nicholas resolved to avoid making a single hospital a test of strength: "We could not afford to gamble, to sustain one defeat before we had 52 elections under our belt." The union would organize across the city; indeed, it had to become "a visible force quickly" to be successful. As in the early years in New York, especially during the PAC period, 1199 tried to give Philadelphia workers a sense of what could be achieved through collective action even before gaining formal recognition. Relying on rank-and-file staff, 1199C held sit-ins and candlelight marches and created a membership structure: "[We] elected shop delegates, [had] delegates' training, Christmas parties for kids, picnics. We had everything that the union usually had."[24] In all 1199C activities the bottom line was worker involvement.

The managers of Philadelphia's hospitals revealed themselves to be determined opponents of unions, hiring antilabor consultants to help plan their strategy. Officials at Hahnemann Hospital, for instance, brought in Dan Rowe Associates of New York, a consulting firm. Just before a scheduled certification vote in May 1971, Hahnemann workers received a "Vote No" recording and were handed fortune cookies that contained messages such as "Union dues sock it to your pocket" and "Save your money, save your dough, put your X in the block marked NO." Such tactics were not entirely successful, though, because on May 5, 1971, Hahnemann service division workers and licensed practical nurses voted 272 to 210 to be represented by 1199C.[25]

Metropolitan Hospital proved to be the union's most stubborn opponent in Philadelphia. After 1199C filed for a representation election in November 1970, the hospital hired legal counsel to advise it on how to resist the union. Ronald Souser of the local firm of Morgan, Lewis, and Bockius devised a strategy built on stalling, that is, on filing a stream of formal protests and requests for clarification, on generating endless testimony at hearings, and on appealing each prounion ruling in court. One former hearing examiner for the Pennsylvania State Labor Relations Board who had heard the various charges against 1199C filed by Metropolitan observed: "The hospital filed protests on everything — on the language of the ballot, on the way the election was conducted, on the fact that somebody was seen making a peace sign."[26]

After it lost the certification election in November 1971, the hospital continued to stall in negotiating a contract. In August 1972 events surrounding 1199C's drive at Metropolitan turned violent: an altercation in the hospital parking lot led to the fatal shooting by a security guard of Norman Rayford, a union organizer. Rayford's death had a galvanizing effect on public officials. Pennsylvania's governor, Milton Shapp, and Philadelphia's mayor, Frank Rizzo, immediately stepped into the dispute, and negotiations began that led to a settlement.[27] However it had come, the settlement, according to Nicholas, marked a turning point for the union in Philadelphia. Three years after its first victory at Inglis House in August 1969, 1199C represented workers at more than thirty hospitals and nursing homes in the city, occupied a new headquarters, and had 7,000 members, second only to 1199 in New York.[28]

The making of 1199C represented a "shift in posture," in Nicholas's view; specifically, the need to "organize all workers and not just service and maintenance [workers]." He told a reporter in 1972, "You can't have an effect on the whole system unless you represent all the workers. And while the service workers may be black, the clerical and technical and professional workers are going to be white."[29] Elliott Godoff concurred, as Bob Muehlenkamp recalled. Godoff contended that "[you] can't organize white America with the bosses pushing an image of 1199 as a 'militant black union.' " However, while Nicholas and Muehlenkamp conceded that in the early seventies 1199 was moving away from the "union power, soul power" theme, both denied any diminution of the union's militancy, especially in its pursuit of larger social goals. There would be no narrow "dollars per hour feeling" in 1199's campaigns, Muehlenkamp insisted, but instead "a sense of liberation."

Changes in the organizing strategy of the national campaign had an impact on 1199 in New York as well. Nowhere was this more evident than in the

1972–73 drive at Columbia-Presbyterian Medical Center, then the nation's largest voluntary hospital with over 1500 service workers. Initially, Godoff was contacted in April 1972 by a rank-and-file group at Columbia-Presbyterian that for more than a year had been trying without success to gain union recognition.[30] Believing that the time was right for an all-out effort there, Godoff assigned union vice president Eddie Kay, then area director for the Queens–Long Island organizing team, to lead the day-to-day organizing drive.

As an organizer Kay was cut very much from the same cloth as Godoff. Determining that the union had gotten nowhere at Columbia-Presbyterian in the past because it had "tried to change the boss instead of organizing the workers first," Kay created a rank-and-file organizing committee that quickly grew to include 150 workers. Previous organizers, he felt, had been "too defensive," too accepting of the hospital's definition of itself as "impregnable. They thought they were hot shit and they could do no wrong. . . . And we always approached them from that angle." One of the first indications that 1199's drive was succeeding was a massive demonstration in November 1972. Workers crowded into the hallway outside the office of the hospital's personnel director and demanded an early certification election.[31]

Hospital management countered 1199's efforts with a campaign that appealed to the workers' economic self-interest. One of Columbia-Presbyterian's first moves after agreeing to an election was to announce a general wage boost of around $8 a week, which was on top of wages that already were comparable to 1199 standards. Still, as one rank-and-file leader observed, "not once did the hospital ever respond to our organizing efforts by trying to meet the workers' biggest beef—the lack of respect for people as human beings. All they could think of to do was to try to pay workers off with money, or use fear and phony buddy-buddy stuff."[32] After the 878 to 507 vote to join the union was announced in March 1973, one laundry worker compared her euphoria to the way she felt after giving birth to her first child: "Now—no more fear. . . . That's over now."[33] By aggressively responding to workers' feelings of powerlessness and to their demands for respect rather than by just meeting their economic needs, however real, Local 1199 continued to invest union campaigns with the "sense of liberation" that Muehlenkamp and other union leaders called for.

With 1199's victory at Columbia-Presbyterian, its membership in the metropolitan area was more than double what it had been following the 1968 contract. By 1974 the union counted 80,000 members in fourteen states and the District of Columbia. Although at least three-quarters of the membership was from New York, New Jersey, and Connecticut (1199NY), the union also represented 7,000 health care workers in Maryland (1199E), 7,000 in

Philadelphia (1199C), and, even after the defeat in Pittsburgh, 3,000 in western Pennsylvania (1199P).[34] Both to celebrate what had been accomplished and to signal its ongoing commitment to organizing, 1199 hosted a convention in New York in December 1973 at which it founded the National Union of Hospital and Health Care Employees.[35]

Problems Operating in the Public Arena

Local 1199's efforts to establish itself in New York had benefited from the expansion of health services fueled by public spending in the 1960s. By the mid-1970s, however, the union found itself operating in a more competitive and combative environment. As a result, 1199's progress slowed considerably in the late seventies. Whereas between 1968 and 1974 union membership increased by 128 percent, by 1980 there was a gain of only 25 percent, to 100,000 members.[36] Opposition to 1199 took many forms in the 1970s, but of particular significance were the growing competition it received from other unions and the antilabor tactics increasingly employed by hospital management. The campaign against 1199 received an unexpected assist in 1974 when federal labor law was revised to include voluntary hospitals.

Even though the 1947 Taft-Hartley Act had exempted voluntary hospitals, the trend throughout the sixties was to include hospital workers under the protection of federal law. In 1964 they were covered by the Equal Employment Opportunity Act; two years later they came under the Fair Labor Standards Act; and in 1970 the Employment Security Amendments called on states to provide coverage for them under unemployment insurance laws. In 1972 the U.S. House of Representatives passed a bill, introduced by Frank Thompson, a New Jersey Democrat, that would have extended collective bargaining rights to hospital workers simply by deleting the exemption provided under Taft-Hartley. This proposed legislation died when the Senate Labor Committee failed to act on it.[37]

Working through the American Hospital Association (AHA) and state hospital associations, voluntary hospitals sought to protect their Taft-Hartley exemption. As they had done so often in the past, administrators cited hospitals' special mandate as health care agencies, which "absolutely cannot afford any interruptions in service caused by work stoppages. Healthcare facilities are not like assembly lines."[38] Acknowledging the unique standing of voluntary hospitals, the Congress, even as it lifted the Taft-Hartley exemption in 1974, still limited union activity in the health care field. For example, under the 1974 amendments both parties in a hospital labor-management dispute involving an initial contract were required to give thirty days' notice to the Federal Mediation and Conciliation Service (FCMS), and an affected institution as well as the FCMS had to be given at least ten days' notice by the union before any picketing or a strike could take place. Most important, the new legislation provided for special boards of inquiry to conduct hearings and recommend settlements in all hospital-labor disputes.[39]

The leaders of 1199 expected the various changes in federal labor law to have the same salutary effect on union organizing that extension of coverage under state labor law had had. "Long a goal" of 1199, this legislation, according to Leon Davis and Moe Foner, would open "the door to the organization of hospital workers on a nationwide scale."[40] At first glance an AHA review entitled "One Year under Taft-Hartley" appears to confirm union leaders' expectations. During fiscal year 1975 (ending June 30), 1,659 representation petitions were filed with the National Labor Relations Board, up sharply from the 461 filed during the previous fiscal year. Moreover, unions won 62.5 percent of the 200 elections, a comparatively high win rate.[41]

Along with finding that union activity had intensified in the wake of hospital coverage under Taft-Hartley, the AHA survey also uncovered evidence that should have been of some comfort to the hospitals: when management "campaigned aggressively," hospital employees chose unions in only 35 percent of the elections. But management had "campaigned aggressively" in only 51 percent of the elections. Similarly, only 30 percent of the hospitals had used outside consultants to direct their antiunion campaigns, yet under such conditions the union had lost 67 percent of the elections; when consultants were not used, the union lost only 44 percent of the elections.[42] These results are indicative of how hospital management transformed the changes in Taft-Hartley into, in Henry Nicholas's words, "a yoke around our necks."

Bob Muehlenkamp, looking back at more than ten years under the revised Taft-Hartley Act, expressed contempt for the "horrible, bureaucratic, endless tangle" imposed by the law. The whole legal process, he claimed, has been used "against us." According to Muehlenkamp, a disastrous campaign during 1974–75 at Henry Ford Hospital in Detroit became the model that other hospitals used against 1199. The word was out, he asserted, to "use the loopholes and defeat union organizing drives by delays." The legal barricades erected by hospital management, including contesting the composition of bargaining units, could postpone elections for up to three years.[43] Testifying before a House subcommittee on labor-management relations in 1980, Muehlenkamp noted that hospitals increasingly were relying on antilabor consultants to help them devise a wide range of tactics to defeat union organizing campaigns. The premier "union buster," with over 500 clients throughout the United States, was Modern Management, Inc., which was said to have kept unions out of 93 percent of its client hospitals in which there was an election.[44]

Management journals reported that hospitals had become "more skilled" in resisting unionization efforts,[45] a "skill" that paid off. Whereas in 1968 unions active in organizing hospitals won about 83 percent of representation elections, the record of victories in the aftermath of Taft-Hartley reform fell to 55 percent. Even though it was doing better than other unions in the industry, 1199 was successful only about half the time in 1980.[46]

Competition with other unions for members, which had been of little significance in 1199's early years, became a second factor complicating the union's ability to organize health care workers in the late 1970s. In fact, during the first year under the revised Taft-Hartley Act, the Service Employees International Union (SEIU) displaced 1199 as the most active union in the field.[47] The antiunion effort at Detroit's Henry Ford Hospital certainly was made easier by the participation of the SEIU as well as by the American Federation of State, County, and Municipal Employees (AFSCME) in the certification election.[48] By 1980 more than thirty unions were actively organizing in health care,[49] and nine of these, including 1199, the SEIU, the AFSCME, the Teamsters, and the American Federation of Teachers (AFT), participated in five or more NLRB certification elections in 1980 alone.[50]

The problem of competition became particularly acute when 1199 began to organize among registered nurses in the seventies. Professional nurses, according to one hospital personnel expert, had become "the primary target of union organizing in the health care industry" by 1980.[51] This is not very surprising, since in New York City hospitals, for example, the number of registered nurses increased by 13 percent between 1975 and 1980, while total full-time equivalent personnel dropped by 6.5 percent.[52] In fact, the U.S. Department of Labor predicted in 1980 that throughout the decade two-thirds of all job openings in health care would be for nursing personnel.[53]

A nationwide shortage of RNs and changes in the hospital workplace put increased job pressure on nurses and made them more receptive to unions. While the "high-tech" medicine of the 1970s was making college-educated and highly skilled nurses more valuable members of the hospital staff, RNs were facing significant challenges to their professionalism. Greater efforts by hospitals to contain costs and increase productivity left the primary nurse with "more work, less time to do it in and no ancillary support."[54] Even as their work loads increased, RNs were conscious of their growing importance in the hospital, which derived in part from their mastery of the new technology but also from the liberating impact of the women's movement. RNs felt, one union official believes, "a gut sense of more power."

In response to the changes, in the same year (1977) that 1199 founded the League of Registered Nurses as a fourth division, the AFT opened its rolls to

In 1977 the union's League of Registered Nurses struck Brookdale Medical Center, eventually winning higher wages and other benefits, including tuition reimbursement.

nonteaching professionals, including registered nurses.[55] Under pressure from labor, the American Nurses Association (ANA) began to take on the functions of a trade union. In New York, for example, the state nurses' association (NYSNA) voted in 1977 to drop its long-standing no-strike policy and accept work stoppages as a valid collective bargaining tool.[56]

The League of Registered Nurses, which initially attracted those no longer satisfied with representation by the ANA, was headed by Sondra Clark. In 1976 Clark and other nurses working at Brookdale Medical Center in Brooklyn had approached the NYSNA for support in their move to get hospital officials to reimburse them for tuition costs for continuing education (a benefit received by 1199 members). The association representative gave them little more than a "professional rap," Clark said, one that they "no longer believed." Frustrated, she met with Leon Davis and with 1199's consent formed an organizing committee for RNs at Brookdale. In February 1977, by a vote of 279 to 214, nurses there chose to be represented by the League of Registered Nurses.[57] Six months later, Brookdale's registered nurses conducted a successful two-day strike; the resulting contract provided, in addition to a 5-percent wage increase and other benefits, tuition reimbursement.[58]

Despite the union's continuing efforts to portray state nursing association leaders as "management" or, alternatively, as "impotent" in their attempts to make "significant inroads in nursing practice and education," the league was unable to dislodge the ANA.[59] In New York, in 1978 and again a year later, the Health and Hospital Corporation conducted elections in which the ANA, the AFT, and 1199 vied to represent RNs in the city's hospitals. Although able to win a plurality, 1199 eventually lost both elections in run-offs with the ANA.[60] Nationwide, in 1980, ANA affiliates represented about 108,000 nurses; the AFT, 12,500; and the SEIU, around 12,000; while the 1199 league had about 6,000 members.[61] According to an AHA survey in 1983, three-quarters of the 14.5 percent of registered nurses who worked under collective bargaining agreements continued to be represented by the ANA.[62]

Legal maneuvers by hospital management as well as opposition from rival unions and state nursing associations contributed to 1199's slow progress in organizing RNs. Hospitals used federal labor law to make the union's job much harder, and in a number of lawsuits they successfully challenged the NLRB-applied "community of interest" standard that had justified holding elections among registered nurses from which other professional employees were excluded.[63] In a 1981 suit won by the Presbyterian–St. Luke's Medical Center in Denver, the U.S. Court of Appeals held that the National Labor Relations Board " 'must expressly consider the congressional admonition (to prevent proliferation of bargaining units in the healthcare industry) in making unit determinations.' "[64] This decision, as the lawyers for Presbyterian–St. Luke's pointed out at the time, should increase "the likelihood of successfully resisting union organizing efforts," because hospitals will have the opportunity, in advance of a campaign, to obtain broad bargaining units.[65]

During 1199's early years in organizing hospital workers, union leaders had frequently looked to government and found an ally. Thus, they appropriately viewed revision of New York State's labor law in 1963 as a positive turning point in 1199's fortunes. They were, of course, not as fortunate with the changes in federal labor law in 1974. Similarly, whereas in 1968 in New York the union had benefited from intervention by city and state officials to break a contract deadlock, during the seventies public officials at both the federal and state levels began to respond with growing alarm to the "skyrocketing" costs of health care. Government attempts to control price increases in the industry frequently began with efforts to curtail "inflationary" hospital contracts by reducing the rate of reimbursement to hospitals for the care of insured or covered individuals.

Government aid programs transformed many voluntary hospitals into, in effect, publicly supported institutions. In fact, by the early 1970s more than 90 percent of the income of U.S. hospitals came from third-party payments (Blue Cross plans, Medicare and Medicaid, and private insurance) derived mostly from reimbursement formulas set by government health care agencies. All increases in hospital employee wage rates and fringe benefits, as well as in expenses for personnel administration, were considered part of the legitimate cost of providing patient services that could be passed along to a third-party payer.[66] As a result, in New York City, for example, approximately 50 to 60 percent of all patient revenue came to hospitals under reimbursement formulas that set per diem limits on charges.[67] Not surprisingly, New York was the first state to attempt to contain health care costs through a rate-setting mechanism.

During its 1969–70 session, the New York State legislature, no doubt mindful of upcoming contract negotiations between 1199 and the League of Voluntary Hospitals, placed all cost-control activities within the office of the state commissioner of health.[68] Moving cautiously, the commissioner developed a reimbursement formula that was expected to hold increases in daily hospital charges for the following year to 12 percent rather than the projected 13 to 18 percent. According to Dr. Donald G. Dickson, then deputy commissioner for community health and hospital affairs, the state wanted eventually to reduce increases to 7 percent a year."[69]

Both union leaders and the voluntary hospital league's representatives predicted that implementation of the new reimbursement guidelines would precipitate "a hospital crisis."[70] Once collective bargaining began in the spring of 1970 both sides resorted to brinksmanship tactics, anticipating that as the talks reached an "impasse" state officials would intervene to avoid a strike and avert a "crisis." Shortly before the strike deadline, Governor Rockefeller assigned Vincent D. McDonnell, chairman of the New York State Mediation Board, to take part in the negotiations. After an intense and often acrimonious weekend of bargaining (which was filmed by the local CBS-TV news station), McDonnell was able to announce a settlement. Apparently, the impasse had been broken after he assured both sides that his compromise recommendations had the governor's backing.[71] Hospital officials and leaders of Local 1199 were both well satisfied. The two-year contract included a $130 minimum weekly salary (close to the $139.71 the union had asked for), a 2-percent hospital contribution from the total payroll to the union's benefit fund, a paid holiday for Martin Luther King, Jr.'s, birthday, and four weeks' vacation after eight years' service.[72]

The outcome of the negotiating process in 1970 confirmed Norman Metzger's opinion that collective bargaining between the union and hospitals entailed little more than finding out how much the government was willing to pay.[73] Despite much rhetoric about the need to contain costs, state officials had in the end, agreed to underwrite the new contract. The next round of contract talks, in 1972, at first followed the same pattern. However, then the federal government stepped in and upset the game plan.

Local 1199 opened contract negotiations in April 1972 by publicly announcing its demands, which included a $155 minimum weekly wage or a 15-percent across-the-board increase (whichever was higher), a thirty-five-hour workweek, and four weeks' vacation after one year of service.[74] Voluntary hospital league representatives quickly labeled the union's proposal "unrealistic" and offered instead an "uncompromisable" $6.00-per-week increase over a three-year contract. Near the end of May, Leon Davis accused the league of refusing to bargain and warned that a strike of "catastrophic proportions" loomed.[75] "On schedule," state officials intervened, but mediation board chairman McDonnell failed to resolve the dispute and the state industrial commissioner, Louis L. Levine, appointed a three-member board of arbitration. On June 30 a settlement was proposed that virtually duplicated 1199's original demands.[76]

Under President Nixon's much ballyhooed national campaign to curb inflation, all labor settlements had to be submitted to the federal Pay Board and Price Commission for review. Approval appeared uncertain. As the *New York Times* pointed out, the 7.5-percent wage increase that was agreed to exceeded the 5.5 percent allowed under federal inflation guidelines.[77] Nearly a year later, in March 1973, the pay board finally announced that the settlement would have to be reduced to 5.5 percent.[78] Although the following month the Cost of Living Council, which replaced the pay board, reinstated the original settlement, it did so only for the first year of the contract.[79]

Union leaders, dissatisfied with the delay and hoping to force a quicker determination on the contract's second-year wage provisions, set October 15, and then November 1, as the deadline for a council response, or otherwise 1199 would strike. At 6:00 A.M. on November 5, 1973, in what was called the most extensive strike ever in the health care industry, some 30,000 workers walked out of forty-eight voluntary hospitals in New York City. Federal officials at first declared that they would not be pressured into precipitous action but then agreed to meet the following day to decide on the proposed wage increase.[80] One week later, on November 12, the Cost of Living Council accepted a compromise—a 6-percent increase—proposed by the advisory Health Wage Stabilization Committee. Union members overwhelmingly ratified the compromise to end the strike,[81] though at least one striker publicly voiced the probably widespread feeling that "we gained nothing—a half percent."[82] Other participants in the dispute also offered harsh assessments. To Dr. Gerald D. Rosenthal, director of the Health Wage Stabilization Committee in 1973, union leaders had simply backed themselves into a corner. Having "sold a lot of people that they were getting screwed," 1199's leaders could not let the momentum for higher wages slip. Most other unions went along with federal wage guidelines, Rosenthal claimed, because they understood that the anti-inflation program would only be temporary.[83]

From 1199's point of view, however, to have been the only labor union to go out against "the Nixon Board" reaffirmed its militant traditions and ongoing commitment to social and political change.[84] After the strike, Leon Davis commented that now "the entire city . . . knows that our members are an important force in New York," while Elliott Godoff insisted that "the strike had a profound impact. I don't think we were aware of our strengths."[85] One of 1199's primary tasks, according to a 1971 review of the union, was to help members "learn how to assert their rights, not only on the jobs through the union, but as citizens of their community and their country." If the nation was "going to be changed in the interests of the people it will not be done by a Nixon and it will not be done for us" but only "in cooperation with millions like us." To union leaders the strike in 1973 offered further proof that "1199 is a good way of beginning that fight."[86]

With the demise of the Cost of Living Council, contract negotiations again took on a more predictable character in 1974. As usual, 1199 demanded wage and benefit increases that the hospital league was sure member institutions could not afford "unless reimbursed." When the negotiations inevitably stalled, the state stepped in and, as it had in 1972, empowered a three-member arbitration panel to break the deadlock. On June 30, 1974, the panel announced a settlement that nearly met the union's original demands.[87]

Acknowledging the fairness of the arbitration panel's award, the *Times* nonetheless expressed deep concern over the "high price of illness."[88] A broad consensus had formed by the mid-seventies among policy analysts, politicians, health care planners, and representatives of the insurance industry that health care costs, which had more than tripled in the ten years that followed passage of the federal Medicare and Medicaid programs in 1965, had gotten out of hand. Indeed, Social Security Administration officials estimated that by 1980 health care costs would reach 10.3 percent of the gross national product, up from 5.9 percent in 1965.[89] Voluntary hospitals had become so dependent on public funds that the New York City commissioner of health, Dr. Lowell E. Bellin, could claim without too much exaggeration, "If I were to wake up one morning in a bad mood and decided to cut off city Medicaid funds, most of [the city's hospitals] would have to declare bankruptcy within 48 hours."[90]

The particular concern expressed over the rising cost of health care became entangled in the more general fiscal crisis that engulfed New York City during the summer of 1975. Unable to honor $792 million in maturing securities, the city, according to one study, "all but declared bankruptcy, placing its finances under quasi-receivership, monitored by corporate and bank leaders."[91] To many observers New York City's financial plight was simply a consequence of "the fact" that its public employees were overpaid.[92] The city's creditors, including the federal government, thus gave special attention to ensuring that total levels of budget support to municipal hospitals would be reduced.[93] State officials clearly decided in 1976 to play a much more aggressive role in the collective bargaining process in New York City in the interests of controlling hospital rates. To increase the power of the state to intervene, New York's newly elected governor, Hugh L. Carey, introduced legislation, which passed in March 1976, that enabled the state's commissioner of health to reduce Medicaid reimbursement rates to hospitals experiencing high inflation of per diem costs. Given that previous negotiations between 1199 and the League of Voluntary Hospitals had turned on the state's willingness to offset the cost of a settlement by increasing the reimbursement formula, the implications of this legislation for collective bargaining should have been self-evident.[94]

In 1976 both the union and the league chose to ignore the likelihood that their contract talks would be very different from those of previous years. Despite repeated warnings from public officials that "the state has no money" and that the cost of any settlement would have to be met through hospital economies, league representatives and union leaders remained convinced that they could force the state to guarantee full financing of any agreement. Their faith did not waver, even after a strike began on July 7 against thirty-three voluntary hospitals.[95] According to management there was only one issue—the hospitals' ability or inability to fund a settlement. In an effort to apply pressure on state officials to raise reimbursement rates, the

In the face of new financial constraints imposed by the state, 1199 found itself in 1976 in the unusual position of engaging in "a militant struggle for binding arbitration."

hospitals refused any compromise with the union, even arbitration. "We would be committing an imprudent management decision," league officials stated, "to commit ourselves to something we don't have the money for and have been told we won't get the money for."[96] Leon Davis came to accept the state's assertion that there would be no "new money" and agreed to enter into arbitration as a way to end the strike. As a result, the union found itself in the highly unusual position of engaging in "a militant struggle for binding arbitration."[97] During the second week of the strike Governor Carey, acting through an aide, finally broke the impasse by threatening hospital management with a cutoff of Medicaid payments unless they accepted arbitration.[98]

Officials of 1199 had good reason to be optimistic: in 1972 and 1974 the union had won most of its demands through arbitration. This was not to be the case in 1976, however. One September 15 the arbitrator, Margery F. Gootnick, announced her decision: following a wage freeze during the first six months of the contract, there would be a 4.5-percent wage "bonus" given in the second six months (the latter was not intended to raise the workers' minimum base pay); funding was to come from a 1-percent savings as a result of reduced hospital contributions to the union's training fund. In making the award, Gootnick stated that she was "persuaded that if I were to grant the majority of union demands, substantial layoffs and closing of medical facilities would result."[99] She seems to have accepted arguments made by state officials linking a higher settlement to a possible city bankruptcy, as well as arguments by hospital management that, denied a higher reimbursement rate, their institutions had no money with which to fund a wage increase.[100] In a real break with previous practice, the cost of the 1976 settlement was not going to be passed along to third-party payers.[101]

Contract negotiations in New York in 1976 marked a trend in American health care away from the expansion of coverage to include ever greater numbers of citizens toward a focus on controlling costs. "In a short time," Paul Starr has observed, "American medicine seemed to pass from stubborn shortages to irrepressible excess, without ever having passed through happy sufficiency."[102] In 1976 the hospital workers' union found itself caught in the undertow of what would be a major changeover in the U.S. health care delivery system, but it chose instead to blame what happened on the arbitrator. Jesse Olson recalled that 1199's prior experience with arbitrators had been good, but in 1976 the union was "sucked in by the state, sucked in to Gootnick as arbitrator." Union leaders believed that after assuring them they "would not do badly," the state had turned around and told Gootnick "not to give [them] an increase."[103]

Determined to avoid being caught again in the contract talks scheduled for 1978, the union renounced arbitration and gave notice of its return to brinksmanship tactics. The disappointing award in 1976 convinced many 1199ers that "in the future they should rely on their strength on the picketline rather than arbitrated decisions."[104] During preparation for the next round of contract talks, Davis told union members: "We have been deceived before, and we do not intend to go the same route again. The results this time will correspond to our strength; and our strength will correspond to our unity."[105] Indeed, 1978 saw "a dramatic last-minute negotiating session," with Governor Carey stepping in to promise the funds necessary to finance the settlement.[106] Based on the recommendations of a federal fact-finder, the workers won a 14.5-percent wage increase over two years, an increase the governor said was well within the state's Medicaid budget. *1199 News* characterized the settlement as "catching up with the cost of living."[107]

Despite the impression of "normalcy" in subsequent negotiations, both 1199 and the League of Voluntary Hospitals found themselves entering what one government official has called " 'the shin-kicker era' " in health care financing.[108] As the system had operated prior to the mid-1970s, the hospitals had had little incentive to control costs. They and other health care providers had received a predetermined share of all their "reasonable costs," including labor, from third-party payers. Thus, the higher the established reimbursement rate, the greater the income both for hospitals and their workers. State officials acted in 1976 on the belief that in limiting hospital income they could hold down the rate at which hospital charges were climbing.[109] As in New York, officials in other states, as well as federal officials, now began by various means to make strenuous efforts to regulate and contain the rising costs of health care.[110]

Perhaps not coincidentally, state action on cost containment occurred first in Connecticut, Maryland, New Jersey, and other states in which, like New York, 1199 was strong.[111] By 1976 four states had created their own independent rate-setting commissions. In Connecticut, for example, hospital officials who had requested a 16.9-percent rate hike for fiscal 1977 found themselves battling with the state's Commission on Hospitals and Health Care for a 10.5-percent increase.[112] The Health Service Review Commission of Maryland, in its first six months after being empowered to approve hospital budgets, slashed more than $40 million from the total amount requested. Of particular importance to 1199, in early 1976 the commission developed a formula for determining hospital costs, including labor, for Johns Hopkins Hospital, which subsequently was applied to all of Maryland's hospitals. The 5.3-percent guideline set by the commission thus became the basis for collective bargaining between the hospital and the union later that year.[113]

The financial restraints imposed on hospitals by government created an incentive for the institutions' managers to cut back on staff.[114] For instance, whereas in New York City in 1975 there were 112 community hospitals with 141,277 full-time equivalent personnel, by 1980 the number of hospitals had declined to 82 and those employed to 134,172.[115] An official of the AHA, upon completing a tour of hospitals in 1984, stated that he could not "think of any place where hospitals are not either letting people go or else not replacing them when vacancies occur."[116] It is hardly surprising, then, that in the 1980s Norman Metzger, vice president for labor relations at Mt. Sinai Medical Center in New York, declared that the most critical issue in contract negotiations was "job security."[117]

The effort to make hospitals operate more efficiently led not only to staff reductions but also, as happened in 1976, to more moderate wage increases for workers. According to a nationwide hospital wage survey conducted by the Vanderbilt University Personnel Department, real wages reached a peak in 1972–73 but generally declined over the entire period from 1970 to 1977. The Vanderbilt data also provide evidence that where hospitals were unionized, workers tended to be better off.[118] Although 1199 did manage to negotiate higher increases than the national average, the union also experienced a slowing down in the late seventies. From the first contract at Montefiore Hospital in 1958 to the breakthrough contract with the League of Voluntary Hospitals in 1968, the minimum weekly salary paid to hospital workers rose from $40 to $100, a 150-percent increase. From the 1968 contract through the 1974 contract, the minimum weekly salary increased to $181, or by 81 percent. But between the 1974 and 1980 contracts, the minimum wage paid to hospital workers rose by only 40 percent.[119] The union responded to these changes in the health care system by focusing on the impact on collective bargaining. In the seventies, for instance, 1199 placed the provision of adequate Medicaid reimbursement funds and a full budgetary disclosure by hospitals on its legislative agenda in New York.[120] In 1977 the union challenged, in an unsuccessful lawsuit, the validity of New York State's freeze on Medicaid reimbursement to nursing homes.[121] The following year 1199 sponsored a conference on "Health Planning: Tool or Weapon?"[122]

While insisting that hospital workers not become "the victims" of government cost-containment reforms, the leadership of 1199 defined the union's role in the organization of the health care industry in ways that did not go much beyond traditional trade unionism, "pure and simple."[123] Although they remained outspoken critics of the cutbacks in health care, the leaders of 1199 have not spearheaded the formation of a progressive coalition to oppose those cutbacks. In a 1976 interview Moe Foner responded to questions about union policy on the structure of health care by observing, "We articulate positions on the hospitals and on health care, but we don't want to insert ourselves in how hospitals should be run." Organizing workers has been "the key for us," he added, and in a sense has been "our contribution to health care, to restructuring health care."[124] Leon Davis cited as the union's "basic and primary responsibility" the amassing of sufficient power "in order to deal with wages, fringe benefits, job security, grievance machinery and dignity on the job."[125] Such "power" would come from organizing, from reaching out and building "one union for all health care workers"—the national union slogan in the next decade.

In the seventies, 1199 had responded to changes in the health care industry by concentrating its energies on organizing workers. The competition from other unions as well as the intensified and increasingly sophisticated opposition from hospital management made that job much harder, especially in a period of contraction for health care services. As Norman Metzger noted, 1199 faced "an altogether different industry, one that is laying off, that is competitive, that is sensitive to the costs of having a union on the premises and that is willing to legally fight harder."[126] Observing these changes, Leon Davis became convinced that the solution for 1199 was to join forces with the SEIU.

The SEIU and 1199 first cooperated during the effort to revise federal labor law in 1974, and sometime after that, Jesse Olson recalled, Davis and Elliott Godoff approached George Hardy, SEIU's president, who at one time had led a health care local in Los Angeles. In 1978 Davis spoke at the SEIU's annual convention and raised the prospect of a joint effort to organize all health care workers into one union.[127] According to Henry Nicholas, Davis initiated merger discussions with the SEIU because "he had achieved what he thought achievable as a single entity." The changes taking place in health care delivery in the late 1970s, according to both Nicholas and Bob Muehlenkamp, only made the merger "objectively" more desirable.

In 1979, as talks on the proposed merger continued, Davis suffered a severe stroke. The union now had to confront as well the highly charged question of his succession. These two issues—merger and succession—dominated the proceedings at the national convention in December 1979.[128] Rather than "one big union for all health care workers," 1199 found itself embroiled in an internal struggle that threatened its survival.

CHAPTER 9

1199 Exceptionalism: Taking Stock of the First Generation

It is the task of the labor leaders to allow and to initiate a union of the power and the intellect. They are the only ones who can do it; that is why they are now the strategic elite in American society. Never has so much depended upon men who are so ill-prepared and so little inclined to assume the responsibility.

—C. Wright Mills

I used to live in New York for 30 year an work at Mount Sinai Hospital for 12 full year and as a union member. I have moved to Miami Florida now for two years. Since I moved to Miami you don't know how much I miss and regret [leaving] 1199. I work in two hospital and one nursing home for the [elderly] and for the reason of having problem with supervisor and director, I have to resign. In many occasion the employees at the hospital are treated like animal or slaves. People in South Miami . . . are waiting for a union like 1199 to have guts to come and fite for them and there right.

—March, 1982 letter to Leon Davis

From Montefiore to Charleston and Philadelphia, from $28- to $100-a-week contracts, from organizing aides and orderlies to enrolling technicians and registered nurses—1199 had, according to *New York Times* labor correspondent A. H. Raskin, established itself by 1970 as "a miraculous organism, a live union."[1] Even in the midst of dramatic achievements, however, some observers began to ask just how different 1199 was from other unions. Were its relations with management, and with its own members, truly exceptional? Were the principles of union democracy and political action as central to 1199 practice as to 1199 rhetoric? Finally, what problems, as well as benefits, beset the attempt to reinvigorate unionism as a social movement in the contemporary period? We try to answer such questions as they relate to the history of the hospital workers' union up to Leon Davis's retirement in 1982. In so doing we trade on several perspectives: the union's image as conveyed by characteristic deeds as well as the public presentation of those deeds; criticisms leveled by outside observers and by disaffected union members; and an understanding of the union's first-generation leaders themselves.

A critical analysis of the union's past is, of necessity, influenced by present-day problems. Thus as we comment on the union's first quarter-century of operation, we self-consciously set the stage for a discussion of the "inner civil war" that began with 1199's merger plans in 1980 and continues in some fashion to the present. That the organization could have cascaded into such agonizing conflict and bitter division among its top cadre necessarily casts a shadow on its history. In particular, the recent problems mandate close attention to race and gender relations, leadership development, and the decision-making process within the union. Yet even while being pulled by a presentist quest for explanation, we must portray the union's development as it was understood at the time. In short, we try to isolate both the strengths and weaknesses inherent in the union's own actions and at the same time identify the range of outside circumstances that at once stimulated and delimited the union's room to maneuver.

In part, of course, from the late fifties through the mid-seventies 1199 shined by comparison to the field around it. The years in which the hospital workers' union grew up generally offered little testimony to the idealism or initiative of organized labor. While already unionized workers took advantage of the last surge of the postwar boom economy to secure unprecedented real earnings, the trade union movement in most other respects had arrived at an impasse. Membership was at a standstill, organizing drives generally appeared anemic, efforts to control automation and technological displacement of workers proved unproductive, and political influence visibly waned. More important, perhaps, union leadership seemed to acquiesce to the deceleration of the labor movement. Unions no longer appeared to represent the advance guard of social change; instead, Big Labor, like Big Business, conjured up (even in the minds of many working people) a bureaucratic and self-interested pressure group. For the era's young, new radicals, the union movement had joined the Establishment, becoming a creaking appendage of the corporate welfare state at home and an agent of third-world exploitation abroad. Writer and former labor correspondent Murray Kempton commented in 1970: "It is a long time since many of us burdened the trade union movement with our hopes or complimented it with our curiosity."[2]

Numerous signs pointed to the torpor surrounding the unions. In 1958, just when the hospital workers' campaign was taking off, Daniel Bell argued that union membership in blue-collar industry had substantially reached its upper limit, while the explosive service, sales, and white-collar sectors were proving all but impenetrable. Meanwhile, the bottom rung of the social ladder, that "Other America" with vast numbers of unemployed and unskilled workers, enjoyed little or no contact with organized labor. Even the unions' major growth area—government employees—derived more from political leverage than grassroots militancy. This new arrow in labor's quill, moreover, not only failed to rekindle the ardor of the labor movement as a whole but eventually spawned a taxpayers' backlash that turned even union households against the favored treatment of public employees. If the "injuries of social class" still defined the American landscape, they were "hidden" by other agendas, even among organized labor.[3]

Within unionized industry, collective bargaining had become a relatively tame affair. During the postwar boom unions continued a trend toward productivity agreements—abandoning the defense of older shop rules and generally deferring to management in areas of work definition and technological innovation in exchange for substantial wage and security benefits. With the focus now on national wage settlements, contract bargaining often became only a shadow play of conflict, climaxed by a last-minute, strike-averting agreement aimed at convincing both company stockholders and union members of the negotiators' backbone and good intentions. Analysts of even such socially conscious unions as the United Auto Workers began to speak of labor-management collusion against the consumer.[4]

The labor movement's loss of outward momentum had its counterpart in the internal desiccation of union life. C. Wright Mills traced the bureaucratization process that had transformed unions from fighting units into stable holding operations of the "new men of power." In Mills's definition, labor leaders, like their counterparts—the "organization men"—of the business world, sought to pursue routine methods toward narrow and predictable ends. Codification of labor relations by the New Deal's Wagner Act and further restrictions added by the Taft-Hartley (1947) and Landrum-Griffin (1959) acts had generally served the process of bureaucratization. By holding union leaders (and union treasuries) accountable for violations, the latter two measures, in particular, nurtured carefully defined, legalistic, centralized decision making.[5]

Aside from political and structural restraints, by 1960 unions seemed afflicted by a deeper moral failing. "If one were to single out the most telling 'personality' weakness of the unions," observed labor economist Neil Chamberlain, "it would be their passion for respectability. The goal most ardently sought by union leaders generally . . . is to be accepted by their communities as good middle-class citizens." To this portrait Daniel Bell added the underside of middle-class ambition: "The real sickness lies in the decline of unionism as a moral vocation, the fact that so many union leaders have become money hungry, taking on the grossest features of business society, despoiling the union treasuries for private gain. . . . where there has not been outright spoliation . . . one finds among union leaders an appalling arrogance and high-handedness in their relation to the rank and file, which derives from the corruption of power."[6]

One other historical factor that affected the purposelessness or "end of ideology" among the labor leadership—a factor Bell notes but does not emphasize—was the expulsion of labor's left wing from the CIO in 1947–48. By generally discouraging socially critical thinking, the purge undoubtedly took its toll on the winners as well as the losers within trade union ranks.

Given the main drift of union practices during the postwar boom years, it is hardly surprising that organized labor should have collided—in mutually incriminating ways—with the new social and political movements of the 1960s. Confrontations over minority entry into the skilled trades, New York City's battle over community control of the schools, as well as the rise of militant black caucuses within industrial unions symbolized not only bitter racial divisions among working-class Americans but also the distance unions themselves had traveled away from their insurrectionary youth. Visceral identification of the AFL-CIO hierarchy with the U.S. role in Vietnam further sealed labor's disaffection from the budding antiwar political opposition. This stubbornly defensive and even openly conservative stance toward the new radicalism was fully reciprocated in the ignorance and disrespect for unions exhibited by much of the New Left, "new politics" liberals, and the Black Power vanguard of the civil rights movement. Although such a sweeping judgment overlooks trends to the contrary—for example, substantial economic assistance offered to civil rights groups by the labor establishment, defections from the Meany-dominated executive council of the AFL-CIO over the Vietnam conflict, revolts against the leadership in several of the industrial unions, and militant strikes by young blue-collar workers in the early seventies—many observers could not resist the notion that changing times had passed the unions by.[7]

It was not surprising, then, that in the face of the conventional image of organized labor, Local (subsequently District) 1199 appeared to many liberals and radicals in the 1960s as a breath of fresh air. Its very being refuted the prevailing view of organized labor as a complacent, white male–dominated labor aristocracy grown conservative after years away from struggle. District 1199's members were precisely those the big unions had failed or neglected to organize. Here was a union that had finally made effective contact with the third-world constituency that lay at the heart of 1960s' radical political strategies. Unlike the AFL-CIO hierarchy, 1199 leaders remained a lean and hungry bunch. Their salaries fixed constitu-

The union with a social conscience: (top) 1199 vice presidents Teddy Mitchell and Jesse Olson lead a Vietnam protest in the mid-1960s. (bottom) Martin Luther King, Jr., appears with 1199 vice president Henry Nicholas at the annual "Salute to Freedom" celebration.

tionally no higher than that of the best-paid union members, 1199 officers repeatedly struck, marched, and went to jail for their cause.

The hospital workers' union also consistently projected a larger social agenda. By their willing identification with social movements—from the early days of the civil rights campaign to participation in New York City rent strikes, through active opposition to U.S. involvement in Vietnam and open aid to the legal defense of Black Panthers, as well as criticism of expansionist Israeli settlements—1199 defined a most unconventional current in the labor movement. Not only what they did, but how they did it set them apart as a union that had assimilated the spirit of protest. The very brashness of this small union, the moralistic zeal with which it operated and its flair for the dramatic and militant gesture, brought the hospital workers' union uncommon and disproportionate public attention. Amid the phenomena of hardhats attacking students, trade union Democrats-for-Nixon, and the continuing decline of unionism within the labor force, 1199 seemed to be keeping faith with an older, more militant ideal. The blue-and-white paper caps of the hospital workers, surfacing at countless rallies and demonstrations, announced one brigade of organized labor still committed to a democratic social vision.

By the 1970s the union had acquired a reputation in liberal circles that separated it, along with Cesar Chavez's heroic group of farm workers, from the "spiritual wasteland" assigned to the mainstream of organized labor. David Livingston, president of District 65 and for years a close observer of the hospital union's development, reflected in 1977 that nothing "in the history of the last fifty years, certainly since the information of the CIO . . . compares with what 1199 has done." Similarly, while campaigning for her husband in the 1980 presidential election, Joan Mondale proclaimed her 1199 hosts "the conscience of the labor movement."[8]

The dynamism of the hospital union began with its grassroots organizing work, where an intense, even frenetic approach characterized its recruitment of new members. "You organize or die" was the oft-repeated catchphrase among the union staff. If one person was the walking embodiment of the 1199 temperament, it was Elliott Godoff, director of hospital organizing for sixteen years, truly an organizer's organizer. Outwardly unassuming, uncomfortable before large crowds, and so myopic that he required a driver on organizing trips, Godoff commanded a passionate loyalty from those who worked alongside him. His followers describe a man whose outer calm and gentle manner masked a ferocious inner resolve. "He was so fucking tough," remembered Bob Muehlenkamp, Godoff's protegeé and ultimate successor in charge of national organizing. "When he decided he wanted something, he never stopped until he got it." A chain smoker, Godoff sometimes also "took pills to calm himself, then again to hop himself up." "He called himself the champion shit-eater of the world," mused Muehlenkamp about the man who assumed many roles and donned many guises. "Over the years he had been beaten so many times . . . but he just wouldn't stop until he got what he wanted." One organizing tactic developed by Godoff was the 1199 "High Noon": to demonstrate union strength in advance of a strike deadline, workers would (at least until the 1974 labor law restricted such "spontaneity"), at a prearranged moment, drop what they were doing and descend on an administrator's office or form a picket line outside the hospital building. The message of the high-noon technique, according to Godoff, was, "You cannot fire, you cannot threaten because an injury to one is the concern for all."[9] It was also a clear signal to the organizer, who kept careful record of the participants, of the strength and motivation of the union's "paper" majority.

A master of detail, Godoff insisted on a relentless, nuts-and-bolts approach to union building. Eddie Kay, who joined the hospital organizing staff in 1968 after four years as a drugstore delegate, recalled some calm counsel at a stressful moment:

[Sometimes I would go] in there and [, angry and frustrated, say,] "Elliott, we have to kill; we have to go there and shoot everybody." You know, I'm getting all excited and . . . he'd sit there and roll his cigarette paper, sit there and not say a thing, and when I finished my tirade, then he'd say, "Well, I guess we gotta do this, we have to do this, and we have to do this." It was the old formula, and I knew fucking well before I got in the room that's what I had to do. But I was frustrated and looking for a gimmick. He had a wonderful ability to just say, "Well, how many cards did you get today and how'd you put the cards together and what committee did you put it into and where is the old rule." . . . It was very simple, yet he never got off that. If you yelled at him, "This doesn't work — that doesn't work — this doesn't work," he'd say, "Of course, nothing's working." Now when nothing's working, the place is not organizable at that particular time — nine out of ten times. He'd get you back in the mold of how to organize no matter what. He wouldn't get off the beaten path.

Sizing up a hospital for organizing, Godoff moved cautiously but methodically in applying pressure on the administrators. "He always considered himself a little conservative in weighing the balance of forces," said Muehlenkamp, recalling his initial experience with the union organizer in Baltimore. "At a certain point you took what you could get, got your foot in the door, then built from there."

Godoff's life was devoted entirely to empowering workers through organization. His wife, Lillian, remembered: "He always worked with goals. He never expected other people to do what he himself couldn't do. . . . By such and such a time you had to organize that number of people, that's how his whole life was." His daughter, Ellen, recalled her father's return from a union-sponsored trip to China: "He came back and the only regret from the whole trip was that the goal wasn't met. This many workers had to be organized that year and he shouldn't have taken the month off. . . . the only thing that bothered him was how many workers didn't get organized." Toward the end of his life, nearly blind and in failing health, Godoff seemed to drive himself that much harder. Crisscrossing the country, he would rush from meeting to meeting of the emergent national union. At the same time he offered the fruits of his experience to workers outside the hospital industry. Fittingly, Godoff's fatal heart attack in 1975 occurred immediately following a meeting with rank-and-file Miners for Democracy in Washington, D.C.

In addition to setting the standard for the perfect organizer, Godoff bequeathed a gentler, nurturing legacy to the young staff he left behind. Doris Turner, for example, remembered him as "a mover and a doer . . . but still a friend." At a tense moment during the 1959 strike, she recalled, he came up and "hugged me and told me not to cry." Within the larger, breakneck schedule of organizing work, within a life that left not enough time for family and almost none for outside friends, Elliott Godoff offered compassionate understanding to those around him. A year after his death, Turner remembered:

> My time with him was a different kind of time. I used to go upstairs and we'd lock the door and get into deep conversations . . . if we didn't close the door I would never get five minutes with him. . . . Many times nobody but his secretary knew I was up there. I could level with him and think he felt that he could [too]. I knew if I asked him something I could get a good answer, but he wasn't around enough, [he was] all over the country. I've only been upstairs [i.e., to Godoff's eleventh-floor office] one time since he's been dead; I made myself go one time.

Godoff was a tough act to follow. Like most unions 1199 has experienced a tremendous turnover in organizers. Long hours, low pay, and constant pressure (many say "abuse") to perform took a serious toll on these captains in the field. The life-style of the hospital organizer made it an over-whelmingly male role even within a largely female work force. The basic directive to the young organizer was simply "sink or swim." Those who survived, even for a few years, tended to adopt personality traits or at least a style of operation appropriate to the strictures of the job.[10] If there was a prototype for the 1199 organizer it was the young man (or extraordinary woman) who combined some of Godoff's attention to details and his no-nonsense approach to the immediate task with a bit of Leon Davis's public swagger. A hard-nosed, rough-and-ready realpolitik characteristically com-mingled in 1199 circles with a sentimental, even maudlin sense of ultimate purpose.

Leonard Seelig, an organizer who died tragically at age forty-one in a 1971 automobile accident, exemplified this 1199 mystique. Before coming to the union he reportedly worked in a somewhat shady junk business, where he would customarily pay building superintendents to "liberate" the pipes of condemned buildings. As union organizer, there was an air of derring-do and unpredictability to the man. "If Lenny hadn't had a little ideological development," Marshall Dubin noted affectionately, "he would have made a wonderful gangster." Indeed, the union's preference for certain personality types was so strong that the organizing staff's most successful recruit was almost overlooked. Henry Nicholas, frustrated for two years in his application to become an organizer ("They suggested I was too quiet and too small"), began a career in 1961 that would bring in thousands of new members and ultimately elevate him to the presidency of the national union.

The combative style evident in 1199 campaigns, from the 1959 strike in New York to the 1969 strike in Charleston, has become only slightly subdued in recent years. Generally, 1199-sponsored walkouts remain well-disciplined but militant affairs. Sy Broomer, organizer and union administrator at Mt. Sinai Hospital during the 1976 strike, recalled with a straight face that "some of the [strikebreaking] volunteers got their clothing messed up by some ruffians, I don't know who." Even in the day-to-day administration of contracts, the assumption of an inherent conflict of interest between managers and workers was evident on the part of union personnel. The relationship between Broomer and Mt. Sinai vice president Norman Metzger is a case in point. Broomer recounted that he was perturbed in March 1977 at the hospital's delay in processing union grievances:

> Norman knows that there's no nonsense with us, that when we feel we have to go to the mat with him, we're going to the mat with him. Today is an example. I called him . . . and said, "I'm coming right up and I'm going to talk with you, 'cause I'm not going to be provoked into bullshit with anybody, and he said, "Who do you think is provoking you?" and I told him, "If you want to play by the book it'll be that way." If necessary I'll give him grievances till [they] come out of his nose. [Referring to one particularly troublesome department head, Broomer continued,] I've been giving him two grievances a night except for Friday when I hit him with four. Some of the grievances are real strong and legitimate, some we know are bullshit, but it annoys them to have to come upstairs to a hearing. You might call it a form of harassment but I'll do it.

The union's concentration on organizing paid off in a high, even extraordinary rate of election successes: an average of 85 percent in consent elections according to a report by Godoff in 1971. Official NLRB figures for the much tougher 1974–79 period show 1199 winning 50 percent of the elections, a more modest score but still higher than those of the eight other national unions competing for health care worker representation. More recent figures indicate that the National Union of Hospital and Health Care Employees has remained the most energetic in the field: out of a dozen unions organizing health care workers in 1984–85, for example, it won the most elections (123) and had the highest percentage of election victories (67 percent), a winning percentage it maintained through the last available figures for 1987.[11]

Beyond the ferocity of organizing campaigns, the union-building process was directed "to develop" (to use the union's own phrase) the union rank and file. Momentum, in the leaders' minds, was all. "You've got to have tasks, goals, all the time," said Moe Foner, "otherwise you dry up." An extraordinary amount of effort was expended on communication, education, and motivation of the membership: "We are always doing something, selling tickets . . . lots of things other unions never contemplate." The union's far-flung voluntary programs, including the Job Training and Upgrading Program established in 1969 and the scholarship and camp programs for members' children, were operated in part to fortify rank-and-file identity with the labor union.

The bedrock of rank-and-file participation remained the delegate system—one delegate per twenty-five members elected from each work group—creating an elaborate communication and administrative netting for union projects. The delegates (a less industrial-sounding term than shop steward) not only passed on all major policy decisions taken by the leadership but were counted on to implement the collective will of the union. Gathering in monthly division meetings and biennial joint assemblies, delegates were expected to meet with their work groups every other month and to attend hospitalwide 'chapter' meetings when scheduled. In principle, it was in such gatherings that the rank-and-file workers exerted influence on union affairs and in turn were motivated by the delegates to do their part.

Clearly, 1199 leaders hoped for more than organizational loyalty from the participatory acts of union members. Activities were gauged to instill certain attitudes, in particular, tolerance, group pride, and social justice, which were constantly being cultivated both formally and informally by the union leadership. Such indoctrination might be seen as a thoroughly practical part of organization building within a labor force otherwise divided by race, skill, and diverse political perspectives. In 1970, for example, 1199 vice president Doris Turner reiterated the union's attention to the details of the annual boat ride up the Hudson River: "I like dances and outings that get everybody together. . . . This local has young militants, both black and white. It has Toms, and middle-class and old people, and a lot of mothers with responsibilities. I figure if we can just keep everybody from throwing each other overboard for a whole evening, that's the first step." The ideal (and practical necessity) of cultural pluralism similarly showed itself in the union's annual

"Salute to Freedom" (formerly, "Negro History Week") celebration, its "Salute to Israel," and its "Latin America Fiesta Night."[12]

Cultivation of the arts was another pragmatic addition to the union-building process. Over the years the hospital workers regularly sponsored labor theater, films (including five produced by the union itself), dramatic readings, art exhibits, dance performances, and lectures. When 1199 moved into its new headquarters, the Martin Luther King Labor Center, in the fall of 1970, the principal room on the first floor became a permanent art gallery, the first in American trade union history. The union's cultural initiatives were capped with the far-flung "Bread and Roses" project, established in 1979, which combined musical and dramatic performances with art and photographic exhibits and even inaugurated an annual Labor Day street fair. Perhaps the most innovative aspect of the project was the scheduling of professionally performed theater and music and poetry recitals in hospitals and nursing homes. Two original musical reviews, based on material developed at workshops with union members, were performed at lunchtime gatherings of some 36,000 hospital workers in four states. Major funding—more than a million dollars—came from public arts and humanities endowments.[13]

Such ambitious cultural programming served several purposes. On the one hand, these "extra" activities strengthened the positive identity and active

The September 1980 Labor Day Street Fair was one of many events organized via 1199's far-reaching Bread and Roses cultural agenda.

association of union members. Moe Foner's modest assessment that "a good union doesn't have to be dull" undoubtedly underestimated the real contributions his direction of "Bread and Roses" and earlier 1199 cultural initiatives brought to the internal life of the union. On the other hand, such efforts had untold public relations value. In fact, over the years 1199 gained more positive public recognition than other unions many times its size. The variety of films, art, and theater extravaganzas particularly impressed journalistic commentators and, especially in New York, the artistic and intellectual community. In an industry ever sensitive to public opinion and political pressure, the union's creativity and keen eye for public relations represented more than peripheral accomplishments. In this sense "having fun" was clearly good politics.

The union's cultural commitment was also one way by which the leadership tried to "teach" a set of ideals and feelings to the members. A cultural milieu that drew upon both the left-wing folk music tradition of the thirties and the rhythms of the civil rights crusade lent 1199 campaigns the spirit of a protest movement—best exemplified by Larry Fox, a young organizer who pulled out his guitar and led workers on picket lines in song during the tense Rochester (N.Y.) nursing home campaign of 1972. Often, the labor-civil rights motif seemed especially designed to close the gap between the heterogeneous ethnic identities of the members, creating a populist celebration of the American common people. It was not surprising that when asked to define the union's goals, Elliott Godoff answered simply, "Rights! Rights! Rights!" To be sure, the reception by the hospital rank and file to such messages was not always exact. At the union's 1976 "We Can't Work for Peanuts" demonstration before the Democratic National Convention at Madison Square Garden, someone strummed the chords of the labor gospel song "We Shall Not Be Moved"; however, among the demonstrators was heard a full-throated Hispanic chorus of "We Shall Not, We Shall Not Remove."[14]

There were other values, as well, implicit in 1199's cultural agenda. Officially it reflected a faith in rational enlightenment, a vision that presupposed the power of ideas and education as a means both to self-improvement and to social progress. With a bow to ethnic and racial particularism, union leaders ultimately emphasized an appreciation of high culture (i.e., "the arts") for the individual as well as "movement culture" for the group. "What we want to do," explained Foner in an interview about the "Bread and Roses" project, "is open up new horizons to our members. I'm not saying they're going to become inveterate theater goers, but like Jewish mothers say about chicken soup, 'It ain't going to hurt.' " He saw the role of the union as an agent of access to the "good things in life" emerge in the "cultural" as well as the "economic" sphere of operation. A union brochure explained that culture is "a right for everyone, not a privilege for a few."[15]

More than an instrumental accoutrement to "real" union business, the cultural enrichment of members lay close to the sentimental heart of the 1199 leadership. This was most evident in the union's college scholarship program, named after union attorney Joseph Tauber and administered for many years by Anne Shore, which signaled its simultaneous faith in individual enlightenment and group economic arrival. Union members, asserted one official publication,

> believe, as their ancestors did before them, that education confers dignity and respect. They believe it can provide leadership, not only to their own ethnic group, but to the nation as a whole. And like their ancestors, the member and their children believe that education can be a vehicle for social mobility. It is for all these reasons that Irish, Italian, Hispanic, Jewish and Black members have utilized the Joseph Tauber Scholarship Program. . . . [It] is attempting to put the children of hospital, drug and health care workers on an equal footing with more affluent, middle-class students. In doing so, it is helping members fulfill the dreams of generations of their ancestors who hungered for knowledge and wisdom so that they could find freedom and dignity.[16]

Paradoxically, such educational idealism at once compelled the leaders toward contact with the rank and file and separated them from the members. Likening 1199's success to a David-and-Goliath struggle, Leon Davis declared in his 1971 "State of the Union" speech: "What occurred is that we wounded the giant and in a relatively short period brought new hope, new social and cultural values and material benefits to thousands of workers." In an offhand moment several years later he said simply, "We took backward people and elevated them."[17]

The Union Difference

Despite its paternalistic overtones, Davis's message contained a considerable measure of truth. Beyond the visions of its leaders and the characteristic spirit of its operations, the hospital workers' union had unquestionably made a difference in members' lives, and on several levels. For most 1199 members, unionization clearly meant a rising living standard. While labor economists dealing with national statistics varyingly calculate the positive payoff of unionization on hospital workers' wages, a recent survey of the literature offers a "modal estimate" for nonprofessionals of "about 10 percent," not counting the difficult-to-quantify spillover effect of the union on nonunion rates of pay.[18] A New York City hospital worker in 1980 who had been in the industry since the 1950s would likely have taken the economists' figure and multiplied it several times over. Starting wages at the city's voluntary hospitals in 1958 ranged from $28 to $34 per week; in

1983, minimum wages under the 1199 contract began at $294 per week. Adjusting for inflation, the gain in real income over a twenty-three-year period amounted to 140 percent.

In 1981 Evelyn Singleton, a dietary technician at Philadelphia's Hahnemann Hospital, more concretely compared her earnings of $6.25 an hour, along with job security and good benefits, with preunion conditions (before 1970) of $1.68 an hour, few benefits, no pension, and no job security: "You were struggling, you really couldn't eat a decent meal. You had a one-room apartment. You couldn't afford a car or a home." To be sure, the union alone did not bring about these dramatic increases. Third-party payment plans, expanded government subsidy of hospitals, a rising national minimum wage, and shifting labor requirements of the hospitals all have some claim as contributors to rising wages. However, the historical record provides ample evidence that collective bargaining, or the threat of it, consistently served as the chief catalyst to change.[19]

Such material changes, of course, found real meaning for workers in the course of daily life. Two surveys of 1199 members in New York City are illustrative. A confidential wage and salary report, undertaken by the union in 1961, locates a historic moment when 1199, concentrating on employer recognition, had made only the most fledgling impact on wages and living standards. The report compared workers' incomes to expenditures and also provided data on weekly savings, savings accounts, and outstanding loans.[20] A second survey, based on our Hospital Workers History Project Questionnaire in 1977, provides a measure of union-generated changes in workers' living standards.[21]

The 1961 figures point to a working-class population basically shut out of the "affluent society," the general economic "feast" characteristic of the long postwar boom.[22] Three-fourths of those polled indicated that their wages did not cover weekly living expenses; 27 percent reported that they had "recently" borrowed money, while only 8 percent maintained savings accounts. Of those surveyed, 47 percent had left formal schooling during the elementary grades, 61 percent had not received a high school diploma, and 97 percent had no instruction beyond high school. These figures correspond closely to national norms: in 1960, 48 percent of the adult black population had not completed eighth grade, 80 percent had not finished high school, and 93 percent had never entered college.[23]

Descriptions of weekly expenditures suggest the limits of material comforts. Julio Q, for example, a Puerto Rican file clerk at Mt. Sinai, earned $43.20 per week and reported that he generally could meet weekly expenses of $10.00 toward rent, $3.70 for lunches (other food not itemized), $4.00 for clothing, and $1.50 for transportation. He even had a few dollars left over to buy jewelry and to enroll in a "study course." However, Julio had not saved anything and had taken out a bank loan to support his mother "because this system of life in this country is too higher." Laundry workers' leader Gloria Arana just "barely" covered her needs on a 1961 income of $45 per week: $15 for rent (not counting gas and electricity), $20 for food for herself and her youngest daughter, and $10 for transportation, "the minimum" on clothing, and "regular donations to the sick, church, etc." Clothes presser Eddie Sanchez found that he fell short at least $5 a week in providing for his young family; payments of $19 a month on $500 worth of living room furniture left nothing for incidentals like "haircut, shoe repairs, medicines, telephone calls, etc." Maintenance mechanic Elon Tompkins earned nearly $20 a week more than the laundry workers, yet he matched the forced frugality of the others in order to send a $20 weekly "surplus" to his grandchildren.

Superficially, the economic profile of hospital service workers in 1977, after sixteen years of unionization, suggests a strong degree of continuity: 67 percent of the workers reported that their wages did not keep pace with weekly expenditures, while 45 percent (a considerable increase) reported that they recently had had to borrow money. The educational achievement of the hospital work force likewise seems to have changed little between 1961 and 1977. Behind first appearances, however, stood a world of difference, indicating that the higher incomes had triggered a quest for security, comfort, and—for one's children—rapid occupational mobility. Savings accounts, for example, were maintained by 57 percent of the workers (a sevenfold increase), with ten of sixteen respondents naming "emergencies," "when needed," "whatever comes," and "retirement" as security-oriented motives for saving; others listed "home," "car," or "new dining room set" as immediate goals. A Puerto Rican seamstress explicitly combined the search for security with the desire for disposable cash, putting aside $30 each week for "emergencies and my personal needs." Even their sources of indebtedness reflected the growing immersion of hospital workers into a consumer economy. Among bills to be paid with loans, workers listed house and car payments, car insurance, vacations, and clothes for school. Insolvency might even be expected in the mid-1970s stagflation years for those with rising material expectations and slowed economic rewards—as indicated by explanations like "everything went up," "due to economy," "due to the high cost of living," and "an unemployed son to take care of." The sense of release from the subsistence-oriented life-style of preunion days was evident in Beth Israel nurse's aide Mae Harrison's comment: "Now I'm able to go places."

To no one's surprise the technical and professional members of the union's guild division reported an even more abundant standard of living than the service workers. By 1977 the traditional complaint regarding "a professional skill without a professional income" had been muted by the impact of a succession of union contracts, bigger hospital budgets, and (one might infer) the two-profession household. Roughly matching the profile for service workers, 64 percent of guild members reported savings accounts, while 46 percent had recently borrowed money. The nature of their consumption, however, set most white-collar workers apart from the others. Some guild members were able to save $50, $66, and in one case $100 a week for such ends as a house, home improvements, education (including, for a few, private schooling for their children), "annuities," "mutual funds," and even "art." Such consumer tastes and capacities coincided with a reading public that regularly chose the *New York Times* over the service workers' literary currency, the *Daily News*. When one lab technician listed "vacation, rent, bills, ordinary necessities" as the motive for taking out a loan, he defined a reality that was still not entirely ordinary for large numbers of service workers.

The revolution that occurred in the lives of hospital workers and their families from the late fifties through the mid-seventies also occurred, as union leaders hoped it would, in the schoolyards. Appeals by the union, as in the civil rights movement, to be "somebody"—to obtain a piece of the American dream as well as the American pie—received an immediate answer in the form of new educational and occupational opportunities which were seized by members' children. Black education enrollment, in general, had greatly improved during the boom years of education and welfare spending, but not as dramatically as it had for union children. By 1980, for example, 75 percent of all black students completed high school, and 22 percent enrolled in college.[24] Our 1977 survey revealed that 91 percent of the age-eligible sons and daughters of 1199 members, less than half of whom had finished high school (only 5 percent progressed beyond a high school diploma), had graduated from high school, and nearly 40 percent had gone on to some form of college training; guild members' children had all graduated from high school, and nearly all had at least entered college. Employment patterns also suggested the upward mobility of hospital workers' families: half of the employed children of service workers claimed white-collar or professional jobs.

The union's messianic educational rhetoric seemed to resonate with the individually less schooled service workers. By 1979 nearly three-fourths of the Joseph Tauber Scholarship winners were the children of hospital service workers. One early winner reflected on the transformative experience: "When I came here, I realized that it was up to me to learn and succeed. No one was going to help me. If I was in Jamaica now I wouldn't have the opportunity. I'd probably be doing something ridiculous. Over here you have more opportunity. You can get ahead if you really want to, but you have to work hard for it."[25]

Unionization for hospital workers was thus part of a larger process of socialization (for some, Americanization) into new patterns of urban, economic life. Nowhere was this more striking than in 1199's summer camp program for members' children. Like the rest of the union's economic, political, and cultural agenda, the summer camp program encouraged individual (and familial) striving, uplift, and general exposure to "new experiences." "We have nine children and were never able to send any to camp," acknowledged one mother in a letter of appreciation. The children's comments, written at the end of their two-week outings in the country, reflect similar feelings of discovery as well as gratitude:

I like it because in the city you can't swim, fish, go frog hunting and snake hunting. (Timothy Thomason, 1972)

I learnd how to milk a goat. I never did it before but I have got good at it. I would like to come back. P.S. I received an Indian name. (John Byrd, 1976)

I had a great time at Camp Leah doing things I never had a chance to do before. . . . I want so much to go back again but Mom says I can only go if 1199 sends me. Please send me, I'm gonna do good in school. (Felix Rivera, 1979)

I liked [Camp] Indian Brook because you could be free. I also like being close to nature and I loved riding the horses. But I think that the counselers should let you play cards with your friends at rest hour. (Kim Crowell, 1972)[26]

Besides sparking material gains and expanding individual desires, the union strongly encouraged participation in the larger public sphere. This was particularly evident in relation to such basic acts of citizenship as registering and voting on election day. A comparison of participation rates for a cross-section ($N = 155$) of 1199 members and stewards with citywide averages in the 1976 presidential election and the 1977 mayoral primary is illustrative of the union's role in political assimilation:

	Citywide average	Hospital division		Guild division	
		Members	Delegates	Members	Delegates
registered	na	64%	100%	62%	70%
voted in 1976 election	51%	61%	93%	69%	80%
voted in 1977 primary	45%	51%	87%	46%	45%

Source: *New York Times* (Dec. 26, 1976; Sept. 1, 1977) and authors' 1977 Hospital Workers History Project Questionnaire.

In the case of 1199 — as with other unions, particularly in the early "organizing" phase — mobilization at the workplace seems to have had a galvanizing effect on citizenship activity beyond the workplace.[27] Moreover, it is surely no accident that hospital division delegates, who typically emerged as rank-and-file leaders during mass mobilizations and remained as organizational captains, exhibited a phenomenal rate of political participation. Clearly, they had been touched by the union message.

The Critique of 1199

Whatever its distinctiveness, 1199 was apt, sooner or later, to disappoint those who celebrated the hospital workers' union primarily for its distance from ordinary American trade unionism. In the years following the attention-grabbing events at Charleston, adulation of the union was mixed with a strain of disillusionment and sometimes bitter disaffection. The most searching exposé of 1199's shortcomings appeared in the writings of three New Left commentators, John and Barbara Ehrenreich (and, more generally, the Health-Pac organization to which they belong) and Elinor Langer. In fact, their published critiques, based on brief but observant contact with the union, have been echoed softly by some of the more educated and politically motivated union members themselves.[28]

The overall critique of 1199 addressed both the ends and the means of union practice. With regard to the former, the real gains harvested did not appear to transcend the "bread-and-butterism" of conventional unions or to affect the systematic inequality of the American health care system. Critics claimed that in pursuing every avenue to higher pay and better benefits for its members, 1199 showed relative indifference to issues regarding the organization of work or to matters affecting the consuming public. While outside analysts often attacked misallocation of research funds and tendencies toward overprofessionalization, fragmentation of function, extreme hierarchy, and ultimate inefficiency in health delivery, one heard comparatively little on these issues within the union. The union also effectively dismissed the question of worker alienation and cooperated with the hospitals' complex differentiation of job definitions and pay ranges, insisting officially (in Leon Davis's words) that "we love our work." At its best, the Job Upgrading and Training Program, established by the landmark 1968 contract to lift workers out of dead-end jobs, succeeded only at the individual level and within the established structure.[29]

Despite its progressive political posture, the hospital workers' union did adopt a cautious, even defensive approach to larger assaults on its own industry. Except for hosting regular health policy conferences, the union paid scant attention to the issue of structural reform of the health care system. Neither the demands of the publicly owned municipal hospitals for a bigger share of medical dollars nor the indictment of the voluntary hospitals by Health-Pac as expansionistic "medical empires" raised much sympathy from 1199. No more than the United Auto Workers pushed for alternative forms of transportation have the hospital workers joined the critics of the voluntary hospitals.

Even in its relation to black and minority issues, the "soul power" union did sometimes upset its more politically inspired supporters. While offering support to community control forces in the 1968 Ocean Hill–Brownsville school fight, only a few years later 1199 opposed the Young Lords (and Health Revolutionary Union Movement) takeovers of New York City neighborhood health clinics on grounds that they violated standing union-management contracts. Discountenancing official union action in such matters, 1199 vice president Jesse Olson reportedly told militants occupying the mental health center at Lincoln Hospital in 1969, "If the workers want to challenge who should be management, who should control the center, that is their own affair."

More generally, tactics and strategies that circumvented the union's normal operating machinery have received a frosty reception. When, for example, a coalition of interns, residents, workers, and community people moved in 1971 to oppose a series of staff cutbacks at the Maimonides Hospital Mental Health Center, the union pressured its members not to get involved. Since no 1199 members were involved initially in the economy moves, according to guild delegate Ezra Birnbaum, union leaders did not "give two hoots in hell" about the matter. Indeed, the very fact that the cuts pointedly avoided union members was used by the leadership as a sign of the organization's strength, regardless of the health care impact. In what Birnbaum termed the "1199 version of red-baiting," individual union sympathizers of the community movement were attacked (in language derived from old-left orthodoxy) as "dissidents," "trotskyists," or "wreckers." Of course, no one denied that in a period of growing retrenchment in social services 1199 did, to a remarkable extent, protect its own. Sometimes, as in bucking the Nixon-ordered wage freeze, it even threw pragmatic caution to the winds. Still, the union did not use such occasions, in one critic's words, to "take on the hospitals in a basic way."[30]

Compared to those levying a frontal challenge to the health care establishment, the union and its priorities sometimes seemed mundane, even downright conservative. Elinor Langer, for example, sided with the community health activists as apostles of "real liberation" versus a union that had revealed itself to her as a supporter, not an antagonist, of the status quo."[31]

Critics also have pointed to deficiencies in the union's decision-making process, particularly the disparity between formally democratic procedures and an effectively centralized chain of command. Not that opposing voices were unfairly silenced; rather, both structure and personality of the union executive encouraged docility by the delegates, sycophantism among the staff, and a general lack of initiative and "critical independence" throughout the organization. In such a context, John Ehrenreich has argued, participation in the formal democratic process of the union as well as in 1199's multiple political, cultural, and educational programs signified less an exercise in real democracy than a "vast recreational therapy program carefully designed and staged by the union's leadership."[32]

Structurally, the problem of democratic process in 1199 likely has several explanations. Delegates convened by the late 1960s in 800-member (by 1980, 1500-member) assemblies, far too large a body to engage in substantive discussion. Moreover, beyond the delegates there was no mid-range elected leadership, only appointed organizers and business agents. Unionwide officer elections, with each nominee required to show supporting signatures from the drugstore division as well as the hospital and guild (and later nursing) divisions, militated against the development of sectional blocs or local power bases. While the system perhaps forestalled some intraunion divisions, it stunted the development of strong chapters and rank-and-file-based leaders.[33]

In a scholarly assessment of "Local 100" (a thinly veiled reference to District 65, whose structure the hospital workers' union practically replicated), industrial relations expert Alice Cook captured the centralizing tendencies within an 1199-style apparatus. She acknowledged that in spirit and grassroots participation Local 100 was almost "without a peer" while emphasizing the gap between a powerful union executive and a distant, though democratically represented, rank and file. In such situations, large "general council" meetings of assembled stewards "are conducted more like educational or revival meetings than as deliberative assemblies" and "are aimed first at developing acceptance of, and commitment to, participation in specific programs. . . ." On the whole, Cook concluded "the communications value of the steward-crew [or for 1199, delegate-chapter] system is mainly in its downward flow of directives, preachments, and invitations to participant activity and that the upward stream at best provides what the president has called a 'barometer of members' feelings.' This is all very well but it is not democratic government in the full sense of the term." With its combination of democratic spirit and "autocratic machination," she warned, "both the morality and the stability of the structure [of Local 100] rest largely on the capacity of the officers."[34]

In 1199 executive power collapsed further into the single office of the president. A scholarly review of the union's institutional order in the early 1970s called the president's constitutional powers "extraordinary": "He presides or can preside at or call all meetings of members, committees, officers at various levels, and can subdivide divisions of the union or appoint officials to strategic and powerful committees. These constitutional provisions result in the absolute concentration of power in the hands of the president and raises his authority far above that of any other officer or unit in the union."[35] In practice, both union structure and personal capacity undoubtedly contributed to the authority of Leon Davis as president. Henry Nicholas recalled that Davis "ran a tight ship," that "there was only one spokesman during his reign as president." Retired national union organizer John Black likewise claimed that only Elliott Godoff and Moe Foner, if anyone, shared real decision-making power with Davis. It is remarkable, indeed, that the two most celebrated "social-movement" unions in the postwar period—Cesar Chavez's farmworkers and Leon Davis's hospital workers—were led by charismatic patriarchs whose unquestioned authority verged on benevolent despotism.[36]

What is perhaps most remarkable is that this state of affairs engendered remarkably little resentment from either staff or union membership during Davis's long tenure. While union vice presidents, organizers, and secretaries privately complained about the volatile temperament of a boss who might snap and roar at them almost as reflexively as at a hospital attorney, they accepted his judgments with an almost reverential respect based on what he had risked and accomplished.[37] It was awe as much as constitutional power that explained Davis's extraordinary authority. If not exactly a pleasant colleague, he nevertheless fostered a spirit of common commitment and mutual sacrifice, as well as a kind of affection-under-duress. For example, Teddy Mitchell, the former drugstore porter and veteran 1199 organizer, at one moment located a general problem of the labor movement in the fact that "old labor leaders don't never try to train those young guys. They [are] so fucking jealous of their role." Yet he quickly exonerated his former boss: "I do know Davis tries. Of course he pushed me. [I] had it tough when I came here. . . . Davis was giving me holy hell. I used to [think] he was picking on me, 'cause I was black, you know? But he wasn't. He wasn't. And I found that out since I got old. I had [phlebitis] in this [leg] . . . and I wanted to retire. But he told me, I don't want you to retire, I won't be able to handle it. . . . And, you know, I've never had another day [when] I'd wake up and want to quit."

Doris Turner expressed a similar admiration for the man who had drafted her into union work. Reassuring union delegates in 1970 of the quality of contract terms that Davis had just negotiated, she spoke of her personal feeling for the union's president:

> On behalf of hospital workers I don't think there's anything in the world he couldn't do. In these terrible and lengthy negotiations, with all the discomforts and all the abuse and mistreatment that we all received, he took the brunt of it. He stood up like the president of 1199 should, in my opinion; he answered for us,

he spoke for us, he fought for us, and he won for us. We are all, or at least we should all, be very proud of our president, and if he does nothing else in the next two years all he has to do in my opinion is come around at negotiation time and bring us home these kinds of settlements.

The combination of selfless, dedicated leadership and rather abject deference by staff as well as rank-and-file members summed up for Elinor Langer "the good and bad truth about 1199."[38]

While in office, Leon Davis and his executive cohorts paid little attention and less respect to the intellectual and political criticisms laid at the union's door. They were only too happy to accept parts of the critique, such as the contention that the union had had only a negligible effect on hospital health care delivery, which substantiated what they had been saying all along. From its very inception 1199 faced down industry charges that collective bargaining would seriously impair the functions of health care institutions, interposing a dangerous third party between patients and health professionals. The union continually argued that it pressed no claims for work reorganization. "We handle the hospitals with great caution," explained Davis in 1976. "We still believe that." Self-confessedly, the union's concerns lay in another direction: "Organizing is the key and everything else is peripheral," explained Moe Foner. "In a real sense we have made a contribution to health care by permitting people [i.e., health care workers] to live decently. We believe that their interests coincide with the idea of good things for the general society." Guild director Jesse Olson emphasized that "the union's concern is to see that workers get a fair share of the pie." In Turner's eyes the larger issues of health care organization seemed peripheral: "I'm not an expert in running hospitals and it would be wrong to tell those who are [what to do] anymore than it would be wrong for those people to run the union."

Informally, there was no shortage of criticism by 1199ers of the American health care system. Without hesitation, Davis said in 1976 that it was "in chaotic condition," a "disaster area," yet he admitted that politically practical solutions were "not easy to come by." For him the intellectual problem was "how to provide a health care system that's rational in a society that's terribly irrational." The union president allowed that he had once placed faith in structured, prepaid medical plans but had discovered that "even our own members won't accept the idea of giving up individual doctors. . . . Insurance won't help; Medicaid is a total disaster—[it] set back health care with all its corruption." The implication, at least for the time being, was that the union ought to tend its own garden. As director of the union's job and retraining program since 1971, James R. O'Brien was more willing than most of the union staff to admit that work fragmentation, professional hierarchy, worker alienation, and hospital inefficiency were all problems that were steadily "getting worse." He saw workers and patients as victims of "the same system." Still, the idea that the union could take a major role in reforming the system struck O'Brien, like his colleagues, as "an impossible dream." He also acknowledged that too much focus on the issue of hospital efficiency could lead to "cutting our own throat."

Many of the specific proposals for health care reform that emerged out of 1960s radicalism did, in fact, leave the union openly unenthusiastic. By 1970–71, when health care decentralization and community control banners were being raised, 1199 had already soured on the idea. The corruption and virulent ethnic politics to which local poverty and school boards had succumbed offered one reason for caution. Of course, the threat to consolidated bargaining between the union and the League of Voluntary Hospitals provided another. An appeal for "open books" (dismissed by hospital administrators as mere contract-time gimmickry), occasional calls for the appointment of "public" representatives to hospital boards of directors, and vague expressions of interest in an "integrated" public-private (i.e., municipal-voluntary) hospital system were as far as 1199 ventured, even rhetorically, into the area of structural change for the industry. On the last point it is worth noting that the voluntary hospital–based union had in mind no submersion into the "public sector" — indeed, quite the contrary — at least as it was currently defined. "Other than the factor of the jobs involved," Moe Foner candidly observed, "we are hard put to find a reason for having the city hospitals. There would be a serious problem in terms of jobs [if the municipal hospitals were merged into the voluntary institutions] but it would be a superior system." While some sort of amalgamation under tighter public scrutiny might theoretically make sense, interests outside the union's control made any such reform most unlikely. In the meantime the union leadership stuck by the superiority of service in the private, nonprofit sector. "The city," noted Davis in a typically acerbic moment, "can't run a shithouse."

Leon Davis was no less emphatic about the importance of a unified command structure. He viewed proposals for more decentralized, delegate-based decision making with the utmost skepticism. "There are no clear answers," he argued, "about how to run a democratic union, unless it's a very small union like the old AF of L craft unions, towns in Vermont, or building trades locals. With a big union and power, what do you do?" On the one hand, Davis and other union leaders regularly bemoaned the lack of initiative flowing upward through the union's elaborate delegate structure; while on the other hand they saw no ready, acceptable alternative to their own practices.[39] Most outsiders, in Davis's view, had "no understanding of what a union is, what makes it go, stop, how it runs." He continued:

The membership can only be a sounding board, even the delegates . . . they can't make decisions. The 1,000 delegates in 1199 can react but they can't make decisions. The most you can do with rank-and-file leadership [the delegates] is as a stopgap to the leadership, to set the bounds [of action]. The idea of wisdom emanating up from the bottom is full of shit, not because the rank and file are stupid but because they have a job which is not running the union and knowing all the intricate business about it. Consequently, their ability to come up with initiatives is limited.

A fear of faction and disunity provided the chief rationale against most recommendations for internal structural reform. Davis's insistence on a strong union executive in fact belied parental fears for the fragile creature he had nursed. He possessed an almost Hobbesian sense that if left to their own devices the members would allow factional interest, personal corruption, and moral weakness to tear the union apart. Without a farseeing guide, the racial and occupational heterogeneity of the membership could lead to a disastrous cycle of inner conflict; the distinctive hospital divisions, in this nightmare vision, would not only chew each other up, but together they would totally trample the tiny drugstore division. Over and over, therefore, Davis emphasized that the membership "needs guidance and coordination." He added, "There is a very deliberate process of filtering issues which are divisive, which may suit one [branch of the union] but not the union in general and to put it in a form which will create the greatest amount of unity among the members."

From early on union leaders worried especially about the fit between the more highly educated guild members and the hospital union's traditional service worker base. Particularly as the guild grew, it triggered resentments of both style and substance from hospital division members. As an example of potential dangers, in 1976 Davis cited the difficulty experienced in getting hospital division members to accept a bargaining demand of shorter hours for guild members because it did not exactly correspond to their own terms of employment. Such tensions, in any case, only hardened the union president's insistence on decision making being coordinated from the top. Only from the union's summit, he reasoned, could one make an informed decision on behalf of all members.

The hospital workers' union's answer to criticism, on the whole, was similar to that of other unions. Abstract goals and principles—like an equitable health care system or workers democracy—are fine, 1199 leaders responded, but the union lives in the here and now, with what works and what doesn't. A union is a union, they pragmatically argued, not a vehicle for transforming society. Advancing and protecting workers' jobs and livelihoods are basic aims; the rest is largely a matter of faith in the long-term march of history. By its refusal to engage in political abstractions, 1199 thus placed itself in the mainstream of American labor ideology. Indeed, on the basis of self-avowed aims, one might think that the AFL's Samuel Gompers and his watchdog, "More!" would have been perfectly at home in the hospital union's high command. Labor journalist A. H. Raskin, in a 1977 interview, noted that the "ideological" edges had gradually worn off 1199 rhetoric, a change he attributed to a general "mellowing" of Leon Davis's own politics. The union itself tended to encourage this impression, as is evident in their documentary film tribute to the outgoing president: *Leon Davis—Practical Dreamer.*[40]

Still, accepting the union's self-definition at face value created problems, and important features of both its early and more recent history receive little explanation. Why, for example, did 1199 venture into the hospital field in the first place? And why their distinctive style of mass militancy, their engagement in so many political issues? What sort of vision lay behind the leaders' militant pragmatism?

The difficulty in answering such questions reflects not only the particular experience of 1199 but larger elements of postwar American labor history as well. McCarthyism and the Cold War placed a veil over political unionism in the United States and even those union leaders who held generally anticapitalist political convictions gave up the attempt to communicate to their members what kind of tacit assumptions and dreams held them to their life's course. As Bert Cochran suggests, the truncated relationship of radicals to the union movement was already apparent in the thirties. For political militants like Leon Davis and his drugstore unionists, "industrial unionism" during the Depression became a kind of catch-all for an acceptable, progressive vision. The term implied class solidarity, industrial fighting power, and the merging of specific political-ideological differences in a common effort. Yet Cochran details how industrial unionism, once embraced by the New Deal and at least indulged by Big Business, lost much of its messianic content: "Industrial unionism did spell greater labor solidarity, but not for anticapitalist assaults; mass political activities, but not for Socialist or Labor Party candidates; the conversion of unions into more socially purposeful, less discriminatory mechanisms, but for social service, not radical purposes." A trend, in Cochran's terms, took place away from "left-wing unionism" toward "no-nonsense" unionism.[41]

The notion of a developmental taming of industrial unionism finds a degree of resonance within the experience of the hospital workers' union. Both the class-solidarity model that informed a commitment to industrywide organizing as well as political priorities had necessarily to be modified in the course of union building. Politically, the union could not be too far out "in front" of its members or influential friends. Thus, while offering moral support on many left-wing issues, 1199 in New York generally accommodated itself to dominant political figures like Nelson Rockefeller or Harry

Van Arsdale; and in Philadelphia, Henry Nicholas and 1199C became adroit municipal political power brokers. Organizationally, the "one big union" ideal of industrial unionism was similarly leavened by pragmatic accommodation to professional identities, evident in the growing number of recognized divisions among the hospital union membership.

If the class-struggle ideology of its founders had been readapted to the realities of the surrounding political culture, 1199's remaining original pillar of idealism—interracialism—had also been affected by the centripetal force of consensus ideology. Communists of the 1930s placed interracial organizing within a larger class analysis, one that viewed race prejudice as *the* impediment to a united working-class movement. As the decades wore on, the fight for racial justice on the part of many of the old radical battlers became an end in itself. The struggle was waged less against the economic system than for full rights and respectability within it, for *entry* into the American way. Within the union the image publicly projected of Doris Turner after 1959 is suggestive: her former poverty was compared to the degree of power, fulfillment, and comfort she had achieved through the agency of the union. This is not to say that interracialism as an article of faith had lost its punch. Indeed, over the years it was perhaps the most powerful emotional chord touched by the union. But, like industrial unionism, the concept became detached from a more thoroughgoing analysis of American society.

The drugstore-cum–hospital workers' union, then, offers one of the more fascinating cases of the retooling of the old radical labor vision. While undergoing the pull toward Cochran's pragmatic, "no-nonsense" version of postwar unionism, 1199 never lost the restless, striving quality characteristic of the movement in earlier days. For the leaders at least, the union remained a crusade, and its ties with the civil rights movement effectively attached its fate as an organization to the larger cause of human freedom and democracy.

Despite their apparent success in adapting to the social realities of postwar America, however, 1199 leaders paid a certain price in discarding older ideological baggage. Perhaps most important was the gulf that developed between the political thought of the leaders and the union's rank and file. The permanent public silence—and therefore contemporary ignorance—about the leaders' political origins and energizing vision could not help but exacerbate the already difficult problems of leadership training and transition for the hospital workers. The first generation could never really pass on its skills so long as it hid, even from itself, an examination of basic assumptions, motivations, and ends.

For the old leaders political thought became, by the force of circumstances, more a matter of personal conviction and private feelings than a guide to public action. The feelings themselves were mixed and usually complicated. Up to the day of his retirement, for example, Leon Davis remained something of a sentimental communist. Long after resigning from the Communist party and signing the Taft-Hartley oath, he noted with pride that he had journeyed three times to the Soviet Union on friendship tours and likewise had entertained visiting labor delegations from the Eastern Bloc. Privately, he still hoped for "basic economic and political changes" and described himself as "certainly not a Social Democrat—that's not a political [movement], that's a cover-up for maintaining the status quo." Likewise, Elliott Godoff's son remembered that although he formally left Communist party circles even before joining 1199, he "never changed his politics." Friends noted that Davis and Godoff, both immigrants from Russia, carried a "touch of Russian nationalism." A final vestige of old political affinities survived in the recruitment of organizing staff: through the early 1980s, party circles or at least past party-connected political experience proved a useful conduit for several individuals who would make their mark on union affairs.

For Davis, Godoff, and Foner, the old ideals, if not explicitly abandoned, nevertheless lost any real link with ongoing union affairs or contemporary political strategy. The plight of the Left in America, what Davis privately called "this problem that I have lived my life through," reduced itself to the unsolved, abstract dilemma of reconciling socialism and freedom—"freedoms which workers will not give up; they just will not give up." Acknowledging that the Soviets had inaugurated a "very destructive" form of socialism—"a dictatorship which is certainly not the wave of the future for any Western country and I'm not sure whether it's good for any country"—Davis suggested, without evident optimism, that only a move by the Soviets "in the direction of [personal and political] liberty" could "reignite positive momentum" in the socialist movements of the West. He readily admitted that he had never tried to communicate to the union membership such dreams and doubts, the fruits of a lifetime of brave and difficult commitment to what he still calls the "workers' struggle."

The peculiar political experience through which 1199 emerged offers a lesson in both faith and disillusionment for the union's leaders. While the "workers' struggle," however transmuted, remains an unsullied ideal, a hard-bitten cynicism has developed about the world that surrounds the struggle—people's motives, means, and ends. Contempt for an exploitative and corrupt corporate and political world has left an abiding impression on 1199 staff, as well as a fear that the corruption could spread to the workers. Indeed, the very success of the American labor movement, together with the comparative affluence of the workers themselves, sometimes seems to have undermined the capacity for mobilization.

Reflecting on an abortive organizing campaign, Davis privately lambasted workers ("They don't deserve a union") for showing insufficient will to fight and to sacrifice for the cause. In his last years before retirement, he complained increasingly about the "dependence" of the membership on the bureaucratic staff, worrying out loud that perhaps the union had "overcompensated" (i.e., done too much for) the poor, "backward" troops it had welded together. Ironically, this life-long advocate of the "social unionism" of the CIO ultimately discovered the virtues of an older, discredited craft unionism. Davis admitted in 1979, "I am beginning to appreciate some of the old conservative unions who expected the worker to stand up for his rights and on his own. I am beginning to think that we . . . overservice the members. Members get a bellyache and two organizers are there to see what it's all about. [That] doesn't build leadership, responsibility, and strength."

By the time Leon Davis retired, 1199 survived in his vision as an irreducible ideal. A frail creature, it required constant vigilance from selfless leaders to protect it from employers, political schemers, selfish workers, and starry-eyed radicals. For the first-generation leaders the protection and extension of tangible organizing and contract gains constituted a measure of the union's progress. These material signs, however, were always linked to a deeper emotional and political reservoir. Beneath the surface, the chords of "struggle" and "solidarity" still made union work a vocation as well as a livelihood.[42] For the old leaders the union was the living vestige of youthful hopes for a better world. A half-cynical, half-sentimental engagement with the issues and forces operating in that larger world contributed in important ways to 1199's uniqueness as a union. But could such a legacy be passed on?

CHAPTER 10

Union Power, Soul Power:
When the Solution Becomes
the Problem

"Our union is like a bed of flowers. Black orchids and white gardenias bloom side by side, and the beauty is in their togetherness."
— An 1199 delegate at the National Hospital Union's 1977 convention

From a distance, one might have expected gala celebrations in 1982 and 1983 by the National Union of Hospital and Health Care Employees to mark first the fiftieth anniversary of the former drugstore local and then the union's twenty-five years' experience in the hospitals. That these same years witnessed the inauguration of a new black leadership in both the national union and the New York district might also have been cause for rejoicing. No theme, after all, had been more important to the union's self-esteem than the social advancement of minority workers. As Leon Davis said from retirement in 1985, "There was a time . . . when promoting the union and promoting the blacks was the same." Thus, the succession of rank-and-file black leaders to fill the positions of departing first-generation officials was not merely an anticipated outcome but might well have served as the symbolic culmination of the union's commitment to social justice.

As it happened, 1199's nearly simultaneous silver and golden anniversaries passed almost unnoticed. The coordinated elevation of Henry Nicholas to the helm of the national hospital union and Doris Turner to the command of District 1199, within a six-month period, took place in an atmosphere of growing tension and foreboding. Just when it might have been looking confidently outward, the union was in fact locked in a bitter internal struggle that spurred racial and ethnic intolerance and was accompanied by violent

Leon Davis and his wife, Julia, at the national hospital union convention in December 1981, in Philadelphia, at which Davis relinquished the presidency.

incidents and a breakdown of respect for constituted procedure (and even federal law). The turmoil accomplished what no hostile hospital administrator had done: it broke the union in two, dividing the old New York base from its newer national outposts. More important, perhaps, the internal conflict seriously set back workers' organizing and negotiating positions and threatened to suffocate the 1199 spirit in a tangle of selfish interests.

The moment of trial has, in fact, been an extended one. As we write these words the leadership and direction of the original New York base of the union are still unsettled. If this chapter must therefore stand at the awkward intersection of history and political journalism, we have sought to emphasize the roots of the crisis while conveying simultaneously something of the feel and complexity of a union coming apart.

That troubles of some sort should have erupted at the end of Leon Davis's fifty-year tenure is not surprising. The problem of succession is a classic one for labor unions, particularly when passing from first-generation charismatic leaders to their inheritors. Seymour Martin Lipset notes in his Weberian analysis of union political process that "the more the power structure was organized around personal allegiance to the 'leader' the more likely it is that his death or retirement will result in major internal conflict." Like the United Steelworkers after Philip Murray or the Amalgamated Clothing Workers after Sidney Hillman, the passage of 1199 into the post-Davis years promised from the beginning to pose a serious challenge to the continuity and stability of the union structure.[1]

Nor was it surprising that the hospital workers' union should have experienced its share of racial tensions. Indeed, against the backdrop of general black frustrations despite civil rights gains, and in particular the demand for leadership and "power" by blacks within multiracial organizations, 1199 under Leon Davis had long delayed its day of reckoning. Citing raging controversies within the transit workers', teachers', and police and firefighters' organizations, a national survey in 1973 of public-sector unionism by Sterling Spero and John M. Capozzola concludes: "Perhaps the most abrasive factionalism that has become part and parcel of the internal politics of unions is racial in nature."[2]

A sensitive observer might even have predicted new frictions accompanying the belated entry of women into top union positions, although no one could have imagined their dimensions. While rarely voiced as an issue by the members, gender inequality—particularly, the heavily male majority among the union staff and exclusively male coterie in policy-making circles—set up a difficult path both for aspiring women leaders and those who sought to integrate them into the decision-making process. On the one hand, the union's democratic rhetoric raised expectations for boosting rank and filers up to the executive ranks. On the other hand, a legacy of male leadership would make it difficult for a female officer to act with the same authority as her male counterpart. A female union president, for example, would likely confront not only her own deficit of experience but the doubts of male officers and staff as to her true qualifications—except as a token reflection of an overwhelmingly female union membership. Thus, if not an inevitable source of controversy, traditional male dominance within the union power structure undoubtedly added to the problem of forming a new regime.

The irony of 1199's fate lay in the terms of its dilemma, that is, the extent to which the union was suddenly impaled on its own petard: a centralized constitution and decision-making structure, previously defended as a bulwark of stability and unity, threatened to serve as an instrument of self-destruction; and the race issue, which for years had ennobled the union by identifying it with a larger social movement, now became the centerpiece of a discourse of division and internal mistrust. In a final irony, the rank-and-file members of 1199, whose direct participation in countless confrontations with management had built a tiny local into a powerful national union, were virtually powerless to halt the process of disintegration. Time and again the unfolding events and decisions, which took place in union executive suites, courtrooms, and even international AFL-CIO corridors, did not include them.

To the extent that he had confronted the issue of leadership succession in any way prior to the late 1970s, Leon Davis, as president of District 1199 and of the national union, had adopted three principles. First, any aspirants for office would have to dutifully wait until he was ready to step down. Second, as he had done at the lower level with organizers, Davis adopted a sink-or-swim attitude toward vice presidents within their own districts. Each geographical district approached what Jesse Olson called "autonomous health care unions," responsible for administering members' problems while Davis and his circle of advisors concentrated on major contract issues, organizing strategy, and political matters. Third, Davis made it clear to those around him that his successor "had to be a black." Moe Foner remembered, "He kept saying this over and over again, that when we go this union is going to be run by blacks and Hispanics."

From the mid-seventies on, both principle and pragmatic political reality pointed to Henry Nicholas and Doris Turner as the eventual heirs. Both were drawn from the black rank and file and were concrete symbols of democratic empowerment, proof that the poorest hospital worker could indeed be "somebody." Nicholas, the former Mt. Sinai nursing attendant who had built his Philadelphia district into 1199's second most powerful geographic center, fully identified with the union's missionary role. "The struggle for us is real," he told a Philadelphia reporter in 1981. "I'm committed to die for this organization if it comes to that." Other unions, Nicholas explained, had "prostituted themselves" by not standing up to employers and political authorities. As a result, "they didn't purchase anything but their tombstones." Slight in appearance and normally soft-spoken, Nicholas expressed self-confidence and sensed the destiny of his own role. "I thought all the time I was a leader," he said in 1981. A year later he commented, "I envisioned since 1961 that I would end up where I was on December 5 [1981, the day he was installed as the national union's president] . . . I clearly understood where the struggle should be and how it should be led."[3]

Doris Turner, vice president of District 1199's hospital division and the top-ranking woman in a union that was still half black and three-quarters female, remained Davis's protégée in New York City. Even as others expressed doubts about her, worrying that she took little interest in affairs beyond her immediate domain, she maintained the confidence of the union president. "I didn't see in her what Dave [Leon Davis] did," recalled Olson. "He saw her as a fighter . . . always said the best organizers were [people who were] just like the workers." Before a delegates' meeting in 1970, Davis tellingly presented Turner as:

> the person who personifies hospital workers more than anyone, herself a hospital worker. You can see yourselves in her more than in me for she is one of you in every way, she'll be with you for many more years than I will. It's

wonderful to have leadership coming from the ranks because that's the leadership in the long run that counts. I don't intend to retire tomorrow but it's our responsibility to get new leadership and you should show them your loyalty and appreciation as she does for you every day.[4]

After Elliott Godoff died in 1975, Nicholas, in addition to his Philadelphia district vice presidency, became secretary-treasurer of the national union, next to Davis the highest-ranking officer outside New York. Forced to reckon with his own mortality, Davis confided to Olson that he planned for Turner to succeed him in New York at the appropriate time. When Davis was temporarily incapacitated after suffering a mild stroke while attending a rally outside the 1976 Democratic National Convention, Olson personally reassured Turner of her informal "annointment."

Despite an avowed commitment to rank-and-file leadership, Leon Davis hesitated for the longest time to transfer the reins of power. Aside from the bureaucratic inertia common to many long-term union regimes, Davis and his first-generation advisors held doubts as well as admiration for the rank-and-file leaders who would necessarily replace them. Dedicated, articulate, and charismatic beyond a doubt, the two heirs apparent were nevertheless flawed, in the eyes of the founders, in some vague yet vital way. As Moe Foner recalled the period, the second-generation leaders seemed not to see "the big picture." Lack of higher education or connection to a broader intellectual culture was part of what separated the newer from the older union generation. So too did the Communist party experience, with its awareness of the relationship between immediate tasks and longer-term dreams and ends. "How do you teach a world view," Foner plaintively asked, recalling the dilemma that Davis faced. "To us it was like breathing."

Those who worked closely with Davis in the 1970s saw him struggle fitfully and with increasing exasperation to "train" Doris Turner as his chosen successor. While Elliott Godoff was a gentle and patient man who had spent considerable time with both Nicholas and Turner, Davis had no such natural instincts. As one of his friends described it, his bare-boned pedagogy boiled down to "Watch me and you'll understand." When such learning by osmosis proved ineffectual with Turner, Davis added some structure, setting aside an afternoon each week for general discussions. But after awhile, according to Foner, Turner absented herself: "She was always being called out. . . . It became clear it was a hopeless thing, she was not interested. I remember [Davis] used to say it was very important to teach her that she had to read a newspaper. He wanted her to become acquainted with broader issues in the world. It never worked. More and more he began to [accept] that this is what she is." Olson considered her "lazy . . . with no political understanding." Looking back on the process, Bob Muehlenkamp blamed Davis for treating Turner as a "token" black leader: "She was not developed, and when he tried, it was too late." Privately expressing fears about the union's future leadership, Davis lay his trust in a cabinet-style governance, where old hands Foner and Olson would lend expert advice during the inevitable changing of the guard.

Henry Nicholas and Doris Turner also felt the pain of 1199's transition experience. Simultaneously celebrated as the heroic, best hopes for the future and patronized as unformed intellects, the younger black leaders held the prestige of union office without commensurate, decision-making responsibility. In one of her few public comments on the subject, Turner bitterly recalled the "standing joke" that "Jesse, Moe, and Dave ran the union driving home in the car to Queens each night."[5] Neither Nicholas nor Turner knew when—or, absolutely for sure, if—they would be called to command. According to Nicholas the two black leaders were sufficiently worried about the danger of being manipulated by whites as to make an informal pact "never to fight each other." While Turner maintained publicly that she had always "loved" Davis, tensions between them surfaced as early as the 1978 city contract negotiations. There, for the first time, a demand passionately adopted by Turner and service employees for every other weekend off (EOWO) had been placed on the table. Piqued when Davis ultimately subordinated EOWO to other contract issues, Turner sullenly distanced herself from union officers during the contract ratification proceedings. She was not forgiven this act of defiance. Meanwhile, Turner herself went quietly about the business of building a loyal district organization. "I saw it, everybody saw it," recalled Nicholas. "Everybody who did not have contempt for her intellectual ability understood it."

When Davis next faced the leadership question, following a more severe stroke in 1979, his approach had changed in two ways. Structurally, the issue of succession was now linked to a bigger project: the nurturing of a long-deferred dream for "one big hospital union," which involved the nationwide merger of 1199 with the hospital workers' division of the much-larger Service Employees International Union (SEIU). Together, the restrictive national hospital legislation of 1974, growing sophistication of hospital management, and the costs and mixed success of 1199's far-flung organizing attempts of the 1970s had convinced Davis that only a merger on the proper terms could open a new era of union advances. Combining complementary geographic strengths, the proposed merger would create the fifth largest union in the AFL-CIO and offer new leverage for nationwide campaigns. Formal discussions between Al Heaps, president of the Retail, Wholesale, and Department Store Union (RWDSU, 1199's parent organization), and retiring SEIU president George Hardy began in early 1979. SEIU vice president John Sweeney, who succeeded Hardy in June 1980 (and who happened to be a family friend of 1199 district officer Jerry Brown), played a key role in encouraging the process.[6]

Although approval at the "international" level would be required, from the beginning the objective of the negotiations was the joining of the health care units.

The merger talks quickly took on a life of their own. More swiftly than anyone expected, SEIU and 1199 negotiators worked through the labyrinthine details of organizational mechanics, finances, and projected power sharing. The smaller union's national leaders were convinced by June 1981, at the time of an 1199/SEIU health care conference, that they were on the verge of a most auspicious agreement. According to the jointly drafted proposal, creation of a new international health care division would follow immediately upon the merger of the two international parent unions (i.e., SEIU and RWDSU). Even though the SEIU, in keeping with its disproportionate size, would control two-thirds of the new division's executive board, both parties agreed to support the nomination of Leon Davis as president for the first four-year term and to back Henry Nicholas as his successor for a second term. The national hospital union was also guaranteed two vice presidents on the five-person executive board (implicitly designated for Turner and Nicholas). Organizationally, Davis and his advisors felt confident that they could stamp the new and more powerful union in their own image. The final sweetener for 1199 was financial: the SEIU would commit $3 million to the new operation, while 1199 would invest $1 million.[7]

While planning for the merger, Davis necessarily touched upon the question of leadership succession since the proposed restructuring would alter the relative authority of 1199's executive officers. The district presidency, in particular, which in the past had dominated the union as a whole, would be diluted by incorporation into a larger, more dispersed national structure. The ever-reluctant Davis was also pushed to establish his version of a future chain of command. Amid serious merger talk during the spring of 1980 he asked the union's executive council to recommend a new national president. An informal black caucus, including Doris Turner and a dozen vice presidents, reached a unanimous verdict: Henry Nicholas. With Davis's support the nomination sailed past the executive board, and Nicholas was formally elected in December 1981, having been nominated from the floor by Turner.

Such formal cooperation barely disguised a growing private estrangement between Davis and Turner. As long as the merger remained an abstraction — and such ideas had been floated about before — Turner was an uncomplaining if disinterested witness to the interunion contacts. As the process hardened, however, so did her suspicions. She knew that a merger would not only weaken the authority of the New York district but, given the ethnic heterogeneity of the national hospital labor force (as well as the SEIU's relative success in attracting professional and technical as compared to service workers) would also lessen black power within the union. A commitment from Davis in the spring of 1981 that he would nominate her for the District 1199 presidency the next year failed to stanch Turner's growing fears that an internal power play had been unleashed against her. By summer she was openly attacking the merger as a racist ploy and rallying hospital division staff to her side.[8] Davis quickly counterattacked and in a series of secret, small-group meetings at his house discussed the means by which Turner might be cut down within the critical New York district. There seemed to be no easy solution. Physically, Davis was too weak to run again for the district presidency; politically, he might lose to Turner in a racially polarized vote. The more dependable Henry Nicholas was virtually unknown in New York City and therefore not a viable candidate. So union leaders reluctantly concluded that they had no choice but to accede to a Turner presidency in April 1982, even while attempting to complete the merger agreement before that date.

The union's internal dispute quickly spilled beyond issues of personality or even policy differences. To Turner and her New York advisors, in particular, the actions of Davis and the national executive reflected racist, paternalistic attitudes they deeply resented. The "plot against Doris," which they located in the proposed merger as well as in the secret meetings at Davis's house, was proof for them that the union's black members could not trust its white leaders. Telbert King, the hospital division vice president Davis had personally recruited, viewed the internal fray as a battle between the rank-and-file forces, led by Turner, and "white leaders trying to pull the strings."

The story of David White, long-time guild vice president who bolted to Turner's side during the merger fight, reveals much about the tensions afflicting an organization built simultaneously on principles of left-wing trade unionism and black empowerment. From childhood White had learned a fierce racial pride. His father, a railroad stevedore and Mason from Virginia (the family moved to Jersey City when David was seven), "was a registered voter his entire adult life—he braved the threats and taught us always to stand up for principle." The family achieved considerable respectability in the black community, thanks to his father's steady employment and his mother's earnings as a domestic. There were many books and newspapers at home, and on Thursday nights the children regularly listened to their father read from the *Chicago Defender,* a black weekly. Politically, David White, Sr., was a follower of Marcus Garvey. His son remembered, "He never let us refer to black kinky hair as bad hair. My sisters were never allowed to have white dolls, no white pictures could hang in our house. If a calendar had a white face on it, you had to take it off. The religious pictures in our home—Jesus and his followers—were all black people." A member of a separate, "colored" railway brotherhood, the elder White was always "very bitter" toward the white craft unions.[9]

The Great Depression drew both father and son to new political commit-

David White figured in many of the power shifts that affected the New York local in the 1980s. His political mixture of Marxism and black nationalism has left him a quixotic figure, battling for "the principles that Leon Davis taught us" but against most of Davis's heirs.

ments. David joined his father in Scottsboro protests and unemployment council agitation, and in 1937, at the age of sixteen, he began a fifteen-year stint as a Communist party activist. Through Popular Front circles he began to work with whites in a common cause, while through institutions like the Jefferson School in New York City he extended his interests in history as well as art and music. During the McCarthy era White refused to be "colonized" (i.e., go underground with a new identity) and thus left the party in 1952, still maintaining a range of political contacts and interests—for example, in the company of old comrades he attended meetings organized by the Congress of Racial Equality for the first freedom rides in 1961.

Indirectly, White's radical political experience also led him to the hospital workers' union. In 1948, after being fired from the navy yard for refusing to sign a loyalty oath, White took a job as an attendant at Bellevue Hospital. With extra training he became a licensed practical nurse and found permanent employment at Manhattan's Hospital for Joint Diseases. In 1964 Local 1199 began an organizing drive at the hospital and White, recruited by his old

Communist party friend Leonard Seelig, quickly offered full support. Two years later, responding to a dare from Leon Davis ("What's the matter, you afraid?"), White joined the hospital union staff as an organizer. Within months he became an area director, helping Jesse Olson administer the technical-professional guild division.

Gradually, White began to chafe under the direction of the union's first-generation white leadership. While participating in various assignments, including the 1969 Charleston campaign, he remained in the same organizational niche. Although he never doubted the abilities of Davis and other top officers, he resented their apparent unwillingness to relinquish real authority to the black and Hispanic staff waiting in the wings. Doris Turner's rise as Davis's heir apparent at first only confirmed White's still-private indictment. In his view, Davis had built Turner up as a "puppet," effectively shielding her from criticism of her "obvious inadequacies." White felt that Turner took little interest in politics and had "no commitment to working people. . . . She'd always been that way and Davis always knew that." Still, after being indulged for so many years, it seemed to White that Turner was being punished when she finally stood up to the white leaders.[10] Thus, when Turner broke with Davis over the merger issue, White eventually came to her side. After initially attending several of the oust-Turner meetings at Davis's house, he attacked "benevolent racism" in 1199 and betrayed the meetings to Turner. "I never believed she would win," White recalled, but as a matter of basic "black consciousness" it seemed "the right thing to do."

Turner's antimerger revolt found a powerful ally in the form of Al Heaps. Although he acceded to 1199 pressure for merger discussions (hospital union members comprised more than half of his international) and expressed support for the idea in principle, he had already acted, on occasion, to delay the implementation process. Even as he expressed apparent satisfaction, in October 1981, with the creation within the proposed merger of a new executive vice presidency for himself (1199 officials said that he and other RWDSU officers also extracted salary and pension concessions) and confirmed joint convention arrangements with the SEIU for the following June, he had begun conferring privately with Turner and her antimerger staff. His first sign of open disengagement came during the December 3 session of the 1199 national convention when, two days before delegates would overwhelmingly ratify the merger decision, Heaps walked off the stage in an unexplained huff. Shortly thereafter he reportedly informed Turner's people that they would be pleased with his final position on the merger question.

On December 30, 1981, a letter bomb exploded in the RWDSU offices, severely injuring Heaps, and from his hospital bed he announced the "suspension" of merger talks. Privately, 1199's Bob Muehlenkamp believed that "Al pointed the authorities in one direction, to us." Whatever the reason for the bombing—no arrests were ever made—it stopped the merger process cold.[10] Officially, the topic remained on the table for a few months, and in March the 1199 rank and file voted 30,888 to 9,739 (including a 2-to-1 margin in New York City) for merger. Constitutionally, however, the decision rested not with the hospital workers but with the RWDSU board. In a final pitch for unity, Leon Davis followed up on his original intention and personally nominated Doris Turner for the district presidency. On the surface this was the logical culmination of many years of achievement. Yet the transfer of office in May 1982 not only closed off Davis's organizational hopes for the future but began an unraveling of the structure over which he had labored for twenty-five years.

Two years of triangulated internal warfare—involving the Nicholas-led national, Turner's district, and Heaps's RWDSU—following Davis's retirement and the collapse of the merger option revealed the weak underside of 1199. A strong centralized leadership has few self-correcting mechanisms when it veers off course, and now the union members were left helpless by the breakdown at the top. No precedent and no machinery existed by which they could humble their leaders into cooperation for the good of all. As a result, the precious unity that 1199 had, over the decades, carved out of a socially diverse drugstore and hospital labor force—a social heterogeneity that matched the larger, perpetually feuding American urban community— was left hanging by a thread. In New York City, the most important seat of power in the hospital union was controlled by Doris Turner but with less than the traditional full authority. Within the district, pro-merger (and effectively anti-Turner) people still headed the guild and nursing divisions. Meanwhile, directly competing with the district leadership, the national union represented both the figurative and material continuation of the Davis regime. Not only top staff but also most of the union's more experienced organizers had supported the merger and were perceived by the Turner forces as a destructive, insidious fifth column. David White later recalled: "We felt they would do anything to undermine her. They had all the ties to labor and political leaders and kept us from making new relationships." Even the official union newspaper was in the hands of the national union forces.

The letter-bombing added a particularly ominous, even paranoid, feeling to the deliberations of the new district leaders. White recalled that Turner provided her staff with guns for self-defense and was herself protected by an armed human shield whenever she left the building. For the first time visitors to the union's Martin Luther King Labor Center headquarters were stopped apprehensively at the door and their comings and goings carefully monitored. The daily tension between national- and district-related personnel grew so unpleasant that the national union moved in January 1983 to the old McGraw-Hill building a block away.[11]

Lacking the instinctual fealty rendered to Leon Davis, Doris Turner resorted to the encompassing powers vested in the presidential office to purify her command. One by one most officials and organizers who had sided with the merger were forced out or resigned under duress. Executive secretary Moe Foner's premature retirement in November 1982 and part-time reattachment to the national staff set a trend for many of the district's old guard. By April 1984, less than two years after the conflict erupted, ten district vice presidents and twelve of fourteen guild organizers had left. Turner herself claimed in 1985 that more than eighty staff personnel had "deserted" her administration.

The requirement of organizational loyalty, which was not entirely new for 1199, was accompanied by subtle shifts in the union's organizational emphasis and operating style. Sondra Clark, who resigned as vice president in charge of the union's nursing division, had long sensed Turner's mistrust of the skilled, mostly white RNs. Backing off from campaigns aimed at professionals, Turner instead emphasized the organizing of lesser-skilled, mostly black "home-care" workers.[12] Rhetorically, she continued to express support for the union's liberal social-political agenda. In practice, however, change toward an unqualified, interest-group pragmatism was apparent—for example, District 1199 was conspicuously absent from the city's giant "No Nukes!" rally on June 17, 1982. Whereas two years before the union had practically provided an alternate campaign headquarters for Mayor Ed Koch's left-liberal primary opponent, in 1982 Turner proposed backing Koch over the more liberal Mario Cuomo in the governor's race.[13]

Turner also shifted the terms of union culture, as the traditional cultivation of black aspirations and ethnic group pride now acquired a more predominant edge. The union president's open display of religious faith, active encouragement of Bible reading among union staff, and invocation of divine providence before contract talks, for example, provided a striking contrast to the secular language of American left-liberalism spoken by the union's former leaders. Establishment of an 1199 gospel chorus, with a repertoire departing from the union's customary labor-folk songs, represented another innovation of the Turner years. When combined with the dislocation of veteran staff and surrender of a left-leaning politics, Turner's style suggested a turning away from movement unionism toward a combination of black nationalism, business unionism, and an ethnic political clubhouse.[14]

Totally outmaneuvered by Turner and her rapid consolidation of district control, the union's old guard quickly sensed its impotence. Within months of his retirement Davis spoke with a mixture of indignation and remorse of the transformation of District 1199. He castigated Turner's style as a divisive and phony "put-on" and, fearing the loss of union principles, sadly acknowledged that "the frustration that blacks had for the role of leadership was something that I underestimated." Jesse Olson asserted that Turner knew her "blackness" made her invincible: "That's her trump card that paralyzed us." Even Davis grudgingly admitted, "If we were victims, we were victims of our own strategy." In fact, neither Turner's visceral identification with a majority of union members nor her political retrenchment in the Ronald Reagan era was likely to undermine her position in New York. As Pearl Cormack, a Turner loyalist and union activist since 1959, put it, "We believe in her. She's a fighter who grew up with her people."[15]

The struggle for power between district and national leaders reached its peak at the December 1983 national convention in Philadelphia. In the weeks leading up to the meeting, pressures to line up the New York delegation behind a Turner challenge to Henry Nicholas's presidency were intense. Turner loyalists, as David White later explained, sought to "drive out" their opponents—"to intimidate them, discredit them with the members, and if that don't work then to withhold their checks." Dennis Rivera, an elected guild division vice president and chairman of the union's Latin caucus, witnessed some eighty staff members swear individual oaths of allegiance to Doris Turner at the annual November district staff retreat. According to Rivera, the union president herself spoke of a coming struggle in which there would "be blood all over the place." During the same period district financial comptroller Roy Anderson resigned his position and sought protection from the courts and the labor board for anonymous telephone threats on his life. He claimed that his problem began with a "Jew pay-docking list," which he said Turner had ordered him to devise as a means of withholding checks from her Jewish political enemies within the union. "People called me a Nazi and gave me this Heil Hitler salute," Anderson reported. Then came the direct threats. He was in no position to say, or discover, whether they were from Turner friends or opponents.[16]

One of the last holdouts from the Leon Davis era was guild director Jesse Olson. Forced by Turner's opposition into an embarrassing runoff in the 1982 district elections, Olson became a lone opposition voice in an ever more polarized situation. With New York area organizer Eddie Kay he took satisfaction at the Philadelphia convention in assembling just enough pro-Nicholas votes among the New York delegation to deprive Turner of the national presidency. Shortly after the convention, however, unnerved by telephoned threats on his life and feeling powerless in his job, Olson resigned, twenty-five years to the day after he had come on staff.[17]

Alongside the tensions between the district and national staff loyalists, a battle raged between the national and the RWDSU. Following his own antimerger stand in early 1982, Al Heaps sought to forestall a possible unilateral move toward merger by the hospital union and generally to neutralize the national's influence within his international. After pushing through constitutional changes that repealed the secession rights of affiliates and facilitated international imposition of "trusteeship" over financially errant locals, Heaps announced in October 1983 his intention to dissolve the hospital workers' union altogether and divide its members into RWDSU locals. A week before 1199's Philadelphia convention, Heaps appointed RWDSU vice president Lenore Miller as temporary trustee to assume control of 1199 finances, prompting the national union's workers to physically bar her entrance to union headquarters. After the U.S. District Court threw out as spurious Heaps's charges of mismanagement of 1199's Strike and Defense Fund, the RWDSU president announced plans for a special July 1984 convention to restructure the union on his terms. The national responded by initialing its own trusteeship clause—a warning to Doris Turner—by countersuing the international, and by authorizing Nicholas to initiate secession moves, whatever the consequences. When the AFL-CIO executive council rejected 1199's request for a separate international chapter in February, the union prepared for the second time in its history to enter labor's wilderness and go it alone, outside the federation.[18]

Further legal complications were occasioned by the April 1984 district elections in New York, the first truly contested officers' race in the union's history. When Turner announced a 13,000-vote margin of victory over a pro-merger slate, opponents charged that the tallies had been rigged to avoid a runoff election occasioned by the actual loss of both guild and nursing divisions. District vice president David White (who replaced Olson as guild director) publicly counterattacked Turner's opponents as "racists" and dismissed their charges as ludicrous. In addition to its still-boiling legal and constitutional imbroglios, a union that had long been acclaimed for the selfless motivation of its leaders now faced the prospect of an extended Department of Labor election fraud investigation.[19]

Brought to a standstill by its internal tug-of-war, the organization Al Heaps labeled "a two-headed monster" finally succumbed to formal division. With tacit approval from the AFL-CIO, the RWDSU agreed in early May to allow the national to disaffiliate and establish its own international charter, within the labor federation. At the same time District 1199 in New York was permitted to detach itself from the national it had itself created, returning as of July 1, 1984, to its old status as Local 1199 of the RWDSU. While some sections of the national hospital union were reportedly upset with the division settlement, national president Henry Nicholas summed up the toll of two years' turmoil with an appeal to the membership, "Let's get on with it!" Within a year, despite financial belt-tightening and some cuts in organizing staff, the national was again reporting steady, if unspectacular, membership growth, with organizing successes in Pennsylvania, Ohio, and scattered sites around the country. Still, there were limits to what could be done with decreased resources. A union that recognized togetherness as the only winning strategy and soul power as a crucial complement to economic organization had come apart in racial animosity and mistrust.[20]

For New York 1199 president Doris Turner the July 1984 expiration of the citywide contract with the League of Voluntary Hospitals, coming on the heels of the settlement within the union, provided the opportunity to do battle with the bosses and reunite Local 1199 members. Substantial contractual gains, particularly something beyond the 4-percent-per-year increase negotiated only weeks before by the national hospital union in Rochester, New York, would help to legitimize and even distinguish the new chief officer. If the union could combine a hefty monetary advance with a symbolic, qualitative breakthrough, such as Turner's long-sought EOWO, then the 1984 contract might measure up historically against Leon Davis's famous $100-a-week contract of 1968. Furthermore, with a citywide round of municipal union negotiations set to follow the hospital talks, Turner and the union could set the pace for hundreds of thousands of public employees.

But there were minefields to cross on the way to a hospital contract. Hospital employers, represented by their league, were in no mood for major breakthroughs on the labor front, and the new governor, Mario Cuomo, was anxious to contain the state health budget. With 90 percent of the contemporary hospital budget deriving from state funds, a "cost trend factor," which was determined by the state's Department of Health and anticipated only moderate wage increases based on an assessment of hospital income, had established the parameters for no-strike contracts in 1980 and 1982. In 1984, however, the governor, through state health commissioner David Axelrod, refused to specify the factor in advance of negotiations. Under these circumstances the hospitals placed tight limits on their negotiators: go no higher than 4 percent per year and tie raises to certain union financial "offsets" (i.e., union absorption of partial contract costs). The hospitals resisted the union's EOWO demand and offered only the administratively more flexible twenty-six weekends off. On July 13, with the two sides far apart, Doris Turner ordered nearly 50,000 union members at forty-one institutions to begin the nation's biggest single hospital shutdown ever.[21]

From the beginning the inexperience and lack of preparation of the new union leaders showed both in the strike's formulation and execution. Treating the contract as a personal test of will, Turner had not even called her executive council together to agree to the terms or provide direction for the strike. In addition to an improbable 10-percent annual wage increase, the union doggedly pursued formal EOWO enactment, even though 80 percent of its members already enjoyed the benefit in practice. The very mechanics of the strike were uncharacteristically rough: picket signs were not ready when the strike began and one member of Turner's negotiating team later related that he and others had spent the prestrike evenings frantically blotting out the national hospital union insignia on 1199 hats. The traditionally dramatic display of worker strength and mastery of public relations were also absent. Picket lines were skimpy at many hospitals, according to widespread reports, and throughout the conflict no clear message of union intent ever appeared in the press. While the union had never been able to sustain elaborate strike benefits, there was, this time around, little relief of any kind offered to the strikers. Specific administration lapses marred the hospital shutdown, including oversight of a ten-day filing notice by 200 striking nurses in Far Rockaway, Queens, which resulted in more than $600,000 in fines against the union. Prestrike frustrations within the nursing division deteriorated during the strike and prompted four requests by nursing groups for union decertification.[22]

As the strike dragged on into August, the union, without any apparent reason for optimism, stubbornly clung to its maximum set of demands. Nineteen days into the strike Turner had rejected an offer that the *New York Times* called a "real 4%" (without benefit freezes and givebacks) as a "terrible insult." She attacked hospital management as "cruel, greedy, wicked, rich, and spoiled." The hospital league warned after the collapse of an apparent compromise on August 20 that it "now appears impossible to conclude an agreement with the present leadership and structure of this union." The hospitals' threat to hire permanent replacements and widespread signs of demoralization among the strikers served to move the strike fitfully toward resolution, though twice in late August Turner rejected agreements hammered out by city mediator Basil Paterson.[23]

Finally, on August 27, before 20,000 members gathered at Madison Square Garden, Turner endorsed a strike-ending two-year agreement. With the throng cheering wildly, the union president pointed with pride to management's acceptance of EOWO and a 5-percent-annual wage increase. Triumphantly Turner added, "we didn't give back a thing . . . nothin'." Alluding to a freeze on minimum salaries for new hires and a lower entering wage for probationary employees, she modified her upbeat tone only slightly: "We traded some things we didn't need for something better but we didn't give back." City union leader Victor Gotbaum echoed the hospital workers' leader, calling the settlement a "clear victory for Doris Turner."[24]

The giveback issue proved much more complicated than hospital workers had reason to suspect. Unknown to all but a few union members, to end the strike Turner had not signed a real contract but rather an incomplete "agreement" that left out important pieces of the financial puzzle. There would, in fact, be no contract until the union committed itself to making up a hospital income shortfall occasioned by the settlement. Norman Metzger later explained that management's bottom line from the first days of the strike had "remained the same," and to get the 5-percent settlement Turner had agreed to choose from a list of offsets (mostly union benefit deferments) estimated at $29 to $45 million, depending on the state's final cost trend factor. League president William J. Abelow noted that, in the end, the union effectively accepted the same financial deal it had spurned earlier. The hospitals would not begin to honor EOWO or pay raises until Turner publicly completed her part of the deal. "It turned out," said Metzger, who had dealt with 1199 since 1959, "that the union was a paper tiger. But paper tigers don't usually go into battle, they go to the brink of battle."[25]

Turner, who presumably had hoped to tie up the giveback issue in prolonged postsettlement negotiations, was caught short by the hospitals' public hard line. While she insisted on August 29 that "the contract is in force now; its immediate implementation is contractually clear," the union president seemed incapable of further action. An exhausted rank and file, which had just sacrificed 13 percent of its annual income on the strike, was not about to walk out again. Indeed, when the hospitals "rationalized" their practices with hundreds of layoffs during the following weeks, the union stood by, powerless to act. Politically, the embattled union leader could not easily take responsibility for a deal she had called a "sham" only weeks before. So the stalemate persisted for months. As late as March 1985, without a penny of wage increases yet having been paid, Turner's annual report to the membership referred to the strike as a struggle of "love, respect and commitment for each other," resulting in a "5% wage increase, Every Other Weekend Off and no givebacks," an example of "trade unionism at its very best."[26]

At least twice before—in New York in 1959 and in Charleston in 1969—the hospital workers' union had limped home from major strikes only to turn apparent adversity to its own advantage. In 1984, however, neither momentum from the ranks nor creativity at the top helped transform defeat into victory. The strike had seriously tarnished 1199's reputation among the membership as well as the general public. With the Turner regime retaining firm control of the administration, by the end of 1984 most signs pointed to a period of slow but irreversible decline for the hospital workers' union.

Under these circumstances the poststrike defection of one of Turner's chief lieutenants was barely noticed. Appalled at what he considered the misdirection and cynical manipulation of members during the strike, David White, director of the guild division and district executive vice president, did not appear at the Madison Square Garden victory rally. He turned in his resignation, effective September 1, and for several months thereafter kept his own counsel, allowing his departure to be imputed to medical causes. However, White's own constant reflections on his career with the hospital workers and what had happened under the new leadership brought him close to the brink of open rebellion. He had chafed at the signs of growing political conservatism, anti-intellectualism, and self-seeking corruption within the district staff, but the strike had been the final straw. White claimed the strike was a strategic "disaster" waged for no other reason than Turner's own image, and it made him physically sick. Nor could he justify the workers' tireless exertions: "For the first time in my life I was ashamed to look at the members."[27]

Bitter in his retirement White struck back at Turner and the local leadership: he went public—in November 1984 to a Department of Labor examiner and in January 1985 to the press—with details of ballot tampering in the contested district officer election the previous spring. In a sworn statement White described the events he "witnessed in the early morning hours of May 7" at the union headquarters "under the supervision and direction of Doris Turner." He alleged that after securing the building union officers formed a human chain, passing ballot boxes from the auditorium where they had been sealed to the elevator. Then, in an upstairs conference room, attended by fourteen or fifteen staff members, the boxes were unlocked and emptied. "Whenever we got a ballot for slate two [the opposition] we'd just throw that away and take a substitute ballot and mark a slate one and include that ballot. Now, you would leave some, because it would look funny if you took them all." Discarded ballots were carted away in plastic garbage bags, while the "new ballots were slipped into the ballot boxes and returned to the auditorium." Triggering the first competitive presidential runoff in the union's history, the opposition votes from the guild and nursing divisions would have been a setback for Turner at a moment of keen intraunion factionalism. "I imagine," explained White, "she felt that [by winning in the first round] her position as a leader would be more secure."[28]

White's charges, confirmed by three other participants, ultimately led the Department of Labor to press for a new election (the only remedy under the law for union voting fraud). Their immediate effect, however, was to plunge the New York union even more deeply into the pits of personal backbiting, centralization, general demoralization, and public relations damage control. Insisting that "we won the election fair and square," Turner called White a "desperate liar" and suggested that he had received a payoff: "I'm told he's running around in a new Lincoln Continental." While expressing a desire to refute all the charges, Turner continually put off requested federal inspection of the suspected ballots until ordered to do so by a federal appeals court in June 1985. In the meantime she pushed through a series of constitutional bylaw changes, including a lengthening of the presidential term and radical reduction in the number of elected union officials. Finally, in a move that undoubtedly served to shore up support from the international, Local 1199 agreed to give up its traditional cut-rate dues assessment (which had allowed it to cover organizing and administrative costs) and pay full per capita dues (an additional $2.5 million) to the RWDSU. Internal opposition to such measures was shunted aside in an atmosphere of increasing intolerance and even physical intimidation.[29]

With her formal powers enhanced, Turner acted boldly to "go out and sell her case" to the public. Flanked by the RWDSU's leaders and Washington-based public relations consultant Victor Kamber, she aggressively struck back against David White and his supposed allies. Ideologically, the counter-attack had two themes: race and communism. First, the pre-Turner union was pictured as a stable of a decrepit white paternalism. RWDSU secretary-treasurer Lenore Miller stated at a press conference. "I guess they [Davis, Foner, et al.] figured that if a group of white Jewish pharmacists do something so altruistic as organizing black women, who's going to question anything they do afterwards?" Kamber asserted simply, "A group of white boys lost power and they don't like it." The early leaders were characterized as not merely white liberal do-gooders but vintage Stalinists of the conspiratorial kind. "You have to remember," said Al Heaps, who for twenty-five years had welcomed Leon Davis's troops into the international union, "that was an old-left union. I'm talking Communist left-wing, all the way." Kamber insisted publicly, "They put ideology before trade unionism," and Turner commented in an interview, "I think he [White] was probably on the other side [a Communist] all along. I think they had him looking in on me."[30]

While Turner might delay the verdict on White's charges, she could not ignore the clear outcome of the 1984 strike: she had not delivered the goods. Agreeing to a Department of Labor–supervised election in April 1986, she struggled in vain to extract some face-saving compromise regarding the "missing 5 percent"—the second half of a two-step raise the workers had never received—from both the hospitals and the state. Governor Cuomo showed no sympathy for a labor politician who had not only backed his Democratic rival but increasingly cozied up to conservative Republicans.[31] Similarly, the voluntary hospital league, which might have been expected to promote the weak and inexperienced status quo within the union, displayed no such inclination. Turner's refusal to uphold the 1984 agreement apparently made even the specter of renewed union strength look better than anarchy in hospital industrial relations.

Forced to turn over union documents to opposition attorneys alleging misuse of funds, the beleaguered president's aides admitted that certain records had already been subpoenaed by a federal grand jury empaneled by the corruption-busting office of U.S. Attorney Rudolph Giuliani. The focus of attention was the union-controlled Ardeon Realty Company, the transfer of $2.4 million from Local 1199 to the RWDSU, and the issuing of $204,739 in checks made payable to cash and a $4,740 payment for groceries. Turner managed to obtain a delay in the federal lawsuit (since she could not use union attorneys or funds to defend herself), but her public image had suffered yet another blow.[32]

The combination of circumstances offered unique opportunity to Turner's opposition. Building on a nucleus of 1984 "slate two" insurgents, the "Save Our Union" coalition formed in November 1985 and nominated Georgianna Johnson, a fifty-five-year-old black social-work assistant, for the union presidency.[33] Raised in Ware Shoals, South Carolina, by her grandmother, who took in laundry for a living, Johnson attended college for one year then left to get married and to move to New York. In 1967, after becoming a Medicare case aide, she took advantage of the union's training and upgrading program and at the same time assumed an active role as a union delegate. A calm, low-keyed presence, Johnson self-consciously separated herself from her charismatic predecessors: "I'm not a person who kicks over the table and I'm not a revival-type leader." Rather, she promised to be a "team" player who would rely heavily on the executive council. Even as she prepared to take on Turner, Johnson expressed sympathy—mingled with criticism—for her beleaguered foe: union leaders had "underestimated" Turner and at the same time "let her go too far—maybe that's the white man's way of dealing with a black woman." Johnson noted that "Doris sat there for twenty-seven years" and "now all that [hostility] is coming out."[34]

In an energetic campaign, Johnson visited scores of hospitals and promised a respectable contract from management and restoration of democratic accountability within the union. Flanked by an ethnically balanced slate of officers—six blacks, four Hispanics, and three whites—she tied the future of Local 1199 to the national union. "Every union that is strong in the country has organized the whole industry," she argued. "I want to follow the idea of Leon Davis and organize health care workers from top to bottom. From doctors to janitors. That's how you acquire power." Davis himself came out of retirement in Florida to campaign with the challenger. Most of the union's long-time friends held to a diplomatic, public silence during the campaign (though many privately contributed to the insurgents via Moe Foner). Actor and civil rights activist Ossie Davis was one supporter who openly declared his allegiance at a Johnson rally: "I cannot in good conscience stand by and see what should be one of the major weapons in our struggle being sullied and soiled and left unused."[35]

Doris Turner was uncharacteristically subdued and nearly unavailable to hospital workers and the press during the campaign. "She didn't say anything," recalled Telbert King. Dismissing Johnson's candidacy as a "front" for "the National Union and the white folks," Turner effectively rested her campaign on the twin themes of racial solidarity and personal loyalty. Her paid staff and professional public relations specialists did not have much to work with. Even a last-minute appearance by the Reverend Jesse Jackson on Turner's behalf—in which Jackson compared her toughness under fire to that of his own mother—failed to stop the inevitable. The largest voter turnout in the union's history helped Johnson unseat Turner, 18,972 to 16,039.[36]

Local 1199 officers, elected on the Save Our Union opposition slate, are sworn in by RWDSU president Al Heaps, in June 1986: (left to right) RWDSU secretary-treasurer Lenore Miller; Heaps; 1199 president Georgianna Johnson; 1199 secretary-treasurer Eddie Kay; 1199 vice presidents Dalton Mayfield, Dennis Rivera, Aida Garcia, Angela Doyle, Betty Hughley, Marshall Garcia, Katherine Abelson, Carlton Yearwood, Harold Curtis, Sylvia Grant-Guiterrez, Frederick Gilliam, and Eustace Jarrett.

The newly installed 1199 leaders had their work cut out for them. Internally, the delegates and organizing staff were in disarray, a function both of the election upset and the previous two years' strife. In June, for example, just before Turner stepped down, only 300 of 1,500 delegates attended a required meeting. Despite public appeals for support of the new leadership by Coretta Scott King, Jesse Jackson, and even Governor Cuomo, old wounds still festered. For months to come a vocal minority of service workers would interrupt union meetings with chants of "Doris! Doris!" Externally, the new president faced September negotiations with the hospitals. To extract the "missing" 5-percent pay hike, the union again tried to capture the moral high ground of contract debate, linking fulfillment of management's 1984 commitment to the commandment "Thou Shalt Not Steal." A local media campaign castigated league-affiliated hospitals while praising John Cardinal O'Connor and the archdiocese of New York, which had already reached a separate agreement with the union for "living up to their ideals of fairness and social justice." However, union leaders, while publicly assertive and self-righteous, were limited by the unwillingness of the membership to risk a strike under any circumstances. "You sent us out with a rubber sword," Georgianna Johnson later told them.[37]

Fortunately for Johnson and the hospital workers, neither the employers nor the state sought to rub salt in union wounds. Negotiations were among the most controlled—on both sides—in years. The governor's office helpfully insisted that the hospitals did indeed have the resources to afford a wage settlement, while the league's president complimented the new union leaders on their "professional" and "responsible" decorum. On October 12, without great fanfare, Johnson spoke for a 400-member rank-and-file negotiating committee in announcing settlement terms: union members would receive 5-percent "back-pay" in a pre-Christmas lump sum and could anticipate a 13-percent wage increase spread over a three-year contract. In return, as a rhetorically downplayed "offset," employers would reduce their contributions to union pension and training and upgrading funds. For a union in disarray and previously without a contract, the agreement, according to one Mt. Vernon x-ray technician, was "the best we could get." However, executive vice president Dennis Rivera described the contract as merely "satisfactory . . . [it] gives us time now to rebuild the union."[38]

The new faces at Local 1199 took steps during the following year to restore the union's faded presence in the workplace and resurrect its old political luster. Hundreds of new delegates were trained by an augmented education staff, and an election victory in February, in Middletown, New York, secured the union's single largest RN unit to date. Meanwhile, Georgianna Johnson acted on her promise to bring the union "back to where we used to be: number one in social activism." In 1986 the union hosted the Nicaraguan health minister and Chilean resistance leaders; at the same time it offered full support to Governor Cuomo's easy re-election bid as well as to the losing Senate candidacy of liberal Mark Green. Johnson herself presided over union-led protests against the December 1986 racist beatings and death in Howard Beach; and the new leadership also promoted the mobilization of a thousand-member delegation to the April 1987 demonstrations in Washington, D.C., against South African apartheid and U.S. policy in Central America. In parallel moves on the cultural front, support was withdrawn from the Turner-endowed gospel chorus, tribute was paid to long-time supporters Ossie Davis and Ruby Dee, regular exhibits in the 1199 gallery were reinstituted, and plans were made to renew theatrical programs in the hospitals.[39]

Outwardly, then, by the beginning of 1987 the hospital workers' union appeared to have weathered an extended leadership crisis. In New York, a division of labor imposed by necessity if not by choice on an inexperienced president and staff suggested that a more democratic if somewhat chaotic leadership style was replacing the traditional deference to centralized authority. There were hints of change in the national union as well. National secretary-treasurer and New England district president Jerry Brown, for example, publicly identified the "problem of member involvement" in the union, criticized a "staff and officer-centered" approach that tended to "suffocate rank and file leadership," and called for experiments with new decision-making structures. Similarly, after a disappointing election showing among state mental health para-professionals in Ohio, the national organizing director, Bob Muehlenkamp, authored a tough, thoroughgoing assessment of the union's strengths and weaknesses, prompting long-time observers to express hope that a chastened organization was gradually recovering its sense of direction if not (yet) its old strength. There was even excited, if informal, talk of reunification.[40]

Inwardly, however, all was not well. Tensions resurfaced similar to those that had waylaid the Turner regime. The basic problem was acknowledged on all sides: Georgianna Johnson led the new slate of officers in name only. It became apparent that she lacked the experience and temperament necessary for organization building, contract negotiations, financial dealings, and public as well as internal leadership. A dedicated delegate, she had been hoisted atop the anti-Turner slate as one of the few available candidates of her race and sex, though she clearly lacked the charisma of her two predecessors and even failed to carry her own hospital in the race against Turner. Once in office, she readily assented to the collective leadership of the new executive council and relied in particular on the union's veteran secretary-treasurer, Eddie Kay, to coordinate most of the nuts-and-bolts tasks of administration. Faced with caring for her ailing mother while she herself recovered from a mild stroke suffered during the campaign, Johnson was neither physically nor emotionally prepared for the exhausting workdays expected of her.

Within the first six months of the new regime tensions were evident; by the end of the second six months they were out of control. To her colleagues Johnson appeared increasingly irresponsible, even unreachable. She neglected the content of her duties (she suspended tutorial sessions setup for her benefit and missed critical delegate meetings) and clung steadfastly to the symbolism of her office, demanding a chauffeur and complaining about her salary. While continuing to represent the union "abroad," the president increasingly appeared irrelevant and ineffectual at home. She was helpless, for example, when one of her aides, Noni Perry, resigned under executive council presure. Union administrative assistant Gerry Hudson acknowledged, "People stopped going to Georgianna for leadership; it could not have been easy for her." To her fellow officers the union president, as Rivera later put it, seemed to have gotten in "over her head." She had become an "embarrassment."[41]

All the while, problems rooted in the union's economic position as well as its past internal political conflicts continued to fester. A liquidity crisis involving the benefit and training funds and a lack of experienced organizers and delegates heightened dependence on outside "experts," including some recruited from the national union, and further exacerbated the racial division of labor within the local. In her appearances at delegate meetings Johnson repeatedly faced verbal harassment and ridicule from recalcitrant Turner supporters for her figure-head role. Eventually, through meeting with other union presidents, Johnson came to realize how little power she actually wielded. In May 1987, at an Amityville, New York, staff meeting, she claims it struck her that she "was never meant to run 1199" but rather to serve as a "conduit" for others. Although she had never projected herself as a strong leader, Johnson began to rebel against the "advice" and indirect authority doled out largely by the men around her. At some point she became convinced that a plot was afoot to force her to resign; and she heard rumors that she was "incompetent," a "mental patient," and an "alcoholic." One day, she says, she even found a voodoo doll in her desk. But the final blow was her colleagues' insistence on bylaw revisions, in tune with their campaign pledges, that would sharply reduce the formal power of the president. A package of sixty constitutional amendments—including the creation of a home care division, election of organizers and rank-and-file delegates to the executive council, and a requirement that the executive council approve all policy decisions—was approved, 12 to 2, by the executive council on September 4 and submitted to the membership at large. Like Doris Turner before her, Johnson had by this time come to view her situation in racial and ideological terms. And like her predecessor she decided to fight back.[42]

Virtually isolated within the local leadership (she could count on only one other vote within the executive council), over the summer of 1987 Johnson discovered new allies. The first and most powerful was Lenore Miller, elected president of the RWDSU after Al Heaps's death in 1986. Miller, never a friend of 1199's old guard, was engaged in merger talks with the United Food and Commercial Workers Union and had good reason to be wary of a hospital local that comprised more than half her 140,000-member international bent on reunification with the national hospital union. Therefore, out of more than sisterly feeling the RWDSU leader quickly offered sympathy and material support to Johnson. For immediate help in day-to-day affairs Johnson hired the retired firebrand David White as her "special assistant." White unhesitatingly analyzed the problem in the local as one of "racist structures" and a "power-mad" Eddie Kay, the one white male on the executive council and the man Johnson admits was responsible for getting her to run for office in the first place. Through Miller, Johnson also brought in the Washington-based legal firm of Jules Bernstein (a business associate of Victor Kamber, who had worked earlier for the RWDSU and Turner forces). A moderate socialist with strong anti-Communist views, Bernstein added to the analysis of racism and power politics an open suspicion of Communist party influence and general "Stalinist" tactics within the executive council.[43]

Emboldened by her new advisors, Johnson acted to assert all of her formal constitutional powers. When the council vetoed her efforts to bring legal counsel to board meetings, rejected her attempts to take control of the union budget and personnel, and even convened without her approval, she filed suit. The internal contradictions of the union's governing principles were never so exposed as in the ensuing thrusts and counterthrusts of a gathering army of labor lawyers. On the one hand the constitution charged the president with far-reaching responsibilities, including the power to call all meetings, appoint all non-elected staff, sign all documents, and cosign (along with the secretary-treasurer) all checks. On the other hand it vested the executive council with the power to "formulate policy," authorize disbursement of union funds, and offer a "binding" interpretation of the constitution. Consensus and/or clear-cut political clout had long overridden any potential fight over the union's formally ambiguous division of powers. A generally passive council had never caused trouble for the president during the Davis years, and under Turner any show of independence was met by a reminder that the president had the power to field and elect her own slate of candidates. In short, there had never before been an opening for the "colonels' coup" that developed in 1987.[44]

While the case against Kay et al. languished in court (a decision never was rendered on the conflicting constitutional claims within the union executive), Johnson and her opponents battled on other fronts. The executive council hurried to get membership approval of the new bylaws, which Johnson's attorneys immediately protested, claiming a lack of due process in the referendum and specifically citing the refusal of council officers to print the president's column in the monthly union newspaper. Then, in late September and at Johnson's initiative, Lenore Miller formally sought to remove Eddie Kay from office as Local 1199 secretary-treasurer, citing both general dereliction of duties and specifically charging Kay as a "dual unionist" who intended to unhitch Local 1199 from the international in order to resurrect the 1199/SEIU merger. With Solomonic discretion, U.S. District Court Judge Robert Sweet temporarily enjoined the move against Kay while requiring that equal time and space be given in official union publications to Johnson's views on the bylaws and inner union crisis. An early, less than professional leaflet denouncing the proposed bylaw changes also attacked Kay and suggested the passions of Georgianna Johnson and her defenders: "This man is evil, he is poison. . . . As a racist and a communist, he hates Black women . . . [and] uses black men to do his dirty work."[45]

Two other factors heightened internal tensions by the time the constitu-

A message to Local 1199 members:

Ossie Davis
Ruby Dee
Paul Robeson, Jr.
Leon Davis

*We Hold These Truths
To Be Self-evident:*

- A more democratic '1199' means a stronger '1199'.

- Greater rank and file participation will help '1199' play a more effective role in the fight for social and economic justice.

- Those who raise the issue of 'racism' in this vote are creating a smokescreen to avoid the real issues.

That's Why We Urge 1199ers

VOTE YES
On the Proposed
Constitutional Amendments

Issued by: 1199 Officers, Staff, Delegates and Members to Save Our Union.

VIOLENCE?	¿VIOLENCIA?
DICTATORSHIP?	¿DICTADURA?
FINANCIAL RUIN?	¿RUINA FINANCIERA?
FACTIONALISM?	¿FACCIONALISMO?
WASTED RESOURCES?	¿RECURSOS DESAPROVECHADOS?
DISGRACE?	¿DESGRACIA?
POLITICS OR TRADE UNIONISM?	¿POLITICA O SINDICALISMO?

Georgianna Johnson
President

LOCAL 1199
Drug, Hospital and
Health Care Employees
Union, RWDSU/AFL-CIO

310 West 43rd Street,
New York, N. Y. 10036
(212) 582-1890

Election mailings to 1199 members from opposing sides during the bylaw referendum, October-November 1987.

tional balloting occurred in late October. First, an October 8 guild delegates' meeting was interrupted by a shoving match between pro- and anti-referendum factions. In the melee the beleaguered president, among others, was sent sprawling. While Johnson participated in the meeting once order was restored, she later entered St. Clare's Hospital complaining of severe neck pain and ultimately charged Eddie Kay with assault. Despite Kay's protestations of innocence (the Manhattan District Attorney's Office later dropped all criminal charges against Kay on grounds of insufficient evidence), a lasting image of violence and abusive behavior—highlighted by a newspaper photo of the union president in traction—hung over the executive council on the eve of the election. "Stop the violence. Vote no," intoned Johnson's mailing to all 1199 members.[46]

Second, Doris Turner returned to the union, declaring that "1199 is the soul of my being" and that she could "not stand by when I could help the union in a time of crisis, no more than a mother can watch her child be torn apart." In her own time of troubles Johnson had slowly come to a new appreciation of the leader she had displaced. "I understood," she confessed, "why she did what she did, why she was angry and autocratic. She had to be 'cause they didn't want her." Johnson also recognized that she possessed little political base of her own within the union and needed any allies she could get. On October 26, just days before the start of the balloting, Turner, now a presidential "special assistant," appeared with Johnson at a news conference to openly oppose the bylaw changes. Both Johnson and White (still condemned by Turner loyalists as "the man who stabbed Doris in the back") insisted that whatever misdeeds Turner had committed paled in comparison to the present state of "plantation-style" management of the union.[47] However, the executive council, on the defensive because of the violence issue, jumped to take aim at a familiar target. For many union members Turner still represented the chief source of the union's era of troubles—"Doris Turner is bad news," the *New York Amsterdam News* quoted one union staffer. The reform forces, in a final mailing before the bylaw vote was taken, barely mentioned Johnson; rather, a visibly worried nurses' aide asked, "Doris Turner negotiating *my* next contract? No way!"[48]

By a slim 600-vote majority, out of 26,500 ballots cast, union members adopted the proposed constitutional changes. The anti-Johnson council members thus managed to effect the proposed structural reforms and save their own positions, gaining new leverage in their power struggles with both their president and the RWDSU. Partly to salvage her own merger negotiations with the Food and Commercial Workers Union, Miller agreed to an entente with local leaders within two weeks of the ballot count. By terms of the formal settlement she would drop efforts to dismiss Kay and abandon trusteeship plans in exchange for at least the short-term organizational loyalty of the local. The biggest loser, of course, was Georgianna Johnson, who refused to accept a postelection "deal" from executive council antagonists (the main item, reportedly, consisting of a hefty salary increase) and was left out in the cold by Miller. "She abandoned me like all the other whites," the local president reflected bitterly. "When everybody comes together and they all white, you're in trouble. I don't trust anybody, anymore."[49]

Union reformers in the Leon Davis tradition had hung onto power, but the old guard had barely survived and at considerable cost. Voting in the bylaw referendum was down a full 25 percent from the presidential poll a year and a half earlier, suggesting the degree of rank-and-file alienation from the entire leadership, and those who did vote reached no clear consensus. Workers at the biggest hospitals in the city—Columbia–Presbyterian, Beth Israel, Montefiore, Mt. Sinai, and Brookdale—were virtually deadlocked, with less than 75 votes separating the two sides. Even more problematic, the tally suggested deep racial cleavages in the organization. The most heavily black Brooklyn hospitals, for example, had produced large pluralities in Johnson's favor, while mostly white Long Island institutions had backed the constitutional reforms. The hospital division, Doris Turner's former base, appeared to be totally at odds with the executive council; indeed, the executive council could not meet a constitutional requirement to hold a general delegate assembly in 1987 for fear of provoking a riot. Even while cleaning up from its last fight, the local faced the prospect of renewed turmoil during its next scheduled officer elections in 1989. In the meantime, devoid of power or meaningful influence, President Johnson daily shut herself in her office, taking private succor from a hand-painted biblical invocation, "If God be for us who can be against us?"[50]

In a formal sense, champions of the old 1199 tradition had something to cheer about in 1988. The "good guys" had won another political round and legal challenges to executive council rule appeared to be collapsing. However, for those whose connection to the hospital workers' union dated back to Montefiore and the strike of 1959, as well as those who identified not only with Davis but with the spirits of Elliott Godoff and Martin Luther King, Jr., exhaustion and an air of sadness were perhaps more likely. The dream of a strong and united hospital workers' movement seemed as distant as ever, and the debris of the past several years made it very difficult for either Local 1199 or the National Union of Hospital Workers and Health Care Employees to lead the way. Speaking amid the Turner debacle in 1985, District 65-UAW president David Livingston expressed a widely felt sense of 1199's lost promise: "What could be worse than a busted Stradivarius?"[51]

In reviewing the issues that sent a once-proud social organization into a downward spiral, we are struck by the larger questions raised as well as by the impact—for good or ill—of individual will and personality. Aside from the principals involved, the heirs to Leon Davis were in no position to "deliver the goods"—and thus ensure rank-and-file-support—as the union patriarch had done for decades. The effective "socialization" of hospital costs, together with the new stringency of state cost controls, deprived the New York–based union of any major material advances. The reality of rising living costs and restricted contract settlements, most obvious in Doris Turner's 1984 "phony 5%" contract, had been felt since the 1976 Gootnick arbitration award. Even after Turner, union reformers could not easily restock the cupboard. With the organization still reeling from the effects of the 1984 strike, tensions between Georgianna Johnson and her "cabinet" arose in part because no one could address rising membership complaints of declining pay packets (measured against the cost of living) and deteriorating union benefits. In truth, neither Davis nor Turner nor Johnson could politically negotiate in the frigid economic climate of the late 1980s according to the 1199 legacy of "mass militancy equals prosperity."

Other issues might have served to unite the membership in a generally hostile economic and political climate. For the long term, perhaps the most ominous developments were those affecting the hospital industry itself. With increasing restrictions on public funding, the 1980s witnessed a dramatic trend toward proprietary (private-for-profit) control of health care institutions. A wave of mergers placed a growing proportion of the nation's health care—and health care workers—under the management of a few large chain operations virtually untouched by unionization. In the meantime, nonprofit institutions, fighting a rearguard action against their aggressive corporate competitors, were themselves bending before the stiff winds of cost containment and general market pressures. Fixed governmental reimbursement rates and more efficient technologies combined to shorten hospital stays, while suburban "Doc-in-the-box" clinics challenged the large institutions for specific services, prompting a nationwide threat of massive layoffs and even the closing of many hospitals.[52] Had worker (as well as union staff) frustrations been turned against management instead of union leaders, internal fratricide might never have occurred. But New York City's voluntary hospitals made a poor, uneven target for the rebirth of union enthusiasm. Indeed, generally assuming a low profile throughout the period of intraunion strife, these semipublic employers seemed to have learned all too well the lessons Mark H. Maier ascribes to the city's public sector labor relations: it is easier (both politically and administratively) to govern with a relatively weak and bureaucratized union than with no union at all.[53]

Aside from wringing economic concessions from employers, "organizing the unorganized" had traditionally provided the magic elixir for upholding the 1199 spirit. Although the possibilities in that direction at the national level remained considerable, they were severely restricted within the New York metropolitan area. The well-publicized fight on behalf of homecare workers hinted at a yawning "underclass" of health care workers, but the physical dispersal of this potential constituency made it an unlikely source of a new union "crusade." Neither were professionally minded RNs, the most obvious alternate target group, likely to harken to the long-running brawl within the hospital workers' union. Here, of course, was the cruelest dilemma of the 1986 split between Local 1199 and the national union: while the national faced the contemporary challenge of new growth and classic trade union engagement with precious few resources, its natural base ("We're their children," plaintively noted one national delegate in 1987) was devouring itself in internecine quarrels.[54]

Among the powerful "outside" agents acting on the hospital workers' situation one cannot overlook urban racial antagonism and general political fratricide, particularly as they operated in New York City. In important ways the deterioration of spirit and the leadership crisis within 1199 mirrored events within the city's public culture as a whole. The powerful ideological currents that in the late 1960s overcame the tendency toward ethnic factionalism in New York politics dissipated in the 1970s. Beginning in 1977, under the municipal regime of ex-reformer Ed Koch, the moral purpose as well as the common interests that had loosely bound a liberal-minority electoral coalition utterly came apart (foreshadowing a rout of the liberal electoral coalition nationally during the Reagan years). A period of conservative political hegemony and general social quiescence was also one of savage ethnic infighting and growing racial mistrust. Writing on "New York racism in the 1980s," Nicolaus Mills declared: "If Howard Beach proves anything, it is that New York City's vaunted recovery from near bankruptcy has left blacks and whites further apart than ever. In the 1980s blacks and whites in New York don't just find it difficult to act in concert. They are not even sure that a lynching strikes them with equal horror."[55]

Race polarization and stagnation of the public-sector economy combined to spell disaster for the peculiar political and social coalition that was 1199. In many ways the achievements of the hospital workers' union may be seen as a slightly radicalized version of the more general liberal-black political advances of the 1960s and 1970s. The union had been built on a tripod of class-combative workplace militancy, establishment liberal sympathy, and the willing sacrifices of a minority rank and file. But now, amid the fiscal crisis of the state, the radical leaders' old economic formulas no longer worked. Similarly, liberal pieties meant little under the Reagan and Koch administrations. As living standards slipped and neighborhoods deteriorated, many middle-class spokespeople for the black community reacted, as Jim Sleeper has poignantly reported, by "withdrawing into a cold, internal, often largely unspoken separatism." Sleeper's representation, at once assertive and suspicious, of the new mood among blacks who had heretofore trusted in coalition politics seems to apply as well to the loyalists of Doris Turner in Local 1199: "Why should blacks allow white liberals and the left to keep using them as stalking horses for compromised and or hopeless agendas? Aren't both liberal pieties about racial integration and leftist dreams of progressive, interracial coalitions ultimately dead ends? And for that reason isn't liberal and left solicitude toward blacks just another dimension of racism itself?"[56]

It would have taken uncommon leadership and a measure of good luck for a multiracial union like 1199 to prosper in the political and racial climate of the 1980s. As it happened, the union—particularly the New York local—has had neither. Thus, black union leaders like Doris Turner, and later Georgianna Johnson and David White, treated white union antagonists as if they were occupying colonialists, racially bent on keeping blacks from any say in union affairs. Meanwhile, the political heirs to the Davis tradition, both black and white, tried studiously to ignore the race issue. Yet they undermined their credibility by publicly stating that leaders were chosen based on competence and personal integrity while privately paying heed to racial and ethnic considerations. Twice in two years the Davis loyalists appealed to the rank and file to reject the counsel of leaders they themselves had chosen. With no acknowledged sense of their own culpability, the old guard asked the members to strike down Turner and then Johnson, in one observer's words, as "evil women who sprang spontaneously from the bowels of hell." Was it any wonder that internal bonds of loyalty to and trust in a once-proud tradition were coming apart?[57]

Tattered as it had become, however, the vision vested in the Davis heirs still carried more integrity than any available alternative. The black ethnic challenge to the old leadership, for its part, appeared ready to use any ally, and any excuse, to seize power for personal again. With a notable lack of inner consistency and commitment, the banners of racism, anticommunism, and union democracy were waved at the opposition on every available occasion. Politically, the black leaders made curious friendships among conservative white unionists at the top of the local's international affiliate. Just as Turner had found succor from the RWDSU's Al Heaps, so Georgianna Johnson later turned to Heaps's successor, Lenore Miller, for financial and political support. Indeed, the structural connection to the international, an expedient arrangement hatched during the drugstore union's flight from McCarthyism, in the end proved something of an albatross. In the 1980s the lackluster international appeared determined to hold onto its golden step-children in Local 1199; and after 1986, it desperately feared reunion of the local with the national hospital union. While apparently short of the necessary muscle to break up or take over ("trustee") 1199—options RWDSU leaders have threatened on more than one occasion—the international, through its compromise settlement with executive council leaders, has at least temporarily scuttled any chance for a nationally powerful amalgamation of health care workers. To be sure, by the end of 1987 there was no place else—short of a risky, expensive, and doubtlessly endless legal process—for Local 1199 "progressives" to go. These apostles of labor as a social movement found, in the end, that the dominant structures of American trade unionism were almost as hostile as any employer.[58]

We suspect that, as a solution to the internal problems of the New York local, the internal constitutional changes mandated by the November 1987 referendum promise only partial relief. The "weak-president" model of the new bylaws—so unlike the model of the Leon Davis years—may or may not stand the test of time. Meanwhile, even at its best the leadership training potential of the constitution's grassroots democracy features will not manifest itself for several years. Most important, however, these structural revisions, even while they offer new avenues for rank-and-file participation and certainly place a firm check on presidential authority, fail to solve the problem of centralism in an organization of 80,000 members. Without provisions for an elected "chief delegate" at each hospital or elected area directors, there is still no structural accommodation to pluralistic power centers within the union and little place for leaders of the future to spread their wings.[59] Communication as well as decision making will still be formulated in a room at the top, even if a few more individuals are let through the door. As in most unions, the articulation and organized expression of dissenting opinion is seldom encouraged; yet because it is considerable, it will either be contained or it will explode.

Whatever the heuristic value of its bylaws, the union, if it is to save itself, must make another kind of "constitutional" change. Quite apart from its formal structures of leadership, decision making, and public presence, Local 1199 desperately needs to rediscover and then nurture the bonds of mutual respect among its members and officials. The "beloved community" that made the early civil rights movement a powerful moral as well as political force in American life has long since dissipated, but its lessons of tolerance, power sharing, and leadership by example need not be lost. Alternatively, a union that has identified itself for years with progressive social movements and whose membership is over three-quarters female might do well to heed one of the elementary lessons of the women's movement. Aside from what it does—contracts, elections, strikes, and so on—the union is what it is, day-to-day, for the people involved in it. Like most other organizations that must define themselves in a male-oriented political world, 1199 has largely failed, recently at great cost, to apply its larger political humanism to its own internal processes. For an organization that has done righteous battle on so many fronts, it would be cruelly ironic if the message "The personal is also political" were its epitaph.

Yet no one should write off 1199's future too quickly. The fate of the hospital workers' union has always been intricately bound up with the interaction of a social vision, a dynamic industry, and a changing social and political landscape. For a considerable time the combination of strategic leadership and boisterous rank and file was able to effect dramatic changes for a previously forgotten sector of the American working class. Despite its troubles, in 1988 the union continued its vanguard role in the American labor movement by its actions on two fronts. First, it led a vigorous political campaign on behalf of the city's 60,000 home health care workers, successfully lifting minimum wages a whopping 42 percent over two years. Union attorney and black political leader Basil Paterson likened the home

Home care workers at a City Hall rally, September 1987.

care contract to the "1950s when Local 1199 . . . [brought] an underpaid army of predominantly black and Latin hospital workers out of the shadows of poverty."

A second sign of life occurred during the U.S. presidential campaign. The national union was the only union in the country to break an AFL-CIO directive and endorse Jesse Jackson for president, while Local 1199 not only endorsed the black activist candidate (with Dennis Rivera coordinating the citywide Latino campaign) but turned an entire floor of its offices over to Jackson for his statewide campaign headquarters. For Jackson's national campaign director, Gerald Austin, the experience was, as he recalled in a letter of gratitude, something of a homecoming: "As you know, I sort of grew up in 1199 where my mother, Mary Austin, worked in the Finance Department for more than 30 years. (And is still active as a retired member.) As a kid, I attended 1199 holiday parties, as a teenager I participated in the Union's Teen Time, and while in high school I marched on 1199 picket lines during the hospital organizing crusade." For those like Austin, happily associated with the union in a high-energy moment, it seemed that Local 1199 was "once again on the road to building the kind of union that made it Dr. King's favorite."[60]

In a larger sense 1199's crisis in the 1980s is one that perhaps ultimately besets every progressive crusade. Beyond the era of movement building and the elan of the grassroots struggle, how does a democratic organization function effectively while maintaining a commitment to first principles? One union's experience suggests that the test comes not only at the workplace, in the streets, and around the bargaining table but also during the long hours of desk work and interminable staff meetings in the front office; and that it is mounted not only over great issues of collective welfare but also over countless unpredictable questions of daily conflict. As with other struggles for human progress, the history of the hospital workers' union mixes instances of personal heroism with individual smallness and moments of collective triumph with tragic setback. Nothing suggests that its future will be less complicated.

Notes

Introduction

1. Seymour Martin Lipset, "Review of Stanley Aronowitz, *Working-Class Hero,*" *New York Times Book Review,* Dec. 11, 1983, p. 3.

2. Charles M. Rehmus, "Labor Relations in the Public Sector in the United States," *Public Employment Labor Relations: An Overview of Eleven Nations,* ed. Charles M. Rehmus (Ann Arbor: University of Michigan Press, 1975), p. 22.

3. The best of the new social histories of American medicine include: Barbara Melosh, *The Physician's Hand: Work Culture and Conflict in American Nursing* (Philadelphia: Temple University Press, 1982); Morris J. Vogel, *The Invention of the Modern Hospital* (Chicago: University of Chicago Press, 1980); Susan Reverby and David Rosner, eds., *Health Care in America: Essays in Social History* (Philadelphia: Temple University Press, 1979); Susan Reverby, *Ordered to Care: The Dilemma of American Nursing, 1850–1945* (Cambridge: Cambridge University Press, 1987). A recent work with some focus on nonprofessionals is Patricia Cayo Sexton, *The Nightingales: Hospital Workers, Unions, and New Women's Issues* (New York: Enquiry Press, 1981). Useful recent analyses of the hospital industry with implications for the labor force include: Thomas Barocci, *Non-Profit Hospitals: Their Structure, Human Resources and Economic Importance* (Boston: Auburn House, 1981); Amarjit Singh Sethi and Stuart J. Dimmock, eds., *Industrial Relations and Health Services* (New York: St. Martin's Press, 1982); Frank A. Sloan and Bruce Steinwald, *Hospital Labor Markets: Analysis of Wages and Work-Force Composition* (Lexington, Mass: D. C. Heath, 1980). The pioneering radical critique of the American health care system is Barbara and John Ehrenreich, *The American Health Empire: Power, Profits and Politics* (New York: Vintage, 1970). A further extension of this New Left perspective is in John Ehrenreich, ed., *The Cultural Crisis of Modern Medicine* (New York: Monthly Review Press, 1978). For a more reformist yet systemic approach, see Irving J. Lewis and Cecil G. Sheps, *The Sick Citadel: The American Academic Medical Center and the Public Interest* (Cambridge, Mass: Oelgeschlager, Gunn and Hain, 1983).

4. One of the few scholarly labor histories to reach into the recent period is Ronald W. Schatz, *The Electrical Workers: A History of Labor at General Electric and Westinghouse, 1923–60* (Urbana: University of Illinois Press, 1983). An important union history is Jewel Bellush and Bernard Bellush, *Union Power and New York: Victor Gotbaum and District Council 37* (New York: Praeger, 1984). For the contemporary period, see also Stanley Aronowitz, *False Promises: The Shaping of American Working-Class Consciousness* (New York: McGraw-Hill, 1973) and *Working-Class Hero: A New Strategy for Labor* (New York: Pilgrim Press, 1983).

5. For an important exception, see August Meier and Elliott Rudwick, *Black Detroit and the Rise of the UAW* (New York: Oxford University Press, 1979). See also Robert Korstad, "Daybreak of Freedom: Tobacco Workers and the CIO, Winston-Salem, North Carolina, 1943–1950" (Ph.D. diss., University of North Carolina at Chapel Hill, 1987).

6. Karen Brodkin Sacks's *Caring by the Hour: Women, Work, and Organizing at Duke Medical Center* (Urbana: University of Illinois Press, 1988) offers a pathbreaking case study of connections between daily work culture and union mobilization within a black and female labor force.

7. The first year's oral interviews were conducted on a contractual basis with the union for the sum of $6,000, split between the authors. That payment represents the first and last time during the course of the project that we were ever directly employed or remunerated by the union.

Chapter 1

1. John S. Gambs, "Hospitals and the Unions," *Survey Graphic* 26 (Aug. 1937): 435 (see also pp. 435–39).

2. Paul Starr, *The Social Transformation of American Medicine* (New York: Basic Books, 1982), p. 335; Adrian J. Menichetti, "A Study of Labor Unions: Their Impact on the Voluntary Non-Profit Hospital" (master's thesis, Xavier University, 1969), p. 5; Norman Metzger and Dennis D. Pointer, *Labor Management Relations in the Health Services Industry: Theory and Practice* (Washington, D.C.: Science and Health Publications, 1972), pp. 7–8, 11.

3. In New York City, for example, by 1957 gifts and private endowments accounted for only 10 percent of voluntary hospital revenue; Blue-Cross third-party payments accounted for nearly 30 percent; and direct patient payments and other insurance claims accounted for a full 40 percent of hospital revenue. The balance was derived from a city subsidy of indigent patients (10 percent) as well as other miscellaneous sources. *New York Times,* May 17, 1959; Metzger and Pointer, p. 7; "Report on Healthcare Workers and the Industry" (prepared for SEIU/1199 Joint Healthcare Leadership Conference, June 1981).

4. Starr, pp. 179, 338.

5. Ibid., pp. 177–79.

6. Metzger and Pointer, p. 15; testimony of Kenneth Williams, American Hospital Association director, "Hearings before the Committee on Education and Labor re.

Extension of Coverage to Laundry, Hotel, Restaurant, Bar and Hospital Workers," House of Representatives, 87th Cong. 2d sess., Oct. 22–26, 1962.

7. Metzger, p. 12; Myron D. Fottler, *Manpower Substitution in the Hospital Industry: A Study of New York Voluntary and Municipal Hospital Systems* (New York: Irvington, 1972), pp. xix–xx, 32, 63, 88.

8. Gambs, p. 436. In an interview with the authors, former Mt. Sinai Hospital director Dr. Martin Steinberg recalled that approximately one-third of the service workers at Mt. Sinai were on public welfare in the late 1950s. See also Williams testimony.

9. Gambs, p. 435. The Puerto Rican influx was, of course, a direct consequence of the postwar "modernization" of the island. In 1940, 61,000 Puerto Ricans lived in New York City; by 1960 the figure was 430,000. Department of Labor (New York State), *Manpower Directions, New York State, 1965–1975*, Special Bulletin No. 241, pp. 3–68. In 1969 black and Spanish-American workers composed 80 percent of the service and craft departments at Montefiore Hospital, 79 percent at Beth Israel, 70 percent at Mt. Sinai, 86 percent at Brooklyn Jewish Hospital, and 66 percent at Misericordia. See Judith Layzer, "Ethnic Survey of Hospital Employees: New Occupational Possibilities" (New York City, Office of the Mayor, Jan. 1970), p. 9.

10. Starr, p. 149. At least as it relates to the unskilled employee, Starr's generalization that "as the hospital has evolved from household to bureaucracy, it has ceased to be a home to its staff, who have come to regard themselves as *no different from workers in other institutions*" (emphasis added) is too schematic. See also Charles S. Bunker, "A Study to Determine the Impact of Unionization and the Threat Thereof on New York City's Voluntary, Non-Profit Hospitals, 1959–1966," (Ph.D. diss., George Washington University, 1968), pp. 21–22.

11. U.S. Department of Health, Education, and Welfare, Public Health Service, Bureau of Health Manpower, *Health Manpower Perspective: 1967* (Washington, D.C.: GPO, 1967), p. 45.

12. *1199 News*, Sept. 1970 (excerpt from *New York Magazine*, July 27, 1970). For the sake of consistency we cite the union periodical as *1199 News*. Its formal name has changed slightly over the years: in the 1950s, *1199 Drug News;* beginning in January 1959, the hospital division published *Local 1199 Hospital News*, which in July 1959 became *1199 Hospital News;* in June 1966 the two papers merged as *1199 Drug and Hospital News*, becoming simply *1199 News* in January 1972. With a split in the union in 1984, *Local 1199 News* re-emerged in New York City. Our references are to the national hospital publication, unless otherwise stated.

13. Ronald L. Miller, "Collective Bargaining in Nonprofit Hospitals" (Ph.D. diss., University of Pennsylvania, 1969), p. 18; Leo B. Osterhaus, "Labor Unions in the Hospital and Their Effect on Management" (Ph.D. diss., University of Texas, 1966), pp. 42–44, 59. With regard to his national survey Osterhaus notes, "A limited number of isolated attempts occurred prior to 1959. However no significant movement existed until the much-publicized drive in the hospitals of New York City in 1959" (p. 46).

14. Gambs, pp. 436–37; E. M. Bluestone, "A Labor Program for Hospitals," *The Modern Hospital* 43 (Apr. 1937): 48 (see also pp. 43–51).

15. A LaFollette Committee investigator had himself collected labor espionage

reports from the trash of the Railway Audit and Inspection Co., the antiunion detective agency. One report, dated August 10, 1936, from the "Jewish Hospital" reads:

> Today I overheard Bert, a porter in the A.A. Building asking Anna (a red-headed girl on the seventh floor serving room) if she was going to the meeting tonight. She said "yes." However, I didn't hear anything else . . . about it. I asked members about [it], but they were not aware of a meeting.
>
> After dark I walked by the union meeting room and [the] hall was lighted up, and shortly after I met Steve and Anna walking back to the hospital, accompanied by two others who I couldn't identify, due to the darkness.
>
> It seems to me that of late the leaders are becoming more secretive. They do not go around talking about the union matters as openly as they were doing when I first came. Now when there is something they want to discuss they go off into a corner. In the dining room they all sit at the same table usually—that is, Steve, John Spleen, Jim Graham, and his brother Leo, Tommy the houseman, and Jimmy from the engine room—but all they talk about is the Olympics, etc.
>
> Regarding the regular members, they don't bother their heads about the union except to read the circulars when they are distributed.

Hearings, "Violation of Free Speech and Rights of Labor," Subcommittee of the Committee on Education and Labor, U.S. Senate, 74th Cong., 2d sess., pt. 1: "Labor Espionage and Strikebreaking," Aug. 21 and Sept. 22–23, 1936 (Washington, D.C.: GPO, 1936); *New York Times,* Feb. 9 and 11, Mar. 9 and 16–18, July 27, Aug. 10, Sept. 23, 1937. Beth Israel Hospital administrators reportedly agreed to wage increases after talks with the Association of Hospital and Medical Professionals and the Maintenance Employees Union. At Brooklyn Jewish the union nucleus was known simply as the Hospital Employees Union, although it may have been part of the organization calling itself the Association of Hospital and Medical Employees of Greater New York, which early in 1938 announced a merger with the State, County, and Municipal Workers Union. *New York Times,* Jan. 10, 1938.

16. Harry Millis and Emily Brown. *From the Wagner Act to Taft-Hartley* (Chicago: University of Chicago Press, 1950), p. 399; Glenn W. Miller, *American Labor and the Government* (New York: Prentice Hall, 1948), pp. 267, 278–87, 363.

17. No reprisals, except a frozen salary, were ever taken against Elliott Godoff, and his twelve years at Maimonedes were, according to his wife, Lillian, and other witnesses, marked by a most ambivalent connection to the hospital administration. "They liked him [personally] even if they hated what he stood for," she said.

18. Many of the early UPWA leaders, nevertheless, would prove quite successful in subsequent careers. President Jack Bigel, for example, became a powerful financial consultant and pension plan expert for the city's trade union establishment. Ewart Guinier, the young secretary of Local 444, would first sell bonds and ultimately emerge as an important figure in the black studies renaissance, with a faculty position at Harvard University.

19. Letter, Elliott Godoff to "Dear Member," Nov. 24, 1953, National Union of Hospital and Health Care Employees Records, 1937–76, Labor-Management Docu-

mentation Center, Cornell University, Ithaca, N.Y. (hereafter cited as 1199 Archives). Letter, Henry Feinstein to Maimonides Hospital Employees, Nov. 1, 1957, 1199 Archives. The tone of benevolent solicitude toward Godoff quickly turned icy when Local 237 allegedly discovered that he had spread the word to his many hospital contacts across the city to give up their Teamster affiliation and join Jerry Wurf's District 37 (on the grounds that only he was serious about organizing). Feinstein actively but unsuccessfully petitioned Leon Davis of Local 1199 to fire his new staff member, Godoff, for "unconscionable treason." Letter, Feinstein to Davis, Oct. 3, 1957; telegram, Feinstein to Godoff, Sept. 4, 1957, 1199 Archives.

20. While others around the union have spoken openly of their former Communist party ties, Leon Davis has always defined his early political experience in vague terms. In interviews with the authors, for example, he once referred to the time he was forced (for the union's good) to leave the party, but he never talked about when he had joined it. Leon Davis interview, June 5, 1979.

21. David Kaufman interview, May 26, 1977.

22. "Leon Davis, Fifty Years of Leadership", *1199 News* 17 (Mar. 1982): 7. For the larger political context for interracial unionism under the Popular Front, see Mark Naison, *Communists in Harlem during the Depression* (Urbana: University of Illinois Press, 1983), pp. 255–78.

23. Leon Davis, "Report to the Distributive Workers Union," Dec. 4, 1950, 1199 Archives.

24. See Leon Davis's remarks at a store chairmen's dinner, Oct. 8, 1947, press release "Drug Affairs—Miscellaneous", 1199 Archives.

25. Leon Davis, "Report to the Membership," Oct. 1, 1947, 1199 Archives; "Investigation of Communism in New York City Distributive Trades," transcript of hearings, Special Subcommittee of the Committee on Education and Labor, House of Representatives, 80th Cong., 2d sess., Aug. 4, 1948, Washington, D.C.; Leon Davis interview, June 5, 1979.

26. "Statement of the Committee That Accompanied President Davis to the Hartley Committee Meeting, Wednesday, Aug. 4th, 1948, in Washington, DC," Davis Papers, 1199 Archives.

27. Jesse Olson telephone interview, May 27, 1985.

28. Leon Davis address re Negro History Week, Feb. 18, 1951, 1199 Archives; Theodore Mitchell interview, March 16, 1976; Davis address, National Pharmaceutical Convention, Aug. 7, 1951, 1199 Archives.

29. Proceedings of the DWU Founding Convention, Feb. 4–5, 1950, New York City, copy in 1199 Archives; Murray Kempton, "Osman the Obscure," *New York Post.* June 2, 1950; Letter, Arthur Osman re DPOW merger, Oct. 13, 1950; report on Local 1199 submitted to Osman, DPOW, Dec. 4, 1950; Leon Davis, report on DWU Convention 1950 to 1199 members; letter, Walter Reuther to Irving Simon, president of RWDSU, and Arthur Osman, president of DPOW, May 13, 1953, statement by Max Greenberg, president of RWDSU, AFL-CIO, re history of 1199 and RWDSU, June 8, 1960, 1199 Archives.

30. Letter, Reuther to Simon and Osman, May 13, 1953; statement by Greenberg,

June 8, 1960. This view of 65–1199 relations was confirmed in an interview with David Livingston, District 65 president, June 23, 1977.

Chapter 2

1. See Dorothy Levenson, *Montefiore: The Hospital as Social Instrument, 1884–1934* (New York: Farrar, Straus and Giroux, 1984), esp. pp. 7–33, 146–200. In the thirties, Bluestone recruited key staff officers from among Jewish refugees from Nazi-occupied Europe. His own social commitments, including a passionate opposition to America's basic fee-for-service medical tradition, attracted like-minded young physicians. About his one-year residency at Montefiore in 1937, in the midst of Spanish Civil War passions, Martin Cherkasky quipped that the "house officers were divided into two groups: half of them were at the hospital and half of them were at Madison Square Garden for the rallies" (ibid., p. 164).

2. Levenson (p. 205) offers a quantified index to changes at Montefiore, 1944–54: average stay in wards dropped from 160 days to 60; admissions up 1,725 to 7,119; major operations up 256 to 1,827; x-rays up 12,602 to 109,309; lab tests up 21,689 to 170,193. In 1958 Montefiore qualified as a large hospital with 638 beds.

3. *New York Times,* Nov. 21, 1958.

4. See letter, Herbert H. Lehman to Victor S. Riesenfeld, [1958], "Montefiore Hospital" folder, 1199 Archives.

5. See A. H. Raskin, "Politics Up-ends the Bargaining Table," in *Public Workers and Public Unions,* ed. Sam Zagoria (Englewood Cliffs, N.J.: Prentice-Hall, 1972), pp. 122–46. Victor Gotbaum ("Collective Bargaining and the Union Leader," in Zagoria, p. 86) writes: "New York City passed a collective bargaining law in 1958. Upon my arrival in 1964 I was under the erroneous impression that collective bargaining was at a mature stage in the city. . . . The city had no negotiating team."

6. Leon Davis to Martin Cherkasky, Nov. 28, 1958, 1199 Archives.

7. Robb K. Burlage, "New York City's Municipal Hospitals: A Policy Review" (Washington, D.C.: Institute for Policy Studies, 1967), pp. 29–52. By 1966 the $200 million from the city's Department of Hospitals required for affiliation agreements constituted 25 percent of the department's budget, while payments to voluntary institutions and medical schools combined claimed 40 percent of the municipal health budget. Requests for municipal reimbursement for city-change payments at voluntary hospitals in the period 1957–64 rose 40 percent (ibid., pp. 435, 436b, 436c).

8. See Levenson, pp. 201–31; "Empire Survey (II): Einstein-Montefiore Bronxmanship," *Health-Pac Bulletin,* April 1969. By 1980 the number of employees at Montefiore had risen to 7,000 (Levenson, p. 203).

9. Martin Cherkasky, "Why We Signed a Union Agreement," *Modern Hospital* 93 (July 1959): 69–70. Levenson (p. 208) comments re Cherkasky's early awareness of new health care financial realities: "He rapidly realized some of the essentials of the hospital business. Like a hotel, a hospital can't make money from empty beds. Heating and lighting an empty ward costs as much as doing the same for a full one. On

the other hand, the coming of insurance as the mainstay of hospital financing made thrift a vice, not a virtue. The reimbursement system did not favor an institution that saved money. A hospital was reimbursed for the money it spent. If it cut its per diem costs, the reimbursement was also cut. He also realized that the days of loose regulation on the part of the insurance companies would not last, that he would take advantage of the existing situation."

Chapter 3

1. General Council Minutes, December 3, 1958, 1199 Archives.
2. *1199 News,* Mar. 26, 1959.
3. David Montgomery, *The Fall of the House of Labor: The Workplace, the State, and American Labor Activism, 1865–1925* (Cambridge: Cambridge University Press, 1987), p. 2.
4. *New York Post,* May 10, 1959.
5. The use of the Jewish expression, along with the peculiar meaning implied here, is linguistic evidence of the syncretism of New York City working-class culture. Nowhere would the mutual borrowing and redefinition of cultural styles and symbols among blacks and Jews likely be more complex than in the hospital workers' union.
6. *RWDSU Record,* Feb. 1959; Executive Council Minutes, Jan. 12 and 26, Feb. 9, 1959, 1199 Archives.
7. *New York Herald Tribune,* Mar. 6, 1959; *New York Times,* Mar. 17, 1959; *Business Week,* Mar. 21, 1959; *New York Daily News* and *New York Times,* Mar. 26, 1959; *New York Post,* Mar. 27, 1959. No more was heard from AFSCME until the end of June, when Local 302 authorized an ill-fated walkout at Brooklyn Hospital on the heels of 1199's strike settlement.
8. *Local 1199 News,* Jan. 15, 1959.
9. Letters dated Mar. 19 and 24, 1959, to Federation of Jewish Philanthropies and Montefiore Board of Governors, Montefiore Medical Center files (names of correspondents withheld at the request of Martin Cherkasky). Mt. Sinai, for example, initially deferred action on the union's request on the grounds that it must first give full consideration to "the profound implications [of union recognition] for the sick and needy patients in our hospital." *New York Herald Tribune,* Mar. 7, 1959; *New York Post,* Mar. 3, 1959; *New York Daily News,* Mar. 5, 1959.
10. Martin R. Steinberg, "Guest Editorial," *Hospital Management* 87 (June 1959): 26.
11. Executive Council Minutes, Mar. 23, 1959, 1199 Archives; *New York Amsterdam News,* Mar. 14, 1959.
12. Local 1199 leaflets, Mar. 10, Apr. 2, 1959, 1199 Archives.
13. Dan Wakefield, "Victims of Charity," *The Nation,* Mar. 14, 1959, pp. 226–29.
14. Taylor was admitted to the negotiating team only as a representative of the Central Labor Council, not directly from 1199. Executive Council Minutes, Apr. 18, 1959, 1199 Archives.
15. The Mt. Sinai board of directors included, among others, Alfred L. Rose of

Proskauer, Rose, Goetz and Mendelsohn; Sheldon R. Coons, an owner of Pepsi Cola; Robert Lehman of Lehman Brothers; and Edwin C. Vigel, a director of the C.I.T. Financial Corporation.

16. Beth Israel Hospital, *Annual Report, 75th Anniversary Edition* (1964).

17. In additional to a close, personal friendship with Frances Cardinal Spellman, Silver gave liberally to Catholic charities. He was honored as vice president of the Alfred E. Smith Memorial Foundation, which, among other things, subsidized St. Vincent's Hospital in Lower Manhattan. *New York Times,* May 13, 1959.

18. L. M. Kahn to Local 1199, undated, 1199 Archives.

19. *New York Times,* May 6, 1959.

Chapter 4

1. *New York Herald-Tribune,* May 10, 1979.

2. The strikers did receive sympathy, and occasionally tangible support and contributions, from individual nurses and residents. Annette Scheider Fisher, former staff nurse and supervisor at Beth Israel, complained in a letter to Local 1199 that nurse's aides in the voluntary hospitals were generally "stepped on and degraded as if they were nothing. . . . *These are human beings* and must be treated as such," she wrote in May 1959, endorsing the strike. The only public demonstration of support from members of a hospital house staff was a letter from Brooklyn Jewish Hospital interns denying their administration's claim that patient services during the strike were perfectly "normal." *New York Times,* May 17, June 10, 1959.

3. *New York Post,* May 12, 1959; *New York World-Telegram,* June 1, 1959.

4. *Strike Bulletin,* no. 2 (May 1959). The bulletin, published approximately twenty times during the strike, in English and Spanish, was a one- or two-page special edition of the regular union periodical, *1199 News.*

5. *New York Times,* May 9, 11, 13, 22, 1959.

6. Ibid., May 18, 1959; *New York Journal-American,* May 19, 1959.

7. *New York Daily News,* May 21, 1959. To be sure, the court judgments proved to be of only limited utility to the hospitals. Once Davis was sentenced for contempt, it technically required only a formal order of commitment from hospital attorneys to have him arrested. But the hospitals feared that jailing the union president would only exacerbate the strike situation and make compromise impossible; as such, all the court orders in the world were hollow threats. Still, it would be inaccurate to suggest that the legal strategy served no useful purpose for the employers. Court costs and appearances acted as a continuing drain on union energies and resources, and the threat of jail introduced an element of uncertainty among the union high command. In addition, the judgments against the union may have had a marginal political impact. For example, after Davis was sentenced for contempt the *New York Times,* which had been reasonably balanced in its denunciation of the behavior of both sides, issued an editorial entitled "This Strike Is Illegal."

8. *New York Times,* June 13, 1959.

9. *New York Tribune,* May 22, 1959; *New York Post,* June 4, 1959.

10. Arnold Beichman telephone interview, January 16, 1976.

11. *New York Times,* May 22, 1959.

12. *New York Times,* May 18, 1959; *Strike Bulletin,* No. 11 (May 24, 1959); "Food Contributions," box 46, 1199 Archives.

13. "Hospital Strike Support," report submitted to New York City Central Labor Council by Local 1199, July 15, 1959, box 47, "Strike" folder, 1199 Archives; *Electrical Union World,* July 1, 1959.

14. *New York Times,* Mar. 27, Nov. 21, 1958; May 2, July 9, 14–31, 1959.

15. Ibid., May 24, 1959; C. Vann Woodward, "Introduction," in Bayard Rustin, *Down the Line: The Collected Writings of Bayard Rustin* (Chicago: Quadrangle Books, 1971), pp. ix–x.

16. "Statement Issued by the Citizens Committee for a Just Settlement of the Hospital Strike," box 47, "Strike" folder, 1199 Archives.

17. Letter from Oakley C. Johnson, *1199 News,* Oct. 1959.

18. *New York Post,* May 26, 1959.

19. *New York Times,* June 13, 1959.

20. *Minutes* of a special meeting, 1199 General Council, May 20, 1959; *Minutes,* 1199 Executive Council, June 3, 1959, 1199 Archives.

21. *New York Daily News* and *New York Times,* June 19, 1959.

22. *New York Times,* May 26, 1959.

23. "Report of the Special Committee to His Honor, Robert F. Wagner, Mayor of New York City . . . , June 8, 1959," box 47, "Strike" folder, 1199 Archives.

24. Ibid.

25. *New York Times,* June 14 and 16, 1959; "Mayor's Memorandum of Understanding of the Statement of Policy of Concurring Voluntary Non-Profit Hospitals Based on the Understanding Reached with Mayor Wagner on June 1959 in Connection with the Discontinuance of the Strike," June 19, 1959, 1199 Archives.

26. Ibid.

27. "Union Proposals," box 48, 1199 Archives; *New York Times,* May 16, 1959.

28. *New York Times,* Mar. 26, 1959. The Toledo settlement was drawn up in December 1956 by local attorney Edward Cheyfitz after two unsuccessful organizing attempts by electrical and building maintenance workers at Toledo hospitals. Stopping far short of union recognition, the plan established an employees committee elected by secret ballot in each hospital to present problems to hospital administrators, mandated a uniform grievance procedure in each hospital, and created a community board of appeals. Toledo unions effectively backed off from their organizing efforts, tacitly agreeing not to place union representatives in the hospitals and offering a no-strike, no-walkout, no-slowdown pledge. *Hospital Topics,* Sept. 1959.

29. *New York Times,* June 23, 1959.

30. Minutes, 1199 General Membership Meeting, June 22, 1959, 1199 Archives.

31. *1199 Hospital News,* June 9, 1959.

32. Ibid.

Chapter 5

1. "The Strike Is Over: A Report to the Hospital aFamily," Mt. Sinai Hospital leaflet, 1199 Archives.

2. Minutes, Mt. Sinai Hospital Coordinating Committee, June 25, 1959, 1199 Archives.

3. "The Strike Is Over."

4. "Hospital Rules," Mt. Sinai Hospital bulletin, 1199 Archives.

5. A copy of this manual is in the authors' possession. The procedures established by Norman Metzger at Mt. Sinai served as the basis for the PAC recommendations for New York City's voluntary hospitals.

6. *Mt. Sinai News,* May and June 1960. Thelma Bowles cited Montefiore's adoption of special insignia for employees as a factor motivating her to become active in the union campaign. See chapter 2.

7. In 1962 there were about ninety voluntary hospitals and nursing homes in New York City; sixteen had contracts with 1199 and fewer than forty participated in the PAC. The thirty-seven hospitals that signed the Statement of Policy ending the 1959 strike included the seven struck hospitals as well as seven Catholic and thirteen denominational and nondenominational institutions. Columbia-Presbyterian and New York hospitals were among the major institutions that never joined the PAC. See Minutes, Executive Council, Mar. and July 23, 1962, 1199 Archives.

8. *New York Post,* Oct. 8, 1959.

9. *1199 News,* Sept. 17, 1959. See also "Statement by Leon J. Davis to the Permanent Administrative Committee," May 31, 1960, and "Statement by A. Philip Randolph, President, Brotherhood of Sleeping Car Porters, to the Permanent Administrative Committee," May 31, 1960, 1199 Archives. The lowest wage paid in city hospitals was $53 per week.

10. For example, see the statements of Dr. Mark A. Freedman, executive director, Beth Israel Hospital; Dr. I. Magelaner, Brooklyn Jewish Hospital; Dr. Arnold Karan, director, Bronx Hospital; and Mt. Sinai Hospital in 1199 Archives.

11. "Report on the Annual Review for 1960," July 1, 1960, and Bob Burke, "Report on Permanent Administrative Committee," December 6, 1960, 1199 Archives. The union's request for a minimum wage comparable to that of municipal hospital workers was $1.32 per hour. The PAC recommendation represented a 23-percent increase over the weekly wage of $40 paid in most voluntary hospitals in New York City after the 1959 strike.

12. Minutes, Mt. Sinai Hospital Coordinating Committee, June 25, 1959, 1199 Archives.

13. Minutes, Executive Council, Sept. 28, 1959, and Minutes, Drug Division, General Council, Oct. 21, 1959, District 1199 Archives.

14. David Livingston was quite candid about his ambitions, discussed in more detail later in this chapter.

15. U.S. Congress, House, Committee on Education and Labor, *Fair Labor Standards Act,* 87th Cong., 2d sess., 1963; House Report, 95989, p. 127.

16. Minutes, Executive Council, June 22, 1959, 1199 Archives. In 1959 the union

set up a stewards council, which Davis claimed would "be the governing body of the hospital division." See Minutes, Hospital Division Stewards Council, Oct. 6, 1959, 1199 Archives. On the role of the stewards in 1199, see chapter 9.

17. That all the workers in Mt. Sinai's laundry paid their dues should be seen as a tribute to Gloria Arana's leadership. Davis complained to the stewards council in 1960 that only one-third of the members were fully paid up. Minutes, Hospital Division Stewards Council, Oct. 4, 1960, 1199 Archives.

18. Minutes, Executive Council, Apr. 11, 1960, 1199 Archives.

19. Minutes, Hospital Division Stewards Council, Jan. 5, 1960, 1199 Archives.

20. Minutes, Hospital Division Stewards Council, July 11, 1961, 1199 Archives.

21. On the importance of union literature during this period, see, for example, Minutes, Hospital Division Staff Meeting, July 22, 1959, 1199 Archives.

22. Mt. Sinai leaflet, Apr. 23, 1962, 1199 Archives.

23. Beth Israel leaflet, Feb. 1960, 1199 Archives.

24. Mt. Sinai leaflet, Nov. 13, 1959, 1199 Archives.

25. Mt. Sinai leaflet, Jan. 20, 1960, 1199 Archives.

26. *1199 News,* June 29, 1959.

27. Ibid., Oct. 8, 1959.

28. Ibid., Feb. 11, 1960.

29. Beth Israel leaflet, May 28, 1962, 1199 Archives.

30. Minutes, Hospital Division Stewards Council, June 26, 1962, 1199 Archives.

31. *1199 News,* Nov. and Dec. 1961.

32. Minutes, Hospital Division Stewards Council, Jan. 5, 1960, 1199 Archives.

33. "Union Goals and Membership Participation," Drug Division General Council, Jan. 11, 1961, 1199 Archives.

34. Minutes, Hospital Division Stewards Council, Oct. 3, 1961, 1199 Archives.

35. Ibid., Feb. 7, 1961.

36. Minutes, Hospital Division Staff Meeting, Mar. 29, 1960, and Minutes, Hospital Division Stewards Council, May 3, 1960, 1199 Archives.

37. From materials supplied by Moe Foner, Apr. 20, 1987. See also Leon J. Davis and Moe Foner, "Organization and Unionization of Health Workers in the United States: A Trade Union Perspective," *International Journal of Health Services* 5 (1975): 21–22.

38. Minutes, Hospital Division General Membership, Mar. 8, 1960, 1199 Archives.

39. On the contract agreed to by Montefiore and 1199, see Sara Gamm, *Toward Collective Bargaining in Non-Profit Hospitals: Impact of New York Law* (Ithaca: New York State School of Industrial and Labor Relations, Cornell University, 1968), pp. 65–67; *Modern Hospital,* July 1959, p. 70.

40. Minutes, Hospital Division General Membership, Mar. 8, 1960 and Minutes, Drug Division General Council, June 1, 1960, 1199 Archives; *New York Times,* Apr. 22 and 25, May 13 and 21, 1960.

41. *New York Times,* Sept. 26, Dec. 31, 1969.

42. Copy of a form letter, May 4, 1960, 1199 Archives.

43. Minutes, Executive Council, May 23, 1960; Minutes, Hospital Division Staff

Meeting, Apr. 26, June 13, 1960; Minutes, Hospital Division Stewards Council, June 7, 1960, 1199 Archives.

44. Minutes, Executive Council, May 23, 1960, 1199 Archives.

45. Letters, Leon Davis to Harry Van Arsdale, May 9, June 7, 1960, 1199 Archives.

46. Letter, Leon Davis to Nelson Rockefeller, June 10, 1960, 1199 Archives.

47. *New York Times,* July 1, 1960; *1199 News,* July 14, 1960; "Statement by Mayor Wagner," June 30, 1960, 1199 Archives.

48. *New York Post,* June 7, 1961. Silver was a personal friend of Francis Cardinal Spellman, archbishop of the Diocese of New York. See chapter 3.

49. Minutes, Hospital Division Staff Meeting, Dec. 1, 1959, 1199 Archives.

50. Minutes, Hospital Division Stewards Council, Oct. 26, 1959 and Minutes, Hospital Division General Membership, Mar. 8, 1960, 1199 Archives; *1199 News,* Mar. 26, 1959, and Feb. 25, 1960.

51. *1199 News,* Nov. 1959 and Feb. 25, 1960.

52. Gamm, p. 7. The founding statement for this group was essentially the same as a public announcement written in support of the 1959 strike by Moe Foner and Stanley Levison for Martin Luther King, Jr.

53. Ibid., pp. 7–9. The legislation required unions representing the employees of a charitable, religious, or educational organization to notify the New York State Labor Relations Board ten days before the date set for a strike. It also provided for the board to appoint a fact-finding commission during a thirty-day cooling-off period.

54. Quoted in Gamm, p. 8.

55. "Statement of the Greater New York Hospital Association," Mar. 16, 1962, 1199 Archives.

56. *New York Post,* Mar. 30, 1962. Henry Paley, legislative aide to House Speaker Joseph Carlino, mentioned the pressure Carlino felt from the Catholic church.

57. *New York Post,* Mar. 30, 1962; *Buffalo Evening Times,* Mar. 21, 1962. Both Foner and Ted Mitchell feel that racism more than compulsory arbitration explained Corbett's opposition to the Albert-McCloskey bill. They both cite Van Arsdale, who recognized that without compulsory arbitration there could be no change in the law.

58. *New York Amsterdam News,* Mar. 8, 1962.

59. Letter, Leon Davis to Robert Wagner, Aug. 18, 1961, 1199 Archives.

60. *New York Times,* Aug. 22, 1961.

61. *New York Times,* Dec. 4, 1961; Minutes, Hospital Division Stewards Council, July 11, 1961, 1199 Archives. According to Foner, 1199 decided to focus on Beth El because the union thought it could get a contract there.

62. *New York Times,* Feb. 14 and May 24, 1962; Minutes, Drug Division General Council, May 31, 1962, 1199 Archives. Davis only stayed in jail overnight. However, during the strike he did serve a thirty-day sentence for contempt for not calling off the strike. See Gamm, p. 9.

63. *1199 News,* May and June 1961.

64. *New York Post,* May 29, 1962.

65. Gamm, p. 10.

66. *New York Times,* June 22, 1962.

67. Letter, Committee for Justice to Hospital Workers to Nelson Rockefeller, June 20, 1962, 1199 Archives.

68. *New York Times,* July 18, 1962.

69. Memo, Henry Paley to Joseph Carlino, Mar. 27, 1962, 1199 Archives. After the settlement was announced, Martin Luther King, Jr., praised Governor Rockefeller for his efforts, while Leon Davis pledged 1199's support for the governor in the upcoming election. See Gamm, p. 11.

70. *New York Times,* July 19, 1962. It was King who suggested that a scheduled July 22 mass march and demonstration be turned into a victory celebration and rally in support of the governor's proposed legislation. Although unable to attend, he sent a taped message. The rally would have been the only time King and Malcolm X appeared together. Foner credits Bayard Rustin with overcoming the strong differences between them.

71. Henry Paley phoned Leon Davis to apprise him of the negotiations. Bayard Rustin, who was unaware of the arrangements to settle the strike, had led a sit-in at the governor's offices, which Foner states he first learned of when he got a call from Rustin, whom he quickly told to "get out of there." The final negotiations came just after Davis's release from jail, and it was arranged that Davis would not have to serve a new six-month jail term to which he had been sentenced. See Gamm, p. 11.

72. *New York Times,* July 23, 1962.

73. Gamm, pp. 16–17. Some hospitals recognized Local 144 of the Building Service Employees' Union, which had been at odds with Local 1199 since the late 1950s. In 1963 Harry Van Arsdale negotiated a compromise, giving 144 jurisdiction over the city's proprietary institutions while 1199 would organize the voluntary hospitals. For examples of the charges made by 1199 and 144, see *Local 144 News,* Oct. and Nov. 1962, and "Mississippi Justice in Bronx Hospital," 1199 Archives.

74. On 1199's efforts to organize professional, clerical, and technical hospital employees, wherever included under the provisions of the 1963 legislation, see chapter 6.

Chapter 6

1. *New York Herald Tribune,* May 26, 1963.

2. Sara Gamm, *Toward Collective Bargaining in Non-Profit Hospitals: Impact of New York Law* (Ithaca: New York State School of Industrial and Labor Relations, Cornell University, 1968), pp. 67–68.

3. *1199 Drug News,* June 1957. Negro History Week was begun in 1925 by Carter Woodson. In 1964 Local 1199 adopted the title "Salute to Freedom."

4. Philip Foner, *Women and the American Labor Movement* (New York: Free Press, 1979), p. 405. The relationship between King and 1199 is discussed in chapter 5.

5. Minutes, Executive Council, July 8, 1962, 1199 Archives.

6. *1199 News,* Sept. 1963; Minutes, Hospital Division Stewards Council, Sept. 10, 1963, 1199 Archives.

7. *1199 News,* Sept. 1963.

8. Gamm, pp. 18–19; *New York Times,* Mar. 11, 1964.

9. *1199 News,* Feb. 1965.

10. *New York Times,* Feb. 28, 1965.

11. Gamm, p. 20.

12. *New York Times,* Feb. 28, 1965.

13. Gamm, p. 19; *New York Times,* Feb. 28, 1965; *1199 News,* Feb. 1965.

14. *New York Times,* Feb. 2 and 28, 1965.

15. The telegram was signed by A. Philip Randolph, president, Negro American Labor Council; Roy Wilkins, executive director, NAACP; James Farmer, national director, CORE; Whitney Young, executive director, National Urban League; Dorothy Height, president, National Council of Negro Women; and Bayard Rustin, director, Randolph Institute. A copy of the telegram is in the 1199 Archives.

16. *1199 News,* Feb. 1965; Leon Fink, "Bread & Roses, Crusts & Thorns: The Troubled Story of 1199," *Dissent* 33 (1986):183.

17. Gamm, p. 20. After the law was passed Moe Foner found that there had been some eighteen editorials in the *New York Times,* the *New York Post,* on WCBS-TV, and so on.

18. The hospital agreed to hold an election in October, after the law was changed, and also to rehire all but seven of the workers who had been on strike. *New York Times,* Mar. 12 and 13, 1965. In terms of tactics and ideology, the Bronxville campaign appears to have been genesis of the later "union power, soul power" national organizing effort.

19. Gamm, p. 21.

20. *New Rochelle* (N.Y.) *Standard Star,* Jan. 21, 1966. On January 27 Davis sent a letter to Bronxville supporters explaining why 1199 pulled out of the election.

21. Minutes, Executive Council, June 19 and 27, 1959, Feb. 15, 1960, 1199 Archives. The union did attempt to organize a professional, technical, and office workers' section of the hospital division but without much success.

22. Minutes, Drug Division General Council, Apr. 3, 1963, 1199 Archives.

23. Ibid.

24. For example, see a leaflet titled "A Message to Technicians and Professionals in the Voluntary Hospital," from the 1963–64 period, 1199 Archives.

25. *1199 News,* June 1963.

26. Ibid., Aug. 1962.

27. Ibid. At this point it was called the Guild of Medical, Diagnostic Research, and X-ray Technicians.

28. Minutes, Executive Council, Sept. 7, 1963, 1199 Archives.

29. *1199 News,* Jan. 1964; Minutes, Executive Council, Oct. 11 and Nov. 9, 1963, 1199 Archives.

30. Gamm, pp. 65–66; Minutes, Drug Division General Council, Apr. 3, 1963, 1199 Archives. Elliott Godoff had begun organizing the guild in July 1962. See his reports in Minutes, Hospital Division Leadership Meeting, Aug. 20 and Sept. 18, 1962, and Jan. 7, 1963; Minutes, Executive Council, July 23, 1962, 1199 Archives.

31. *1199 News,* Jan. 1964.

32. See note 24.

33. "Professionals and Economic Security," leaflet, District 1199 Archives.

34. *1199 News,* Oct. 1965.

35. See Gamm, p. 45. A successful organizing drive in the first four months of 1967 resulted in guild membership for 66 clerical and office employees at Knickerbocker Hospital, 7 social workers at Gouverneur and Judson clinics, 150 licensed practical nurses at Brooklyn Jewish Hospital, and 300 employees at Einstein and Lincoln hospitals. See *1199 News,* June 1967.

36. An unsigned informational leaflet to the AEEO, May 1967, 1199 Archives. Albert Einstein is a medical school operated by Yeshiva University with affiliated units at Jacobi, Van Etten, and Lincoln hospitals and at Bronx neighborhood health centers.

37. Much of the information on the AEEO comes from an interview with Diane Bianculli, May 28, 1982.

38. See note 36.

39. *1199 News,* Nov. 1967.

40. Letter, Sidney Schutz, general counsel of Yeshiva University, to Leon Davis, July 18, 1967, 1199 Archives.

41. Letter, Leon J. Davis to Sidney Schutz, July 19, 1967, 1199 Archives; *New York Times,* July 20, 1967.

42. *New York Times,* July 22 and 24, 1967.

43. "Sense and Common Sense," a leaflet distributed by the Executive Committee AEEO/1199, Oct. 12, 1968, 1199 Archives.

44. Ibid. Bianculli gave as one example that professional but not technical workers received support for going to conferences. After discussion by all members the issue became a contract demand.

45. *1199 News,* June 1963.

46. Minutes, Executive Council, Sept. 7, Oct. 11, and Nov. 9, 1963, 1199 Archives.

47. *1199 News,* June 1967.

48. Minutes, Review of the Union-Administration, May 15, 1967, 1199 Archives. In 1976 the union established a fourth division, the League of Registered Nurses. Although Bianculli conceded that without a separate division organizing the RNs probably "would never have gotten off the ground," she nevertheless felt that once in the union RNs should be "educated" to understand that "we don't need" separate divisions.

49. "Why Mt. Sinai LPNs Should Join the 1199 LPN League," leaflet, July 23, 1970, 1199 Archives.

50. Minutes, Executive Council, Sept. 7, 1963, 1199 Archives. Through the 1970s the union appeared to have in many ways fulfilled Davis's aspirations. Only recently have the economic and cultural differences recognized in the formation of discrete divisions begun to haunt 1199.

51. Minutes, Hospital Division Stewards Council, Jan. 8, 1963, 1199 Archives; *1199 News,* July and Sept. 1964.

52. Gamm, pp. 42–43, 51–52. The union had some members in Westchester County, on Long Island, and in New Jersey.

53. Ibid., p. 52.

54. *1199 News,* May 1964.

55. Ibid., Mar. 1967.

56. Ibid., Sept. 1967.

57. *New York Times,* Feb. 17, 1969; *The Nation,* July 14, 1969; *1199 News,* Aug. 1973.

58. Pagan and Mitchell also insisted that many Catholic hospitals hired new immigrants who were Catholic as a way to hold off unionization. For example, according to Pagan, St. Vincent's Hospital hired mainly Haitians and assigned them to a French-speaking supervisor who would threaten to "call Immigration" if they got involved with a union.

59. Gamm, p. 56.

60. *New York Times,* Jan. 22, 26, and 31, and Feb. 6, 1969.

61. Gamm, pp. 65–68. The first contracts signed in 1963 by those hospitals that bargained with 1199 used the Montefiore agreement as the standard.

62. *1199 News,* Feb. 1966. The existing five-year contracts contained a reopener clause, for wages only, at the start of the fourth year. If a wage increase could not be agreed to, the contract provided that the issue be arbitrated.

63. Ibid., Sept. 1966.

64. Ibid.; *New York Times,* July 13–14, 1966; Gamm, pp. 66–68, 74.

65. *1199 News,* Sept. 1966; Gamm, pp. 74–77; *New York Times,* July 13–16, 1966.

66. *New York Times,* July 14, 1966; Gamm, pp. 74–77.

67. *New York Times,* July 13–14, 1966.

68. Ibid., July 21, 1966.

69. In the three years that followed the 1965 race riot in the Watts section of Los Angeles, some 300 racial disturbances took place, marked by 50,000 arrests and more than 800 casualties. In 1966 alone more than a score of riots in cities across the nation had required the national guard to restore order. See Harvard Sitkoff, *The Struggle for Black Equality, 1954–1980* (New York: Hill and Wang, 1981), pp. 200–202.

70. *New York Times,* July 19, 1966.

71. "The Hospital Surrender," ibid., July 20, 1966. See also Odin Anderson, *Blue Cross since 1929: Accountability and the Public Trust* (Cambridge, Mass.: Ballinger, 1975), pp. 81–86; Herbert E. Klarman, *Hospital Care in New York City: The Role of the Voluntary and Municipal Hospitals* (New York: Columbia University Press, 1963), pp. 414–35. Between 1950 and 1970 national health care expenditures increased from $12.7 billion to $71.6 billion; at the same time the medical work force more than tripled, from 1.2 million to 3.9 million people. In the five years after Medicare the rate of growth in the cost of medical services rose by 7.9 percent annually, compared to a 3.2-percent yearly increase in the previous seven years. See Paul Starr, *The Social Transformation of American Medicine* (New York: Basic Books, 1982), pp. 335, 384. For a discussion of the impact of these changes in the 1970s, see chapter 8.

72. In 1952 insurance paid only 15 percent of all private expenses for health care. See *Source Book of Health Insurance* (New York: New York Health Insurance Institute, 1976), pp. 145–47; *Hospitals,* Oct. 16, 1973.

73. On New York's municipal unions, see Raymond D. Horton, *Municipal Labor Relations in New York City: Lessons of the Lindsay-Wagner Years* (New York: Praeger, 1973); Mark H. Maier, *City Unions: Managing Discontent in New York City* (New Brunswick, N.J.: Rutgers University Press, 1987); A. H. Raskin, "Politics Up-Ends the Bargaining Table," in *Public Workers and Public Unions*, ed. S. Zagoria (Englewood Cliffs, N.J.: Prentice-Hall, 1972), pp. 122–46. Horton points out that with the exception of the transit workers, salaries for the city's civil servants generally rose twice as fast as the consumer price index between 1967 and 1972. On Lillian Roberts, see Susan Reverby, "Hospital Organizing in the 1950s: An Interview with Lillian Roberts," *Signs* 1 (1976): 1053–63.

74. *New York Times*, Mar. 7, 1968. John Connorton, director of the GNYHA, maintains that the league took a different approach, a more "rock-'em, sock-'em attitude."

75. See *New York Times*, June 21 and 27–28, 1968.

76. *Wall Street Journal*, June 19, 1968. At this point workers in municipal hospitals were earning a minimum weekly salary of just over $96.

77. *1199 News*, May 1968. The Poor People's Campaign was the ongoing Southern Christian Leadership Conference demonstration in Washington, D.C.

78. *Wall Street Journal*, June 19, 1968.

79. *New York Times*, June 24, 1968.

80. Ibid., June 27 and July 19, 1968. Relations between the police and the black community were already tense. In November 1966, after numerous charges of police brutality, the city reinstated its Civilian Complaint Review Board. For an account of a mass meeting attacking this board, see ibid., Aug. 22, 1968.

81. Ibid., June 28, 1968.

82. Ibid.

83. Ibid., July 2, 1968; *1199 News*, June 1968.

84. *New York Times*, June 21, 1968.

85. Ibid., July 2, 1968.

86. Ibid., June 24, 1968.

87. Ibid., June 28, 1968. Citing government statistics, Foner stated that it cost $272.50 per month, or the equivalent (allowing for taxes) of $85 per week take-home pay, for a family of four to live in New York City.

88. *1199 News*, Sept. 1966.

89. *Wall Street Journal*, July 2, 1968.

90. Minutes, Executive Committee, July 17, 1968, 1199 Archives.

Chapter 7

For their help with key aspects of research in this chapter we would like to thank Steve Hoffius, David Garrow, Jack Bass, and George and Randy Kaiser. In addition, Robert Korstad and Harry Watson provided useful editorial criticisms.

1. *American Statistical Index*, 1976 S.V. "Southeast Regional Reports, 6946–133," "Work Stoppages," "Union Membership and Employment for the Southeast";

"Employment and Economic Growth: Southeast," *Monthly Labor Review* 91 (Mar. 1968): 18–19; telephone interview with George Kaiser, field representative for the AFL-CIO in South Carolina since 1965, Apr. 29, 1963; South Carolina Department of Labor, *Annual Report, 1978–79,* pt. 2: *S.C. State Budget Control Board: Departments and Resolutions,* pp. 77–82.

2. Jamie W. Moore, "The Lowcountry in Economic Transition: Charleston since 1865," *South Carolina Historical Magazine* 80 (Apr. 1979): 156–71; Frederic Cople Jaher, "Antebellum Charleston: Anatomy of Economic Failure," in *Class Conflict and Consensus: Antebellum Southern Community Studies,* ed. Orville Vernon Burton and Robert C. McMath, Jr. (Westport, Conn.: Greenwood Press, 1982), pp. 207–31; *U.S. Census, 1950,* vol. 2: *Population,* pt. 40 (South Carolina), pp. 46, 168–70; *U.S. Census, 1970,* vol. 1: *Population,* pt. 42 (South Carolina), pp. 23, 198, 204, 208.

3. See Kay Day, " 'My Family Is Me': Kin Networks and Social Power in a Black Sea Island Community" (Ph.D. diss., Rutgers University, 1983); *Washington Post,* June 16, 1969.

4. Sanford Sherman, "The Charleston Strike" (ms. in possession of Moe Foner, n.d.), p. 7; *Business Week,* Apr. 5, 1969.

5. *Congressional Quarterly Weekly Report* 28, no. 51 (Dec. 11, 1970): 2951–2; Robert Coles and Harry Huge, "The Way It Is in South Carolina," *New Republic* 159 (Nov. 30, 1968): 17; see also pp. 17–21.

6. This pattern of racial containment is described by William Chafe, *Civilities and Civil Rights: Greensboro, North Carolina, and the Black Struggle for Freedom* (New York: Oxford University Press, 1980); Stephen O'Neill, "The Struggle for Black Equality Comes to Charleston: The Hospital Strike of 1969," *Proceedings of the South Carolina Historical Association,* 1986, p. 83.

7. Interview with Rev. Thomas Duffy, Feb. 18, 1980; *New York Times,* Sept. 3–4, 1963; *New York Times Index,* 1964.

8. Letter, Alice Cabaniss to Leon Fink, Aug. 1, 1983; telephone conversation with Joseph W. Cabaniss, Feb. 13, 1985.

9. *New York Jet,* June 5, 1969.

10. For a more liberal interpretation of public employee law by two legal counselors representing 1199 in Charleston, see Eugene G. Eisner and I. Phillip Sipser, "The Charleston Hospital Dispute: Organizing Public Employees and the Right to Strike," *St. John's Law Review* 45 (Dec. 1970): 254–72. *Los Angeles Times,* Apr. 14, 1969. Haynesworth was a cousin of Clement Haynesworth, a federal judge who later that year was nominated, then contested and defeated, for appointment to the U.S. Supreme Court.

11. "Review of the Union Meeting," July 22, 1968, Davis Correspondence, 1199 Archives.

12. Convincing evidence of the Charleston workers' seriousness was reported by visiting 1199 vice president Doris Turner. She was scheduled to meet with organized workers one evening at the tobacco workers' hall but because of airline delays did not arrive until after midnight. Before she went to the hotel she decided to stop by the meeting hall, just in case someone had waited for her, and found it full of hospital workers.

13. *Charleston News and Courier,* Feb. 27, 1969; *Charleston Evening Post,* Mar. 5, 1968.

14. *Charleston News and Courier,* Mar. 20–21, 1969; *Charlotte Observer,* Apr. 4, 1969; interview with Henry Nicholas, Jan. 11, 1978; "Case Study: The Charleston Hospital Strike," *Southern Hospitals,* Mar. 1971, pp. 16–18; *Business Week,* Apr. 6, 1969.

15. *The Medical College of Charleston* v. *Drug and Hospital Union, Local 1199B,* 52, slip op. at 596 (S.C.C.P. Ninth Judicial Circuit, July 9, 1969); Sherman, p. 63.

16. *The State,* (Columbia, S.C.) May 10, 1969; J. H. O'Dell, "Charleston's Legacy to the Poor People's Campaign," *Freedomways* 9 (Summer 1969): 201; *Charleston News and Courier,* Apr. 9, 1969.

17. See David J. Garrow, *The FBI and Martin Luther King, Jr.* (New York: W.W. Norton, 1981), esp. chap. 1; Adam Fairclough, *To Redeem the Soul of America: The Southern Christian Leadership Conference and Martin Luther King, Jr.* (Athens; University of Georgia Press, 1987), p. 30; interview with Moe Foner, Mar. 9, 1979.

18. Levison's continuing role in strike strategy discussions as well as backbiting and personality conflicts within SCLC were relayed to the FBI through "confidential sources." Memos, Mar. 31 and Apr. 24, 1969, secured through the Freedom of Information Act (File No. 54688 80514 73518) by David Garrow and shared with the authors.

19. *Charleston News and Courier,* Apr. 2, 1969; interview with Henry Nicholas, Apr. 14, 1982.

20. *Charleston News and Courier,* Apr. 25–26, 1969; "Case Study"; *New York Times,* May 30, 1969. An FBI memo, dated May 2, 1969, reported: "Young sees the SCLC capitalizing on a framework they have laid in the citizenship schools and feels it is important, to call in their citizenship contacts from other counties. Young recommended that win, lose, or draw they will mobilize South Carolina politically in the process. . . . Young mentioned that they have done more underground work in South Carolina than any other state in the South and that the citizenship schools have trained people in every county. He estimated six to seven hundred people have attended these schools in the last five years."

21. O'Neill, p. 86.

22. *New York Times,* May 4, 1969.

23. *Charleston News and Courier,* Apr. 24–25 and 28, 1969; *New York Times,* Apr. 26 and 29, 1969.

24. Jack Bass, "Strike at Charleston," *New South,* Summer 1969, pp. 35–44. The poem is quoted on p. 44.

25. Moultrie speech, Charleston file, 1199 Archives; *Baltimore Afro-American,* May 31, 1969.

26. *New York Times,* Apr. 30, 1969; Coretta Scott King speech, May 6, 1969, Charleston file, 1199 Archives.

27. Letters from Charleston strikers, Charleston file, 1199 Archives.

28. Ibid.

29. *New York Post,* June 26, 1969.

30. Letters from Charleston strikers.

31. Ibid.

32. Annie Scott to 1199, May 19, 1969; list of monetary contributions to Charleston strike, Aug. 1, 1969, 1199 Archives.

33. Ann Fay (Brearly School) to Mrs. King, June 4, 1969; Eleanore Levenson (I.S. 70) to Mrs. King, May 9, 1969; Charles Serota et al. (University of Rochester) to Mrs. King, May 8, 1969, Charleston file, 1199 Archives.

34. Sherman, pp. 53–54, 60–61.

35. *Park East,* June 12, 1969.

36. Interview with Naomi White and Gloria Frazier, July 25, 1979, by Steve Hoffius (transcript courtesy of interviewer); *Charleston News and Courier,* Apr. 30, 1969; "Case Study."

37. *Business Week,* May 17, 1969. See, e.g., *New York Times,* Apr. 21 and 29, May 14–15, June 6, 12, and 18, 1969; *The State,* May 30, 1969.

38. *New York Times,* Apr. 23, 1969; *Newsweek,* May 5 and 12, 1969.

39. *New York Post,* June 27, 1969; letters from Charleston strikers.

40. While acknowledging in a June 23, 1982, telephone conversation with Leon Fink that he had been on hand for nearly every day of the hospital workers' strike, Chief Strom declined to be interviewed on the subject. Nevertheless, the hints about his role in Charleston seem of a piece with his documented initiatives during other civil disturbances. Strom, who had gained a reputation as "the J. Edgar Hoover of South Carolina," had helped to break up the Ku Klux Klan in the 1950s, and in 1964 he headed off violence when students picketed an appearance by George Wallace in Columbia. For his subtle efforts before the deadly confrontation at Orangeburg, S.C., on February 6, 1968, see Jack Nelson and Jack Bass, *The Orangeburg Massacre* (New York: Ballantine Books, 1970), pp. 31, 202.

41. County Council Resolution, n.d., Charleston file, 1199 Archives; *Charleston News and Courier,* Apr. 26, 1969.

42. *Charleston News and Courier,* June 3, 1969; *New York Times,* June 4, 1969; statement by Bishop Unterkoefler, n.d., Charleston file, 1199 Archives.

43. *Charleston News and Courier,* May 1, 1969.

44. Sherman, p. 61.

45. *Charleston News and Courier,* May 30, 1969; letters, Hugh S. Brimm to William McCord, Sept. 19, 1968, and June 4, 1969, Charleston file, 1199 Archives.

46. O'Neill, p. 88.

47. Cf. *Washington Post,* June 16, 1969; *Charleston Evening Post,* June 13, 1969; Bass, pp. 35–44; Leon E. Panetta and Peter Gall, *Bring Us Together: The Nixon Team and Civil Rights Retreat* (Philadelphia: Lippincott, 1971), pp. 183–87; Harry S. Dent, *The Prodigal South Returns to Power* (New York: John Wiley and Sons, 1978), pp. 130–31.

48. *Charleston News and Courier,* June 21, 23, and 26, 1969; *Charleston Evening Post,* June 10, 1969; *New York Times,* June 26, 1969; O'Dell, pp. 205–8. The textile trade paper, the *Daily News Record* (June 26, 1969), called the strike "a bombshell set to explode at the back door of the South Carolina textile industry."

49. *Charleston News and Courier,* June 21, 1969; *New York Times,* June 25, 1969.

50. Dent, pp. 130–31; *New York Times,* June 28, 1969; interviews with Moe Foner, Mar. 9, 1979, and Andrew Young, Jan. 31, 1980.

51. *New York Times,* June 28, 1969; *1199 Drug and Hospital News,* July 1969. On the Memphis sanitation workers' settlement the previous year, see Philip S. Foner, *Organized Labor and the Black Worker, 1619–1981* (New York: International Pubs., 1981), p. 384.

52. On the poststrike unraveling process, see Steve Hoffius, "Charleston Hospital Workers' Strike, 1969," in *Working Lives: The Southern Exposure History of Labor in the South,* ed. Marc S. Miller (New York: Pantheon, 1980), pp. 225–58.

53. Carl E. Farris, "The Steelworkers' Strike in South Carolina," *Freedomways* 11 (2d quart., 1971), p. 189; see also pp. 178–91. The increasing numbers of blacks in the southern industrial labor force likely did create a window of opportunity (at least until the oil shock, stagflation, and textile import crisis of the mid-seventies) for the wider application of "union power, soul power." The Oneita strike at Andrews, S.C. (1971–73), the J. P. Stevens campaign at Roanoke Rapids, N.C. (1974), and the Farah strike and boycott at El Paso, Tex. (1972–74), also drew heavily on civil rights themes but without the involvement and resuscitation of a national civil rights movement. See Carolyn Ashbaugh and Dan McCurry, "On the Line at Oneita," *Southern Exposure* 4 (1976): 30–37; Bill Finger and Mike Krivosh, "Stevens vs. Justice," pp. 38–44; Bill Finger, "Victoria Sobre Farah," ibid., pp. 45–49.

54. Fairclough, pp. 11–35, 385–405. In painting the outcome of the Charleston strike as one of undiluted union victory (p. 396), Fairclough himself was apparently misled by the union's and the SCLC's immediate poststrike enthusiasm.

55. A postscript to the 1969 Charleston strike suggests that objective conditions for hospital worker organizing in South Carolina have not improved much. In 1981, following an NLRB election of the previous year, 1199 negotiated a contract in Tuomey, S.C., reportedly the first unionized voluntary hospital in the South. When that contract expired, management proposed to remove both the arbitration-of-grievances clause and the dues checkoff; they also subcontracted out the housekeeping department (where the union had over 95-percent membership) and threatened to do the same with the dietary department. Before the next contract expired in June 1984 the hospital laid off 16 nurse's aides, 14 of them black union members, and replaced them with all-white LPNs who had been told not to join the "Black Union"; other black union members also were replaced with white part-time workers. A one-year contract was signed in September 1984 that called for a meager 2-percent raise for most workers. Then, on October 5 the hospital laid off 53 nurse's aides, most of whom were union members. In four years' time the bargaining unit had dropped from 426 workers to 300, and union membership was down to less than 70 voluntary dues-payers. In January 1985 the hospital filed a decertification petition, and by March the last 30 union dues-payers voted unanimously to officially disavow their representation by the union. In April 1985 Tuomey Hospital hired back many of the aides it had previously laid off—at $3.35 an hour (a $2.00-an-hour wage cut). See *Officers' Report to the Seventh Convention of National Union of Hospital and Health Care Employees (AFL-CIO),* December 9–12, 1987, Hartford, Conn., p. 38.

Chapter 8

1. *Baltimore Sun,* May 3, 1969.
2. James Griffin telephone interview, Feb. 4, 1988. According to Griffin, a physical therapist whose first organizing effort was in 1963 at the Granada Nursing Home, in Baltimore, the Maryland Freedom Union had by 1968–69 largely petered out.
3. *New York Times,* Aug. 31, 1969.
4. *Baltimore Sun,* Aug. 28, 1969.
5. Ibid., July 10 and 12, 1969. Speaking for his own institution but articulating the feeling at all of the target hospitals in Baltimore, the chairman of Lutheran's board of trustees explained, "We don't expect any trouble with the union, but we don't want another Charleston on our hands . . . either." See *Baltimore News American,* July 9, 1969.
6. *Modern Hospital,* Oct. 1969; *New York Times,* Aug. 31, 1969.
7. *Hospitals* (Journal of the American Hospital Association), Mar. 1, 1970; *1199 News,* Jan. 1970.
8. According to Nicholas, who had recruited Punch, Davis asked Punch to be an area director in the Bronx but Punch refused, wanting instead "to go where the action is." Muehlenkamp says that Godoff was aware of the problem of poorly trained union staff, but under the circumstances it was "sink or swim. He didn't know what else to do." This paucity of experienced organizers would continue to plague the union.
9. *1199 News,* Oct. 1969.
10. Copy of a press release, Mar. 18, 1970, 1199P District Office, Pittsburgh; *Modern Hospital,* Feb. 1970; *Pittsburgh Post-Gazette,* Jan. 13, 1970.
11. Quoted in *Wall Street Journal,* Mar. 3, 1970.
12. *Modern Hospital,* Feb. 1970.
13. *New York Times,* Mar. 21, 1970; *Pittsburgh Press,* Mar. 20, 1970. Presbyterian-University Hospital had about 700 service and maintenance employees (see ibid., Feb. 17, 1970). On the eve of the strike, the hospital agreed to recommend an increase in the minimum base pay of service workers from $1.75 per hour to $1.95 per hour, effective May 1 (see ibid., Jan. 9 and Mar. 15, 1970). The evidence suggests that hospital management in Pittsburgh had prepared to meet a union organizing drive even before 1199 came to the city. Most of Pittsburgh's hospitals belonged to the Hospital Council of Western Pennyvania (HCWP). Three years prior to the events of 1969–70, the council hired Hay Associates, a Philadelphia-based management consulting firm, and based on the firm's report had launched "Operation WE [Wage Equalization]," a program for raising the wages paid hospital workers until they matched the pay for workers holding comparable jobs in private industry.
14. *1199 News,* Apr. 1970; *Pittsburgh Press,* Mar. 23–25, 1970; *Modern Hospital,* Apr. 1970. A strike at Uniontown Hospital, about forty miles outside Pittsburgh, which had begun on February 26, did continue but had no greater success. See *New York Review of Books,* Apr. 9, 1970; *1199 News,* Apr. 1970.
15. *Modern Hospital,* Nov. 1970.
16. See *Pittsburgh Press,* Jan. 6, 1970. A *New York Times* (Jan. 4, 1970) report on a

demonstration before the vote at the Jewish Home and Hospital states that a majority of the workers were black.

17. According to Black, Nicholas misled Godoff on the strength of union support among Pittsburgh hospital workers. At the rally the night before the strike, Nicholas informally polled the workers by asking those who supported the strike to stand up, hospital by hospital. Black says that Nicholas then gave Godoff, who was at the meeting but was virtually blind, an inaccurate (much higher) count.

18. *Wall Street Journal*, Mar. 3, 1970.

19. U.S. Bureau of the Census, *Census of Population, 1970*, vol. 1: *Characteristics of the Population* (Washington, D.C.: GPO, 1973), pt. 40 (Pennsylvania), sec. 2, and pt. 34 (New York), sec. 2. John Black estimates that about 40 percent of Presbyterian-University Hospital workers were black.

20. *Wall Street Journal*, Mar. 3, 1970. Public support for 1199 was led by the Citizens Committee to Secure Justice for Hospital Workers, an umbrella organization of area liberal, labor, and civil rights groups, but many leading Pittsburgh unions were not represented. Tillow recalls that unions in the city were not "anxious to help. [They] saw it as a kind of intrusion on their territory by a union that was not local." In fact, in trying to capitalize on its affiliation with the University of Pittsburgh, officials at Presbyterian-University Hospital attempted to block 1199 by recognizing Local 29 of the SEIU. First for a nurses' residence and later for its Western Psychiatric Institute and Clinic, they claimed that Local 29 already had jurisdiction because that union had represented workers at the University of Pittsburgh since 1941.

21. On 1199D, see *Modern Hospital*, June 1970; on 1199H, see ibid., Aug. 1970.

22. The racial composition of hospital workers in Dayton was similar to that in Pittsburgh; Durham, however, was predominantly black. Again, looking specifically at health service workers, in Dayton 25 percent of them were black, while in Durham the number was much higher—over 70 percent black. See *Census of Population, 1970*, vol. 1, pt. 37 (Ohio), sec. 2 and pt. 35 (North Carolina), sec. 2. Organizing in Durham was complicated by divisions between older and younger black workers, as well as by competition between 1199 and Local 77 of the American Federation of State, County, and Municipal Employees. See Karen Brodkin Sacks, *Caring by the Hour: Women, Work, and Organizing at Duke Medical Center* (Urbana: University of Illinois Press, 1988), pp. 54–57.

23. *Philadelphia Inquirer*, Oct. 25, 1970; *Modern Hospital*, Nov. 1970.

24. At this point 1199C did everything except collect dues. The union, Nicholas told a reporter, always let the workers know that "*we* can't get them a raise. . . . they can only get what *they* are prepared to fight for." See *Philadelphia Magazine*, Oct. 1972.

25. Ibid.; *1199 News*, June 1971.

26. *Philadelphia Magazine*, Oct. 1972.

27. Ibid.; *Philadelphia Inquirer*, Aug. 29–31, 1972.

28. *Philadelphia Inquirer*, Sept. 3, 1972. Other evidence indicates that the 10,000 members claimed for 1199C was too high. See note 34.

29. *Philadelphia Magazine*, Oct. 1972.

30. The rank-and-file group at Columbia-Presbyterian called themselves Sisters and Brothers United.

31. Columbia-Presbyterian Medical Center stretched over ten buildings. Kay organized by building and by area within each building. See *1199 News*, Apr. 1973.

32. Ibid.

33. Ibid.

34. By mid-1973 the union represented some 55,000 workers in voluntary hospitals and nursing homes in New York, New Jersey, and Connecticut. See ibid., Dec. 1979; *Modern Healthcare*, May 1974.

35. *New York Times*, Dec. 2, 1973. In a review of the national hospital union's first decade, *1199 News* (July 1983) noted that in 1973 more than 10,000 hospital workers in seven states were organized in addition to those in Local 1199. In addition to the other districts the convention established 1199/New England. Muehlenkamp claims that the district structure represented Davis's belief that the health care industry should be organized over large geographic areas, not by city or by institution.

36. See *1199 News*, Dec. 1979; *Modern Healthcare*, Sept. 1980.

37. *1199 News*, Sept. 1972; *Modern Healthcare*, May 1974.

38. *Modern Healthcare*, May 1974.

39. Ibid.; *Hospital Health Services Administration*, Jan. 2, 1982; American Hospital Association, Taft-Hartley Amendments: Implications for the Health Care Field (Chicago: American Hospital Association, 1976), pp. 3–7. In disputes involving business and industry there is no obligation to file such notification.

40. Leon J. Davis and Moe Foner, "Organization of Unionization of Health Workers in the United States: The Trade Union Perspective," *International Journal of Health Services* 5 (1975): 19.

41. Joseph Rosmann, "One Year under Taft-Hartley," *Hospitals* 49 (Dec. 16, 1975): 64.

42. Rosmann, p. 66.

43. *Modern Healthcare*, Sept. 1980. Of course, labor union membership in general was declining by the 1970s. Economic dislocation and an estimated $100 million spent annually by corporations to defeat labor cost the unions 350,000 members between 1974 and 1976. In the seventies, the percentage of the industrial work force belonging to unions dropped to its lowest point since the late 1930s. See James R. Green, *The World of the Worker: Labor in Twentieth-Century America* (New York: Hill and Wang, 1980), pp. 236–38.

44. U.S. Congress, House, Committee on Education and Labor, Oversight Hearings before the Subcommittee on Labor-Management Relations, 9th Cong., 1st and 2d sess., 1979 and 1980. In his testimony Muehlenkamp referred to "3M." Originally the labor relations law firm of Melnick, McKeon, and Mickins, this firm was called Modern Management Methods (or 3M) in 1975; by 1980 the firm was known as Modern Management, Inc. See *Modern Healthcare*, Sept. 1980.

45. See, e.g., *Hospital and Health Services Administration*, Jan. 2, 1982.

46. Ibid.; John Kilgour, "Union Organizing Activity in the Hospital Industry," ibid., Nov./Dec. 1984, pp. 82–83; Daniel S. Freeman and Bradford L. Kirkman-Liff, "Trends in Hospital Unionization and a Predictive Model for Unionizing Success," ibid., p. 112.

47. AHA, *Taft-Hartley Amendments,* p. 54.

48. *Modern Healthcare,* May 1974.

49. Ibid., Sept. 1980.

50. Kilgour, pp. 86–87.

51. *Hospitals,* Apr. 1, 1980. Health care unions in the eighties would find that their chances of winning an election in professional and technical units, which included registered nurses under the NLRB code, were more than twice as good as their chances of winning in the units that covered service and maintenance workers. See Kilgour, "Union Organizing Activity in the Hospital Industry," p. 84.

52. *Hospital Statistics,* 1975 ed., pp. 168–70; 1980 ed., pp. 170–71.

53. U.S. Department of Labor, *Occupation Outlook Handbook, 1980–81* (Washington, D.C.: GPO, 1980), p. 395.

54. *Modern Healthcare,* Sept. 1980. According to James C. Velghe, president of Management Science Associates, organization of nurses was on the rise because "the issues affecting professional nurses today are more volatile and sensitive than those affecting other hospital employees." He cited, in particular, the hospitals' use of temporary RNs from nurse registries and the overall pressures of the job caused by a nationwide nursing shortage. Cost controls have led to even greater reductions in the numbers of LPNs, a job category that some predict may eventually disappear. See Barbara Melosh, "Nursing and Reaganomics: Cost Containment in the United States," in *Political Issues in Nursing: Past, Present, and Future,* vol. 2, ed. Rosemary White (Chichester, England: John Wiley and Sons, 1986), pp. 160–61.

55. *New York Times,* Aug. 28, 1977.

56. Ibid., Dec. 11, 1980. Despite forming a committee on "Unions in Nursing" in January 1937, the ANA board continued to oppose nurse membership in unions. Still, by 1946 it did sanction collective bargaining by professional associations. See Susan M. Reverby, *Ordered to Care: The Dilemma of American Nursing, 1850–1945* (New York: Cambridge University Press, 1987), pp. 197–98. According to Barbara Melosh, by 1960 only some 8,000 nurses were covered under seventy-five contracts, all of which were initially negotiated by state nursing associations. See *"The Physician's Hand": Work, Culture and Conflict in American Nursing* (Philadelphia: Temple University Press, 1982), pp. 198–201. Even as late as 1980 only 5 percent of the ANA budget was allocated to collective bargaining. See *Modern Healthcare,* Sept. 1980.

57. *1199 News,* Sept. 1977 and June 1978.

58. *New York Times,* Aug. 26, 1977.

59. League of Registered Nurses organizing brochure in possession of authors; *1199 News,* Sept. 1977.

60. In each case the AFT, after being eliminated, supported the ANA against 1199 in the runoff election.

61. *Modern Healthcare,* Sept. 1980.

62. Cited in Melosh, "Nursing and Reaganomics," p. 164. The league has been more successful organizing nurses outside New York, especially on the West Coast. In May 1983, for example, 1,200 RNs from Seattle, who had been represented by the Washington State Nurses Association, voted to affiliate with the national hospital

union (see *1199 News*, July 1983). In April 1987 the 4,700-member Nurses Association of California also voted to join the national union, bringing the total number of nurses in the union to 25,000.

63. Two cases stand out: *N.L.R.B.* v. *St. Francis of Lynwood*, 601 F.2d 404 (9th Cir. 1979); and *Presbyterian/St. Luke's Medical Center* v. *NLRB*, 107 LRRM 2953 (July 8, 1981). See Clifton L. Elliot and Gina Kaiser, "Court Gives Hospitals an Important Victory on Bargaining Units," *Modern Healthcare*, Oct. 1981, pp. 124–28; Norman Metzger, "Hospital Labor Scene Marked by Union Issues," *Hospitals*, Apr. 1, 1980, p. 105.

64. Quoted in Elliot and Kaiser, p. 124.

65. Ibid. Hospital experience has been that unions thrive when bargaining units are small rather than large. See Kilgour, pp. 82–86.

66. *Hospitals*, Oct. 16, 1973.

67. Carl J. Schramm, "The Role of Hospital Cost-Regulating Agencies in Collective Bargaining," *Labor Law Journal* 28 (Aug. 1977): 520.

68. Ibid., pp. 520–21. Schramm noted that these changes, as well as the three-year freeze on Medicaid rates, had little impact until 1976. As will be clear, New York was not the only state to attempt to contain health care costs in this way. But since New York was at the forefront of this effort, and because 1199 was strongest there, we focus on collective bargaining in New York City.

69. *Modern Hospital*, Oct. 1969, pp. 31–34. Norman Metzger warned the legislators that any attempt to carry out the cost-cutting measures "will surely lead to a disastrous confrontation" between the hospitals and unions in New York City. See "Statement Concerning Reimbursement Principles and Cost Controls," League of Voluntary Hospitals, Oct. 3, 1969, 1199 Archives.

70. *New York Times*, June 17 and 25, 1970; *Modern Hospital*, June 1970.

71. *New York Times*, July 2, 1970. Rockefeller had assured the hospitals that the settlement would be "recognized as a legitimate element of a reasonable cost for reimbursement." See also *Hospitals*, July 16, 1970.

72. *New York Times*, July 2, 1970.

73. On the 1968 settlement, see chapter 6. A very different view of the 1970 contract negotiations is offered by Elinor Langer in a series of articles in the *New York Review of Books* (May 20 and June 3, 1971). Langer is critical of 1199 for failing to pursue such nonwage contract issues as training and upgrading programs and career ladders, and for not challenging the hospitals on finances. For more on New Left criticism of 1199, see chapter 9.

74. *New York Times*, Apr. 26, 1972.

75. Ibid., May 25, 1972.

76. Ibid., June 30, July 1 and 5–6, 1972.

77. Ibid., July 1, 1972.

78. The union appealed this decision. See ibid., Nov. 6, 1973; *1199 News*, Aug.–Oct. 1977, Feb.–Mar. and May–June 1973.

79. *New York Times*, Nov. 6, 1973.

80. Ibid., Nov. 9, 1973.

81. Ibid., Nov. 10–13, 1973; Al Nash, "Labor-Management Conflict and Change in

a Hospital," *Hospital and Health Services Administration,* Spring 1976, p. 48. The vote was 13,852 for, 3,839 against. The union was fined $723,500 for violating a federal antistrike injunction. See *1199 News,* Dec. 1979.

82. *New York Times,* Nov. 13, 1973.

83. Telephone interview with Gerald D. Rosenthal, Sept. 1985.

84. Davis and Foner, p. 124.

85. *New York Times,* Nov. 12, 1973; *Modern Healthcare,* May 1974.

86. *1199 News,* Feb. 1971.

87. *New York Times,* June 18, 28–30, 1974; Nash, p. 53. The minimum wage for hospital workers was raised from $154 to $181 per week. Among the demands that the union did drop was for every other weekend off (EOWO), an issue that would become controversial for 1199. Jesse Olson believes that Doris Turner's "disillusionment" with 1199's leadership began with the union's unwillingness to push EOWO, which she felt was important to hospital service workers. As president of the New York district, Turner made it a key issue in the 1984 contract negotiatons.

88. Ibid., July 6, 1974.

89. Schramm, p. 519; *Modern Healthcare,* May 1976.

90. Quoted in Toby Cohen, "Medicaid Fraud Reconsidered: How Hospitals Got on Welfare," *Dissent,* Mar. 1978, p. 391.

91. Mark H. Maier, *City Unions: Managing Discontent in New York City* (New Brunswick, N.J.: Rutgers University Press, 1987), p. 170.

92. Ibid., p. 187. Maier makes the point that even with the more liberal contracts secured by District Council 37 of AFSCME in the late sixties and early seventies, the workers in city hospitals earned less than the federal minimum for an "adequate" standard of living ($10,487). In 1976 minimum base pay for 1199 members was $9,412 per year; the average pay was $10,920, or slightly higher than the federal standard-of-living guideline.

93. Schramm, p. 521. In October 1975 Governor Carey ordered the city's Health and Hospital Corporation (which administered municipal hospitals) to reduce spending by $200 million. See *New York Times,* Oct. 25, 1975. See also George W. Bohlander, *Impact of Third-Party Payors on Collective Bargaining in the Health Care Industry* (Los Angeles: Institute of Industrial Relations, 1980), p. 89.

94. Schramm, p. 521.

95. *New York Times,* June 15 and 21, July 7, 1976.

96. Ibid., July 13, 1976.

97. Ibid.

98. Ibid., July 16, 1976. Having agreed to arbitration, league representatives sought assurances that the process would include a comparison of the wages of voluntary hospital workers with those paid to workers in other quasi-public and public employment, as well as consideration of "the employer's ability to pay as affected by the reimbursement in effect in New York." After first rejecting these conditions, 1199 finally agreed to them but on condition that the arbitrator also take into account the recommendation for a cost-of-living increase that had already been made by a federal mediation panel.

99. Gootnick had left the second year of the contract for another arbitrator to settle

(see *New York Times,* Sept. 16, 1976). Among the contract provisions set by the second arbitrator, Maurice C. Benewitz, were that the 4.5-percent increase would continue through 1977 and that a 5-percent increase would take effect on January 1, 1978. In addition, as of July 1, 1977, the employers' contribution to the national union's benefit fund was to go up from 8.5 percent to 9.9 percent of the gross payroll. Davis called the award "too little, by far" and announced that the union had had enough of arbitration (ibid., June 29, 1977).

100. Schramm, p. 522; Bohlander, p. 84.

101. Schramm, p. 522; Bohlander, p. 84.

102. Paul Starr, *The Social Transformation of American Medicine: The Rise of a Sovereign Profession and the Making of a Vast Industry* (New York: Basic Books, 1982), p. 378.

103. *1199 News,* May 1978.

104. Ibid., Dec. 1979.

105. Ibid., May 1978.

106. Ibid., July–Aug. 1978; *New York Times,* July 7, 1978. The union has tended to be more successful in contract bargaining before election years, when the governor looks for support or simply wants to keep the peace. Elected in 1975, Carey ran for re-election in 1979.

107. *New York Times,* July 7, 1978; *1199 News,* July–Aug. 1978. During negotiations the union pointed out that the wages of workers in league hospitals had risen only 9.5 percent over the previous three years, although the cost of living had gone up 17.3 percent.

108. Quoted in C. Ellis, "Prospective Reimbursement: Pain or Panacea?," *Modern Healthcare,* May 1976, p. 31.

109. The labor costs were calculated to be about 70 percent of a hospital's operating costs. See Schramm, p. 521.

110. The Reagan administration has taken the lead in developing incentive systems as a way to cut costs. In 1983 it created a prospective payment system presided over by the Health Care Financing Administration, which divided medical care into 467 diagnosis-related groups, a system of categories used to assign benefits (see Melosh, "Nursing and Reaganomics," pp. 147–48). Michael Greenberg also considers federal efforts to encourage the privatization of health care in the eighties in "Blind Faith: The Movement toward a Free Market in Health Care," ms., authors' files.

111. *1199 News,* Sept. 1977.

112. Anne Myerson Ayers, "A Tough New Breed of Rate Setters Regulates Hospital Charges, Budgets," *Modern Healthcare,* Nov. 1976, p. 44.

113. Ibid., p. 44; Schramm, pp. 522–23. Local 1199E won a 5.3-percent increase— 3.8 percent in wages and 1.5 percent in benefits.

114. Suzanne LaViolette, "Nurse Shortage Spurs Trend-Setting Contracts," *Modern Healthcare,* Sept. 1981, p. 32.

115. See note 54. Similar employment reductions occurred among city workers as a consequence of cutbacks in municipal services imposed by the Emergency

Financial Control Board. The city's labor force, which between 1954 and 1970 had grown by 60 percent, was cut by 20 percent through the mid-seventies.

116. Quoted in *American Journal of Nursing,* Aug. 1984, p. 1050.

117. LaViolette, p. 32.

118. Frank A. Sloan and Bruce Steinwald, *Hospital Labor Markets Analysis of Wages and Work-Force Composition* (Lexington, Mass.: D. C. Heath and Co., 1980), pp. 105–21.

119. Information on minimum salaries was compiled from the *1199 News* and the *New York Times.* In calculating the increases, the final amount awarded was used even though it usually took two steps to reach that level. For example, the $181 minimum secured in 1974 was reached via an 11-percent increase in the first year of the contract and a 10-percent increase that took effect on July 1, 1975.

120. *1199 News,* Sept. 1977.

121. Bohlander, pp. 90–91.

122. *1199 News,* July–Aug. 1978.

123. The union's concern about hospital workers' victimization is reminiscent of its stand against their being "involuntary philanthropists" (See chap. 2). For further discussion of 1199's role in health care, see chapter 9.

124. When asked about the union's role in health care, Foner referred us to Judy Berek, 1199's legislative representative in Albany, who he said would give us some "position papers." An example of union leaders' participation in a progressive coalition in New York City is provided by the 1981 campaign for mayor waged by Frank Barbaro. Barbaro, a state assemblyman who chaired the Labor Committee, forged an alliance in support of his candidacy among tenant and welfare rights groups, educational and environmental groups, the city's black leaders, and unions such as District 1199 and District Council 37. As Eric Lichten notes, once the coalition was defeated, the unions withdrew and "were not willing to continue the progressive alliance." They defined the Unity party, he continues, as a short-term coalition, organized solely for one purpose — to defeat Mayor Koch. See Eric Lichten, *Class, Power and Austerity: The New York City Fiscal Crisis* (South Hadley, Mass.: Bergin and Garvey Publishers, 1986), pp. 227–28. For a further discussion of the limited political role played by 1199, see chapter 9.

125. Quoted in Barbara Ehrenreich and John H. Ehrenreich, "Hospital Workers: Class Conflicts in the Making," in *Organization of Health Workers and Labor Conflict,* ed. Samuel Wolfe (Farmingdale, N.Y.: Baywood Publishing Co., 1978), p. 45.

126. *Wall Street Journal,* Aug. 27, 1985.

127. Moe Foner recalls a similar progression of informal contacts leading to merger talks.

128. *1199 News,* Jan. 1980.

Chapter 9

1. A. H. Raskin, "A Union with Soul," *New York Times* magazine, Mar. 22, 1970, p. 24; see also pp. 25, 38–46.

2. Murray Kempton, "Sticking to the Union," *New York Review of Books,* Apr. 9, 1970, p. 6. See also Ronald Radosh, *American Labor and United States Foreign Policy* (New York: Random House, 1969), esp. pp. 435–52; James Weinstein and David W. Eakins, eds., *For a New America: Essays in History and Politics from Studies on the Left, 1959–1967* (New York: Random House, 1970), esp. pts. 1 and 2.

3. Daniel Bell, *The End of Ideology* (Glencoe, Ill.: Free Press, 1960), esp. chap. 11; Michael Harrington, *The Other America* (New York: Macmillan, 1962); Richard Sennett, *The Hidden Injuries of Class* (New York: Vintage, 1973).

4. See, e.g., William Serrin, *The Company and the Union* (New York: Alfred A. Knopf, 1973).

5. C. Wright Mills, *The New Men of Power* (New York: Harcourt Brace & Co., 1948), esp. pp. 84–108, 223–38, See also Sidney Lens, *The Crisis of American Labor* (New York: Sagamore Press, 1959), esp. pp. 47–69. For a recent refinement of these views, see Christopher L. Tomlins, *The State and the Unions* (New York: Cambridge University Press, 1985).

6. Quoted in Harold Vatter, *The U.S. Economy in the 1950s* (New York: W. W. Norton, 1963), p. 247; Bell, p. 218.

7. Cf. Andrew Levison, *The Working-Class Majority* (New York: Penguin Books, 1975), pp. 213–47.

8. Raskin, "A Union with Soul'" Mondale quote verified by Moe Foner in a letter, July 17, 1984, authors' files.

9. Quoted in Norman Metzger and Dennis D. Pointer, *Labor-Management Relations in the Health Services Industry: Theory and Practice* (Washington, D.C.: Science and Health Publications, 1972), pp. 261–62.

10. Ibid., p. 262.

11. Ibid., pp. 263–64; Edmund R. Becker, Frank A. Sloan, and Bruce Steinwald, "Union Activity in Hospitals: Past, Present and Future," *Health Care Financing Review* 3 (June 1982): 2, 4, 5, 8, 10. Figures for 1984–85 are drawn from NLRB monthly reports as reprinted in *The Organizer* 1 (Feb. 1986): 4; National Union Organizing Status Reports, 1985–87, copy in authors' possession.

12. Elinor Langer, "Inside the Hospital Workers' Union" (pt. 1) *New York Review of Books* 16 (May 20, 1971): 36.

13. *Business Week,* Jan. 15, 1979, p. 108. Films produced by 1199 include: *Hospital Strike* (about the 1959 strike), *I Am Somebody* (about the Charleston strike), *Like a Beautiful Child* (1967), *Bread and Roses, Too* (national organizing campaign, 1980), and *Practical Dreamer* (farewell to Leon Davis, 1980). In addition the union helped to arrange the CBS-TV production of "Countdown to a Contract" (1970).

14. Metzger and Pointer, addendum Vi-A.

15. A recent study emphasizes the union's extensive use of the arts "as organizing tools, as educational aids, as environments for social interaction . . . and as pure entertainment." See Peter H. Gordon, "District 1199: A Study of the Cultural Arts in a Trade Union Context: (master's thesis, Hunter College, 1977), p. 4. See also *Business Week,* Jan. 15, 1979, p. 108.

16. William J. Taylor, Anne Shore, James E. Nelson, and Mark Hirsch, "A Study

of the Joseph Tauber Scholarship Program" (1199 publication, July 1979), pp. 5–6, authors' files.

17. Gordon, p. 115; *1199 News,* Feb. 1971; Leon Davis telephone interview, Oct. 13, 1984.

18. Becker et al., pp. 1–13, esp. p. 10. They acknowledge the difficulties of measuring the "spillover effect" of wages among unionized hospital workers on nonunionized workers.

19. *Philadelphia Inquirer,* Mar. 3, 1981. Minimum weekly wages (and the percentage of increase) established in successive New York City contracts between 1959 and 1982 are: 1959, $42; 1965, $65 (50 percent); 1968, $100 (53 percent); 1970, $130 (30 percent); 1972, $154 (15 percent); 1978, $195 (26 percent); 1982, $294 (51 percent). These figures do not reflect a growing parallel increment in benefits (e.g., retirement, health care). Percentage increases are measured from selected previous contract terms (i.e., omitting intervening contracts, as in 1974 and 1980).

20. Thirty-eight responses to the confidential Wage and Salary Report drawn from three hospitals (Beth Israel, Mt. Sinai, and Grand Central) were located in the union files. While incomplete, the data nevertheless indicate the economic status of hospital service workers at the time.

21. Distributed at chapter meetings at Beth Israel and Mt. Sinai hospitals, our survey, which elicited 155 responses (81 from hospital division members and 74 from the guild), reproduced the categories raised in 1961 and added several new ones.

22. See John Kenneth Galbraith, *The Affluent Society* (Boston: Houghton-Mifflin, 1958); David Potter, *People of Plenty* (Chicago: University of Chicago Press, 1954); William Leuchtenburg, *A Troubled Feast: American Society since 1945* (Boston: Little-Brown, 1979).

23. U.S. Department of Commerce, Bureau of the Census, *Statistical Abstract of the United States* (Washington, D.C.: GPO, 1986), Table 216, p. 133.

24. Ibid.

25. Taylor et al., p. 44.

26. Letters from 1199 summer camp program participants, 1199 Archives. The delightfully unvarnished view of "Mario Smith," son of a Queens, New York, hospital laundry worker, on a union summer camp stipend was recorded in a literary remembrance by his Vermont camp counselor:

He got off the bus with other kids from New York and looked around.

"Where the hell ya'all get them mountains from?" he said, in a raspy voice like a boy Ray Charles or a boxer punch-drunk before his voice has even changed. Nobody answers him so he went to find his bunk.

I was assigned to his table for meals. The first night at dinner he bent his head down over his chicken and rice and ate without saying a word and with furious concentration, so that by the time he had finished his first helping his face was shiny with chicken grease and grains of rice were stuck in the curls of his hair.

"Pass the napkin, please," he said.

I asked him what his name was. "Mah-rio," I said when he told me. He puckered up his face and punched me in the arm with a balled-up skinny fist and all of his strength. "Listen," he said, "you long-headed white Puerto-Rican honky, ain't no MAHrio, it's MArio."

"That's better." He rolled his eyes up into his head and smiled with all his teeth. "What's your name?" (Anthony O. Scott, Harvard College application essay, 1983)

27. See, e.g., Gene Norman Levine, "Workers Vote: The Political Behavior of Men in the Printing Trade: (Ph.D. diss., Columbia University, 1959), pp. 92–93. See also William Kornblum, *Blue Collar Community* (Chicago: University of Chicago Press, 1974), esp. pp. 207–28.

28. See John Ehrenreich, "Local 1199: Where Is It Going?" *Health-Pac Bulletin,* July-Aug. 1970, pp. 7–15; John Ehrenreich and Barbara Ehrenreich, "Hospital Workers: Class Conflicts in the Making," in *Organization of Health Workers and Labor Conflict,* ed. Samuel Wolfe (Farmingdale, N.Y.: Baywood Publishing, 1978), pp. 41–48; "Hospital Workers: A Case Study in the New Working Class," *Monthly Review* 24 (Jan. 1973): 12–27; Langer, pp. 25–33 and pt. 2 (June 3, 1971), pp. 30–37.

29. Langer, pt. 1, p. 28.

30. Ehrenreich, "Local 1199," p. 11, 14. According to Birnbaum, the Maimonides Mental Health Center, like other soft-money facilities, was threatened with extinction by the budget cuts of 1975. A building takeover again ensued, and again the 1199 leadership came down hard on dissident supporters of radical activity. One union official reportedly broke up a meeting of union members and "community types." Intrinsically wary of the unpredictable behavior of the community radicals, 1199 representatives made it clear that they would sanction no militancy other than official union militancy.

31. Langer, pt. 2, pp. 24, 37.

32. Ehrenreich, "Local 1199," p. 11.

33. Constitutional changes in 1970 allowed for a limited number of elected organizers, but districtwide elections did little to break down dependence on the central administrative apparatus.

34. Alice H. Cook, *Union Democracy: Practice and Ideal: An Analysis of Four Large Local Unions* (Ithaca: Cornell University Press, 1963), chap. 3, esp. pp. 63, 73, 75.

35. Al Nash, "Local 1199, Drug and Hospital Union: An Analysis of the Normative and Institutional Orders of a Complex Organization," *Human Relations* 27 (June 1974): 557.

36. John Black telephone interview, Jan. 22, 1987. Others would add Jesse Olson to this list of insiders. On the contradictory leadership style of Cesar Chavez, see Cletus E. Daniels, "Cesar Chavez and the Unionization of California Farm Workers," in *Labor Leaders in America,* ed. Melvyn Dubofsky and Warren Van Tine, eds. (Urbana: University of Illinois Press, 1987), p. 380.

37. Davis's curmudgeonly style was evident in a March 29, 1973, rebuke to his trusted field commander, Elliott Godoff: "I see that we are financing the taxi cab companies in Massachusetts. Evidently, there is no bus transportation. I believe this is

a hell of a way of operating. If we have to rent a car, then that should be done." Leon Davis file, 1199 Archives.

38. Langer, pt. 2, p. 36.

39. Leon Davis's report to the executive council, Jan. 12, 1979, includes the following criticisms: executive council—"too preoccupied with details . . . doesn't play an overall leadership role . . . lacks information and education;" organizers—"lack leadership qualification and initiative with the delegates and rank and file generally;" delegates—"not effective enough to provide rank and file leadership." Moe Foner nevertheless insisted that the "best organizers"—he cited Vivian Gioia and Paul Friedman—were, in fact, able to bring ideas forward out of rank-and-file meetings.

40. *New York Times Magazine,* Mar. 22, 1970.

41. Bert Cochran, *Labor and Communism: The Conflict that Shaped American Unions* (Princeton: Princeton University Press, 1977), p. 332. See also Frances Fox Piven and Richard Cloward, *Poor People's Movements: Why They Succeed, How They Fail* (New York: Vintage, 1969), esp. chap. 3.

42. For further elaboration on these themes, see Nash, pp. 548–54. Davis, like David Dubinsky, Sidney Hillman, Philip Murray, and Walter Reuther, would fit the "committed" extreme of Seymour Martin Lipset's "committed-careerist" index of labor leadership. As Lipset notes, "leaders characterized by a calling are usually men who have helped to organize their union from the start, have come to power as a result of taking part in an internal 'revolution' against an entrenched dictatorial oligarchy, or have entered the labor movement as a result of a commitment to a political ideology which views the labor movements as an instrument to be used to gain a desired social goal." "The Political Process in Trade Unions: A Theoretical Statement," in *Labor and Trade Unionism,* ed. Walter Galenson and S. M. Lipset (New York: John Wiley and Sons, 1960), pp. 231–32.

Chapter 10

1. Seymour Martin Lipset, "The Political Process in Trade Unions: A Theoretical Statement," in *Labor and Trade Unionism,* ed. Walter Galenson and S. M. Lipset (New York: John Wiley and Sons, 1960), pp. 228–29.

2. Sterling Spero and John M. Capozzola, *The Urban Community and Its Unionized Bureaucracies: Pressure Politics in Local Government Labor Relations* (New York: Dunellen Publishing, 1973) p. 120.

3. *Philadelphia Inquirer,* Mar. 3, 1981.

4. Elinor Langer, "Inside the Hospital Workers Union" (pt. 2), *New York Review of Books* 16 (June 3, 1971): 36.

5. Joe Klein, "Labor Pains, Turmoil Grips an Old Left Union," *New York,* 18 (Mar. 25, 1985), 44; see also pp. 40–47.

6. Jerry Brown, who would shortly replace Nicholas as secretary-treasurer of the national union, had risen to prominence as an aggressive organizer, directing the national's fastest-growing New England district.

7. "Chronology, SEIU/RWDSU Merger Discussions," prepared by SEIU staff, May 1982, copy in authors' possession; "Merger Agreement" and "Health Care Division By-Laws," Nov. 1981, copy in authors' possession; financial details courtesy of Moe Foner.

8. Moe Foner telephone interview, June 25, 1985.

9. David White interviews, June 5, 1979, and Oct. 14, 1984; telephone interview, Jan. 5, 1985.

10. Off the record, 1199 sources speculated that either unhappy RWDSU local officials, who would lose their power in a merger, or personal motives were behind the bombing.

11. David White telephone interview, May 16, 1985.

12. Sondra Clark interview, Aug. 11, 1982; Jesse Olson interview, Apr. 17, 1985; *Unity and Progress,* Sept. 1984.

13. *New York Times,* May 13, 1982. The new district president's first journalistic visitor found Turner "a spirited person with a hearty laugh and a friendly manner." Consistent with 1199 tradition, Turner expressed concern for "dollars spent adversely on war toys" and emphasized the union's simultaneous outreach to skilled RNs and less-skilled home care workers.

14. David White interview, Oct. 14, 1984; Moe Foner interview, May 21, 1985. Under the Turner administration David White and other district staff members received unsolicited copies of the religious tract *The Daily Word,* while indirectly the new values also received encouragement from Turner's daughter, Adrienne, who held Bible classes and prayer meetings at the union headquarters (confirmed July 22, 1985, by David White). In certain respects, however, Turner continued to react to the Leon Davis tradition. Not to be outdone by her union forebears, for example, she determined not only to send 1199 kids to summer camp but to charter an official union camp, purchasing land for Camp Noinu ("union" spelled backward) for an estimated $600,000.

15. Leon Davis interview, Aug. 12, 1982; Jesse Olson interview, Apr. 17, 1985; Pearl Cormack telephone interviews, Oct. 15, 1984, and Jan. 28, 1985.

16. David White telephone interview, May 16, 1985; Dennis Rivera telephone interview, Feb. 7, 1985; Roy Anderson telephone interview, Jan. 17, 1985; Petition, 2d Cir., New York Court of Appeals, *Roy Anderson v. The Honorable Constance R. Motley et al.,* 84 Civil 0801. Anderson said that he refused to make up a list of Jewish staff members and that Turner then ordered him to withhold money from specific individuals (he recalled the names of Rona Shapiro and Sylvia Grant, non-Jewish Turner opponents). Other adversaries, like Dennis Rivera, also experienced a cutoff of salary. Anderson sought a contempt citation as early as November 29, 1983, but his petition was ultimately ruled to have no legal standing.

17. Jesse Olson interview, Apr. 17, 1985. Roy Anderson reports a conversation between himself, Turner, and organizer James Emporer in which Turner reiterates prior instructions to Emporer "to make death threats against Jesse Olson" (see *Anderson v. Motley et al.* testimony).

18. Joshua B. Freeman, "Hospital Workers, Heal Thyselves," *The Nation,* Mar. 31, 1984, pp. 379–82; *New York Times,* Feb. 3 and 11, 1984; *Business Week,* Feb. 20,

1984; U.S. District Court, Southern District of New York, *RWDSU* v. *National Union of Hospital and Health Care Employees,* Judge Leonard B. Sand, decision, Dec. 2, 1983.

19. *In These Times,* May 23–29, 1984; Eleanor Metcalf telephone interview, Feb. 18, 1985.

20. *1199 News,* May 1984, June–July 1985, Oct. 1985.

21. As a practical step, in 1984 management transferred control of negotiations from the labor relations experts grouped around the league to attorneys from the big hospitals who were prepared for confrontation. See Wayne Barrett, "A Wounded Strike," *The Village Voice,* Aug. 28, 1984, pp. 16–17; Bureau of National Affairs, *Daily Labor Report,* no. 168 (Aug. 29, 1984): A-11 to A-13; *New York Newsday,* Aug. 7, 1984; *New York Times,* July 15 and 18, 1984.

22. District 1199 Negotiations Bulletin, July 18, 1984, authors' files; *New York Times,* April 28, 1984; Barrett, pp. 16–17.

23. *New York Newsday,* Aug. 23, 1984; *New York Daily News,* Aug. 1, 1984; *New York Post,* Aug. 20, 1984.

24. WCBS-TV News, Aug. 28, 1984; *Daily Labor Report,* Aug. 29; *New York Times,* Aug. 28, 1984.

25. Norman Metzger interview, Oct. 15, 1984; *New York Newsday,* Aug. 6, 1984; *New York Post,* Aug. 30, 1984.

26. *New York Daily News,* Aug. 30, 1984; *1199 News,* Mar. 1985.

27. David White interview, Oct. 14, 1984. White said that due to a nervous stomach, he lost thirty-five pounds during the strike. He initially excused Turner's depoliticized style and appeals to Bible Christianity as ways of reaching the union rank and file, but he was not prepared to hear capital punishment, prayer in the schools, and antiabortion arguments voiced from within the highest councils of the union. Even the divestment of funds from South Africa was initially opposed by Turner on the grounds that such investments created jobs. White also reported that during the strike, while union members received only twelve cents a day on the picket line, Turner's staff entertained themselves with imported champagne in $150-a-night hotel suites.

28. Ibid.; transcript, David White interview by Dennis Rivera, Dec. 1984, authors' files; David White affadavit before Department of Labor investigator Steven George Biller, Nov. 16, 1984, authors' files. See also Leon Fink, "Blowing the Whistle on 1199 Vote Fraud," *In These Times,* Jan. 23–29, 1985. Another possible motive was offered by Herman Benson, director of the Association for Union Democracy: on the eve of the 1199 ballot counting, a district court had ruled (responding to preballoting complaints by union insurgents) that "if the District 1199 election required a runoff, that runoff had to be supervised by the American Arbitration Association. By forestalling a runoff, Turner avoided an election in which ballots would have been printed, distributed, cast, and counted under outside control, a process that limits opportunities for would-be ballot jugglers." *Union Democracy Review,* no. 45 (Mar. 1985): 3.

29. *New York Times,* Jan. 8, 1935; Joe Conason, "1199: Prognosis Poor," *The Village Voice,* Jan. 15, 1985, pp. 20–21; Maria Laurino, "Turner's Union Support: In

Critical Condition," *The Village Voice,* Feb. 5, 1985, p. 5. For a more extended treatment of inner conflict following the 1984 strike, see Leon Fink, "'Turnergate' at 1199: A Union Divided against Itself," *The Nation* 240 (Feb. 23, 1985): 209–10.

30. Victor Kamber telephone interview, Apr. 22, 1985; Klein, pp. 40–47.

31. Fred Brown, national chairman of the Council of Black Republicans, attended a March 1986 awards ceremony for Turner at which he blamed the Democratic governor for the union's problems. In addition, Turner and Telbert King reportedly attended a $1,000-a-plate luncheon in April for Alphonse D'Amato, a Republican U.S. Senator. *New York Amsterdam News,* Mar. 22, 1986.

32. *The Village Voice,* May 6, 1986, p. 18; *New York Newsday,* Mar. 28, 1986.

33. The SOU platform committed Johnson to a series of democratic revisions in 1199's centralized structure, including "representation of rank and file members on the executive council"; "elections of all officers, organizers and area directors by their constituency"; and "membership right to a recall petition for all elected officials." "Proposal for Discussion, Ten Point Program to Save Our Union," pamphlet in possession of authors.

34. Georgianna Johnson interview, Dec. 28, 1985; telephone interview, May 19, 1986.

35. Ossie Davis speech, April 5, 1986, transcript in authors' possession.

36. Pro-Turner election leaflets asked, among other things, "Should a majority of 90,000 Black and Hispanic workers allow a White minority of 170 members and outsiders to take over leadership of this still powerful union that is valued at $2 billion?" and "If the Union is being run so badly, why not challenge our President with a *white supremacy* [ticket]? But 'puppet black' Ms. Georgianna will be a front for Leon Davis, Jesse Olsen and Eddie Kaye [*sic*]." Concerned 1199ers at St. Luke's–Roosevelt Hospital Center, leaflets in possession of authors. A $10,000 check payable to Jesse Jackson for his appearance was stopped by victorious SOU officers as an unfair use of union funds. Moe Foner telephone conversation, Feb. 25, 1987.

37. In July Jesse Jackson publicly counseled former Turner supporters: "Pastors come and go but the church remains inviolate." *1199 News* 4 (Aug. 1986): 8–9. At formal installation ceremonies for the new union officers on August 26, a tape-recorded message from Coretta Scott King noted the similarities between Johnson's victory and that of Corazon Aquino in the Philippines: "Wherever men and women get together to decide what is right, the power of the people cannot be denied." On the same occasion Governor Cuomo responded to the booing of some pro-Turner delegates: "If you are dumb enough to continue to work against each other, you won't get anywhere but backward." Ibid., Sept. 1986, p. 6; Local 1199 advertisement in the *New York Times,* Sept. 28, 1986.

38. *New York Newsday,* Nov. 12, 1986; *1199 News,* 4 (Oct.–Nov. 1986): 2–3, 5; *New York Daily News,* Oct. 14, 1986; *New York Times,* Oct. 14, 1986.

39. *1199 News* 4 (Oct.–Nov. 1986): 2–3, 5; *New York Newsday,* Nov. 12, 1986. Citing excessive costs, Johnson's executive council also terminted Camp Noinu.

40. *Health Care Union News,* Apr. 1986; *The Organizer* 1, no. 1 (Feb. 1986); "Report from the Ohio Organizing Staff to Pres. Henry Nicholas," ms., in possession of authors.

41. *New York Times,* Nov. 30, 1987; Gerry Hudson telephone interview, Oct. 18, 1987.

42. Georgianna Johnson telephone interview, Oct. 5, 1987; Jonathon Tisini, "Turmoil at 1199," *The Village Voice,* Oct. 20, 1987. Johnson's motivations seem essentially to have derived from a deeply wounded sense of self-respect. In interviews with the authors, she readily admitted that she had originally experienced no higher calling for the office of union president. Indeed, referring to a public health group trip to the Soviet Union arranged shortly after her election, she self-mockingly recalled that she had initially accepted assignments rather passively: "I was pleased with a big victory . . . and I like to travel." At the same time, however, Johnson was not about to be hoodwinked or "humiliated"; she would stand up for herself if need be. "I have two degrees," she told the authors, "one from LIU (Long Island University), the other from UCLA (that's the University at the Corner of Lenox Ave). . . . the second taught me to call motherfuckers by their real name." In a June 30, 1988, memorandum to the executive council, Johnson poignantly complained: "I can take the rough-and-tumble of *unbiased* criticism and engage in constructive debate, but not the ferocious, naked, obscene, biased personal attacks bordering on physical assault directed at me when I attend Council meetings. . . . Would any of you men, especially the black men on the Council, treat your mothers, wives, daughters, etc. the way you treat me?" Georgianna Johnson telephone interview, Oct. 5, 1987; interview with Fink and Greenberg, July 14, 1988; Johnson memorandum to executive council, copy in authors' possession.

43. Telephone interviews: David White, Aug. 29, 1987. Jules Bernstein, Oct. 3, Nov. 9 and 19, 1987. Discussions with a number of people in the union indicate that the inference Bernstein draws from the political orientation of certain executive council leaders, rather than their politics, is subject to dispute. Moe Foner, Gerry Hudson, and attorney Eugene Eisner all acknowledge close ties of some of the new leaders to Communist party circles. Most speculation in this regard focuses on Eddie Kay, although Georgianna Johnson, who at one point claimed that she was the victim of a party-inspired "coup," includes not only Kay but Dennis Rivera, two other executive council members, and several union organizers. Rivera identifies himself as a "democratic socialist, not a Communist" and calls the Communist party role in 1199 "greatly overestimated." The executive council, he says, includes members from a range of political persuasions, "members of the Communist party to bitterly anti-Communist members." According to Rivera, the "Communist" issue resurfaced among pro-Turner "black nationalists" who "cannot understand why politically committed whites would work with a minority union unless they were party zealots." Interestingly, one of the most vociferous of the "black nationalist" voices is inclined to agree with Rivera, at least on this one point. David White, ex-party member and no friend of the current executive council, nevertheless dismisses the Communist party as irrelevant in the current drama: "Some of the best people and some of the worst people in the world are in the party," he says. In our view, the important question for union members and those concerned with the union's fate is not the political ideology of individual members but whether undeclared political organizations or associations play a substantial role in union policy making. On balance, given the vagueness of the

charge and the general weakness of the party itself as a contemporary political instrument, we too are inclined to doubt its significance as an independent player in the events at hand. However, within the vacuum of leadership left by Turner's ouster, a party-based network, a kind of "club within a club," probably did reassert itself. Whether these individuals strengthened operation of the local by their dedication to principled trade unionism or weakened it by a thirst for power will have to be judged from hindsight. Telephone interviews: Jules Bernstein, Oct. 3, Nov. 9 and 19, 1987; Gerry Hudson, Oct. 18, 1987; Moe Foner, Nov. 28, 1987; Eugene Eisner, Dec. 11, 1987; Georgianna Johnson, Oct. 5 and Nov. 30, 1987; Ezra Birnbaum, No. 26, 1987; David White, Nov. 28, 1987; Dennis Rivera, Feb. 3, 1988. It proved impossible to speak directly to Eddie Kay on this subject. Interestingly, in the authors' final meeting with Johnson, on July 14, 1988, she downplayed the issue. "I don't care about a person's political beliefs," she said, "as long as they don't use their influence unfairly. Some of my best friends are Reds."

44. Four conflicting orders to show cause had been filed by September 16. The court battle involved some of the nation's top prolabor legal talent: the Washington D.C., firm of Connerton & Bernstein pressed Johnson's claims while Kay and the executive council were represented by New York's Eisner & Levy; Rabinowitz, Boudin, Standard, Krinsky & Lieberman; and Gladstein, Reif, Meginnis. See *Johnson* v. *Kay*, U.S. District Court, State of New York, 87 Civ. 6482; Local 1199 constitution, art. 7, secs. 2, 10; Local 1199 constitution, as amended in 1985, in possession of authors.

45. In 1986, to protect itself from "secessionist" sentiments within 1199, the RWDSU affixed a "dual unionism" clause (art 25) to its constitution which authorized removal from office (for any officer) or trusteeship (for any local) "for actively supporting or advocating" any "dual union" that "attempts to . . . displace this International or an affiliate thereof." Cited in a Sept. 17, 1987, letter from Georgianna Johnson to Lenore Miller, in authors' possession. See also Bureau of National Affairs, *Daily Labor Reports* 188 (Sept. 30, 1987): 4–5; Judge Sweet's Oct. 8, 1987, opinions in *Johnson* v. *Kay* (Opinion 87 Civ. 6432 RWS) and *Local 1199* v. *RWDSU* (Opinion 87 Civ. 6862 RWS), copies in authors' possession. In blocking Kay's suspension from office while insisting on the electoral rights of Kay's opponents, Judge Sweet took eloquent note of "how fragile union democracy can be." He also carefully dispatched with the RWDSU's dual unionism "gag rule," locating in other sections of the international union's constitution the clear legitimacy of discussion of disaffiliation-related issues. See Local 1199 leaflet, n.d., in authors' possession.

46. *New York Amsterdam News,* Oct. 31, 1987. As a result of the union fracas, Johnson sued Kay for a million dollars; Kay responded with a two-million-dollar suit of his own, charging defamation of character.

47. Statement to the news media, Doris Turner, Oct. 26, 1987, in authors' possession; "Doris Turner . . . It's Time to Come Home," leaflet, Commitee for Justice and Democracy for 1199 Members, n.d. authors' files; *New York Times,* Nov. 30, 1987. "Now is the time for our International union, the RWDSU, to take over 1199 . . . and run it by strong leadership," counseled the pro-Turner Committee for

Justice for 1199 Members in a leaflet, n.d., authors' files; Georgianna Johnson interview, Oct. 5, 1987.

48. Save Our Union, leaflet Oct. 27 or 28, 1987, in authors' possession.

49. Telephone interview with Local 1199 counsel Eugene Eisner, Dec. 11, 1987. According to Eisner, the unpublished legal agreement between Miller and the executive council maintained the local's right to cast a negative decision on a prospective UFCW-RWDSU merger. Given the national hospital union's continuing interest in merger talks with the SEIU, openly discussed at the December 1987 convention in Hartford, a faint possibility still exists for Davis's "one big union" of hospital workers. A more likely scenario, however, involves parallel Local 1199–RWDSU merger into the UFCW and 1199 national union merger into the SEIU. Under such circumstances interunion cooperation would, at best, be informal, perhaps coordinated through a special AFL-CIO national health care department, as advocated by Lenore Miller (*New York Times*, Nov. 30, 1987). Even Johnson's lawyers, who had reportedly billed her for more than $300,000, remained unpaid by the international Georgianna Johnson (telephone interview, Nov. 28, 1987). Turner joined Johnson in an appeal to black clergy (calling "the black church and its ministers, from the days of slavery . . . the oasis in the desert of despair"), excoriating Miller as well as factional foes for stealing "their union" (letter from Turner and Johnson to New York City ministers, Dec. 21, 1987, copy in authors' possession). RWDSU president Lenore Miller emphatically denied Georgianna Johnson's charges of a racially inspired "betrayal." In a letter dated January 11, 1988, Miller asserts that after extensive negotiations between parties representing Johnson, Local 1199's executive council, and the international, Johnson had agreed to a settlement guaranteeing her the "respect" of the presidency, a higher salary, payment of legal fees, and certain staff appointments. At the last minute, Miller claims, Johnson killed the deal: "You told us your mother was ill, and we should 'dump you' [i.e., leave her out of the agreement] because six members had called threatening you if you settled with the Executive Council." Lenore Miller to Georgianna Johnson, Jan. 11, 1988, copy in authors' possession.

50. Official election tally sheets, courtesy of Jules Bernstein, copy in authors' possession; telephone interviews with Jules Bernstein, Nov. 19, 1987 and Eugene Eisner, Dec. 11, 1987. The constitution, in fact, mandates at least two such meetings per year (Local 1199 constitution, art. 7, sec. 11). On February 4, 1988, Judge Sweet sided with Georgianna Johnson and ruled that the 1199 executive council must sanction and pay for a general delegate assembly (at which Johnson intended to challenge the bylaw election results) on a date of her choosing.

51. David Livingston telephone interview, Mar. 1, 1985. In a May 10, 1988, decision, Special Master Eric J. Schmertz, appointed by Judge Sweet, dismissed objections to the bylaw election on grounds of insufficient evidence.

52. The merger wave was highlighted by the March 1985 "supermerger" of the 420-plant Hospital Corporation of America with the American Hospital Supply Corporation. *1199 News*, May 1985.

53. The hospitals adopted a cautious posture toward the intraunion conflict, at

once letting Turner take the rap for the workers' "missing 5%," blocking hospital access to her opponents, and all the while subtly shifting the wage reimbursement issue onto the state's shoulders. Asked which union faction the employers would prefer to deal with, veteran hospital negotiator Norman Metzger replied with a terse "No comment." Norman Metzger telephone interview, June 29, 1988. See also Mark H. Maier, *City Unions: Managing Discontent in New York City* (New Brunswick: Rutgers University Press, 1987), pp. 137–50. This view of a "tolerant" management does not imply that on a day-to-day, grassroots level hospital workers did not sense an erosion of union strength. Rather, union losses were experienced incrementally (e.g., a new subcontract here, replacement of full- by part-time workers there, as well as chronic understaffing). Marion Feinberg telephone interview, Nov. 26, 1987.

54. *1199 News* 23 (Jan. 1988): 4.

55. On the changing politics of New York City, see the Fall 1987 special issue of *Dissent,* "In Search of New York," especially Jim Sleeper, "Boom and Bust with Ed Koch," pp. 437–52; Jim Chapin, "Who Rules New York Today?," pp. 471–78; Michael Oreskes, "Is It Still a Union Town?," pp. 436–91; and Nicolaus Mills, "Howard Beach—Anatomy of a Lynching: New York Racism in the 1980s," p. 485.

56. Jim Sleeper, "The Resegregation of America: Promise and the Underclass," *Communal* 114 (Nov. 6, 1987): 620.

57. Marion Feinberg telephone interview, Nov. 26, 1987. Feinberg is a Montefiore technician and member of an independent rank-and-file caucus within the union.

58. In their report to their national convention in December 1987, 1199 national leaders, committed in principle to "One Union for All Health Care Workers," openly expressed bewilderment about the organizational future: "With the recent agreement between Local 1199 and RWDSU, certain questions arise with regard to unity of health care workers: Does that agreement institutionalize a split of organized health care workers, i.e., with some in the UFCW and some in SEIU? Does our own National Union decide to either join with the Local in the UFCW or to reinstitute the discussions with SEIU and join with the health care workers in that Union? Are there other unions we should talk with? Should we remain a National Union with our own AFL-CIO charter?" See "Officers' Report to the Seventh Convention of National Union Hospital and Health Care Employees (AFL-CIO)," Dec. 9–12, Hartford, Conn., p. 51, authors' files. By the fall of 1988, the questions raised above had boiled up into a fractious dispute among national union officers over whether to merge with SEIU or AFSCME.

59. One promising decentralizing feature of the new constitution should not go unnoticed: for the first time "elected organizers" (whose numbers are still to be fixed by the executive council) will be elected "by area" rather than in unionwide elections. In these organizers the possibility exists for greater independence and variety of decision making.

60. *New York Newsday,* May 9, 1988. Vice presidents Aida Garcia and Dennis Rivera led Local 1199's efforts in what they called the home care "crusade." With public relations help from Moe Foner, Rivera reached out to John Cardinal O'Connor, Jesse Jackson, and Manhattan borough president David Dinkins to support the Labor Home Care Council jointly organized by Local 1199 and Municipal Workers' District

Council 1707. Ultimate responsibility for changes in Medicaid funding rested with Governor Mario Cuomo. *1199 News* 23 (Jan. 1988): 3, 6–7. AFL-CIO secretary-treasurer Thomas R. Donahue canceled a scheduled appearance at the national's December 1987 convention to protest the union's violation of the official request that affiliates wait for coordinated executive council action on the question of endorsement; Gerald Austin to Dennis Rivera, Apr. 20, 1988, copy in authors' possession. On Austin, see Sol Stern, "Jesse's Jews," *The New Republic* 198 (June 20, 1988): 18–19.

Interviews

The following list comprises all formal research interviews conducted for this volume. Telephone interviews are included in the text and chapter notes. The tapes and transcripts, where available, have been deposited at the Labor-Management Documentation Library, Industrial and Labor Relations School, Cornell University, Ithaca, N.Y.

Arana, Gloria—Mar. 23 and 31, Apr. 25, 1977

Balancia, Charles—Mar. 2, 1976

Barker, Sylvia—Apr. 26, 1977

Barkum, Marie—Apr. 4, 1977

Bennett, Isaiah—Feb. 29, 1980

Bianculli, Diane—May 28, 1982

Birnbaum, Ezra—Aug. 3, 1977

Bloch, Jacques W.—Mar. 2, 1976

Boshell, Thomas—Aug. 3, 1977

Bowens, Ernestine—Mar. 23, 1977

Bowles, Thelma—Dec. 2, 1975

Brand, Rose—Apr. 26, 1977

Broomer, Sy—Mar. 31, 1977

Brown, Joseph—Nov. 12, 1975

Bryant, James—Mar. 23, 1977

Burgess, Clifton—July 29, 1977

Cameron, Ida—Apr. 25, 1977

Cherkasky, Martin—Apr. 8, 1976

Clark, Sondra—Aug. 11, 1982

Cole, Annie—Nov. 13, 1975

Connorton, John B.—June 22, 1977

Cooper, Grosvenor—Dec. 19, 1975

Cordero, Salvadore—Dec. 15, 1975

Cormack, Pearl and James—July 26, 1977

Cosby, Cassie—Mar. 23, 1977

Cruz, Emeriot—Nov. 12, 1975

Danielli, Andrew—Apr. 25, 1977

David, Aberdeen—Nov. 8, 1976

Davis, Leon J.—Jan. 5 and 6, Apr. 1, 1976; July 27, 1977; Jan. 13, June 5 and 7, 1979; Aug. 12, 1982

Downs, Kenneth—Sept. 23, 1975

Dubin, Marshall—Nov. 12, Dec. 3, 1975; Mar. 25, 1976; Feb. 18, 1977

Duffy, Rev. Thomas—Feb. 28, 1980

Epstein, Harry—Mar. 7, 1977

Ferrara, Claude—Mar. 16, 1976

Field, Fritz—Mar. 31, 1977

Fitzpatrick, Msgr. James—July 11, 1977

Foner, Moe—July 22, Dec. 22 and 23, 1975; Apr. 1, July 22, Oct. 26, 1976; Apr. 13, July 1, 1977; Mar. 9, 1979; Oct. 15, 1984

Fox, Gladys—Oct. 24, 1975
Garcia, Edith—July 1, 1977
Glassberg, Grace—Mar. 23, 1977
Godoff, Ellen and Harvey—Nov. 12, 1976
Godoff, Lillian—Nov. 12, 1976
Goldstein, Sarah—Sept. 16, 1976
Gottshagen, Irving—Jan. 16, 1976
Grant, Rev. Henry—Feb. 27, 1980
Harris, Harold—Nov. 12, 1975
Harrison, Mae—July 13, 1977
Hodara, Morris—[Jan.] 1976
Johnson, Georgianna—Dec. 28, 1985; July 14, 1988
Joquin, Hilda—June 20, 1977
Kamenkowitz, Phillip—Nov. 29, 1976
Katz, Morris—Jan. 16, 1976
Kaufman, David—May 26, 1977
Kay Edward—July 29, 1977
King, Telbert—Dec. 20, 1982; Oct. 16, 1984
Kosloski, Al—Dec. 9, 1975
Landsberg, Arthur—July 8, 1977
Lichtenstein, Howard—June 29, 1977
Livingston, David—June 23, 1977
Malave, Ramon—Dec. 6, 1976
Metzger, Norman—Apr. 25 and 29, 1977; Oct. 15, 1984
Michelson, William—June 22, 1977
Mitchell, Theodore—Nov. 24, 1975; Mar. 16, 1976
Morris, Nellie—Jan. 8, 1976
Moultrie, Mary—Feb. 28, 1980
Muehlenkamp, Robert—Dec. 10, 1976; Aug. 11, 1982; Oct. 15, 1984

Nicholas, Henry—Jan. 11, 1978; Apr. 14, June 8, 1982; Apr. 12, 1985
Olson, Jesse—Oct. 26, 1976; Nov. 17, 1982; Apr. 17, 1985
Ortiz, Arguilla—July 11, 1977
Pagan, Julio—Apr. 20, 1977
Phillips, Marjorie—July 1, 1977
Raskin, A. H.—June 15, 1977
Rath, Karl—Nov. 3, 1976
Reeves, Mildred—May 3, 1977
Riley, Mary—July 6, 1977
Rivera, Calletono—Mar. 31, 1977
Rosoff, Betty—Dec. 8, 1975
Rustin, Bayard—June 20, 1977
Sanchez, Edward—Mar. 23, 1977
Saunders, William—Mar. 1, 1980
Schmuckler, Samuel—Apr. 4, 1977
Sheps, Cecil G.—July 12, 1979
Singletary, Clarence E.—Feb. 27, 1980
Steinberg, Martin—May 13, 1977
Stern, Irving—Jan. 6, 1976
Taylor, William—Dec. 15, 1976
Tillow, Kay—Oct. 21, 1980
Tompkins, Elon—Mar. 23, 1977
Turner, Doris—Oct. 26, Nov. 23, 1976
Van Arsdale, Harry—Sept. 1 and 9, 1977
Volk, Cornelius "Bill"—July 15, 1977
Wagner, Robert, Jr.—July 12, 1977
Weingarten, Victor—Feb. 6, 1976
White, David—June 5, 1979; Oct. 14, 1984
Wise, John E.—Feb. 28, 1980
Works, Lucille—July 26, 1977
Young, Rev. Andrew—Jan. 31, 1980

Index

A Note on the Authors

LEON FINK teaches history at the University of North Carolina at
Chapel Hill. He is the author of *Workingmen's Democracy: The
Knights of Labor and American Politics* and essays on American
working-class history and life in the *Journal of American History,
Labor History, Social History, Dissent, Labour/Le Travailleur,
The Nation, Southern Changes,* and *In These Times.* Currently, he
is studying the subject of intellectuals and labor reform.

BRIAN GREENBERG teaches labor and social history at the University of Delaware. He is the author of *Worker and Community:
Response to Industrialization in a Nineteenth-Century American
City, Albany, New York, 1850–1884* and several essays on labor
and social history, and is the guest editor for a special issue on
labor of *The Public Historian.* Currently, he is working on a study
of the evolving ideas about labor and society in nineteenth- and
early twentieth-century America.

Books in the Series
The Working Class in American History

German Workers in Chicago:
A Documentary History of Working-Class Culture
from 1850 to World War I
Edited by Hartmut Keil and John B. Jentz

On the Line:
Essays in the History of Auto Work
Edited by Nelson Lichtenstein and Stephen Meyer III

Upheaval in the Quiet Zone:
A History of Hospital Workers' Union, Local 1199
Leon Fink and Brian Greenberg